Sketches of the Nineteenth Century

Sketches of the Nineteenth Century

European Journalism and its *Physiologies*, 1830–50

Martina Lauster

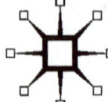

© Martina Lauster 2007

All rights reserved. No reproduction, copy or transmission of this publication may be made without written permission.

No paragraph of this publication may be reproduced, copied or transmitted save with written permission or in accordance with the provisions of the Copyright, Designs and Patents Act 1988, or under the terms of any licence permitting limited copying issued by the Copyright Licensing Agency, 90 Tottenham Court Road, London W1T 4LP.

Any person who does any unauthorised act in relation to this publication may be liable to criminal prosecution and civil claims for damages.

The author has asserted her right to be identified as the author of this work in accordance with the Copyright, Designs and Patents Act 1988.

First published 2007 by
PALGRAVE MACMILLAN
Houndmills, Basingstoke, Hampshire RG21 6XS and
175 Fifth Avenue, New York, N. Y. 10010
Companies and representatives throughout the world

PALGRAVE MACMILLAN is the global academic imprint of the Palgrave Macmillan division of St. Martin's Press, LLC and of Palgrave Macmillan Ltd. Macmillan® is a registered trademark in the United States, United Kingdom and other countries. Palgrave is a registered trademark in the European Union and other countries.

ISBN-13: 978-0-230-51803-2   hardback
ISBN-10: 0-230-51803-6   hardback

This book is printed on paper suitable for recycling and made from fully managed and sustained forest sources. Logging, pulping and manufacturing processes are expected to conform to the environmental regulations of the country of origin.

A catalogue record for this book is available from the British Library.

Library of Congress Cataloging-in-Publication Data
Lauster, Martina.
   Sketches of the Nineetenth Century : European Journalism and its *Physiologies*, 1830-50 / by Martina Lauster.
     p. cm.
   Includes bibliographical references and index.
   ISBN-13: 978-0-230-51803-2 (cloth)
   ISBN-10: 0-230-51803-6 (cloth)
   1. City and town life—Press coverage—Europe—History–
–19th century. 2. Journalism—Social aspects—Europe—History–
–19th century. 3. Flaneurs—Europe—History—19th century. I. Title.
PN5110.L35 2007
302.2309409'034—dc22

2006052960

10 9 8 7 6 5 4 3 2 1
16 15 14 13 12 11 10 09 08 07

Printed and bound in Great Britain by
Antony Rowe Ltd, Chippenham and Eastbourne

Contents

List of Illustrations	vii
Acknowledgements	xi
Note on Translations	xii
Introduction: Nineteenth-Century Sketches and the Problem of Walter Benjamin's Legacy	**1**
1 The Dynamic Present: Sketches and Print Media	**23**
Edward Lytton Bulwer, 'The valet and the mechanic' (*England and the English*)	24
The serialisation of word and image	28
Wood engraving	33
French-English cross-connections	39
German and Austrian developments	43
Verbal-visual wit	48
2 The Mobile Observer: Sketches and Optical Media	**59**
Dickens's 'Rapid Diorama' (*Pictures from Italy*)	60
Panorama in motion: Balzac's 'Histoire et physiologie des Boulevards de Paris' (*Le Diable à Paris*)	65
The cosmopolitan point of observation: Eduard Beurmann's panorama of Frankfurt and August Lewald's panorama of Munich	75
Microscopic viewing	82
3 Physiology, Zoology and the Constitution of Social Types	**85**
Honoré de Balzac, 'L'Épicier' (*La Silhouette*)	94
Kenny Meadows / William Howitt, 'The Country Schoolmaster' (*Heads of the People*)	108
Stereotype or typological portrait?	110
The paradigm of Life Science	114
Karl Gutzkow, 'Naturgeschichte der deutschen Kameele' (*Phönix*)	119
'Quiz' [Edward Caswall] / 'Phiz' [Hablôt Knight Browne], *Sketches of Young Ladies*	124

4 The Devil in Europe: Sketches and the Moralist Tradition — 129
Asmodeus — 129
La Bruyère and the *histoire des mœurs* — 140
'Tableaux de Paris' — 144
'Mr. Spectator' — 149
City Cries, the world as a stage and the magic lantern — 153

5 Turning Insides Out: An Anatomy of Observation — 173
The *flâneur* re-examined — 175
Edward Lytton Bulwer, 'Asmodeus at Large'
(*New Monthly Magazine*) — 179
Charles Dickens, 'Shops and their Tenants' (*Sketches by Boz*) — 188
Ernst Dronke, *Berlin* — 194
George Sand, 'Coup d'œil général sur Paris' (*Le Diable à Paris*) — 205

6 The Panoramic Order: Piecing Together the City — 211
The Asmodean view and the inverted traveller's view — 212
Le Diable à Paris — 216
Wien und die Wiener, in Bildern aus dem Leben — 226
Gavarni in London — 239

7 The Encyclopaedic Order: Reviewing the Nation and the Century — 251
Variations of the classifying view: museums, reviews and encyclopaedias — 253
Edward Lytton Bulwer, *England and the English*, and Karl Gutzkow, *Die Zeitgenossen* — 260
The national review directed by London journalism and its European impact: *Heads of the People, Deutschland und die Deutschen, Wien und die Wiener* and *Les Français peints par eux-mêmes* — 268
The *Physiologies*: a meta-order of encyclopaedism — 288

Conclusion: Sketches as a Grammar of Modernity — 309

Bibliography — 329

Index — 348

List of Illustrations

1. Gavarni, frontispiece for *Le Diable à Paris* (1845).
   Private collection. 7
2. Vignette in V.J.E. de Jouy, *L'Hermite en Italie* (1824).
   © Courtesy of the University of Exeter Library (848.6 JOU-9). 34
3. 'Printing-Machine', in *The Penny Cyclopædia* (1841).
   Private collection. 36
4. 'Great Events and Odd Matters [for April 1837]', *The Comic Almanack*. Private collection. 38
5. Cartoon of 'the woodcutter', *Düsseldorfer Monathefte* (1847). 44
6. Karl Gutzkow, 'Papilloten', and Brennglas [Adolf Glaßbrenner], 'Der Journal-Kirchhof', *Berliner Don-Quixote* (1833).
   © Georg Olms Verlag, 2001, with kind permission. 50
7. Gavarni, vignette in Maurice Alhoy, *Physiologie de la Lorette* (1841). Private collection. 53
8. 'Pen and Palette Portraits', *Punch* (1841).
   © Courtesy of the University of Exeter Library
   (Brooks P/050 P75). 55
9. Gavarni, vignette in Maurice Alhoy, *Physiologie de la Lorette* (1841). Private collection. 56
10. Bertrand, vignettes in Honoré de Balzac, 'Histoire et physiologie des Boulevards de Paris', in *Le Diable à Paris* (1846). Private collection. 68
11. *Boulevards de Paris*. Section of foldout panorama (1846).
    © Courtesy of the University of Exeter Library (BDC 46198). 70
12. Bertall and Bertrand, vignettes in Honoré de Balzac, 'Histoire et physiologie des Boulevards de Paris', in *Le Diable à Paris* (1846). Private collection. 72
13. Bertall, vignettes (as in illustration 12). 74
14. Kenny Meadows, frontispiece in *Heads of the People* (1840). Private collection. 86

viii List of Illustrations

15. Gavarni, 'type' for Honoré de Balzac, 'L'Épicier', in *Les Français peints par eux-mêmes* (1840). Private collection. 95

16a. 'The Schoolmaster', in Alexander Walker, *Physiognomy Founded on Physiology [...]* (1834). Private collection. 107

16b. Kenny Meadows, 'The Country Schoolmaster', in *Heads of the People* (1841). Private collection. 107

17. Gavarni, vignettes in Maurice Alhoy, *Physiologie de la Lorette* (1841). Private collection. 112

18. 'Phiz' [Hablôt Knight Browne], frontispiece for 'Quiz' [E. Caswall], *Sketches of Young Ladies* (1837). Private collection. 126

19. Title illustration of *Satan* (Berlin, 1848). 136

20. Title vignette of *Charivari* (Leipzig, 1845). Private collection. 137

21. Pauquet, vignettes for first and last page of contents table in vol. 1 of *Les Français peints par eux-mêmes* (1840). Private collection. 138-9

22. Gavarni, frontispiece for vol. 2 of *Les Français peints par eux-mêmes* (1840). Private collection. 141

23. Gavarni, 'The Orange-Girl', in *Gavarni in London* (1849). Private collection. 157

24. Theodor Hosemann, frontispiece for A. Brennglas [Adolf Glaßbrenner], 'Nante Nantino [...]', in *Berlin, wie es ist und – trinkt* (1843). 159

25a/b. A.S. Henning's and Kenny Meadows's volume covers for *Punch* (1841 and 1843). 165-6

25c. Wilhelm Böhm, wrapper design for *Wien und die Wiener*. © Adalbert-Stifter-Institut des Landes Oberösterreich. 167

26. Henry Monnier, title vignette in *Paris, ou Le Livre des Cent-et-un* (1831-4). Private collection. 168

27. Robert Seymour, cover illustration (1838 [?]) for *Sketches by Seymour*, vol. 4. Private collection. 171

28. Tony Johannot, frontispiece in Alain René Le Sage, *Asmodeus; or, The Devil on Two Sticks* (1841). Private collection. 172

29. Frontispiece for A. Brennglas [Adolf Glaßbrenner], 'Köchinnen', in *Berlin wie es ist und – trinkt* (1845). 196

List of Illustrations   ix

30. Kenny Meadows, 'The Chimney-Sweep', in *Heads of the People* (1840). Private collection. 199

31. Bertall, 'Paris, le 1ᵉʳ Janvier. Coupe d'une maison parisienne le 1ᵉʳ Janvier 1845. Cinq étages du monde parisien', in *Le Diable à Paris* (1846). Private collection. 203

32a/b. Français, vignettes for George Sand, 'Coup d'œil général sur Paris', in *Le Diable à Paris* (1845). Private collection. 204-5

33. Gavarni, frontispiece, and Champin, head vignette in *Le Diable à Paris* (1845). Private collection. 217

34. Champin, vignette in Théophile Lavallée, 'Géographie de Paris, in *Le Diable à Paris* (1846). Private collection. 219

35. Gavarni, part 4 of 'Les Gens de Paris: Parisiens de Paris', in *Le Diable à Paris* (1845). Private collection. 222

36. Bertall, vignette in P.-J. Stahl [J. Hetzel], 'Conclusion', in *Le Diable à Paris* (1846). Private collection. 224

37. Wilhelm Böhm, 'Beinelstierer', in *Wien und die Wiener, in Bildern aus dem Leben* (1844). © British Library Board. All Rights Reserved (1459.k.6). 235

38. Gavarni, 'Acrobats'. Frontispiece in *Gavarni in London* (1849). Private collection. 242

39. Gavarni, 'The Casino', in *Gavarni in London* (1849). Private collection. 244

40. Mʳ *Albert Smith's Ascent of Mont Blanc*. Programme cover. © Courtesy of the University of Exeter Library (BDC 17418). 252

41a. Gavarni and Gilbert / Henning, vignettes in Albert Smith, *The Natural History of the Flirt* (1848). Private collection. 257

41b. 'Chæton vagabundus'. Illustration in *The Penny Cyclopædia* (1836). Private collection. 258

42. Kenny Meadows, sequence of illustrations in *Heads of the People* (1840). Private collection. 269-70

43. Kenny Meadows, vignettes for 'Preface', in *Heads of the People* (1840). Private collection. 272-3

44. Gavarni, illustrations in Balzac, 'L'Épicier', in *Les Français peints par eux-mêmes* (1840). Private collection. 278

x List of Illustrations

45. Page from table of contents, vol. 3, of *Les Français peints par eux-mêmes* (1841). Private collection. 280

46. Hippolyte Pauquet, vignettes in table of contents, vol. 2, of *Les Français peints par eux-mêmes*. *Province* (1841). Private collection. 286-7

47. Covers of *Physiologie de l'homme de loi* (1841) and *Physiologie du gamin de Paris* (1842). Private collection. 291

48. Henry Émy, illustrations in Louis Couailhac, *Physiologie du théâtre* (1841). Private collection. 298

49. Frontispiece in *Physiologie de la presse* (1841). Private collection. 299

50. Archibald S. Henning, vignette in Albert Smith, *The Natural History of the Ballet Girl* (1847). Private collection. 302

51a/b. Illustrations in Albert Smith, *The Natural History of the Ballet Girl* (1847) and in Louis Couailhac, *Physiologie du théâtre* (1841). Private collection. 304

52. Gavarni, 'The Street Beggar', in *Gavarni in London* (1849). Private collection. 313

53. Illustration in Honoré de Balzac, 'Monographie de la presse parisienne', in *La Grande Ville* (1844). Private collection. 316

54. Honoré Daumier, illustration in Paul de Kock, 'Les Champs-Elysées', in *La Grande Ville* (1844). Private collection. 322

55. Bertall, vignettes in P. Pascal, 'Comment on se salue à Paris', in *Le Diable à Paris* (1845). Private collection. 324

56. 'A Grammarian Declining To Be'.Vignette in *Punch* (1841). © Courtesy of the University of Exeter Library (Brooks P/050 P75). 326

Acknowledgements

My thanks go to the colleagues and friends whose shared interests have been a source of inspiration for this long-term project. David Bellos (Princeton), David Amigoni, John Bowen and Anthea Trodd (Keele) advised me in the early stages, and Carol Adlam, Mary Orr, Michael Pakenham, John Plunkett, Gert Vonhoff, Gar Yates as well as the late Chris Brooks helped me with their expertise and moral support at Exeter. Wulf Wülfing (Bochum) supplied invaluable feedback on my 'Panorama Chapter', Wolfgang Rasch (Berlin) assisted me as a bibliographer and fellow collector of nineteenth-century printed works, Hugh Ridley (Dublin) kindly reminded me that even long books had to be finished some time, and my husband David Horrocks, reader of and adviser on countless drafts, has become a virtual co-author. I would also like to thank Henk de Berg (Sheffield) for our fruitful exchange about Benjamin and the anonymous readers of the book proposal whose comments were a great help.

I am grateful to the former AHRB for funding four months' study leave at the beginning of my project (1999-2000), to the Modern Humanities Research Association for allowing me to make use of materials from my article 'Walter Benjamin's Myth of the "Flâneur"', *Modern Language Review* 102:1 (January 2007), 92-109, and to the University of Delaware Press for permission to re-use parts of my contribution 'Physiognomy, Zoology and Physiology as Paradigms in Sociological Sketches of the 1830s and 40s', in *Physiognomy in Profile: Lavater's Impact on European Culture*, ed. by Melissa Percival and Graeme Tytler (Newark: University of Delaware Press, 2005), pp. 161-79. Should I have failed to trace a copyright holder, I apologize for any apparent negligence and will make the necessary arrangements at the first opportunity.

Finally, I would like to thank staff in the Rare Books Reading Room of the British Library, in the Rara-Lesesaal of the Staatsbibliothek zu Berlin, in the Adalbert-Stifter-Institut, Linz, and Michelle Allen in the Special Collections section of the University Library at Exeter for supplying reproductions of nineteenth-century originals. Special thanks to Helmuth Meyer (Stifter-Institut) for bibliographical help with *Wien und die Wiener*.

A Note on Translations

Unless otherwise indicated, all translations from German and French are my own, with the relevant passages from the original texts supplied in footnotes.

Introduction
Nineteenth-Century Sketches and the Problem of Walter Benjamin's Legacy

Sketches in words and images published during the heyday of the journalistic revolution, the 1830s and 40s, are an ephemeral and seemingly amorphous genre. As such, they have hitherto not attracted much critical interest. It is the contention of this study that sketches occupy a central space in the networks of knowledge that are so characteristic of the Victorian Age and its European equivalents. The century's pronounced cognitive orientation is inseparably bound up with the 'visual imagination', recognised today as a key to the nineteenth century.[1] Seeing and knowing were thought to be in close correlation, even if they were neither conceived nor experienced as identical. What places sketches in the centre of a visual-cognitive culture is their multiple nexus between the visible and the invisible; between observation and abstraction, entertainment and education, popular culture and science, journalism and high art, fragmentary and totalising views, commercial interest and the dissemination of encyclopaedic knowledge. The French *Physiologies* of the early 1840s epitomise this pivotal role of the sketch throughout Europe, the medical term indicating a transfer of methodology from life science to the humorous study of contemporary mores.

The crucial visual appeal of the genre is highlighted by the abundance of illustrations adorning a *Physiologie*. Although only a minority of European sketches were published under the title of 'Physiology' or 'Natural History', the quasi-scientific method of observing the social body, taking the visible world as its point of departure for the categorisation of types, is common to all of them, and this is why sketches are implicitly subsumed under the genre of *Physiologies* in the subtitle of this study. The reference there to European journalism is also to be understood in a comprehensive sense. While the press

---

1 See, also for the following points, Kate Flint, *The Victorians and the Visual Imagination* (Cambridge: Cambridge University Press, 2002), a study which links the century's fascination with the visible strongly to its culture of knowledge.

and its *feuilleton* provided an important outlet for sketch publications, their most significant media were periodical and serial collections, an innovative form of publishing between journal and book. Nevertheless, it is in the context of the 'journalistic revolution', the unprecedented expansion of ephemeral print media and graphic journalism during the period in question, that the sketch acquires its meaning. Sketch-writers were also very often, at least for some time, active as journalists, journal contributors or editors.

Although text-image relationships in nineteenth-century sketches involve printed images, in other words, graphic reproductions, not original drawings, the derivation of the term 'sketch' from painting is important because it carries certain connotations. The Oxford English Dictionary glosses 'sketch' (German 'Skizze', French 'esquisse') as presumably deriving from the Latin 'schedius' or Greek 'σχέδιος', meaning 'done or made off-hand', 'extempore'. In use from the seventeenth century, the expression denoted a 'rough drawing or delineation', giving 'the prominent features without the detail' and often serving as the first draft for a painting. At a later stage, 'sketch' also signified a genre in its own right, 'a drawing or painting of a slight or unpretentious nature'. In England, as Richard Sha has shown, the visual sketch became prominent as an independent form of art during the second half of the eighteenth century and the first decades of the nineteenth, at a time when the genre's seeming artlessness appealed to Romantic notions of the picturesque, of subjective genius, fragmentariness and truth to nature.[2] The emergence of an analogous, essayistic form in the sphere of letters was heralded, according to Sha, by Launcelot Temple's *Sketches or Essays on Various Subjects* (1758), 'the very first book with sketch in its title'.[3] Sha sees the visual and the verbal sketch as an essentially rhetorical form which seeks to persuade the viewer or reader that 'less is more' while allowing a whole range of ideological agendas to work beneath the surface of spontaneous observation.

Such hidden ideological strategies are in fact the focus of attention in the few studies that have been produced of the verbal-visual sketch. One recent example is Sha's article on the rhetoric of appropriation in which he concentrates on English nineteenth-century sketches of landscapes and colonial cultures. He argues that the 'seeming innocuousness' of 'taking', 'seizing' or 'snatching' a scene from nature constitutes an ingredient of expansionist prac-

---

2 See Richard C. Sha, *The Visual and Verbal Sketch in British Romanticism* (Philadelphia: University of Philadelphia Press, 1998), esp. Chapter 1 (pp. 22-72).
3 Ibid., p. 5.

tices at home (as appropriation of land through enclosure) and overseas.⁴ The present study seeks to demonstrate that sketches are indeed a crucial, vastly underestimated form of cultural negotiation in the nineteenth century, but that their capacity for self-reflection makes them an essentially critical genre when applied to urban home environments. The metropolitan sketch of the 1830s and 40s lies at the heart of a major review of middle-class civilisation on the brink of modernity, a review that all European centres underwent at the same time and which involved major cross-cultural exchange. The rapid expansion in print media was both an indication and an engine of the dynamism that sketches thrived on. In other words, their epistemological subtlety predestined them to be cognitive tools in a culture that was increasingly organised by media.

Until now, no thorough-going examination has been made of the metropolitan sketch as a printed medium associated with the revolution in reproductive technology. The pioneering investigations of Walter Benjamin have, it is true, proved a valuable stimulus to some recent work in the field, but it is also arguable that unquestioning acceptance of his ideological critique has prejudiced the findings of such research. Urban sketches have thus often been seen as part and parcel of a middle-class attempt to gain control over a threatening social body. One example is Alison Byerly's 'Effortless Art', a study devoted to Dickens's *Sketches by Boz* and Thackeray's *Paris Sketch Book*. Following Benjamin, Byerly aims to demonstrate that the 'passive pose' of the *flâneur* in these metropolitan sketches, comparable to the leisurely sketching of the gentleman artist (who nevertheless needs a 'buyer'), masks the 'commodified nature of the sketch itself'.⁵ Unfortunately, even when discussing the sketch as a visual form, Byerly leaves out of account the actual illustrations in the works, that is to say Cruikshank's steel engravings and Thackeray's own copper and wood engravings. Yet these illustrations, as reproducible commodities in themselves, cast a very different light on the written sketches they accompany. Another scholar to echo Benjamin is Carol Bernstein who ascribes to urban sketches of the nineteenth century a 'reassuring' function, since they give the impression that the jungle of the city is knowable and therefore controllable. In this view, the observer, threatened by 'effacement', introduces order into the 'heap of available images', thus stripping the urban experience of all menace. For Bernstein, it seems the only adequate response to such

---

4 See Richard Sha, 'The Power of the English Nineteenth-Century Visual and Verbal Sketch: Appropriation, Discipline, Mastery', *Nineteenth-Century Contexts*, 24:1 (2002), 73-100 (p. 75 and p. 80).
5 Alison Byerly, 'Effortless Art: The Sketch in Nineteenth-Century Painting and Literature', *Criticism*, 41:3 (Summer 1999), 349-64 (p. 350).

experience would be to reject mere observation in favour of fictional representation. Hence Boz is the only sketcher she regards as approaching the point where 'the novelist might want to part with the journalist, the sociologist, or the statistician, insofar as the latter three share in an enterprise of collecting and classifying on the one hand, and of reassuring the public about the possibility of knowledge on the other'.[6] What Bernstein does not consider is the potential of the verbal sketch, precisely by virtue of its fluctuating status *between* journalism, sociology, literature and the visual arts, to organise knowledge and imagery in such a way as to communicate with the reader on a more ambiguous and sophisticated level than that of mere reassurance. Moreover, the sketches she discusses, almost entirely from the second half of the nineteenth century, continue the tradition of Mayhew's *London Labour and the London Poor*, in other words, they are investigations of poverty by 'social explorers',[7] and as such make an uneasy comparison with Boz's 1830s portraits of *Every-day Life and Every-day People* through the medium of a 'speculative stroller'.

Curiously, given the general reliance on Benjamin, there are only very few generic studies of the metropolitan sketch which examine textual semiotics in relation to that of the printed image. One of them, Richard Sieburth's of the *Physiologies*,[8] is again restricted by its own ideological preconceptions based on Benjamin's notion of the *flâneur*. These preconceptions obscure the dynamism of text-image relationships which makes the *Physiologies* the most advanced journalistic meta-medium of the time. This achievement can, however, only be fully grasped within the vibrant context of sketch production. Sketches became *the* genre of an intellectual culture driven by publishing and the 'diffusion of knowledge'. The sketch's rhetoric of modesty and authenticity, to take up Sha's point, coupled with the triumph of new journalistic media, made it a prime vehicle for promoting a comprehensive and self-referential concept of 'type'. Thus the actual significance of advertising *Sketches by Boz* in its subtitle as *Illustrative of Every-day Life and Every-day People* lies in the awareness that the sketcher (himself identified as the professional hack, 'Boz', who first published the sketches in journals) provides an 'illustrative' medium for a world of undistinguished, 'typical' contemporaries like himself. Middle and lower-class life is, as it were, the humble daily

---

6 Carol Bernstein, 'Nineteenth-Century Urban Sketches: Thresholds of Fiction', *Prose Studies*, 3:3 (1980), 217-40 (p. 229 and p. 235).
7 Ibid., p. 219. Bernstein here refers to the subtitle of P.J. Keating's collection, *Into Unknown England, 1866-1913: Selections from the Social Explorers* (1976).
8 See Richard Sieburth, 'Une idéologie du lisible: le phénomène des "Physiologies"', *Romantisme*, 47 (1985:1), 39-60.

newspaper to which *Sketches* – Boz's and Cruikshank's – offer the illustrations. Developments in graphic art, especially the triumph of wood engraving, supported this move towards 'typology', so that sketches of the 1830s and 40s have to be understood as intermedial genre-painting and exercises in early sociology on a massive scale. The ostentatious slightness of the sketch form lends credibility to an ambition which could otherwise be seen as hubristic. Nothing less than a 'moral encyclopaedia' of the century is attempted by one of the most famous sketch publications of the 1840s, *Les Français peints par eux-mêmes*, on the basis of hundreds of 'pen and pencil' portraits of professional types. Another encyclopaedic sociological study, Edward Lytton Bulwer's *England and the English* (1833), is peppered with the author's own verbal 'illustrations' in the form of dialogue scenes and character portraits. Lightness of touch and a visually appealing, entertaining style are marketed as characteristics of highly ambitious and 'serious' contemporary literature. An advertisement of 1848 for *Gavarni in London* praises its texts as 'delineations of every-day character and every-day life' in the form of 'light sparkling essays'. As creations of writers who 'hold an important place in the literature of the age',[9] they are thought to be worthy complements to the 'Illustrations', with a capital i, by the celebrated Gavarni. The wording of the advert as well as the joint publication of written and graphic sketches alludes to *Sketches by Boz*, published more than a decade earlier, a sign that the prominence of the visual-verbal sketch in the domain of literature is now something of which its practitioners are well aware. Ephemeral publications have taken the place of 'great' works. In *England and the English*, Bulwer observes that the present is indeed 'a great literary age', but that its significant works must be sought 'not in detached and avowed and standard publications, but in periodical miscellanies'. Such is the import of journal publishing in the sphere of letters that, according to Bulwer, nothing less than a 'revolution' has been 'effected by Periodical Literature'.[10] Journalism has become the literary emblem of the age, and the fact that sketches focus so strongly on cities and their populations is linked to the metropolitan nature of journalism itself.

The rapidity with which innovative, often collaborative journalistic publications were received, translated and adapted across national boundaries is indicative of a European *feuilleton* culture that was relatively evenly developed. The journalistic revolution helped to map out the European world in a new way. International metropolitan topographies supplanted the historical nation

---

9 Publisher's advertisement in Albert Smith, *The Natural History of the Flirt* (London: Bogue, 1849), [p. 113].
10 Edward Lytton Bulwer, *England and the English* (Paris: Baudry, 1833), pp. 282-3.

states, just as the Parisian Revolution of July 1830 had swept away the system of Restoration. The omnipresence of capitals through their journalism, together with the advent of the railway and the electric telegraph, seemed to make real what Karl Gutzkow still considered a fool's telegraphic fantasy in 1832, in other words, that it should be possible for the same individual to have 'one foot in London, the other one in Paris' and to 'act as a correspondent from both cities simultaneously'.[11] A similar image is employed by Gavarni to illustrate the frontispiece for the serial *Le Diable à Paris* (1844-46). It shows a portrait of the devil as a journalist-cum-sketcher towering over a map of the French capital on which he straddles the right and the left bank of the river Seine. This demonic observer who is dressed *à la mode* as a Parisian dandy – a *flâneur*, one might be tempted to think – transmits the results of his vision to the rest of the world in the form of collected loose-leaf sketches and laterna magica images (illustration 1).

This image sums up the central role of sketches, written and graphic, in redrawing the map of Europe in terms of cityscapes and in exploring the changing social body inhabiting them. Without this cognitive re-orientation in the 1830s and 40s – decades framed by the July Revolution and the Reform Bill at one end and the European revolutions of 1848 at the other –, the cultures now most closely associated with the nineteenth century, that of the Victorian Age and of the Second Empire, would be unthinkable. Gavarni's figure is at once a reader and a creator of a completely new urban sign-system layered upon a historical landscape.

Does this map represent an attempt to make legible, harmless and reassuring what, in Benjamin's understanding, is fundamentally 'shocking', in other words, the new world of the city? Since the French sketches of the period, such as the *Physiologies*, are known today mainly because Benjamin discussed them, and since his ideas have been uncritically absorbed into a vast body of scholarship, it seems worth going back to some of his particularly influential passages, mainly from the chapter 'The *flâneur*' in the essay 'The Paris of the Second Empire in Baudelaire', and stating precisely where the present study offers a different and, it is hoped, liberating view.

The crucial significance of the fashionable stroller, the reader of city physiognomies, was not discovered by Benjamin, nor indeed first evident in the

---

11 'Wie der Koloß von Rhodus stehst Du in partieller Allgegenwart mit dem einen Fuße in London, mit dem andern in Paris. [...] so müßtest Du zu gleicher Zeit aus beiden Städten correspondiren können.' Karl Gutzkow, *Briefe eines Narren an eine Närrin*, ed. by R.J. Kavanagh (Münster: Oktober Verlag, 2003), p. 117. See Bibliography for internet edition.

Introduction 7

Illustration 1   Gavarni, frontispiece in *Le Diable à Paris. Paris et les Parisiens. Mœurs et coutumes, caractères et portraits des habitants de Paris, tableau complet de leur vie privée, publique, politique, artistique, littéraire, industrielle, etc., etc.*, 2 vols (Paris: Hetzel, 1845-6), I (1845), opposite p. i. Wood engraving by Brugnot.

works of Baudelaire and Poe, the authors which his interpretation mainly focuses on.[12] However, Benjamin's *flâneur* has become firmly identified with the type and turned into an icon of modernism. This figure prefers arcades and gaslight, follows traces among the crowd in the manner of a detective, turns the boulevard into an *intérieur* and, as a bohemian prostituting himself on the literary market, shows an affinity with the commodities he gazes at in window displays. A critic cannot be held responsible for what posterity does with his ideas, but in Benjamin's case the iconographic cliché has to be seen as a result of the critic's own blinkeredness. John Rignall has remarked that Benjamin's *flâneur* is 'the object of the materialist historian's gaze', in other words, that he is viewed entirely 'as a social phenomenon', a manifestation of the era of high capitalism, regardless of the nature of the sources with which this 'historian's gaze' operates. These sources are not factual accounts, but highly fractured literary reflections, to be precise, Baudelaire's reflections on Poe's reflections, situated in the context of a discussion of the draughtsman Constantin Guys, 'Le Peintre de la vie moderne'. Benjamin thus fails to emphasise the essential, namely, that the *flâneur* is himself 'an exponent of a certain kind of vision',[13] of literary and visual perspectives of the city.

Benjamin the materialist historian *could* have drawn extensively on expository sources (rather than on Poe's story 'The Man of the Crowd' or Baudelaire's essay) which deal with the *flâneur* as a new social type. That is to say, he could have exploited the sketches of the 1830s and 40s. Aware of their existence, however, he makes no use of them but dismisses their cognitive claims as superficial. Not surprisingly, because the whole genre, subsumed under the broad heading of *feuilleton*, is seen by him as socially and ideologically suspect and therefore unreliable. Since I intend to foreground the function of journalism as an engine of social knowledge, I approach sketches as a valuable cognitive resource, more or less the opposite of what Benjamin sees in them. The portrait *they* present of the observing city stroller is rather different from the artistic Second Empire type drawn by Benjamin. The pre-1850 *flâneur* is not the bohemian outsider moving in the jungle of the city, but, on

---

12 'Das Paris des Second Empire bei Charles Baudelaire' (1938), 'Über einige Motive bei Baudelaire' (1939) and 'Paris, die Hauptstadt des XIX. Jahrhunderts (1935; Benjamin's exposé for the *Arcades Project*). Translated by Harry Zohn as 'The Paris of the Second Empire in Baudelaire' and 'Some Motifs in Baudelaire' and by Quintin Hoare as 'Paris – The Capital of the Nineteenth Century'; all in Walter Benjamin, *Charles Baudelaire, a Lyric Poet in the Era of High Capitalism* (London: Verso, 1983). This edition will in the following be referred to as CB.

13 John Rignall, *Realist Fiction and the Strolling Spectator* (London: Routledge, 1992), p. 14.

the contrary, one of a countless number of ordinary city dwellers who read metropolitan surfaces.

One publication of sketches Benjamin mentions dismissively is the collective serial *Paris ou Le Livre des Cent-et-un* (1831-34). It features a sketch of the *flâneur* which reads in parts like something well ahead of its time. The type is described as able to sharpen contemporaries' perceptions of the 'moving panorama' surrounding them: 'Nothing escapes his investigative view [...], everything interests him, everything is to him a text of observation.'[14] The suggestion that the city constitutes a quasi-filmic 'text' whose language is learnt through observation is, however, by no means singular in Parisian sketches of the 1830s and 40s, as the following incisive comments by Richard Burton make clear:

> To describe the *flâneur* as a semiologist *avant la lettre* is in no sense [...] to read back into the past preoccupations of the present. On the contrary, the belief that urban life consisted of a multiplicity of interlocking semiotic systems and that everything in the city was, by definition, meaningful was so widespread amongst writers on pre-1850 Paris as to be virtually platitudinous [...].[15]

Reading surfaces was one thing; another was the awareness of a 'multiplicity of interlocking semiotic systems' which no single act of reading could make available. The interpreter of signs was therefore necessarily also one of a 'multiplicity' of readers engaged in the same business. Significantly, the anonymous author of 'Le Flâneur à Paris' in the (also significantly titled) *Livre des Cent-et-un* (Book of the One Hundred and One) is himself listed as 'un flâneur'. Anonymity here does not imply a Baudelairean 'man of the crowd', but *the new social type*. The portrait of the professional decipherer of the city by a professional decipherer, in a collective medium which is itself characteristic of the changing social fabric of the July Monarchy, therefore possesses the highest cognitive interest both for writers and the reading public at the time and for nineteenth-century specialists today.

---

14 'Sous quel aspect inattendu s'offre à vos yeux, avec un pareil démonstrateur, le panorama mobile qui vous environne!' 'Rien n'échappe à son regard investigateur [...], tout l'intéresse, tout est pour lui un texte d'observations.' Un flâneur, 'Le flâneur à Paris', in *Paris, ou Le Livre des Cent-et-un*, 15 vols (Paris: Ladvocat, 1831-4), VI (1832), 95-110 (p. 102 and p. 101).
15 Richard D.E. Burton, *The Flâneur and his City. Patterns of Daily Life in Paris 1815-1851* (Durham: University of Durham, 1994), p. 2.

Although Burton thus draws attention to this social and semiotic meaning of the *flâneur* and although he clearly differentiates the type from his post-1850 variant, 'the *homme des foules* as described by Baudelaire',[16] he makes no criticism of Benjamin whose concept is determined by the latter. Instead, there are the obligatory nods in the direction of the master.[17] One of them, to be found in almost any more recent study of urban portraiture, is an unquestioning acceptance of Benjamin's point, itself derived from Georg Simmel, that human relationships in the big city are characterised by a preponderance of visual over aural activity. The observer's speculative faculty, which seems at least as important as the activity of the eye, is totally left out of account. It would probably be overstating the case to argue that the fixation of today's criticism on the legibility of surfaces goes back to this particular point in Benjamin's study of Baudelaire. However, there can be no doubt that Benjamin's fascination with the visual world of Paris, culminating in his *Arcades Project*, is at least partly responsible for a neglect of the cognitive dimensions in nineteenth-century city portraits. My study seeks to rectify this by focusing on *the scientific paradigm of discursive urban portraiture between 1830 and 1850, that of physiology*. It enables 'physiognomists' of city life to link their interpretation of surfaces to a context of unseen social, intellectual, moral and semiotic interaction.

Benjamin's scant regard for the publishing industry of the July Monarchy which produced both the concept of the *flâneur* and the genre of the *Physiologie* seriously limits the value of his comments, as others have also pointed out.[18] Measured against Baudelaire, with his poetic apotheosis of the *flâneur*, the journalists who treated the subject in a more mundane way two or three decades before are condescendingly labelled 'minor masters' ('Kleinmeister').[19] Or worse: the acknowledgment of the great serial publications of

---

16 Burton (note 15), p. 5.
17 See ibid., p. 4.
18 For example, Kai Kauffmann: Benjamin's 'criticism of journal literature, publishing and the press, evidently derived from the romantic ideal of immediate experience and communication, is decidedly biased.' ('Seine offensichtlich von der sentimentalischen Idealvorstellung unmittelbarer Erfahrung und Kommunikation abgeleitete Kritik an der Gebrauchsliteratur und der Publizistik/Presse ist ausgesprochen einseitig.') K. Kauffmann, *"Es ist nur ein Wien!" Stadtbeschreibungen von Wien 1700 bis 1873* (Vienna, Cologne, Weimar: Böhlau, 1994), p. 28.
19 See 'The Paris of the Second Empire in Baudelaire', CB, p. 39, and 'Some Motifs in Baudelaire', CB, p. 121. The same kind of value judgement inherent in Benjamin's terminology can be observed elsewhere. He juxtaposes the journalistic 'writings' ('Schrifttum'), destined not to survive, to the 'literature' of the detective story which 'was to have a great future' (CB, p. 39 and p. 40). Baudelaire's *flâneur* is

sketches, including the *Livre des Cent-et-un*, as 'panorama literature' contains a sting in the tail since the collectively produced panorama is seen as a market place where the professional writer, without admitting it to himself, is looking for a buyer.[20] To put it mildly, this does not do justice to the panorama or to panoramic sketches, and although the critic admits that there is a 'store of information' ('informatorische[r] Fundus') in this kind of literature, from which he himself happily profits in the *Arcades Project*, he will only concede 'background' function to it. The 'foreground' of the panoramic collections, for him, is the 'anecdotal form' of sketches. What he sees as background is, as I will argue, in fact the structural principle. Panoramic collections organise a 'store of information' so that it becomes a *body of knowledge* about the city, and this system of order is to be seen as distinct from encyclopaedic collections, a category Benjamin does not develop. The eye-catching foreground of collective sketch publications is not provided by the easy, chatty, anecdotal style, but by the precise observation and delineation of the subject that is the hallmark of the genre, and relationships between written and graphic sketches (not considered by Benjamin) are very important in this respect.

The translators of *Charles Baudelaire. A Lyric Poet in the Era of High Capitalism*, Zohn and Hoare, tend to render Benjamin's consistently used term 'panorama' as 'diorama'.[21] Panoramas (introduced in the 1790s) were circular paintings viewed from a platform in the middle, while dioramas (introduced in the 1820s) were screens viewed from an auditorium, showing a particular vista with changing light (and often sound) effects which, in their most developed form, suggested movement. Despite their shared ending in '–rama', the two media had 'very little in common', as Bernard Comment points out:

---

then, of course, seen to be conceived substantially on the basis of a high-literature detective story, Poe's 'The Man of the Crowd' of 1840 (which, lacking a crime, is not a detective story in the strict sense, but, as Benjamin has to admit, a kind of 'X-rayed' version; CB, p. 48).

20 See 'The Paris of the Second Empire in Baudelaire', CB, p. 35. Similarly, 'Paris – the Capital of the Nineteenth Century', CB, p. 170. Here a mistranslation of Benjamin's sentence, 'Das Warenhaus ist der letzte *Strich* des Flaneurs' (my emphasis) occurs. 'Strich' has obviously been misread as 'Streich', strike or *coup*, whereas it signifies the 'haunt' of the *flâneur* while also bearing clear connotations with prostitution in its allusion to the expression 'auf den Strich gehen'.

21 See 'The Paris of the Second Empire in Baudelaire', CB, p. 35, and 'Paris – the Capital of the Nineteenth Century', CB, pp. 161-2.

[I]n the word *panorama*, 'pan' is the constituent that creates the idea of totality, the total vision of a given reality dependent on a circular horizon. Yet the diorama, because it was flat and like a painting [...], did not contain either the same logic or, more importantly, the same aim. Its main concern was to incorporate the passage of time and movement into a representation whose themes were often connected to the transition from day to night or vice versa, to the changing seasons, to natural disasters.[22]

Translating Benjamin's term 'panorama' as 'diorama' is in fact a silent correction of the critic's loose terminology, since the visual medium he calls 'panorama' includes dioramic effects, such as suggesting 'the changing time of day [...], the rising of the moon, or the rushing of the waterfall'.[23] While thus making Benjamin's text in some ways more precise, the English version loses the connotation of a circular painting which is essential to Benjamin's comparison of socially all-embracing sketch collections with the all-round view of the panorama. Therefore the translation 'socially *dioramic*',[24] with reference to these sketches, makes no sense. This terminological problem shows that Benjamin's imprecision in lumping panoramas and dioramas together is crucial, in that it enables him to conflate two things: the suggestion of a) an overview, turning the city into a 'landscape',[25] and b) an early cinematic mass medium imitating 'Nature' to perfection – both, in his understanding, expressive of middle-class false consciousness. However comparable sketch collections are with visual mass media, this analogy cannot be constructed in such a foreshortened and oblique way. Examining precisely in what respects sketches exploit the paradigms of visual media in order to establish their own distinctive, which is to say cognitive, engagement with the visual world, I will show that the model of the panorama (and of travel literature) works for sketches piecing together the city in a collaborative effort. That of the magic lantern, on the other hand (together with that of the periodical Review), informs encyclopaedic collections reviewing the nation and the century. Here, the emphasis is by definition on *knowledge*, and it is interesting to see that the idea of 'passing in review' before the reader/audience, connected as it is to magic lantern performances and to lectures accompanied by dioramic views, attaches so closely to *cognitive* processes. The sketch industry combines entertainment with instruction, and this instruction is almost always amusingly and critically self-observing. The middle classes laugh

---

22 Bernard Comment, *The Panorama* (London: Reaktion Books, 1999), p. 61.
23 See Benjamin, 'Paris – the Capital of the Nineteenth Century', CB, p. 161.
24 Ibid., p. 162 (my emphasis).
25 Ibid.

about their own thumbnail images and cartoons, as they would laugh in a stage revue. Panoramic (and also, in my definition, encyclopaedic) sketch collections are social 'idylls' for Benjamin.[26] For the last time, he seems to suggest, the working man and woman are depicted here as part of a body of *citoyens*; they are soon to emerge as a class of their own which can no longer be integrated into a bourgeois panorama. A politically radical serial such as *Le Diable à Paris* hardly qualifies as an 'idyll', while even the more moderate *Les Français peints par eux-mêmes* and its European counterparts present an exercise in self-scrutiny by the middle class which is difficult to surpass. A versatile draughtsman and author of dialogical and dramatic sketches such as Henry Monnier, the inventor of the archetypal Monsieur Prudhomme, is dismissed by Benjamin as a 'philistine endowed with an uncommon capacity for self-observation'.[27] The critic is obviously unwilling to view middle-class self-observation as a worthwhile intellectual and creative activity or to concede that it was by no means 'uncommon', but absolutely central to the sketch industry. This industry is to be understood precisely as an attempt by the century's dominant class to review its potential for social inclusion, in other words, its capacity to serve as a social model in an increasingly stratified class system. Since Benjamin's dialectical materialist approach rejects all such self-scrutiny on the part of the bourgeoisie as superficial, he does not investigate the physiological paradigm of early sociology or of sociological sketches at all. Instead, he points to the dubious 'science' of physiognomy as their model, arguing that Lavater and Gall were at least genuine empiricists, whereas the *physiologues* simply 'lived on the credit of this empiricism without adding anything of their own'.[28] I will show just how much further the model of physiognomy is taken by the sketches. Transformed into physiology, it becomes an instrument of *sociological*, not characterological, insight. 'Character' is superseded by 'type', and the Lavaterian business of deciphering virtues or vices from individual features gives way to an anatomy of the living social body. Of course, physiognomy remains an important paradigm within social physiology. 'Physiognomic' study from a 'physiological' angle usually means a non-moralising, yet engaged reading of social surfaces (avocational types, habits, modes, cityscapes, significant developments and so forth) and an analysis of the condition of society.

Consistently, then, Benjamin denies, or suppresses evidence of, the cognitive orientation and achievement of the sketch. This tendency has a particu-

---

26 Ibid., p. 162.
27 'The Paris of the Second Empire in Baudelaire', CB, p. 36.
28 Ibid., p. 39.

larly counter-productive effect on his discussion of the *Physiologies*, a discussion perpetuated by Richard Sieburth in his much-noted article of 1985.[29] A cheap pocket-book genre inundating the Parisian market between 1840 and 1842, the *Physiologies* are dismissed as sedatives for the *petite bourgeoisie*, designed to divert any political caricature that might still have emerged under the tightened press laws of 1835 into innocuous portraits of social types, and to make a disturbing, dangerous urban world look familiar.[30] Supported by the authoritative work of Nathalie Preiss on the *Physiologies*, I argue that, on the contrary, these publications were in their very conception a parodistic form, wittily subverting the portrayal of Parisian and French types in the serial *Les Français peints par eux-mêmes*, and that if the mordant caricature of the earlier July Monarchy found a place anywhere, it was in these illustrated booklets.

In the context of his comments on the *Physiologies* Benjamin also formulates the idea of the *flâneur* using the street as a nature reserve for his botanical studies and turning the boulevard into an *intérieur*, where he is at home just like the bourgeois within his own four walls. Arcades, representing an intermediate space between interior and exterior, are therefore the *flâneur*'s ideal territory.[31] There are at least three objections to be made against this argument:

1. It is inconsistent with Benjamin's own line of enquiry, as is revealed by the discussion of Poe's story 'The Man of the Crowd' and its Baudelairean reflections in which the chapter on the *flâneur* culminates. Here Benjamin asserts that Poe's unknown man (wrongly identified by him as a *flâneur* anyway),[32] who wanders aimlessly through a department store, has lost his way in the 'labyrinth of merchandise' just as the earlier type of *flâneur* had lost his way in the labyrinth of the city.[33] This flatly contradicts the former assertion about the city being made a homely place by the *flâneurs* of the *Physiologies*, yet Benjamin even reiterates this point here. He argues that

---

29 'Une idéologie du lisible' (note 8).
30 See Benjamin, 'The Paris of the Second Empire in Baudelaire', CB, pp. 36-40.
31 See ibid., p. 37.
32 John Rignall has pointed this error out. In the chapter 'The *flâneur*' of his first Baudelaire essay, 'The Paris of the Second Empire in Baudelaire', Benjamin misreads Baudelaire's reading of Poe's 'Man of the Crowd', assuming Baudelaire sees in the unknown man, not in the narrator following him through the crowd, a *flâneur*. In his second essay, 'Some Motifs in Baudelaire', Benjamin 'corrects' the error, saying that the man of the crowd is not a *flâneur*, but still assumes that this is how Baudelaire saw the figure. See Rignall (note 13), p. 13.
33 Benjamin, 'The Paris of the Second Empire in Baudelaire', CB, p. 54.

while the arcades had represented the kind of interior as which the street offered itself to the observing stroller, the department store into which the arcades are degenerating, now becomes a street or 'labyrinth' for him.[34] Even allowing for the associative freedom of Benjamin's thought, this argument borders on the nonsensical, though it has not prevented the idea of streets being turned into interiors from becoming part of the critical canon.

2. Arcades are, at best, of extremely marginal interest to the observers of Parisian life in the 1830s and 40s, as Karlheinz Stierle has shown; their fascination is with street life proper, for example, omnibuses (introduced in 1828),[35] on which Benjamin amasses materials in his *Arcades Project* but remains silent in his two relevant essays. Dickens's *Sketches by Boz* confirm the supreme significance of metropolitan transport in the changing social universe of the 1830s.

3. Assuming streets *are* turned into interiors, the *flâneur* must be someone who has abandoned his 'proper' private space. The dwindling of privacy is in fact a much more fruitful concept for an understanding of social processes and methods of observation during the period in question. I will show that the way in which sketches perform social anatomy suggests a turning inside-out, in other words, a defamiliarisation, of private, internal spaces, rather than a turning outside-in, that is to say, a familiarisation, of public, external space. In the same context one could point to the fact that a perception of the urban environment as nature (see Benjamin's likening of the panorama to landscape and of the *flâneur* to a botanist) has ideological connotations that are alien to the observers of Parisian life. Yes, they do analyse urban environments in terms of natural history, but only inasmuch as 'life science' (anatomy, physiognomy, zoology and physiology) is a paradigm for social science. No *Physiologie* or related publication would at any point suggest that a place shaped by human history is to be understood as natural space. This kind of understanding, which does also exist in metropolitan sketches, has, as it were, an axe to grind. It is a reactionary view formulated against the Western, historical and dynamic interpretation of the city; – an argument I develop in my section on the Viennese panoramic collection, *Wien und die Wiener*.

On the basis of my argument so far, readers could be forgiven for thinking that this book deals mainly with Parisian portraits. It does not. Equal attention is devoted to English, French and German/Austrian sketch publications of the 1830s and 40s. What will not be perpetuated is the myth of 'Paris – the Capi-

---

34 See ibid.
35 See Karlheinz Stierle, *Der Mythos von Paris. Zeichen und Bewußtsein der Stadt* (Munich, Vienna: Hanser, 1993), pp. 208-14.

tal of the Nineteenth Century', analysed but also cemented by Benjamin through the very choice of title for his *Arcades Project* essay. Instead, I will seek to unravel at least some of the dense network of cross-national connections in European journalism of the time and show that Parisian developments were at the cutting edge, but by no means avant-gardist compared to the rest of Europe. In fact London publishing was in many ways ahead of Paris. Thus I will be able to show, for example, how an English sketch collection, *Heads of the People*, which started in autumn 1838, was able to become the model for the famous *Les Français peints par eux-mêmes*, the first instalment of which appeared in spring 1839, and of *Wien und die Wiener* which was published from 1841 but conceived probably from about 1840, the year of the first German translation of the English original.

Readers whose awareness is conditioned by Benjamin will be under the impression that nineteenth-century German letters are more or less devoid of modern readings of urban surfaces as epitomised by the *flâneur*. Benjamin suggests that one of the few approximations to be found is E.T.A. Hoffmann's late story 'Des Vetters Eckfenster' (My Cousin's Corner-Window) of 1822, an example to which he gives great prominence, referring to it in both his essays on Baudelaire, each time in explicit comparison with Poe's story 'The Man of the Crowd'.[36] Hoffmann's observer is a paralyzed writer who takes pleasure in studying life in Berlin's busy market square below his window and in drawing conclusions from the observation of people's appearances (helped by a pair of opera glasses). Benjamin sees the limitations of this view, compared to *flâneurs* in the Poe/Baudelaire mode who observe life from the pavement and mingle with the crowd, as symptomatic of 'the difference between Berlin and London', that is to say, of Germany's less advanced socio-economic situation.[37] However, his argument makes little sense because Poe's 'Man of the Crowd' and Baudelaire's relevant reflections postdate Hoffmann's story quite considerably.[38] The only other German examples Benjamin discusses are Adolf Glaßbrenner, Friedrich Engels and Heinrich Heine. The first two fit conveniently the cliché of the 'private individual' of the German *Biedermeier* or of the provincial German visitor whose city por-

---

36 See Benjamin, 'The Paris of the Second Empire in Baudelaire', CB, pp. 48-9, and 'Some Motifs in Baudelaire', CB, pp. 129-30.
37 'The Paris of the Second Empire in Baudelaire', CB, p. 49.
38 The interesting question Benjamin does not ask is how an author of the German Romantic period was capable of conceiving literature based on precise observation at such an early date – especially since he himself remarks that Hoffmann's could be 'one of the earliest attempts to capture the street scene of a large city'. 'Some Motifs in Baudelaire', CB, p. 129.

traits lack the equanimity, wit and precision of their English or French counterparts. Heine is an exception, the reason being that, as a writer living in Paris, he has adopted a metropolitan outlook and learnt to read the city.[39] In the case of Engels's description of London (in *The Condition of the Working Class in England*, 1845), Benjamin is attracted by the socialist's incorruptibly critical view of poverty, but regards as provincial the sense of unease and the moral indignation in his description of the masses rushing past each other on the pavements. Any Parisian *feuilletoniste*, Benjamin remarks, could have produced an urbane and aesthetically advanced crowd portrait from the *flâneur's* point of view, but not Engels. Yet, had Benjamin taken notice, for example, of the letters from Berlin (1822) of Heinrich Heine or, perhaps more importantly, of the metropolitan portraits (1846) of Ernst Dronke, a writer who collaborated with Marx and Engels from 1848, but was in fact viewed not without a degree of suspicion by Engels, he would have encountered classic examples of city portraiture from a *flâneur's* perspective. The urbaneness of Dronke's socialism, a kaleidoscopic mixture of the latest left-wing theory forged together with physiognomic observation, was exactly what Engels found objectionable.[40]

In other words, the German (and Austrian) sociological sketches which did produce equivalents of Parisian observation, and in an exact historical parallel to French and English developments, are a blind spot on Benjamin's map, which is astonishing in such an avid collector of even quite obscure nineteenth-century documents.[41] The fact that he, of all critical theorists, did not take account of these sketches goes some way towards explaining the complete neglect of an important German contribution to the nineteenth-century culture of knowledge. It has also cemented the image of nineteenth-century German literature as one that only reluctantly engages 'directly with the contemporary world in the manner of a Dickens or a Balzac'.[42] Yet, by the mid-

---

39 See 'Some Motifs in Baudelaire', CB, pp. 121-2 and 129-31.
40 See Rainer Nitsche, 'Nachwort', in Ernst Dronke, *Berlin*, ed. by R. Nitsche (Darmstadt, Neuwied: Luchterhand, 1987), pp. 202-11 (p. 205).
41 With the exception of writings by Marx and Engels, the German sources of the 1830s to 50s consulted by Benjamin for his *Arcades Project* are predominantly works about Paris.
42 Rignall (note 13), p. 17. Rignall's judgement of Benjamin's blinkeredness in the discussion of the *flâneur* (to which I have referred above) is very illuminating. Yet he follows Benjamin in considering 'Hoffmann's view from the window' as 'characteristic' of 'German literature in the nineteenth century and its marginal relationship to the mainstream of European realism', maintaining that 'it is not until the early twentieth century that the *flâneur* has any resonance in German literature' (ibid.).

1840s the art of deciphering urban physiognomies was widely practised in German letters, no longer restricted to the musings of Romantic genius watching the world from on high, or to travel literature such as Heinrich Heine's and Ludwig Börne's letters and observations from London and Paris. Urban sign-reading was performed rigorously at home, against the odds of censorship and despite the lack of a national capital. Thus one of my aims is to show that much of the ephemeral writing in the German-speaking world of the mid-nineteenth century was not parochial compared to Western Europe, however much this may be suggested by the literature of 'Poetic Realism' that became the canon.[43]

The ambition of this study is to present as full a picture as possible of the cognitive and epistemological qualities of the sketch industry, covering publications from three different national cultures, but deliberately excluding travel sketches from abroad. The eyes of the 'foreign' traveller will be shown to be at work in the depiction and analysis of *home environments* – an inversion of the visiting observer's perspective that is distinctive of the sociological orientation of sketches. Their analysis of the social body, following physiological patterns of cognition, focuses on the nineteenth-century urban citizen's social behaviour and moral values. In the terminology of the time, this central area of observation is denoted most happily by the French expression *les mœurs*; the German equivalent, understood in all its nuances by nineteenth-century contemporaries but far less so today, is *Sitten*, whilst English, for want of a better expression, has to resort to the Latin *mores* to capture the full sense. Neither 'manners' nor 'customs' nor 'habits' are sufficient in themselves, but they are all meant by the term *mœurs*. In nineteenth-century usage, however, *manners* does seem to cover more or less the semantic field of *mœurs* or *Sitten* (as can be gleaned, for example, from the first book Bulwer's *England and the English*, entitled 'Society and Manners'). Another terminological difficulty I have to contend with is today's narrow understanding of the noun 'moralist' as someone preaching morality or at least adhering to a set of values, whereas I am using it in the older sense of 'an observer of mores' (and hence the adjective 'moralist' is also understood in this way). When using the adjective 'cognitive', I refer to the use-value of the sketch as a form of knowledge. However, as will at least be implied in parts of my interpretation

---

43 As has been brought to light by Dirk Göttsche's monumental work on the nineteenth-century German *Zeitroman*, a genre that engages directly with the times as well as evincing an awareness of 'time' as the governing factor, this canon must be one of the most selective ever. See D. Göttsche, *Zeit im Roman. Literarische Zeitreflexion und die Geschichte des Zeitromans im späten 18. und im 19. Jahrhundert* (Munich: Fink, 2001).

(see, for example, pp. 260-8), the sketch tradition also belongs to the prehistory of cognitive science, constituting an early form of sociology of knowledge.

By focusing on sketches as a form mediating and shaping social knowledge, outside the discipline of sociology which is emerging as their academic counterpart in the 1830s, I portray them as a distinct type of literature in their own right, not as 'practice pieces' eventually merging into the great realist novels. I am therefore not considering the relationship between, say, Balzac's or Dickens's sketches and their works of fiction. What I am hoping to convey is that the 1830s and 40s were decades of an intensely critical, discursive and international writing process in which, amongst a host of journalists who are now obscure or forgotten, authors of novels and narratives such as Balzac, Bulwer, Dickens, Gutzkow, George Sand and Stifter participated as sketchwriters. Outlooks and preoccupations during this period were different from the aesthetic concerns as well as from the national, often local perspective of the realist novelists of the 1850s and beyond. To lay the foundations for further detailed research on the 'culture of knowledge' between 1830 and 1850 I provide a select bibliography of sketch publications in England, France and Germany/Austria.

Since by far the most characteristic form of sketch publication during this period was the collective serial, my focus will be on works bringing together a multitude of writers and, in fortunate circumstances, also of draughtsmen and engravers, mainly *Heads of the People, Les Français peints par euxmêmes, Wien und die Wiener, in Bildern aus dem Leben* and *Le Diable à Paris* (appearing, between them, from 1838 until 1846). The *Physiologies*, the illustrated booklets which created a vogue in 1841-42, formed a kind of series of their own. Journals will be of interest inasmuch as they were the locus of the first (and sometimes the only) publication of a sketch, but will not, apart from some introductory considerations, be considered as a subject on their own. To explore the sections devoted to sketches in European periodicals of the time, as well as determining their aesthetic and cognitive significance in relation to the specific character of each periodical, would require a separate study. The central importance of journalistic publishing is, of course, discussed throughout. I approach the sketch as a form that implies the plurality of 'sketches' and hints at its own status as a multipliable, open medium; more precisely, as a collectable publication that is neither journal nor book. Hence sketches fulfill their function most evidently en masse, after being revised, ordered and arranged to form a body of observations. Where possible, this body became, or was conceived from the start as, a verbal-visual ensemble. The single-authored collection, and, of course, even the individual, uncollected sketch, have their place in this study, as do unillustrated collections.

After all, what Günter Oesterle has argued with regard to the 'performative' aspect of *feuilleton* writing applies eminently to the sketch, in other words, that it is a form always implying a text-image relationship even if there is no graphic image to relate to.[44]

To highlight the phenomenon of the sketch as central to our understanding of nineteenth-century epistemology, I discuss a different epistemological and/or medial context in each of my chapters. Beginning with an interpretation of sketches' response to the dynamic developments in print media, which they themselves both represent and reflect upon, and outlining the European cross-connections in print culture (Chapter 1), I move on to an analysis of optical media, more precisely, their significance for popular entertainment and instruction, and their reflection in sketches (Chapter 2). The mobility and dynamism represented by both print and visual media is shown to be re-enacted and cognitively transcended by the meta-medium of the sketch. It is important to understand how the visual-verbal genre engages with processes of change happening 'before the eyes' of contemporaries. 'Sketching' implies a present-tense form of writing that depicts and interprets what is seen, thereby joining the act of 'reading' – in the literal sense – to the process of seeing and interpreting enacted on the page. In this way the sketch establishes itself as a specific form of present-day cognition, a science of society without being scientific.

Yet there are scientific paradigms, those of physiology, zoology and geology, which sketches appropriate and transform, making possible insights into a social body in transition. The way in which they achieve a blend of life science with early forms of sociology in an innovative essayistic study of 'type' is then addressed (Chapter 3). While borrowing from physiognomy and physiology as proto-sociological disciplines, sketches constitute types in a way that differs from scientific methods where illustrations serve the text. By allowing dynamic relationships between image and text, sketches perform a process of insight which is appropriate to a fluctuating social universe. Despite the apparent fixity of their systems of classification, the types they constitute are equally subject to dynamic perception and change. These types are often depicted by parodying verbal-visual clichés or stereotypes, thus establishing the sketch once more as a meta-medium.

The performative nature of the sketch, making it enact its own epistemology, is then linked to a long tradition of moralist writing and graphic art re-

---

44 See Günter Oesterle, '"Unter dem Strich". Skizze einer Kulturpoetik des Feuilletons im neunzehnten Jahrhundert', in *Das schwierige neunzehnte Jahrhundert*, ed. by Jürgen Barkoff, Gilbert Carr and Roger Paulin (Tübingen: Niemeyer, 2000), pp. 229-50 (p. 239).

volving around the topos of the 'theatre of the world' (Chapter 4). The theme of human beings as actors and stock characters in a divine comedy, stripped of its religious connotations and understood as a 'comédie humaine', provides the basis of the sociological and typological conception informing sketches. The tradition of associating the comic and satirical depiction of mores with the Devil (who has the freedom to transgress against moral codes) forms the background to a plethora of metropolitan publications of the 1830s and 40s with satanic titles, alluding mainly to Le Sage's moralist novel *Le Diable boiteux* (1707). Devilish insight into the inner life of the city is here combined with a totalising overview, and Gavarni's spectator from *Le Diable à Paris*, 1845-46 (illustration 1, p. 7), documents the significance of this 'panoptic' tradition beautifully.

Sketches, as is shown in Chapter 5, do not simply suggest that everything is knowable and therefore controllable by the privileged observer. Thanks to the sketch industry, the demonic, semi-criminal, dispassionate dandy spectator of the early sketch period is superseded by the empathetic, involved middle-class observer of the 1830s, Dickens's 'speculative stroller', a Mr Anybody, who is not omniscient. Along with the Parisian *flâneur*, he provides the egalitarian formula for the collections of the period. Since any connotation of transgressiveness is lost from penetrating viewing, social anatomy becomes a mundane business. Viewers such as George Sand are aware, however, that the dehumanising effects of industrial deprivation seriously limit the value of surface-reading, and that a new 'science' of society, which does not primarily depend on visual paradigms, is needed to address the problem. It seems significant that the more complex visual-verbal ensembles of sketches – the great illustrated serial collections – all emerge around 1840. They allow for considerable speculative and theoretical scope beyond reading surfaces.

The systems of order according to which these collections are arranged follow a panoramic or an encyclopaedic principle. The question of what these publications achieve in presenting bodies of knowledge, and in empowering their middle-class readership, is addressed in Chapters 6 and 7. While the panoramic order projects a many-faceted all-round picture (a 'peinture multiple', according to its prototype, the Parisian *Livre des Cent-et-un*), the encyclopaedic one generates a classifying structure whose closest cognates are print media such as reviews and serially published reference works. Although the panoramic collections focus on cities and the encyclopaedic ones on the mores of the nation or the century, their common concern is a self-reflective inspection of middle-class civilisation on the verge of industrial modernity. Therefore differences in the process of modernisation between Western and Central Europe are strikingly and self-consciously expressed in the collection *Wien und die Wiener* which presents itself as a panorama informed not by life science (in other words, by the socio-physiological mode), but by earth science (a geo-theological concept). The *Physiologies*, discussed as an encyclopaedic enterprise at the end of Chapter 7, are at the forefront of middle-class self-inspection. Contrary to what Benjamin sees in them, they head a powerful self-reflective trend in sketch production that brings to light not only the affinity between social types and the stereotyping techniques of print, but also the print medium's own lack of originality, its multipliability and commodification. The Conclusion considers the semiological achievements of sketches as studies of social codes. A fully commodified civilisation recasts social identity not only in terms of buyers and sellers of labour. It frees an individual's social existence from any fixed 'use value', providing it instead with an arbitrary 'exchange value'. Social acting therefore becomes role play, not in the old moralist, but in a purely materialist sense, a condition Brecht famously exploited for his stage plays. The sartorial and sign language of material success (or lack thereof) can be studied and learned by anyone, and hence the sketches of the 1830s and 40s revolve around the phenomenon of deception. Recognising the social relativity of behavioural codes, modes and manners, they formulate a grammar of modernity which can also be seen as an epistemology of the moment.

I am convinced that the modernity Benjamin so tirelessly sought to trace in his work on the Parisian nineteenth century, and which he has come to represent himself in critical theory, is still lying partly buried in the journalistic sketches of the period with which this study is concerned – and not just those of Paris.

1
The Dynamic Present: Sketches and Print Media

What powers the journalistic production of sketches in words and images for which the 1830s and 40s are so remarkable? A possible answer is provided by Bulwer in *England and the English*. It is the perception of the present as an age of 'visible and violent transition'.[1] Processes of change that used to take decades or centuries and were imperceptible to contemporaries are now happening within a fraction of the time, bursting to the surface of society and confronting it with a scenario of revolutionary development. A world in visible transition develops a whole universe of signifiers, signifying techniques and viewing methods, including urban physiognomies, graphic typology, typography and advertising, telegraphic abbreviation, proto-cinematic animation, pantomime, melodrama and revue, as well as microscopic and panoramic viewing. The techniques required for such a reading of 'transition' are formulated and promoted partly by print media (for example, illustrated periodicals and serials), partly by the media of visual entertainment (for example, moving panoramas, dioramas and dissolving views). Sketches are at the hub of 'visible transition', and the present chapter argues that the ephemeral, sharply delineating form was able to engage with visual surfaces and journalistic print in a particular way and thus became both a key generator and an intellectual meta-medium of print culture. To achieve this capacity, a sketch does not need to be illustrated; in fact some of the most powerful sketches work solely in the textual medium. Yet it is important to bear in mind the vigorous developments in illustrated print which no doubt spurred the imagination of writers when presenting text in terms of a visually and aurally present 'scene'.

---

1 Edward Lytton Bulwer, *England and the English* (Paris: Baudry, 1833), p. 310; see also pp. 352-3.

Edward Lytton Bulwer, 'The valet and the mechanic' (*England and the English*)

Just how effectively a discursive work can be 'illustrated' by verbal sketches, and how crucial these are as a genre exploiting print as a medium of social transformation, is exemplified by *England and the English* itself, published in two volumes in 1833. Targeted at an educated readership, the work gives great prominence to 'the revolution effected by periodicals' since the eighteenth century, and especially to the social impact of the press, including the recent penny publications created for the education of the lower class.[2] The so-called 'March of Intellect', denoting the activities of the Society for the Diffusion of Useful Knowledge, 'the rise of mechanics' institutes' and 'the spread of literacy and of unstamped as well as stamped periodicals appealing to the working classes',[3] has to be seen as one of the main causes as well as one of the main effects of the publishing revolution of the 1830s. The general transition 'from polite to mass culture' is certainly a mobilising force behind sketch production.[4] This can be shown in one of the sketched 'scenes' or character portraits with which Bulwer intersperses his reasoning and which help to extend the educational progress apparently made by the lower classes to the middle-class reader. He or she is put in the position of a social observer 'instructed' by what is seen.

A mini-dialogue, embedded into the first chapter of the fourth book which deals with 'the Intellectual Spirit of the Time', embodies the social and intellectual dynamism of printed media. Its presentation as a 'scene' acts out the dramatic present of 'transition':

A nobleman's valet entertained on a visit his brother, who was a mechanic from Sheffield. The nobleman, walking one Sunday by a newspaper office in the Strand, perceived the two brothers gazing on the inviting announce-

---

2　See Bulwer (note 1), Book 4, Chapter 2, 'Literature', esp. pp. 282-6, on the boom in periodical publishing; the header of p. 283 points to the 'revolution effected by periodicals'.

3　Robert L. Patten, *George Cruikshank's Life, Times, and Art*, 2 vols (New Brunswick: Rutgers University Press, 1992), I, 308.

4　See Brian Maidment, *Into the 1830's. Some Origins of Victorian Illustrated Journalism* (Manchester: Polytechnic Library, 1992). The transition 'from polite to mass culture' (p. 5) is discussed as a process initiated by the cheap illustrated octavo magazines of the 1820s, featuring as forerunners of the *Penny* and *Saturday Magazine* and *Chambers' Journal*.

ments on the shop-board, that proclaimed the contents of the several journals; the crowd on the spot delayed him for a moment, and he overheard the following dialogue:

'Why, Tom,' said the valet, 'see what lots of news there is in this paper! – "Crim. con. extraordinary between a lord and a parson's wife – Jack — 's (Jack is one of our men of fashion, you know, Tom) Adventure with the widow – Scene at Crocky's." Oh, what fun! Tom, have you got sevenpence? I've nothing but gold about *me*; let's buy this here.'

'Lots of news!' said Tom, surlily, 'D'ye call that news? What do I care for your lords and your men of fashion? Crocky! What the devil is Crocky to me? There's much more for my money in this here big sheet: "Advice to the Operatives – Full report of the debate on the Property Tax – Letter from an emigrant in New South Wales." That's what I calls news.'

'Stuff!' cried the valet, astonished.

My lord walked on, somewhat edified by what he had heard.[5]

Sketching technique turns a past-tense narrative (the experience of the lord walking down the Strand) into a dialogue scene and thereby into an observed present. The reader's imagination is guided to the two characters gazing at the board, then to the eye-catching writing on the board, and finally to the two figures themselves who are characterised by their speech – the snobbish, politically uninterested servant of the fashionable elite, expressing himself in posh language and flaunting his familiarity with high-society club life and scandal, versus the cocky working man whose ungrammatical English belies his political nous. To him, 'news' means hard political instruction, the opposite of the gossip in which the valet has a vital interest. The impression of hearing and seeing a short scene hinges on the presence of the mute observer, through whom the position of witness and passer-by is transferred to the reader. The moment of 'overhearing' a dialogue in the bustle of a Sunday morning on the Strand, captured in the sketch itself, gives pause for 'edifying' thought before the nobleman continues his walk and the reader moves on in the text. The dramatic narrative of the sketch is thus set into a dynamic relationship with its discursive context in the manner of an image inserted into the text. This entirely textual 'image-text' relationship, different from the illustrated *Penny Magazine* which supports the 'March of Intellect' of the lower classes, underscores the highbrow sensibility of Bulwer's publication. Its effect is nonetheless pedagogical in that the reader is enlightened about the 'March of Intellect' and perhaps made to think about his or her own class position as an educated member of society in relation to the more enlightened

---

5 Bulwer (note 1), pp. 248-50.

parts of the aristocracy and the increasingly educated working class. Reading has rendered class distinctions more diffuse. And reading includes not just learned discourse, but the 'text' of social life as presented by the sketch. The characteristics of the actors are enriched by a set of details which make them sociologically 'legible'. The reader becomes a social decoder.

Thus, the price of the paper the valet wants to buy, sevenpence, indicates that it is stamped,[6] in other words, too expensive as a regular paper for his working-class brother. The valet, however, carries no smaller metal currency than gold sovereigns or half-sovereigns (20 or 10 shillings respectively), obviously considering it below his dignity to have silver or copper on him. In a cutting manner learnt from his masters, he makes it clear that he needs to 'borrow' sevenpence, thus showing off his social superiority. He shows it in other ways, too, condescendingly explaining who is meant by 'Jack', a familiarity only granted to initiates of fashionable circles. To the valet, the scandal-mongering rag, which no member of these circles would buy, provides essential knowledge. It offers key information to a social inferior whose status depends on copying aristocratic manners. To the mechanic, the same information is useless. What attracts *his* attention is the advertisement of a 'sheet', in other words, of a one-page publication which is exempt from the tax,[7] publishing the matter-of-fact or instructive kind of articles (entitled 'Advice', 'Report', 'Letter') that communicate 'useful knowledge' to the 'Operatives'. To each brother the 'news' contained in the paper of his choice is an important means to pursue his social interest. While it is the valet's interest to identify himself with a class to which he does not belong, mainly by cultivating a manner of exclusiveness, the mechanic's interest is to consolidate his sense of class identity as a man of 'labour'. His power of assertion owes everything to the ethos of self-interest and utility. He insists not only on acquiring knowledge useful to *him*, but he makes a point about buying much more value than his brother would, and for far less money. The publications addressing his class are innovative; they have a future because their materialist message corresponds to the materialist class interest which, for the foreseeable future, will fuel progress. (Later in the same book, these publications will be identified as direct descendents of the utilitarian, Benthamite 'spirit'.) The

---

6 Before the stamp duty on newspapers was reduced to one penny per copy in 1836 it was fourpence. If the price of a paper without the tax was below sixpence it was liable to be stamped. The standard price of stamped newspapers was sevenpence or sixpence-halfpenny. See Collet Dobson Collet, *History of the Taxes on Knowledge*, 2 vols (London: Fisher Unwin, 1899) I, 18-19.

7 Under the press legislation introduced in 1815, one-sheet pamphlets were not classed as newspapers and therefore not subject to stamp duty. See ibid., pp. 25-6.

valet's interest is that of a parasite living off a doomed class guarding its privileges, that of the mechanic one of an ascending, productive class which is about to enter the sphere of politics in the wake of the middle class and which future state policy has to reckon with. In a final interpreting sentence which corroborates this reading, the valet's world is associated with closed-in spaces (saloon and pantry), that of the mechanic with processes (legislature, weaving). What is considered news in the servants' quarters of an aristocratic household or at the loom of a cotton mill will come from a corresponding sphere. The sketch characterises class interest essentially in terms of what is considered worth knowing. Thus, Bentham's category of self-regarding interest which, according to Bulwer, has had a profound social effect, has also provided him with an essential tool for deciphering types.

In the same way as the press is shown to promote social change, the act of reading provokes the reader/observer to review class prejudice just as the nobleman walks away 'somewhat edified' because he has been able to correct one of his assumptions. Wont to see his own exclusive circles as the only thing the masses would want to find out about, he thought that 'the papers to please the rabble must descend to pander the vulgar passions' by publishing gossip about the upper crust. After witnessing the scene on the Strand he knows that there are other papers for the lower classes, that the 'passions' of the 'rabble' are in fact not as uniformly 'vulgar' as he assumed, and that there must be vast parts of the population outside the metropolis which could not care less about the aristocracy. That he obviously finds this fact worth knowing shows that he can rise above, if not his class interest, then at least above the perceptions typical of his class. He may not come to Bulwer's own conclusion that 'vulgarity' is just the other side of the coin of aristocratic 'frivolity', and that scandal-mongering 'Society' papers 'are supported alone by the excrescences of aristocracy' such as the lord's own valet.[8] However, this is a conclusion the reader is invited to come to, and in doing so s/he would also break the English middle-class habit of aspiring to aristocratic airs, an aspiration Bulwer never tires of exposing critically in *England and the English*. Making his middle-class reader view the scene through the eyes of an aristocratic stroller is therefore highly significant regarding the reader's ambiguous class position within the dynamic present.

Bulwer's sketch is presented as an anecdote from real life, involving imaginary 'characters' or 'types'. The status of many of his character sketches is explicitly referred to as 'illustrative' in the contents table of *England and the English*. They are neither fiction nor factual accounts, but pointed characterisations comparable to cartoons illustrating the text. Written sketches thus

---

8 Bulwer (note 1), p. 249.

offer themselves as pictures to a cognitive context which may or may not be presented in the form of a learned book. By virtue of their non-fictionality, present-tense and/or dramatic narrative, implicit or explicit reference to print and graphic images and frequent association with periodical or serial publication, they play a central part in embodying, capturing and decoding a present consisting of a multitude of signs that indicate movement and change. The nature of their depiction 'before the reader's eyes', which parallels the process of 'reading' both literally and in terms of making sense, means that the reader of a sketch is always an observer and therefore involved in the dynamic present. This relates the genre closely to the ways in which contemporary visual and print media address spectators and readers.

Bulwer's sketch appeared in the context of a major sociological study in conventional book form. To make palpable the full impetus of sketches as a visual-verbal meta-medium in the 1830s and 40s, it is, however, necessary to outline how sketch publications interacted with the most important developments in printing and publishing during these decades, and in what ways they are distinct from novels in this respect. These developments in turn cannot be understood without considering their European dimensions.

The serialisation of word and image

Serialisation, one of the great commercial revolutions of the nineteenth century and itself an indication of the increasing preponderance of dynamic over static paradigms, was actively promoted by text-image publications. This can be seen, for example, from Balzac's 'Prospectus' (1830) for the satirical journal *La Caricature*. Balzac soon extended serial publication to his own literary production; in England, the serialisation of novels was similarly pioneered by Dickens after the success of the monthly numbers of his *Pickwick Papers*, the novel that had started as a series of sporting sketches. Literary culture was fundamentally changed by serialisation, and it is rewarding to compare the different ways in which novels and sketches profited from this.

According to Linda K. Hughes and Michael Lund, the form of the novel benefited from serial publication because it helped it to become less of a fictional artefact. It meant moving away from a linear principle of composition which gave meaning to plots in the light of their ending, towards a more 'open' structure where the ending was not the vantage-point. The long drawn-out publishing process with its interim criticism and reader response might prompt an author to revise the future course of the story and its conclusion. What is more, the individual instalments were potentially all 'self-contained units' within a 'larger aesthetic structure',[9] and criticism that considers novels first published as serials in terms of 'volume editions' and 'whole texts' misses the point. What has traditionally been viewed as the weakness of a serialised novel, in other words, its 'fracturing' or 'impeding' a 'unified' plot,[10] can be seen as its strength in today's terms, particularly those (as the authors argue) of feminist theory. Without referring to the affinity of the serial form to contemporary critical assumptions, Robert L. Patten makes a similar observation about Dickens's *Pickwick Papers*, the novel that famously established the model for Victorian serial fiction. Each of the monthly parts enacts 'a kind of *petit mort*' and the plot often seems to come to a dead end;[11] yet death and disjunction are also the propelling forces of the narrative: 'the text reexamines its premises, its persons and actions, having in a sense got to the end of the alphabet of types and situations quite early on and then subjected them to revision [...].' It is not so much the characters that change through the story, but 'the serial installments that reconsider their own materials, and in so doing grow up, change from an assemblage of disconnected documents [...] into a story, one marked always by the same wrapper design yet continuously reexamining its initial alphabet in the light of the experience of reading'.[12]

What Patten analyses here with regard to fiction – a process in which the story takes hold of the parts while these parts always remain visible as 'materials' to be 'reexamined' and 'revised' – applies particularly to the literature of sketches, from which, after all, the *Pickwick* project originated. Self-consciously fragmented studies, sketches are assembled and reassembled in a process of prolonged revision. Their 'alphabet' of signifiers is reviewed many times and the individual components are regrouped accordingly. The fluidity of the medium and the plurality of elements made early reviewers of *Pickwick* characteristically perceive the work as a 'magazine' rather than as a 'novel'.[13] Not surprisingly, given the affinity of sketch collections with journals, Karl Gutzkow wondered, in the introduction to his two-volume *Die Zeitgenossen* (Our Contemporaries) of 1837, about the genre this work was going to belong

---

9 Linda K. Hughes and Michael Lund, 'Textual/sexual pleasure and serial publication', in *Literature in the Marketplace. Nineteenth-century British Publishing and Reading Practices*, ed. by John O. Jordan and Robert L. Patten (Cambridge: Cambridge University Press, 1998), pp. 143-64 (p. 149).
10 See ibid., pp. 143-4.
11 Robert L. Patten, 'Serialized Retrospection in *The Pickwick Papers*', in *Literature in the Marketplace* (note 9), pp. 123-42 (p. 127).
12 Ibid., p. 132.
13 See Dennis Walder, 'Introduction', in Charles Dickens, *Sketches by Boz*, ed. by D. Walder (London: Penguin, 1995), pp. ix-xxxiv (p. ix).

to. Having been collected in book form from twelve bi-monthly numbers, it still did not seem to be finished and might yet revert to something like 'a monthly journal'.[14] Although modelled on *England and the English*, with character sketches enlivening the argument, and actually appearing as an alleged translation of a new work by Bulwer, *Die Zeitgenossen* was, in its serial form, almost certainly a direct response to Dickens's unheard-of success as a serial author.

The *Pickwick* success made Dickens and his publishers experiment with the publication form of the slightly earlier *Sketches by Boz*. Hence this collection, reverting from volumes to 'shilling monthly numbers', offers an (admittedly extreme) example of fluidity between book, journal and serial as well as of work-in-progress revision of the constituent parts. First the original journal sketches (1833-36) were altered for the two-volume book edition, while being provided with illustrations by George Cruikshank. Another volume, *Second Series*, assembled reworked sketches of a later date and was rounded off by a tale, 'A Drunkard's Death', especially written 'to finish the volume with éclat'.[15] In the light of the current *Pickwick* success, these three collected volumes were, so to speak, taken apart again and the sketches re-released in the medium of a monthly serial. In its twenty parts the individual sketches were completely rearranged, before being revised once more for the definitive one-volume edition of 1839. This preserves the sequence of the serialised version, but divides the sketches into the now familiar four sections: 'Seven Sketches from our Parish', 'Scenes', 'Characters' and 'Tales'. For the serial, Cruikshank 'had twenty-seven plates to make over again' and 'thirteen new ones plus a wrapper design to etch'.[16] The process of revision therefore affects not only the written material in this case, but extends to the text-image relationships. Yet, however many times the elements are re-examined, the result will not be a narrative construction. The medium that binds them together at every stage – and here lies the crucial difference of *Sketches by Boz* from the *Pickwick Papers* – is not a finite plot, but a discursive process to which a potentially infinite number of observations could be added. Flexibility and potential infinity of composition is the hallmark of sketch collections, comparable to

---

14 '[...] ob es ein abgeschlossenes Buch oder ein Journal werden wird'. [Karl Gutzkow], *Die Zeitgenossen. Ihre Schicksale, ihre Tendenzen, ihre großen Charaktere. Aus dem Englischen des E.L. Bulwer*, 2 vols (Stuttgart: Verlag der Classiker, 1837), I, iii; '[m]öglich, daß meine Z e i t g e n o s s e n, nachdem sie ein Buch gewesen sind, sich zuletzt in eine Monatsschrift verwandeln' (ibid., p. xxiii).

15 Dickens in a letter of 7 December 1836, quoted in *Sketches by Boz*, ed. by D. Walder (note 13), p. 635.

16 Patten, *George Cruikshank's Life, Times and Art* (note 3), II, 61.

the form of the journal and hence at odds with the closed form of the volume edition. Periodicals and serial publications are therefore the true medium of sketches. If they eventually do appear in book form, the covers act merely as binding material. The plurality of the elements will never yield to a unitary concept of 'form'. Hence the plural, *Sketches*, frequently found in the title of collections, is absolutely consistent with their content, and Dickens's feeling that 'Sketches by Boz and Cuts by Cruikshank' or 'Etchings by Boz and Wood Cuts by Cruikshank' would be an unassuming, but all the more appropriate title, very justified.[17] Such plurality is not compatible with the character of fiction as a 'work', even if the provenance of the *Pickwick Papers* from a series of sketches is still preserved in the novel's title. Novels, even when serialised, are conceived as 'books'; this is where the unresolvable conflict originates between the draughtsman Seymour, envisaging a loose series built on his sporting sketches, and his provider of 'copy', Dickens, intent on a continuous narrative governed by the text.

Resistance to fictionalisation, a focus on observation and the interaction between discursive text and visual surface (whether verbally suggested or graphically presented) are therefore characteristics of sketches.[18] More often than not, graphic sketches precede, temporally and spatially, the written ones which follow them as a kind of commentary; such is the case, for example, in the collections *Heads of the People* (its serial numbers starting in 1838; two volumes appearing in 1840 and 1841), *Wien und die Wiener* (serial running from 1841, book edition 1844) or *Gavarni in London* (monthly numbers from 1848, book edition 1849). This visual-verbal ensemble, arranged in the manner of a picture book or gallery of metropolitan life and types, makes it strictly impossible to speak of visual sketches in terms of 'illustrations'. They

---

17 Ibid., p. 12.
18 The focus on observed type rather than fictional (stereo)type was already seen by contemporaries as the distinguishing feature of a sketch collection. John Forster referred to *Sketches by Boz* as a work that paints things 'literally as they are', without the 'condescending air which is affectation'; this was presumably meant as a criticism of 'Society' novels: *The Life of Charles Dickens* (London: Chapman and Hall, 1893), p. 47. The *Heads of the People*, too, were commended for their accuracy of delineation, suiting the needs of 'the philosophic observer', and contrasted with the false images of Englishmen 'dreamt of by the fashionable novelmonger', in an advertisement contained in the monthly parts of *Nicholas Nickleby*. See Gerard Curtis, 'Dickens in the Visual Market', in *Literature in the Marketplace* (note 9), pp. 213-49 (p. 232). Ironically, the advertisement praising sketches as a more accurate and scientific medium than fiction uses serialised fiction as its vehicle, but this could also be an indication of the extent to which Dickens's serialised novels were perceived as part of the 1830s culture of sketches that he had himself helped to establish.

are indeed paramount in all the major collaborative sketch publications appearing from around 1840 which form a main focus of this study. Usually issued in serial form, these 'pen and palette' compilations can be seen as the culmination of a development in European publishing since the early 1830s, following the prototype of the 15-volume *Livre des Cent-et-un*, a collective portrait of Parisian mores (1831-34). This sketch collection was, however, not illustrated and in the 1830s had no direct English or German equivalents. So what contributed specifically to the flourishing of hybrid text-image sketch production in the first half of the 1840s?

Here one must point to periodical ventures typical of the 1830s, notably satirical journals, many of them founded just before or after the July Revolution or in the climate of Reform, for example, the main precursor of *Punch*, à Beckett's and Mayhew's *Figaro in London*, illustrated by Seymour and Isaac Robert Cruikshank, or Philipon's *La Caricature* on which Monnier, Balzac, Daumier, Grandville and many others collaborated. Through them, the graphic image lost its independence as a satirical broadsheet sold individually by the print dealer, to become part of a text-image compilation marketed by the publisher. Celina Fox has shown how in English graphic journalism of the 1830s, caricature and letterpress came together in periodical form, replacing the rather 'chaotic' one-off production of broadsheets earlier in the century, so that by the mid-1830s 'the satirical print had become the newspaper cartoon'.[19] Journals containing graphic satire had, of course, existed earlier in the century, but it is important to bear in mind the relative autonomy of the caricature print at that time. *The Scourge*, *The Satirist* and other magazines of the 1810s contained a fold-out coloured plate which was also sold independently as a 'self-contained and self-explanatory' picture.[20] By contrast, magazines of the 1830s, for example, *La Caricature*, integrated the cartoon – in this case, two full-page lithographs per number – into a written context of recurrent sections that referred to a whole range of more or less satirical depiction ('Croquis', 'Caricatures' and 'Charges').

Another factor feeding into periodical text-image production is the illustrated penny press. There clearly exists an analogy between the sketch as 'cheap' instructive literature and the penny publications of the early 1830s, which is most obvious in the *Physiologies* of 1840-42. These individually published pocket booklets, often richly illustrated by vignettes, were mass-produced, sold at the price of 1 franc and constituted a loose series rivalling

---

19 Celina Fox, *Graphic Journalism in England during the 1830s and 1840s* (New York: Garland, 1988), especially her chapter 'The Development of Political Caricature 1830-1836', pp. 73-119 (p. 76).
20 Patten, *George Cruikshank's Life, Times, and Art* (note 3), I, 101.

and parodying the instalments of the 'serious' national work, *Les Français peints par eux-mêmes*. They quintessentially embody the sketch culture of the 1830s and 40s, and particularly so in their innovative text-image relationships which this culture as a whole represents. The illustrations of *Physiologies* can be seen in more or less direct connection with the mass-produced illustrations of the *Penny Magazine*, the *Saturday Magazine* and the *Penny Cyclopædia* (and their European counterparts). Turned into social sketches, the 'useful', encyclopaedia-type illustrations of the penny publications, appearing within the text rather than alongside it, precisely fit the bill. One could argue that, just as verbal sketches occupy a space between the finite book and the infinite periodical, or the lasting and the ephemeral, graphic sketches are located between highbrow art and the illustrations of a manual that, once read, can be disposed of.

While many illustrated sketches featured pictures outside the text (*Sketches by Boz* again being a prominent example), the most intricate connections between words and graphic art arose through the immediate insertion of images into the text. Standard wood-cut or wood-engraved ornaments to break up the page had been in use for a long time; the innovation therefore consisted in integrating small images specifically drawn to correspond to the text. This crucial development in the technique of illustration was owed to the progress in wood engraving (xylography).

Wood engraving

Turned into a successful method by the Northumbrian Thomas Bewick in the late eighteenth century, xylography took off on a grand scale, in the whole of Europe, during the second half of the 1830s and first half of the 1840s,[21] with English engravers initially exporting their art abroad. From 1817, for example, Charles Thompson, brother of the better-known illustrator John Thompson, engraved some of the earliest French designs specifically relating to the text. Significantly, they illustrated the depictions of Parisian and foreign *mœurs* in the popular *Hermite* books by Victor Joseph Etienne de Jouy.[22] The following vignette portrays a female innkeeper met en route to Italy in a

---

21 See Jakob Kainen, 'Why Bewick Succeeded: A Note in the History of Wood Engravings', *United States National Museum Bulletin* 218, Paper 11 (1959), esp. pp. 197-201.

22 See Remi Blachon, *La Gravure sur bois au XIXe siècle* (Paris: Les Éditions de l'amateur, 2001), p. 49. The third volume of *L'Hermite de la Guiane* (1817) was the first French book with proper wood-engraved illustrations, not simply ornamental vignettes, which Thompson executed after drawings by Alexandre Desenne.

French provincial town and described in *L'Hermite en Italie* (1824), one of the many sequels to the Parisian tableau *L'Hermite de la Chaussée d'Antin* (1812-14):

46 CHAMBÉRI.

dit-on, été dans les bonnes grâces de tous les généraux de l'armée française, et même de son plus illustre général en chef. Elle n'avait guère plus de trente ans, mais elle en paraissait presque le double, et je ne me rappelle pas avoir vu une femme plus laide. Bien loin de faire mystère de toutes ses illustres amours, elle en raconta les divers épisodes avec une liberté qui aurait bien pu déplaire à ceux qui en étaient les héros. Le voyageur dont j'ai parlé souriait de pitié; on nous servit un souper détestable, mais que notre appétit nous fit trouver excellent.

Illustration 2 Vignette in V.J.E. de Jouy, *L'Hermite en Italie, ou Observations sur les mœurs et usages des Italiens au commencement du XIXe siècle*, 4 vols (Paris: Pillet ainé, 1824-5), I (1824), 46. Wood engraving by Charles Thompson.

Charles Thompson's skill was still required for the title vignette, designed by Henry Monnier, of the *Livre des Cent-et-un* (see illustration 26, p. 168), while English xylographic expertise in general continued to support the development of illustrated print on the Continent during the 1830s, with publishing houses such as Charles Knight supplying stereotypes. Thus, in 1833, the Paris firm Édouard Charton and the Leipzig branch of Bossange in Paris (managed by the publisher J.J. Weber) received casts of wood engravings to illustrate the *Penny Magazine's* French and German equivalents, *Le Magasin Pittoresque* and *Das Pfennig-Magazin*.[23] Xylography also made it possible to reproduce text and image as one integrated, stereotyped 'form' quickly and in high print runs on the steam-powered printing machine. The metal casts were taken from the whole page of type into which the block was inserted.

Like its older relative, the woodcut, the wood engraving was cut on a printing block so that the image would show in relief (with the areas to be printed protruding from lower-lying areas remaining white). Unlike in wood-'cutting', however, the block of durable boxwood was incised with burins instead of knives. This could only be done by working the wood on the hard end grain, not on the plank as had been the case in wood-cutting. Although the technique was thus much refined, so that very thin lines could be used to create subtle tonal effects, xylographed images were and still are often referred to as 'woodcuts'. Unlike copper or steel plates and, for that matter, lithographs, which were not printed in relief and could thus not be reproduced together with type, wood engraving was destined to become the visual arts equivalent of letterpress and the ideal medium for illustrating mass-produced print. Illustrated works therefore became affordable by the less well-off. Charles Knight's *Penny Cyclopædia of the Society for the Diffusion of Useful Knowledge* (27 volumes, 1833-43), itself an illustrated publication in instalments championing the democratisation of the printed image, comments on the advantages of the medium as follows:

> For the purpose of illustrating books wood-engraving is peculiarly adapted. Being worked in the same manner as type, impressions are produced with great rapidity. Any number of cuts may be printed at once on a sheet of paper that will come into the press or machine, and an almost infi-

---

23 For the trade in stereotypes of illustrations from the *Penny Magazine* see Fox (note 19), p. 51. See also 'Stereotype' in *The Penny Cyclopædia of the Society for the Diffusion of Useful Knowledge*, 27 vols (London: Knight, 1833-43), XXIII (1842), 42-4 (p. 44): 'By the help of this art copies of the wood-cuts in the 'Penny Magazine' and other works are supplied, at a very moderate cost, to publishers in America and on the Continent. This diffusion of engravings has been carried to such an extent, that casts of some illustrations executed for British periodicals have been transmitted to as many as seventeen different countries, for use in similar works'.

nite number of impressions may be taken off without material injury to them. This seems the proper purpose of the art.²⁴

The article on the steam-powered printing machine, able to produce with such 'great rapidity' and first used in Britain in 1814, is itself illustrated by a full-page wood engraving:

Illustration 3   'Printing-Machine', in *The Penny Cyclopædia* (note 23), XIX (1841), 19. Wood engraving.

The sketch industry particularly of the 1840s would be unthinkable without this technological advance in text-image reproduction. The insertion of images into the text so that words and illustrations constitute, literally, the same surface of print is also one precondition for the semiotic subtlety of sketches. Reading the text-image surface involves viewing and vice versa. The whole process may become one of deciphering text or letters as images and images as letters or text.

In actual fact, the medium thanks to which wood engraving was helped to its revolutionary breakthrough was not book illustration, as the quotation from the *Penny Cyclopædia* implies, but the kind of serial 'penny' publication

---

24 'Wood-Engraving', in *The Penny Cyclopædia* (note 23), XXVII (1843), 522-6 (p. 526).

that the *Cyclopædia* itself represents.[25] Before sketches could exploit the new facilities of illustrated print, however, a semantic development in the mass-produced image had to take place. The 'useful' (usually zoological, botanical or technological) illustration thriving in the early 1830s needed to be transformed for the purpose of social and political commentary. This transformation took place in London and Paris during the second half of the 1830s and culminated, as far as London is concerned, in the creation of *Punch* in 1841. Wood engraving had, of course, been used for genre pictures, cartoons and political caricature well before *Punch*; the illustrations for Jouy's *Hermite* books produced from 1817 are a case in point. Pearce Egan's *Life in London*, a monthly serial (1820-21, book edition 1821) which depicted the metropolitan adventures of the 'swells' Tom, Jerry and Bob Logic, owed its huge success mainly to the coloured aquatint plates of the Cruikshank brothers, but they were already complemented by little wood engravings in the text. Moreover, in Hone's *Political House that Jack Built* (1819) and *A Slap at Slop* (1821), George Cruikshank had used wood engraving for caricature to great effect. Most importantly, the *Comic Almanack*, appearing from 1834, featured from its 1837 volume not only the usual Cruikshank steel etching for each month, normally depicting an urban scene, but also tiny, xylographed visual puns which anticipate those of *Punch*, an essential part of its witty visual-verbal vocabulary (see illustration 4, p. 38).

It is significant that the *Almanack* regarded itself as a publication supporting the 'March of Intellect' in 'poking fun at superstition' (that is, by parodying an almanac with zodiacal predictions for each month). A circulation of nearly 20,000 copies bears out its importance for enlightened mass culture,[26] and it must be seen as one of the agents opening the field of contemporary mores to the inquisitive minds of a huge readership. The medium of wood engraving also served *Punch's* main predecessor, *Figaro in London* (1831-39), costing a penny and having a 'reputed sale of 70,000 copies', as well as a number of small, very short-lived satirical weeklies and 'a host of provincial imitators'.[27] Nevertheless, the right pictorial-verbal language, the right team of collaborators and, perhaps, a stable target audience to support a satirical

---

25 Fox (note 19) comments that it was only with the production of Charles Knight's *Penny Magazine* 'that wood engraving's main advantage – that it could be printed by machine in the same sheet as letterpress – was successfully exploited for periodical publications' (p. 50). See also Kainen (note 21) who observes that 'wood engraving did not really flourish' until it could serve 'popular publications' such as *The Penny Magazine* and the *Saturday Magazine* (p. 197).
26 See Patten, *George Cruikshank's Life, Times, and Art* (note 3), II, 8-9.
27 Fox (note 19), p. 77 and p. 75.

Illustration 4
'Great Events and Odd Matters [for April 1837]', in *The Comic Almanack. An Ephemeris in Jest and Earnest, Containing Merry Tales, Humorous Poetry, Quips, and Oddities. By Thackeray, Albert Smith, Gilbert à Beckett, the Brothers Mayhew. With Many Hundred Illustrations by George Cruikshank and Other Artists. First Series, 1835-1843* (London: Chatto and Windus, [1874]), p. 85. Wood engravings.

weekly still had to be found, as the relatively short run of the London *Figaro* suggests. Its emulation of the hard-hitting verbal satire of the (unillustrated) Parisian *Le Figaro*, founded in 1826, indicates that the acidic journalism of the French capital provided a model. And it is again with a Parisian, European appeal that *Punch, or the London Charivari* developed its virtuosity in integrating images engraved on wood piquantly into the text.

French-English cross-connections

The formula came from *Le Charivari*, the illustrated satirical Parisian daily (although *Punch* appeared once a week). It was itself a product of an Anglo-French exchange revolving around composite visual-verbal, collaborative and serialised creations. Founded by Charles Philipon in 1832, *Le Charivari* was one of three periodicals of the early July Monarchy that sought to unite the visual arts with political and literary criticism under the umbrella of 'esquisses' ('sketches'). According to Roland Chollet, this project of sketching in words and writing in sketches, which *La Silhouette* (1829-31), *La Caricature* (1830-35)[28] and *Le Charivari* engaged in, found in the painter and writer Henry Monnier its true spokesman.[29] Monnier had spent some of his formative years in England and had learnt from George Cruikshank how to combine a penetrating grasp of class with an unmistakable, comic visual rendering.[30] Cruikshank, moreover, in his collaboration with the radical pamphleteer and publisher Hone and then with his own brother Robert and with Pierce Egan on *Life in London*, was also associated with the earliest serial publications of texts and caricatures (or rather, in the case of *Life in London*, of a 'meld of caricature and social observation').[31] Since the declared aim of *La Silhouette*, soon to be imitated, was to serialise graphic art in combination with texts, to present 'a true *Album* in which the Fine Arts, the Theatre and *les Mœurs* will be passed in review and subjected to criticism, sometimes by witty writers,

---

28 *La Caricature. Journal politique, morale, religieuse, littéraire et scénique* appeared from 4 November 1830 until 27 August 1835, its discontinuation being due to the suppression of political caricature from 1835 as well as the competition of the increasingly successful *Charivari*. See Susanne Bosch-Abele, *La Caricature (1830-35). Katalog und Kommentar*, 2 vols (Weimar: VDG, 1997), I, 61-4.
29 See Roland Chollet, *Balzac journaliste. Le tournant de 1830* (Paris: Klincksieck, 1983), pp. 186-7. On the foundation of *La Silhouette* and *La Caricature* as well as Balzac's and Monnier's involvement in them, see pp. 175-220, 389-404 and 405-57.
30 Monnier met Cruikshank twice, according to Robert Patten, 'first during an 1822-25 stay, second in 1828'. *George Cruikshank's Life, Times and Art* (note 3), II, 191.
31 Patten, *George Cruikshank's Life, Times and Art* (note 3), I, 190.

sometimes by our best artists',[32] there was 'no-one in Paris', in Chollet's view, 'better suited than Monnier to guide the first steps of a satirical album that took its inspiration from English models'.[33] When *La Caricature* was launched in 1830, Balzac, who was collaborating on several journals during his 'journalistic turn' of that year and contributed some of his wittiest sketches to them, wrote the prospectus. He emphasised the plan to unite pen and pencil portraits of Parisian *mœurs* and to make graphic art affordable to everyone by means of serialisation. This concept was supposed to fuel nothing less than a national project satisfying the needs of all concerned:

> In France as in England, caricature has become a power. [...] Since 1789, it has also been a need in our country. It is eminently popular here, and if, up to now, it has not presented itself in periodical form [...] it is because the price of engraving prohibited this speculation. It is not that our prints have lacked people who like to laugh, but people who like to laugh have been lacking prints. [...] By supporting our enterprise, subscribers will associate themselves with a national work. Nowadays the arts have only very little remuneration to expect from those in power. Only the people can pay artists lavishly. In England, a fortunate idea, a piece of just satire, will be bought by everybody, and the most modest sum, given a thousand times, recompenses the artist or businessman generously. Thus, favouring our journal means, in some way, paying our artists nationally [...].[34]

---

32 '[...] "un véritable *Album* où les Beaux-Arts, le Théâtre et les Mœurs seront passés en revue et critiqués tantôt par des écrivains spirituels, tantôt par nos meilleurs artistes".' Quoted in Chollet (note 29), p. 183.

33 'Personne, à Paris, n'était donc mieux désigné que Monnier pour guider les premiers pas d'un album satirique d'inspiration anglaise [...].' Ibid., p. 186.

34 'En France, comme en Angleterre, la caricature est devenue un pouvoir. [...] Aussi, depuis 1789, la caricature a été un besoin pour notre pays. Elle y est éminemment populaire; et si, jusqu'à présent, elle ne s'est pas rendue périodique [...], c'est que le prix de la gravure interdisait cette spéculation. Ce n'étaient pas les rieurs qui manquaient aux estampes, mais les estampes aux rieurs. [...] En soutenant notre entreprise, les abonnés s'associeront à une œuvre nationale. En effet, aujourd'hui, les arts n'ont que très peu de salaire à attendre du pouvoir. Le peuple sait, seul, solder les artistes avec magnificence. En Angleterre, une idée heureuse, une juste satire, sont accueillies par tout le monde; et la plus faible somme, mille fois donnée, y récompense largement l'artiste ou l'industriel. Ainsi, favoriser notre journal, c'est, en quelque sorte, nationalement rémunérer des artistes [...].' Balzac, 'Prospectus' [for *La Caricature*], in *Œuvres diverses*, ed. by Pierre-Georges Castex (Paris: Gallimard, 1990–), II (1996), ed. by Roland Chollet and René Guise, 795-8 (pp. 795-6).

The reference to England as a country where it pays an artist to have his work reproduced and sold as cheap print is plausible when one considers Hone's retrospective remarks of 1824 about his collaboration with Cruikshank:

> By showing what engraving on wood could effect in a popular way, and exciting a taste for art in the more humble ranks of life, they [the parodic pamphlets] created a new era in the history of publication. They are the parents of the present cheap literature, which extends to a sale of at least four hundred thousand copies every week, and gives large and constant employment to talent in that particular branch of engraving which I selected as the best adapted to enforce, and give circulation to my own thoughts.[35]

This is an astonishingly early praise of wood engraving as an effective mass medium. Balzac, however, had lithography in mind, not xylography, for the 'national work' in which subscribers were about to be involved. *La Caricature* and *Le Charivari* therefore featured full-page lithographic 'designs' in each number, as had been the case with the short-lived *Silhouette*. The lithographic technique of reproduction, allowing the artist to draw on the stone from which the prints are directly taken, does indeed provide for greater proximity to an original 'design' than engraving during which the original is transferred to a plate or block and incised, in most cases by a different hand. What Hone states as the great achievement of wood engraving, in other words, its artistic appeal as a cheap medium, is clearly distinct from the artistic 'aura' of lithography. Interestingly, the mordant political satire of *La Caricature* and *Le Charivari*, now associated mainly with the name of Daumier, was expressed through the more artistic medium of lithographs. However, when political caricature was severely restricted following the Fieschi affair of 1835 and criticism sought a vent in social observation, wood engraving became the preferred medium.

Two things have to be stressed with regard to the deflection of political satire into social observation which, according to Benjamin, is tantamount to a dumbing-down of Daumier's and Grandville's biting criticism to the harmless joke-cracking of Monnier and the *Physiologies*.[36] First, this view obscures the fact that satire found a new and virtually unlimited subject in the *social* impact of the political changes of 1830 and beyond, and that 'the imposed turn' to the depiction of *mœurs* therefore did *not* lead to a 'political no-

---

35 Quoted in Patten, *George Cruikshank's Life, Times and Art* (note 3), I, 186.
36 See Walter Benjamin, *Charles Baudelaire. A Lyric Poet in the Era of High Capitalism* (London: Verso, 1983), p. 36.

man's land, but opened to caricature the whole spectrum of society in all its depth'.[37] Secondly, the social focus goes almost hand in hand with the disappearance of broadsheet caricature and its allegorical qualities, and the emergence of the cartoon which, because of its 'charged' mimetic nature, is often indistinguishable from the printed social genre picture of which the verbal sketch is the equivalent. Broadly speaking, and to refer to England as an example, the pictorial language of the satirical prints of the Regency and 1820s, exemplified in the work of the Cruikshank brothers, was adapted to the expressive needs of typology. It has to be said that wood engraving was indeed congenial to the purpose, lending a 'typed' language to the analysis of types while also drawing attention to the printed types on the page. In other words, xylographed illustrations both represented and highlighted early mass society, including many aspects of its cultural superstructure, not least the printed media. From 1838, at a time when the 'English tutorship' amongst Parisian engravers was beginning to bear fruit,[38] *Le Charivari* showed an increasing number of wood engravings in its columns. It was under these conditions that this journal, having been conceived, like its suppressed relative *La Caricature*, as a composite visual-verbal periodical 'in the English style', and having in turn been considered a model for an English satirical magazine since 1835 by the future *Punch* founders or collaborators Henry Mayhew, Douglas Jerrold and W.M. Thackeray,[39] finally did produce an English equivalent. Together with Mark Lemon and Ebenezer Landells, 'newspaper projector', draughtsman, wood engraver and former pupil of Thomas Bewick,[40] Mayhew launched *Punch* in July 1841.

Under these circumstances, too, and in the slipstream of the international print revolution heralded by the English penny press, visual-verbal sketches as thumbnail social studies thrived and traversed medial and national boundaries with ease. For example, while *Heads of the People*, edited by Jerrold from 1838, became the model (via a French translation) for *Les Français peints par eux-mêmes* and (via a partly pirated German translation) for *Wien*

---

37 'Die erzwungene Wendung führte demnach gerade nicht [...] ins politische Niemandsland, sondern öffnete der Karikatur das ganze Spektrum der Gesellschaft in seiner Tiefe.' Karl Riha and Gerhard Rudolph, 'Nachwort', in *Düsseldorfer Monathefte* (repr. Düsseldorf: Schwann, 1979), pp. 471-82 (p. 476).
38 See Blachon (note 22), Chapters 5 ('Charles Thompson'), pp. 47-62; 6 ('La Tutelle anglaise'), pp. 63-71, 7 ('La Génération de 1830'), pp. 72-87 and 8 ('Débuts des périodiques illustrés'), pp. 88-100.
39 See Michael Slater, *Douglas Jerrold* (London: Duckworth, 2002), pp. 119-20.
40 M.H. Spielmann, *The History of 'Punch'* (London, Paris, Melbourne: Cassell, 1895), p. 15.

und die Wiener, it also combined the efforts of a number of future 'Punchites'. Kenny Meadows, the artist who drew *Heads of the People* (engraved on wood by Orrin Smith), was involved in *Punch* from its beginnings,[41] and also created the *Heads from 'Nicholas Nickleby'*, a portrait gallery which made Dickens's novel a commodity on the visual arts market while closely relating to the series of English popular *Heads* in which 'original essays by distinguished writers' were written to the portraits.[42] Whereas in England, all the energies of sketch production seem to converge in *Punch*, its model *Le Charivari* assembled well-nigh the complete 'équipe' that was to write *Physiologies* for Aubert,[43] the main publisher of this genre, and conveniently also brother-in-law of Philipon. The Leipzig *Charivari* of Eduard Maria Oettinger (published 1842-51) copied French illustrations (as did *Punch*), including many wood engravings after Grandville, Gavarni and Daumier, and provided them with its own verbal sketches. This constitutes one of the examples of cross-national sketch production where the image is assimilated to the national context of the respective satirical journal, but thanks to the recognisably Parisian provenance of the image, the text of the sketch also vibrates with cosmopolitan sentiment.

German and Austrian developments

German sketch-writers learnt a great deal from French and English models, as is indicated, for example, by the paradigmatic status of Bulwer's *England and the English* in the 1830s. By the late 1840s draughtsmen, too, were in command of a snappy visual language able to compete with that of *Punch* and *Le Charivari*. The following wood engraving of 1847, taken from *Düsseldorfer Monathefte*, a satirical monthly with an astonishing circulation of 5,000,[44] may serve as an example, especially since it treats the subject of socially

---

41 See Spielmann (note 40), esp. pp. 284-98 (Jerrold) and 446-9 (Meadows), as well as Slater (note 39), esp. pp. 119-40.
42 The full title of the collection edited by Jerrold was *Heads of the People: or, Portraits of the English. Drawn by Kenny Meadows. With Original Essays by Distinguished Writers*. As a serial it ran from 1838 until 1840 and therefore more or less coextensively with the monthly parts of *Nicholas Nickleby* (1838-39), in which both series of *Heads* drawn by Meadows were advertised. See Curtis (note 18), p. 232.
43 See Andrée Lhéritier, 'Les Physiologies. Introduction', *Etudes de Presse*, 9:17 (1957), 1-11 (pp. 6-7).
44 See Riha and Rudolph, 'Nachwort' (note 37), p. 481. The circulation of *Le Charivari*, from 1836 to 1880, was only 2,000 to 3,000: see Ursula Koch and P.-P. Sagave, *Le Charivari* (Cologne: Informationspresse – Leske, 1984), p. 25.

committed graphic art in relation to the widespread poverty of the 1840s. The man in rags, a lumberjack, is looking for work as a woodcutter ('Holzschneider') in the xylographic studio of the Brothers Holzbock, as can be gleaned from the sign on the wall ('Holzbock' meaning both 'wooden stand, trestle' and a certain species of tick or beetle whilst, in figurative usage, indicating dumbness or insensitivity):

— „Sie! ich wollt' Sie fragen, ob man noch Holzschneider annimmt?" —

Illustration 5
"Sie! ich wollt' Sie fragen, ob man noch Holzschneider annimmt?"
("Mister, I meant to ask if you were still taking on woodcutters?"),
Düsseldorfer Monathefte, 1 (1847), [119]. Wood engraving.
Repr. vols 1-2 (1847-9) in one vol. (Düsseldorf: Schwann, 1979), [p. 119].

The army of wood-engravers, concentrating on their precision work with the help of magnifying glasses,[45] may in fact be producing images very like the one we have in front of us. But they literally have no eyes to see the pauper in the flesh; they produce reproducible images from drawings on wood and are as numb to the plight of the poor as their wood blocks. Could this be a commentary on the blunting, dehumanising effects of art printed on an 'industrial' scale for illustrated periodicals? Another question the viewer could be invited to ask is whether the minute size and the punning humour of state-of-the-art cartoons really convey the magnitude of the social problem they tackle.

To achieve this degree of self-referential interplay between visual and verbal wit, which is so characteristic of wood engravings and text, a rapid development had to have taken place in Germany since the early forties with regard to xylographic technique, the creation of dynamic text-image relationships and the 'critical mass' needed to support illustrated periodicals.[46] The first studio for wood engraving was established in Munich in 1844, co-founded by the artist and xylographer Kaspar Braun who received his training in Paris in the late 1830s.[47] By the late forties, a number of major illustrated satirical magazines offered a sufficient infrastructure from which a national serial of sketches, a German equivalent to *Les Français peints par eux-mêmes*, could have materialised. But it did not. A great obstacle apart from censorship was, of course, the lack of a national capital and therefore of an intellectual and artistic centre which would also have been the centre of publishing. As it hap-

---

45 Another noteworthy detail is the small bag filled with sand on which the engraver rests the block of boxwood so that it can be turned easily. As box, cut on the end grain, never produced blocks of great size, the piece of wood was held by hand during the process of cutting.

46 Even in 1843, J.J. Weber still had, at least initially, to rely on stereotypes received from London and on English wood engravers who had settled in Leipzig, in order to supply pictures for his counterpart to the *Illustrated London News*, the *[Leipziger] Illustrirte Zeitung*. See Wolfgang Weber, *Johann Jakob Weber* (Leipzig: Lehmstedt, 2003), p. 48; also Blachon (note 22), p. 68-9, who mentions seven English wood engravers working in Leipzig between 1839 and 1848. As one of three German firms publishing Dickens in translation in the 1830s, Weber became one of the earliest publishers of humorous graphic sketches on the German book market; he brought out *Sketches by Boz* as *Londoner Skizzen von Boz* in 1838, with plates after Cruikshank.

47 See Blachon (note 22), p. 78; also Eva Zahn, 'Die Geschichte der Fliegenden Blätter', in *Facsimile Querschnitt durch die Fliegenden Blätter* (Munich: Scherz, 1966), pp. 8-18 (pp. 10-11), and Heidegert Schmid Noerr, 'Die illustrierte Presse', in *Kunst der bürgerlichen Revolution*, ed. by Volkmar Braunbehrens and others, 2nd edn (Berlin: Neue Gesellschaft für Bildende Kunst, 1973), pp. 151-6 (p. 154).

pened, Munich and Düsseldorf, which produced three important illustrated satirical magazines between them in the second half of the 1840s, were cities of art, but scarcely writers' haunts. On the other hand, Berlin, the 'city of intellect' ('Stadt der Intelligenz')[48] about which a great number of sketches was written, could not generate the co-productive energy for an illustrated national serial of sketches because of the restrictions of Prussian censorship. Hence, illustrated sketch publications were normally two-men enterprises between a writer and a draughtsman and featuring lithographs or etchings rather than wood engravings.

Given the circumstances impeding collaboration in and across the German states, it is perhaps not surprising that the one sketch collection matching the great European serials of the early 1840s came from Vienna. Capital of a multinational state, a centre of theatre, fashion and good living as well as home of an illustrated journal of national standing, the *Wiener Theaterzeitung*, Vienna produced an answer to *Heads of the People* in the form of *Wien und die Wiener* (Vienna and the Viennese). The work was based on a series of steel plates and appeared at the height of the vogue from 1841 on, its uncritical ideological colour making it pass even under the extremely strict regime of Austrian censorship. Yet purely in terms of the range and scale of its assembled sketches, there is nothing remotely comparable for the Prussian capital, which only produced single writer / single artist serials, such as Adolf Glaßbrenner's long-lived *Berlin wie es ist und – trinkt*, featuring engravings by (mainly) Theodor Hosemann and focusing on plebeian scenes, or the little-known *Berlin und die Berliner*. This work of 1840-42 encompasses a variety of types and locations, with texts written by Ludwig Lenz (first series) and Ludwig Eichler (second series) and graphic types supplied by Hosemann, but contains only eight parts altogether.[49] Germany's leading journalist by the late 1830s, the Berliner Gutzkow, seems to put his finger on it when, in 1834, he laments the lack of a German metropolitan centre and hence the lack of sufficiently developed 'Sitten' as well as of an appropriate style of observation as the reason why Germans were unable to create a grand metropolitan serial of sketches:

> The French, with their *Livre de* [sic] *Cent et un*, set the mode of portraying contemporary life in as glaring colours as possible. The English

---

48 Ernst Dronke, *Berlin*, 2 vols (Frankfurt a. M.: Literarische Anstalt [J. Rütten], 1846), I, 5.
49 Ludwig Lenz, *Berlin und die Berliner. Genrebilder und Skizzen*, parts 1-3 (Berlin: Klemann, 1840-1). Ludwig Eichler, *Berlin und die Berliner. Neue Folge. Schilderungen*, parts 1-5 (Berlin: Klemann, 1841-2).

and the Russians followed their lead; we Germans needed a few national examples first before venturing on character portraits of this kind. But these examples did not come forward because we have no Paris, no big cities, no nuances in our manners [...] and too little talent for observation among our writers. The one hundred painters of mores the French could boast frightened us, for we were unable to muster, from the number of those who handled their pen with some routine, even ten who could have achieved something in this genre.[50]

Even if the attempt proved futile in the end, there must at least have been a serious effort in 1832 to get a Berlin-based collective serial of sketches, conceived explicitly as a counterpart to the *Livre des Cent-et-un*, off the ground: 'Every writer who has a name in the literary world will contribute to it', according to an announcement in the *Berliner Figaro*.[51] This was edited by the same Eduard Maria Oettinger who was later in charge of the Leipzig *Charivari* and had been a 'disciple' of the arch punster Moritz Saphir who, having collaborated on the *Wiener Theaterzeitung*, brought life to the stale journalism of the Prussian capital in the late 1820s and early 30s.[52]

The French *Figaro*, model also for à Beckett's and Mayhew's *Figaro in London*, was the epitome of a small oppositional paper in which the literary intelligentsia was able to practise, 'under the guise of literary criticism, a ferocious art in which innuendo replaced analysis'.[53] Its collaborators from

---

50 'Die Franzosen gaben mit ihrem *Livre de Cent et un* den Ton an, das Leben der Zeitgenossen in möglichst grellen Farben zu portraitiren. Die Engländer und Russen folgten ihnen; wir Deutsche bedurften erst einiger einheimischen Beispiele, ehe wir Charakteristiken dieser Art zu entwerfen wagten. Die Beispiele kamen aber nicht, weil wir kein Paris, keine großen Städte, keine Nüancen in unsern Sitten [...] und bei den Schriftstellern wenig Beobachtungsgabe besitzen. Die hundert Sittenmahler der Franzosen versetzten uns in Schrecken; denn wir konnten unter den routinirten Schreibfedern wohl keine zehn aufweisen, welche in jenem Genre hätten etwas leisten können.' Karl Gutzkow, 'Vorrede', in *Novellen*, 2 vols (Hamburg: Hoffmann & Campe, 1834), I, v-xxii (pp. xix-xx). See also reference to internet edition of *Gutzkows Werke und Briefe* in the Bibliography.

51 'Auch in Berlin soll ein *Livre de* [sic] *Cent-et-un* erscheinen. Jeder Schriftsteller, der einen Namen in der literarischen Welt hat, wird einen Beitrag liefern.' *Berliner Figaro*, 21 (25 January, 1832). I am grateful to Wolfgang Rasch (Berlin) for this information.

52 In the 1840s Oettinger edited, from Leipzig, another version of *Figaro*, but, more importantly, the German *Charivari* which survived until 1851.

53 '[...] les bravi du *Figaro* ou du *Corsaire* pratiquent en guise de critique littéraire un art féroce où le sous-entendu tient lieu d'analyse'; Chollet (note 29), p. 62.

1826 included its founders Etienne Arago and Maurice Alhoy (both future writers of *Physiologies*), as well as Henri de Latouche, Jules Janin, Balzac and the young Mme Dudevant, the later George Sand. Latouche, the only Republican amongst the French Romantics of the Restoration, wrote, together with Thiers, the protest note against the *ordonnances* of 26 July 1830 which was 'signed by forty-three journalists representing eleven newspapers'.[54] Janin, of course, was already established enough by 1831 as the first of critics to write the opening essay for the *Livre des Cent-et-un* and, like Balzac, was hardly absent from any of the major collaborative sketch collections following in its wake. *Le Figaro* was therefore a flagship of oppositional writing between politics and literature and, despite its small size, a symbol of the power of critical journalism whose hallmark was wit.

Given their close spatial relationship with the puns, riddles and charades often found in the *feuilleton* section or fill-up column of journals, sketches are a prime vehicle for exploiting the visual, semiotic and cognitive potential of witty codes without having to recur to images. For example, the way in which print is laid out on the page can itself be suggestive of the world of visual surfaces in which the dynamic present of the sketch unfolds. Under strict political censorship, such a quasi-visual allusive technique conditions the reader to look between the lines and across the columns. Illustrations, on the other hand, can, in their most sophisticated use, become a xylographed visual text and thus contribute their part to the 'vocabulary' with which sketches signal their key status in the culture of print.

Verbal-visual wit

The young Adolf Glaßbrenner was another collaborator of Moritz Saphir in his Berlin years. His short-lived *Berliner Don Quixote* is a typical example of a satirical journal founded in the atmosphere of political excitement after 1830. In it, on 19 September 1833, the editor's former schoolmate Karl Gutzkow, then twenty-two, published 'Papilloten', a sketch that makes use of paper metaphors in combination with its own appearance on the page. The French 'papillote', meaning curl-paper, is supposedly derived from 'papillon', butterfly,[55] and the sketch therefore alludes to its own ephemeral nature as a journal publication read by a considerable number, perhaps even a majority,

---

54 Philip Mansel, *Paris between Empires 1814-1852* (London: Phoenix, 2003), p. 238. See also Raymond Manevy, *La Presse française* (Paris: Foret, 1958), pp. 138-43.

55 See 'Papillote', OED. It is almost certain that this sketch was inspired by witticisms published under the same title and in the same year by Moritz Saphir: 'Papillotten', in *Gesammelte Schriften*, 4 vols (Stuttgart: Hallberger, 1832), IV, 195-248.

of women. In four disjointed sections, it illuminates contemporary journalistic writing and at the same time presents the writer in a veiled self-portrait while also offering humorous advice to budding authors. Young almost by definition, yet already in possession of all the ideas that will sustain a lifetime's work, the precocious literary genius is harnessed to the vehicle of journalism and has to observe an industrious routine to earn his living. Just as the butterflies of his witty, allusive imagination will flutter away when an unwelcome visitor disturbs him at nine o'clock in the morning, his resources as a writer are released in butterfly-fashion. They are published leaf by leaf over a long period, according to 'chance or a bookseller's speculation', rather than being put into one (unreadable) first book. The bittiness of journalistic publishing and the materiality of printed paper are further referred to in a self-ironic passage describing how the young genius spends a feverish few weeks to produce the first 'gift of his muse', a 'paper bridge of a hundred sheets' which conducts him back to earth from his creative delirium.[56] This 'convolute', to remain unpublished according to the author's advice, is also the young writer's capital and 'fool's motley coat' which will miraculously generate and 'clothe' many more of his future brainchildren. It also anticipates the mortality of its creator: 'The first hundred sheets from your pen must never become known, and when you die, instruct your heirs to have them burnt. On these holy ashes let your dead head be bedded in your coffin!'[57]

The romantic image of the dead poet resting on the cinders of his first creation is, however, itself reduced to ashes by the following three columns. The first of them contains a dozen or so aphorisms which offer variations on the theme of the writer and his readership, and in their loose, associative sequence, present another illustration of journalistic writing, the piecemeal release and circulation of ideas. While thus emphasizing the snappiness of 'youthful', contemporary journalism, these aphorisms also graphically enact the ephemeral by showing at the beginning of each sentence a printer's dagger (†) which looks like a Christian cross (illustration 6, p. 50).

---

56 'Einige fiebernde Wochen, [...] und die erste Bescheerung der Muse liegt vor ihm. Auf einer Papierbrücke von hundert Bogen kehrt er in die irdischen Räume zurück.' Karl Gutzkow, 'Papilloten', *Berliner Don Quixote*, 146 (19 September 1833), [p. 2].

57 'Für dieses Convolut [...] suche keinen Verleger! Es ist ein Heckthaler für deinen künftigen Reichthum. Es ist eine Hanswurstjacke, deren Lappen groß genug sind, daß du alle die nachgebornen Kinder deiner Phantasie darin kleiden kannst. [...] Die ersten hundert Bogen deiner Feder müssen nie bekannt werden, und wenn du stirbst, so befiehl deinen Erben, daß man sie verbrenne, und auf diese heilige Asche im Sarge dein todtes Haupt lege!' Ibid.

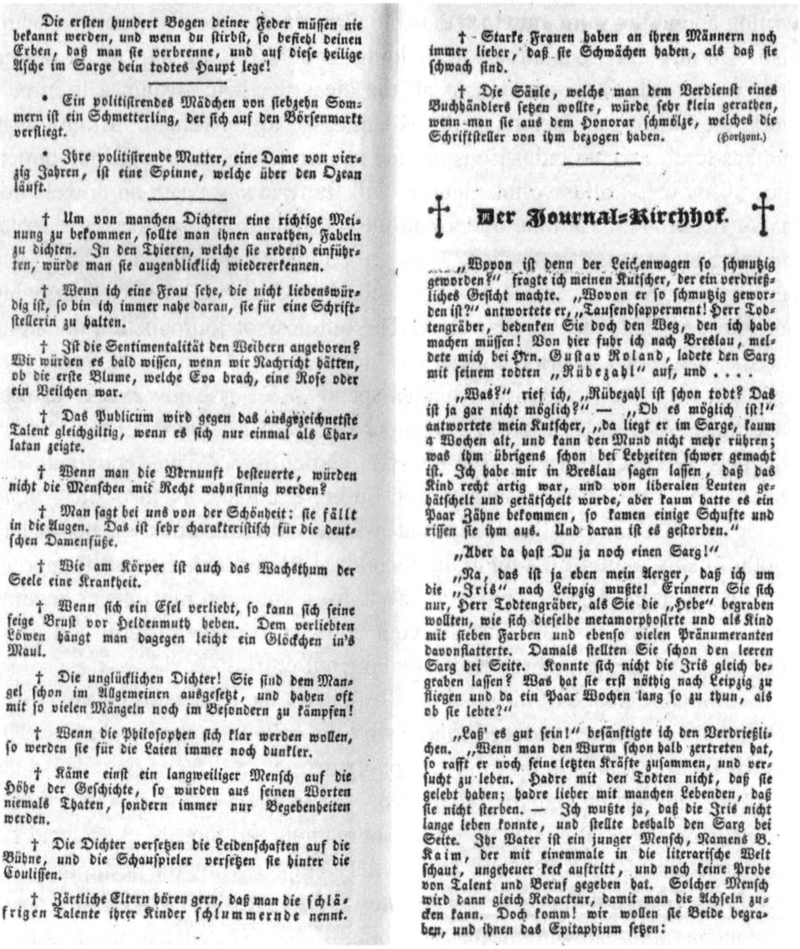

Die ersten hundert Bogen deiner Feder müssen nie bekannt werden, und wenn du stirbst, so befiehl deinen Erben, daß man sie verbrenne, und auf diese heilige Asche im Sarge dein todtes Haupt lege!

* Ein politisirendes Mädchen von siebzehn Sommern ist ein Schmetterling, der sich auf den Börsenmarkt verfliegt.

* Ihre politisirende Mutter, eine Dame von vierzig Jahren, ist eine Spinne, welche über den Ozean läuft.

† Um von manchen Dichtern eine richtige Meinung zu bekommen, sollte man ihnen anrathen, Fabeln zu dichten. In den Thieren, welche sie redend einführten, würde man sie augenblicklich wiedererkennen.

† Wenn ich eine Frau sehe, die nicht liebenswürdig ist, so bin ich immer nahe daran, sie für eine Schriftstellerin zu halten.

† Ist die Sentimentalität den Weibern angeboren? Wir würden es bald wissen, wenn wir Nachricht hätten, ob die erste Blume, welche Eva brach, eine Rose oder ein Veilchen war.

† Das Publicum wird gegen das ausgezeichnetste Talent gleichgiltig, wenn es sich nur einmal als Charlatan zeigte.

† Wenn man die Vernunft besteuerte, würden nicht die Menschen mit Recht wahnsinnig werden?

† Man sagt bei uns von der Schönheit: sie fällt in die Augen. Das ist sehr charakteristisch für die deutschen Damenfüße.

† Wie am Körper ist auch das Wachsthum der Seele eine Krankheit.

† Wenn sich ein Esel verliebt, so kann sich seine feige Brust vor Heldenmuth heben. Dem verliebten Löwen hängt man dagegen leicht ein Glöckchen in's Maul.

† Die unglücklichen Dichter! Sie sind dem Mangel schon im Allgemeinen ausgesetzt, und haben oft mit so vielen Mängeln noch im Besondern zu kämpfen!

† Wenn die Philosophen sich klar werden wollen, so werden sie für die Laien immer noch dunkler.

† Käme einst ein langweiliger Mensch auf die Höhe der Geschichte, so würden aus seinen Worten niemals Thaten, sondern immer nur Begebenheiten werden.

† Die Dichter versetzen die Leidenschaften auf die Bühne, und die Schauspieler versetzen sie hinter die Coulissen.

† Zärtliche Eltern hören gern, daß man die schläfrigen Talente ihrer Kinder schlummernde nennt.

† Starke Frauen haben an ihren Männern noch immer lieber, daß sie Schwächen haben, als daß sie schwach sind.

† Die Säule, welche man dem Verdienst eines Buchhändlers setzen wollte, würde sehr klein gerathen, wenn man sie aus dem Honorar schmölze, welches die Schriftsteller von ihm bezogen haben. (Horizont.)

† Der Journal-Kirchhof. †

... „Wovon ist denn der Leichenwagen so schmutzig geworden?" fragte ich meinen Kutscher, der ein verdrießliches Gesicht machte. „Wovon er so schmutzig geworden ist?" antwortete er, „Tausendsapperment! Herr Todtengräber, bedenken Sie doch den Weg, den ich habe machen müssen! Von hier fuhr ich nach Breslau, meldete mich bei Hrn. Gustav Roland, ladete den Sarg mit seinem todten „Rübezahl" auf, und ....

„Was?" rief ich, „Rübezahl ist schon todt? Das ist ja gar nicht möglich?" — „Ob es möglich ist!" antwortete mein Kutscher, „da liegt er im Sarge, kaum 4 Wochen alt, und kann den Mund nicht mehr rühren; was ihm übrigens schon bei Lebzeiten schwer gemacht ist. Ich habe mir in Breslau sagen lassen, daß das Kind recht artig war, und von liberalen Leuten gehätschelt und getätschelt wurde, aber kaum hatte es ein Paar Zähne bekommen, so kamen einige Schufte und rissen sie ihm aus. Und daran ist es gestorben."

„Aber da hast Du ja noch einen Sarg!"

„Na, das ist ja eben mein Aerger, daß ich um die „Iris" nach Leipzig mußte! Erinnern Sie sich nur, Herr Todtengräber, als Sie die „Hebe" begraben wollten, wie sich dieselbe metamorphosirte und als Kind mit sieben Farben und ebenso vielen Pränumeranten davonflatterte. Damals stellten Sie schon den leeren Sarg bei Seite. Konnte sich nicht die Iris gleich begraben lassen? Was hat sie erst nöthig nach Leipzig zu fliegen und da ein Paar Wochen lang so zu thun, als ob sie lebte?"

„Laß' es gut sein!" besänftigte ich den Verdrießlichen. „Wenn man den Wurm schon halb zertreten hat, so rafft er noch seine letzten Kräfte zusammen, und versucht zu leben. Hadre mit den Todten nicht, daß sie gelebt haben; hadre lieber mit manchen Lebenden, daß sie nicht sterben. — Ich wußte ja, daß die Iris nicht lange leben konnte, und stellte deshalb den Sarg bei Seite. Ihr Vater ist ein junger Mensch, Namens B. Kaim, der mit einemmale in die literarische Welt schaut, ungeheuer keck auftritt, und noch keine Probe von Talent und Beruf gegeben hat. Solcher Mensch wird dann gleich Redacteur, damit man die Achseln zucken kann. Doch komm! wir wollen sie Beide begraben, und ihnen das Epitaphium setzen:

Illustration 6 Karl Gutzkow, ‘Papilloten’, and Brennglas [Adolph Glaßbrenner], ‘Der Journal-Kirchhof’, *Berliner Don-Quixote*, 146 (19 September, 1833), [p. 2 and p. 3; inside columns]. Repr. 2 vols (Hildesheim, Zurich, New York: Olms, 2001), II, [n.p.].

These butterflies, in other words, are doomed to die on the day they hatch, thus representing the epitome of day-publishing, journalism in the literal sense. There is also a political subtext. The crosses continue, much enlarged, into the next two columns where the editor Glaßbrenner, assuming the persona of a grave-digger, runs his series ‘Der Journal-Kirchhof’ (‘The Journal Churchyard’), a witty obituary of ‘deceased’ periodicals and therefore necessarily also a faithful record of the victims of censorship. This time, the deaths of a Silesian journal, *Rübezahl*, at the age of barely four weeks, and of the Leipzig *Iris* are to be recorded. The demise of *Rübezahl* is due to the violent removal of its critical teeth, and that of *Iris* to the inexperience of its young editor. Glaßbrenner signs their 'epitaphs' by his punning *nom de plume*, Brennglas, meaning 'burning-glass'. This satirical incineration of competing journals, ritually performed by the editor, is ultimately applied to his own *Don Quixote*, forced out of existence by the authorities at the end of 1833 after a run of two years. Its last number ends with a self-epitaph, under the vignette of a butterfly,

Of all the rags that ever lived the worst is buried here;
It sank into the grave it dug for others in its sphere.[58]

In an act of politically subversive self-reference, the journal disappears into its own graveyard column for periodical 'butterflies'. Would the target readership, that is to say, 'men, women, children, old men, young men, mothers, fathers, sons and daughters' according to *Don Quixote's* first numbers, have remembered Gutzkow's 'Papilloten', published only a few months before the journal's suppression, where the fluttering paper world of male journalism was imaginatively related to the curl-papers of its female audience? In 'Papilloten', women seem to be ironically invited to regard the value of the periodical sketch as nothing more than that of its paper and to use it for their own fashionable hairstyles. But this is an invitation to read between the lines. Gutzkow's first two aphorisms, significantly not marked '†' but '*', concern women discussing politics and thereby performing a double transgression, firstly because politics is considered a male business and secondly because it is a taboo subject in a public sphere throttled by censorship, and anathema especially in the columns of a 'cultural' family journal such as *Don Quixote*. The two aphorisms that are obviously not designed for the graveyard read:

* A politicising girl of seventeen summers is a butterfly fluttering astray on the stockmarket.

* Her politicising mother, a lady of forty, is a spider crawling across the Ocean.[59]

---

58 'Das schlecht'ste Blatt, das je gelebt, man scharrte es hier ein; / Wer Andern eine Grube gräbt, fällt endlich selbst hinein.' *Berliner Don Quixote* [31 Dec. 1833], [p. 3].
59 '* Ein politisirendes Mädchen von siebzehn Sommern ist ein Schmetterling, der sich auf den Börsenmarkt verfliegt.' '* Ihre politisirende Mutter, eine Dame von

The insect metaphors, linking the sphere of 'butterfly' journalism with the young and the older politicising woman, make it possible to read these aphorisms against the grain of gender prejudice. Politicising women of any age are as serious an offence against the existing order as a lightweight periodical straying into politics.

While this sketch engages with its own ephemeral and politically subversive medium of print through its associative variations on the theme of 'papillotes' and through the visual responses between its aphorisms and the 'graveyard' rubric, inviting the reader to act as a detective in a visual-verbal conundrum, others exploit the interplay between the printed image and type to achieve a similar self-referential effect. Gerard Curtis has argued that the Victorian reader's skill in deciphering an innovative 'conflation of word and visual image' was to no small extent developed by the wrappers of serialised fiction. Their surface appeal of lettering, advertisements and images required and fostered reading as an act of 'typographical seeing', which was tantamount to acknowledging 'the visual value and visual semiotics of material signifiers, print, and the book itself'.[60] But I would argue that it is rarely within the text of a serial novel that the reader can practise 'typographical seeing' and 'visual semiotics' by decoding 'material signifiers' of the print revolution, in other words, the types on the page. To exercise this faculty through a particular form of visual writing and to offer analytical tools at the same time is the prerogative of sketches.

Gavarni's emblematic three silk top hats, around which is printed the opening of the chapter 'Les Arthurs' in Maurice Alhoy's *Physiologie de la Lorette* (1841), may serve as an example of the interplay between print and text where the subject is a sartorial item. 'Arthurs', plural, is the 'generic' name of a *Lorette's* lovers (illustration 7). The vignette and its accompanying text provoke the reader's 'typographic' and 'semiotic' viewing by indicating the particular intimacy between letter and image. The crescent shape of the capital letter C, half illustration, half text, comments on the text-image printing technology by representing 'the second half' of a *Lorette*'s 'soul', as we are informed by the lines running below the vignette.[61] The male 'being' who fulfils this function is metonymically present in the multiple copies of the same model of hat, left on a circular hall table. A *Lorette* will have several 'other halves' (the C also casts a double in the form of a shadow) and they

---

vierzig Jahren, ist eine Spinne, welche über den Ozean läuft.' Gutzkow, 'Papilloten' (note 56), [p. 2].

60 Curtis (note 18), p. 215, p. 214 and p. 217.

61 '[...] l'être que la Lorette nomme la seconde moitié de son âme'. Maurice Alhoy, *Physiologie de la Lorette* (Paris: Aubert, Lavigne, [1841]), p. 38.

typically sign themselves by the same, quite rare Christian name, 'Arthur', when writing *billets doux*. An 'Arthur' matches the *Lorette*'s 'soul' inasmuch as like her, he is a type, made and multiplied by signifiers such as fashionable accessories:

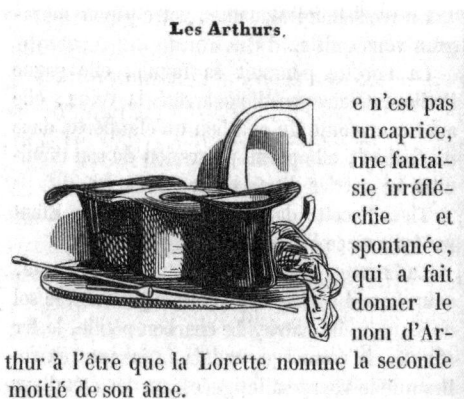

Les Arthurs.

e n'est pas un caprice, une fantaisie irréfléchie et spontanée, qui a fait donner le nom d'Arthur à l'être que la Lorette nomme la seconde moitié de son âme.

Illustration 7   Gavarni, vignette in Maurice Alhoy, *Physiologie de la Lorette* (Paris: Aubert, Lavigne, [1841]), p. 38. Wood engraving.

The black top hat only comes in one different shade, which is white; colour is absent from the civil uniform of the nineteenth-century male, as it is from the printed types on the page. Both are reproducible. Ségolène Le Men has commented on this analogy between social and printed type, pointing to its significance for the production and reading of sketches. Indirectly referring to Benjamin, Le Men argues that the reproducibility of types is inseparable from semiotic awareness:

> Type is, first of all, the proof printed from the same matrix in multiple copies; it is the object in the age of its mechanical reproduction, whether as a minted coin or as a print, as a daguerreotype or as the types and characters of the printer. The type finally implies a reflection on the very nature of the sign [...].[62]

---

62 'Le type, c'est avant tout l'épreuve, tirée d'une même matrice à de multiples exemplaires; c'est l'objet à l'ère de sa reproductibilité technique, qu'il s'agisse de la pièce de monnaie ou de l'estampe, du daguerréotype ou des types et caractères de l'imprimeur. Le type implique enfin une réflexion sur la nature même du signe, que

Reproducibility also means that the same series of illustrated sketches can appear in two different countries; for example, as an English 'original' and as a French 'reproduction'. Le Men refers to the translation of the *Heads of the People* as *Les Anglais peints par eux-mêmes*, which reproduced Kenny Meadows's / Orrin Smith's popular portraits with French versions of the accompanying essays and thus gave rise to the famous *Les Français peints par eux-mêmes*. Douglas Jerrold's introduction to the first volume of *Heads of the People* contains reflections on reproduction and on the significance of multiplied images which bear out Le Men's from the point of view of a nineteenth-century contemporary. Jerrold remarks that '[t]he "Heads of the People", of the numerous family of John Bull, are to be seen gazing from the windows of French shopkeepers', that is to say, from the windows of Parisian print sellers who displayed the 'Heads'. It is likely that these images were made available in the form of stereotypes from which prints were taken. The reproduction of English social types abroad, Jerrold considers, with the 'Heads' of the nation's ordinary people 'gazing [...] at our "natural enemies"', is unlikely to reinforce national 'antipathy'. On the contrary, it effects transnational understanding. Not only are the texts of *Heads of the People* translated into French, but the whole serial is assimilated, forming 'the model of a national work for the essayists and wits of Paris' – in other words, of *Les Français peints par eux-mêmes*.[63] The multiplication of the signifiers indicating social 'types' means that the signified, 'the People', 'les Anglais' or 'les Français' respectively, becomes interchangeable. The printer's stereotypes help overcome national ones. 'John Bull' pales into insignificance vis-a-vis sharply observed, sketched, engraved social types which are reproduced abroad and thereby assimilated. The witty, self-referential manner in which the cross-nationality of 'type' is handled can be demonstrated, for example, in the textual-graphic language of *Punch*.

A sketch entitled 'Portrait of the Lover' in *Punch's* 22nd and 23rd number (11 and 18 December 1841) shows the close relationship between *Punch* and the *Physiologies*, products of a two-way Anglo-French cultural transfer, with regard to their virtuoso treatment of the text-image surface. The sketch appears in the section 'Pen and Palette Portraits. (Taken from the French.) By Alphonse Lecourt' and is introduced by a letter of this spoof Parisian congratulating the 'London Charivari' on the wit contained in its every line. Al-

---

Saussure le premier avait défini par rapport au signe monétaire.' Ségolène Le Men, 'Peints par eux-mêmes ...', in *Les Français peints par eux-mêmes* (Paris: Éditions de la Réunion des musées nationaux, 1993), pp. 4-46 (p. 46).

63 [Douglas Jerrold], 'Preface', in *Heads of the People: or, Portraits of the English*, 2 vols (London: Tyas, 1840-1), I (1840), iii-vi (p. iv).

bert Smith's running series, 'Physiology of the London Medical Student', which has apparently been translated into French, comes in for particular praise: 'the avidity' with which it is read in Paris 'has suggested to me that sketches of French character might be equally popular amongst English readers'. Hence *Punch* is presented with a 'Physiological and Pictorial Portrait of "THE LOVER"', although this type is supposedly not particular to the French, but universal.[64] The sketch thus being set against the background of illustrated *Physiologies* as an intercultural business, its second instalment shows a bearded male figurine in top hat, puffing his cigar, playing with his cane and leaning against the opening letter A, illustrating the distracted look of the man in love who is described in the first paragraph, that is to say, in the block of text facing the figure:

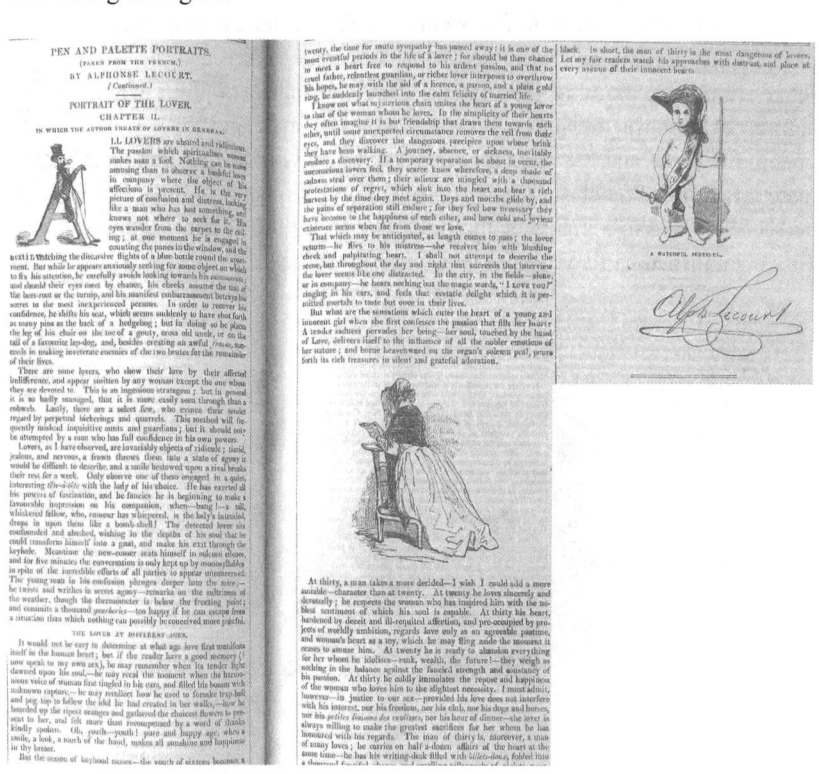

Illustration 8   'Pen and Palette Portraits', *Punch*, 1 (July-December 1841), 274-5. Wood engravings.

---

64 'Pen and Palette Portraits. (Taken from the French.) By Alphonse Lecourt. Portrait of the Lover. Chapter I', *Punch*, 1 (July-December 1841), 262-3 (p. 262).

The woman in love, by contrast, is depicted as inward-looking, expressing her emotions in religious contemplation and hence turning her face from the reader. Again the written word is visualised immediately through the body language of the inserted vignette. In the way the illustrations are arranged, the lovers face one another across the columns of text, yet they are not a couple. The reader's interest is not engaged in a narrative of love, but in a description of the typical male and female middle-class lover. The Napoleonic cupid placed at the end of the text echoes the male figure with his hat and cane at the beginning. Yet this little nude, looking out of the text, signifies the 'watchful sentinel' that female readers are advised to deploy against the advances of the man around thirty who, having grown out of youthful adoration of the other sex, 'regards love only as an agreeable pastime, and a woman's heart as a toy, which he may fling aside the moment it ceases to amuse him'.[65] The visual cross-references constitute a witty sign-system, with the 'Alpha' of male desire and the 'Omega' of female vigilance framing the text. A florid signature of the alleged French author, 'Alph[onse] Lecourt', connects with the man and the 'Alpha' in the opening vignette and literally authorises the borrowing of the 'Pen and Palette' materials from a French source. The original of the kneeling woman is indeed to be seen in Gavarni's image of the praying *Lorette* in Maurice Alhoy's *Physiologie*, published half a year previously in July 1841:[66]

Illustration 9 Gavarni, vignette in Maurice Alhoy, *Physiologie de la Lorette* (Paris: Aubert, Lavigne, [1841]), p. 27. Wood engraving.

---

65 'Pen and Palette Portraits. (Taken from the French.) By Alphonse Lecourt. Portrait of the Lover. Chapter II', *Punch*, 1 (July-December 1841), 274-5 (p. 275).
66 See Andrée Lhéritier, 'Répertoire des Physiologies', *Etudes de Presse*, 9:17 (1957), 13-58 (no. 34, p. 18).

It is of course doubtful whether, the bohemian 'Punchites' themselves apart, anyone would have recognised this literal borrowing from French graphic journalism. But given the intercultural discourse set up at the beginning of the sketch, the reader cannot have failed to be aware of the French implications in its sign-system, as well as that of *Punch* in general, which here transcends what can be seen on the page. Drawing on the French, that is to say, physiological mode of social interpretation, 'Portrait of the Lover' subjects *mœurs* to witty analysis and draws conclusions in a quasi-scientific manner. Just like the *Physiologie de la Lorette*, it is concerned with unmarried love as a social phenomenon breaking the norm of female chastity. In the *Physiologie*, the emphasis is on the 'free' woman who has many lovers, while in the *Punch* sketch it is the male of a certain age whose 'writing-desk filled with *billets-doux*' addressed to his 'many loves' shows disregard for the norm. The *Punch* female, by contrast, and in an absolute reversal of the *Lorette's* role, conforms to expectations by her spiritual sublimation of desire: 'her soul, touched by the hand of Love, delivers itself to the influence of all the nobler emotions of her nature; and borne heavenward on the organ's solemn peal, pours forth its rich treasures in silent and grateful adoration.'[67] But this conventional image of female spirituality as a safeguard against the dangers of sensuality is somewhat undermined by the advice to young women to guard themselves against advances of the 'Arthur' type, in other words, the older man of means who would 'keep' women as a symbol of his own social and sexual success. The warning implies that once seduced by one of them, a woman will be considered 'fallen' and presumably, if she should be so lucky, have to lead the life of a *Lorette* whose social status is recognised, even romanticised. Alhoy's / Gavarni's *Lorette* prays in the church after which her 'class' is named, Notre-Dame-de-Lorette, built in the northern vicinity of the Boulevard des Italiens between 1823 and 1836. The context of the *Physiologie* makes it clear that the church is frequented by the loose women of the quarter who seek spiritual refuge – however temporary – from their lot, and that *Lorettes* are among the most generous financial supporters of the new church. 'Taken from the French', the devout 'Catholic' posture of the woman in the *Punch* sketch invites a reading which could be seen to be subtly offering another layer of interpretation than that suggested by the text.

Sketches, as has been shown, offer an excellent vehicle for engaging producers of texts and images as well as their audiences in dynamic aspects of the print revolution. The printed surface itself becomes eloquent; it bespeaks a revolutionary present in which boundaries of all kinds have become fluid,

---

67 'Pen and Palette Portraits' (note 65), p. 275.

notably those between national cultures, 'educated' and 'uneducated' classes, book and journal, as well as image and type. 'Viewing' and 'knowing' is another distinction that has become uncertain, and the relationship between these two faculties requires intense renegotiation. Here again sketches, thanks to their discursive and visual potential, can be found right at the core of a process in which the speedy transition of the visible world discloses meaning more readily than ever before, but also encodes it in much more complex ways. In responding to the visual challenges, sketches find themselves in competition with pre-cinematic media to which, as will be shown, they constitute a meta-medium.

2
The Mobile Observer: Sketches and Optical Media

The mental processes associated with the nineteenth-century explosion in ocular activity have been subsumed under the category of 'visual imagination'. This mildly pleonastic expression, indicating that the viewer's imagination is constantly furnished with images, seems nevertheless highly appropriate. Such is the challenge of an external world where every surface hints at movement and transition, that the imagination appears to overreact somewhat. Things already 'imagined' are once more translated into pictures so that a heightened mental-visual imprint is achieved.

At the core of an age of 'visible transition' is the very materiality of vision. The 'profound transformation' that processes of viewing underwent through the discovery of 'subjective vision' early in the nineteenth century has been pointed out by Jonathan Crary in *Techniques of the Observer*.[1] An understanding of the eye's capacity to retain afterimages, in other words, of the relative independence of human perception from the objective world, revolutionised the production of optical apparatuses, many of them creating the illusion of movement on the basis of rapidly changing static images. Others suggested transformation with the help of sophisticated projection effects, including, for example, the diorama, the phantasmagoria and the dissolving view (the latter two being developments of the magic lantern show). All these media fostered the century's entertainment industry and in turn influenced the way in which contemporaries viewed and imagined the world.

The acceleration of change means that the present is superseded by a new present ever more quickly, so that what 'is' can be vividly imagined in terms of what 'will have been' and of what 'was'. Kate Flint refers to writing that

---

1 Jonathan Crary, *Techniques of the Observer* (Cambridge, MA: MIT Press, 1990), p. 78; see also his whole chapter 'Subjective Vision and the Separation of the Senses', pp. 67-96.

imagines a simultaneous presence of different layers of history as a 'palimpsest'.[2] The proximity of this type of writing to the new popular visual media was exploited by Dickens, for example, in his 'Travelling Sketches Written on the Road', published in the *Daily News* from January until March 1846 and in book form during the same year.[3] I will thus, exceptionally, include in my discussion a travelogue from abroad, that of Dickens's Italian sojourn in 1844-45. Its last chapter enacts a particular type of contemporary picture show and differs from the others in being written entirely as a dramatic present-tense account.

Dickens's 'Rapid Diorama' (*Pictures from Italy*)

Describing the author's journey from Rome to Naples, visit to Pompeii and Herculaneum, ascent of Mount Vesuvius, arrival back in Naples, onward travel to Florence and final departure from Italy, the chapter is entitled 'A Rapid Diorama'. As a genre traditionally recording a gentleman's impressions during the 'grand tour', sketches of Italy are here catapulted into the age of technically produced images; their artistic paradigm has changed from private drawing to public, even popular medium. Performances of dioramic views usually presented travel destinations such as the Alps, the Rhine, cathedrals, ruined abbeys and, of course, Italian volcanoes,[4] with changing light effects that suggested the passage of a day within a quarter of an hour. In addition to this atmospheric modification of the scene, the so-called double-effect diorama made certain elements of the picture appear and disappear by lighting the surface, painted with diaphanous as well as opaque media, from the front and from behind. For instance, Daguerre's famous diorama of *St. Etienne du Mont* (1834) showed the interior of this church with daylight gradually fading and the congregation appearing for midnight mass as night falls and candles and lamps are lit.[5] Like a diorama, Dickens's travel writing visualises the presence of different layers of time under one and the same surface. Flint comments on his Italian sketches precisely in terms of palimpsest-type writ-

---

2 See the chapter 'The Buried City' in Kate Flint, *The Victorians and the Visual Imagination* (Cambridge: Cambridge University Press, 2002), pp. 139-66.
3 With four illustrations by Samuel Palmer, as *Pictures from Italy* (Bradbury & Evans, 1846).
4 See Richard Altick, *The Shows of London* (Cambridge, MA: The Belknap Press of Harvard University Press, 1978), p. 171.
5 See Heinz Buddemeier, *Panorama, Diorama, Photographie* (Munich: Fink, 1970), chapter 'Die Sujets der Dioramen', pp. 41-8, and Altick (note 4), chapter 'The Diorama', pp. 163-72.

ing in her chapter 'The buried city'.[6] Thus, for example, the landscape dominated by Mount Vesuvius discloses visions of ancient history as well as of the future, a rising from the ashes of new life, which has a clear political implication in an oppressed country 'biding its terrible time'.[7] The ancient everyday objects, excavated at Pompeii and Herculaneum, particularly the theatrical masks, constitute an immediate link with the daily pantomime in Italy's streets which often communicates abject poverty and degradation. But these two thousand year-old traces of life also connect with the hope of rebuilding a civilised state in a description which guides the reader's mental eye through direct address:

> Stand at the bottom of the great market-place of Pompeii, and look up the silent streets, through the ruined temples [...], over the broken houses with their inmost sanctuaries open to the day, away to Mount Vesuvius, bright and snowy in the peaceful distance; and lose all count of time [...] in the strange and melancholy sensation of seeing the Destroyed and the Destroyer making this quiet picture in the sun. Then, ramble on, and see, at every turn, the little familiar tokens of human habitation and every-day pursuits; the chafing of the bucket-rope in the stone rim of the exhausted well; [...] the marks of drinking-vessels on the stone counter of the wine-shop; the Amphoræ in private cellars, stored away so many hundred years ago, and undisturbed to this hour – all rendering the solitude and deadly lonesomeness of the place, ten thousand times more solemn, than if the volcano, in its fury, had swept the city from the earth, and sunk it in the bottom of the sea.
>
> After it was shaken by the earthquake which preceded the eruption, workmen were employed in shaping out, in stone, new ornaments for temples and other buildings that had suffered. Here lies their work, outside the city gate, as if they would return to-morrow.[8]

The ancient market place offers the present observer/reader an auditorium from which the 'Destroyed' and the 'Destroyer' are visually imagined as one-time actors, now part of the same 'quiet picture', and thus irresistibly evoking empathy; first with human dwellings whose 'inmost sanctuaries' are revealed to the eyes of posterity, and then with the ordinary life that has left its marks in stone. The Romantic dream of cities buried under the sea is as nothing compared to the Realism of visual imagination connected with this archaeo-

---

6   See Flint (note 2), pp. 145-9.
7   Dickens, *Pictures from Italy* (note 3), p. 247.
8   Ibid., pp. 243-4.

logical site in the socially and politically tense atmosphere of the 1840s. The stonemasonry of workmen repairing buildings after an earthquake represents the most 'solemn' reminder of the human reality connecting past, present and future. Dickens's sketch thus corresponds to the picturesque subject matter, the time gradations and the life-like effects of the diorama. However, it also puts this visual model into perspective. The description of the excavations is, after all, only one of a multitude of 'scenes' captured by his 'rapid diorama'. A *rapid* diorama is a contradiction in terms since the medium distinguished itself precisely by the *gradual* change effected within one and the same picture. The switch from picture to picture (usually two) was also slow, with a complete blackout during the transition.[9] This leisurely pace associated with the dioramic mode of vision and its relationship to strolling and concepts of the picturesque is communicated by the French translation (1823) of Pierce Egan's *Life in London* as *Diorama Anglais, ou Promenades pittoresques à Londres*. Yet even this publication, alluding to the launching of Daguerre's and Bouton's diorama in 1822 and thus to the *dernier cri* in optical entertainment, indicates that it is discursively at the head of significant developments in the visual media. In the mid-1840s, then, Dickens's 'rapid diorama' of sketches signals a further step in the evolution of the written and printed medium which performs a mode of viewing not provided by the slow-moving diorama.

It must be conceded that visual media since the beginning of the nineteenth century *had been* able to represent continual change or even relatively fast movement in so-called 'moving panoramas'. If one allows for the looseness of contemporary terminology,[10] Dickens's expression 'rapid diorama' might therefore indicate the affinity of his writing with this particular kind of performance. The moving panoramas consisted of long strips of painted scenery moving past the stationary spectators, thus creating in them too the illusion of moving along.[11] Dickens's travel sketches, however, differ from both the diorama and the moving panorama in requiring, and not merely suggesting, the observer's own mobility. The phrase 'Written on the Road', added to the title 'Travelling Sketches', says it all. A mode of viewing is developed here that is akin to dioramic and panoramic modes, yet deviates in one crucial respect. The 'pictures' presented as part of the 'rapid diorama', while being in themselves palimpsest-like and theatrical, in other words, non-static representations, also presuppose non-fixity in the act of viewing. Befitting his status as a

---

9 See Altick (note 4), pp. 169-70.
10 See ibid., p. 174.
11 See ibid., pp. 203-10; also Bernard Comment, *The Panorama* (London: Reaktion Books), 1999, pp. 63-5.

traveller, Dickens's observer conveys a sense of insecurity which is constitutive of the very 'pictures' painted of Italian life. This sense of exposure to the things observed transfers itself to the reader whose act of reading is also an act of viewing, just as depiction, writing and reading coincide in sustained present-tense narrative. The following scene describes the passage through Fondi, the first, wretchedly poor town on Neapolitan territory, where the travellers' coach is surrounded by a population of beggars:

> Look at them as they gather round. Some, are too indolent to come down stairs, or are too wisely mistrustful of the stairs, perhaps, to venture: so stretch out their lean hands from upper windows, and howl; others, come flocking about us, fighting and jostling one another [...]. A group of miserable children, almost naked, [...] discover that they can see themselves reflected in the varnish of the carriage, and begin to dance and make grimaces, that they may have the pleasure of seeing their antics repeated in this mirror. A crippled idiot, in the act of striking one of them who drowns his clamorous demand for charity, observes his angry counterpart in the panel, stops short, and thrusting out his tongue, begins to wag his head and chatter.[12]

The phrase inviting the reader to 'look at' the scene of deprivation as its description unfolds, apparently from the safe position of the observers in their coach, is in fact an invitation to share the foreigners' unsettling experience of *being* looked at by starving crowds. Nor does the observation immediately focus on those gathering around the vehicle, but, as if to seek an impossible escape, on the upper windows of the decrepit houses from which begging hands appear. It is only then that the view takes in the people closer to the carriage as they seem to crowd in on it ever more threateningly. The half-naked children mirroring themselves in the high varnish, and the insane man sticking out his tongue at a reflection then constitute a mirror image of the traveller's own fluctuating perception. As the quasi-medieval, yet uncomfortably present poor see themselves reflected in the polished exterior of the modern travel coach, so their wretchedness and 'bad bright eyes glaring at us'[13] highlight the traveller's own contemporary middle-class status and, most importantly, his status as an observer 'on the road' who is both the subject and the object of viewing. The timeless fool's tongue is also stuck out at him. Both parties are, each in their own way, equally reduced to the human condition.

---

12 Dickens (note 3), pp. 335-6.
13 Ibid., p. 236.

As a travelogue in which not only the observed, but observation itself is subject to mobility and multi-perspectivity, the 'rapid' written diorama comments on the visual medium to which it alludes as limited, that is to say, as a mere substitute for travelling. Optical media can effectively stand in for, and even imaginatively anticipate, the experience, but they are not the real thing.[14] However much they may suggest reality through change and movement, the viewer can only experience foreign places when s/he is himself or herself moving and exposed to the things seen by direct, not mediated, vision. Of course, the reader of a sketch travels as vicariously as a diorama viewer. However, by making mobility a constitutive factor of perception and depiction, sketches can translate into narrative technique and thereby into a mental process the double-edged viewing associated with travelling. Moreover, they can reflect on modes of transport that make mobility and viewing of this kind possible in the first place. In other words, by referring to the diorama as a cognate visualising and popularising medium, Dickens's sketches only underline the medium's constraints which are grounded in its purely visual nature and in the static position of the viewer. If, as Günter Hess has argued, the development of technical media of illusion had a decisive influence on nineteenth-century modes of viewing in that they fixed large audiences' visual expectations into 'optical stereotypes',[15] one could argue that sketches, as a textual meta-medium engaging with these visual media, were able to comment, at least implicitly, on such stereotypes. Most importantly, they were able to relate the observer's own movement, made easier and speedier, directly to the observed simultaneous 'presence' of various layers of history. Thereby they reveal the historical relativity of their own vision; vision in the age of speed and 'visible transition'. They also anticipate an aspect of modernism which centres on the mobility of the metropolitan observer afforded by speedy public transport rather than by strolling, in other words, they foreshadow what Ana Parejo Vadillo has termed 'the late-Victorian aesthetics of transport'.[16]

---

14 Richard Altick has drawn attention to the panorama as a form of vicarious travelling, enabling large parts of the population who could not afford a journey to the Continent or more distant places to engage in 'tourism' *avant la lettre*, before it became a phenomenon in the 1850s with Thomas Cook's organised tours. See Altick (note 4), p. 180 and p. 478.
15 Günter Hess, 'Panorama und Denkmal. Erinnerung als Denkform zwischen Vormärz und Gründerzeit', in *Literatur in der sozialen Bewegung*, ed. by Alberto Martino (Tübingen: Niemeyer, 1977), pp. 130-206 (p. 165).
16 See Ana Parejo Vadillo, *Women Poets and Urban Aestheticism. Passengers of Modernity* (Basingstoke: Palgrave Macmillan, 2005), p. 25.

An illustrated sketch by Balzac, 'Histoire et physiologie des Boulevards de Paris', published in 1845 in *Le Diable à Paris*, demonstrates how a sense of vertical layering interacts with the observer's own linear movement, imagined as that of an omnibus passenger, to culminate in the imagination of unprecedented simultaneity between past, present and future. The allusion to a contemporary visual medium, although not explicit here, is to the moving panorama.

Panorama in motion: Balzac's 'Histoire et physiologie des Boulevards de Paris' (*Le Diable à Paris*)

Parisian street surfaces are described as alive with a sense of what lies underneath and of what lies ahead. Just as today's asphalt is reverberating with the passions of the stock market, the earth that the city's people have walked on since about 1500 has been humming with the passions of historical change. But over the last forty years the intervals of change, formerly centuries, have dwindled to decades. It is only since 1800, when the royal centre of power vanished, that the boulevards (created in the seventeenth century along the line of Charles V's city walls) have been the property of the people and have therefore yielded presentiments of the whole city's future: 'In 1860, the heart of Paris will stretch from the Rue de la Paix to the Place de la Concorde', while at present it is still closer to the centre of the 1820s, the Boulevard des Italiens (or Boulevard de Gand, as it was called under the Restoration). With popular culture, commerce and traffic growing in significance, the centre of life is moving all the time; Balzac speaks of '[c]es déplacements de la vie parisienne'.[17] This mobility reflects fluctuations of the market and of fashion, but even more significantly, the increasing social status of the lower classes. If in the near future, the rue de la Paix will be a centre of life, this means a social shift, as this street, now socially mixed and bordering on the posh

---

17 See [Honoré] de Balzac, 'Histoire et physiologie des Boulevards de Paris. De la Madeleine à la Bastille', in *Le Diable à Paris*, 2 vols (Paris: Hetzel, 1845-6), II (1846), 92: 'La vie de Paris, sa physionomie, a été, en 1500, rue Saint-Antoine; en 1600, à la place Royale; en 1700, au pont Neuf; en 1800, au Palais-Royal. [...] La terre a été passionnée là, comme l'asphalte l'est aujourd'hui sous les pieds des boursiers [...] Le Boulevard ne fit pressentir ce qu'il serait un jour qu'en 1800. De la rue du Faubourg-du-Temple à la rue Charlot [...] sa vie s'est transportée en 1815 au boulevard du Panorama. En 1820, elle s'est fixée au boulevard dit de Gand, et maintenant elle tend à remonter de là vers la Madeleine. En 1860, le cœur de Paris sera de la rue de la Paix à la place de la Concorde. Ces déplacements de la vie parisienne s'expliquent.'

Madeleine quarter, is to turn into a modern version of the working-class rue Saint-Denis in the north-east and into the 'antagonist' of the wealthy rue Richelieu. At present, however, the 'pulse' of Paris is still most strongly felt on the luxurious Boulevard des Italiens and Boulevard Montmartre, which are part of a long thoroughfare between the upper-class west and the lower-class east. It is this historical semicircle of tree-lined avenues, 'the boulevard', consisting of many differently named sections and not to be confused with Haussmann's later creations, that the sketch depicts. The reader is invited to come and fly along it from the Madeleine right down to the Bastille 'as if we were in an omnibus'. This is in fact *the* omnibus, as the first-ever service had been installed precisely between the Madeleine and the Bastille in 1828. Transport seems of the essence if the river of asphalt and stone, 'this second, dry Seine', is to show its full 'physiognomy',[18] a key expression Balzac uses only in the singular as if to underline the unity of the visual experience from start to finish. This is only possible if the observer keeps moving and does not get distracted, for example, by the 'three thousand shops' that 'are glittering', combining into a 'great poem of window display (étalage)' which 'is singing its stanzas of colours from the Madeleine to the Porte Saint-Denis'.[19] 'Étalage' is indeed not the sole characteristic of the boulevard, given that its eastern sections are much poorer. Its socially varied aspects will become fully palpable and mutate into living time-lines if the observer is fortunate enough to experience them in the shortest possible time, being taken at full trot from one end to the other by that status symbol of dandy fashion, an English horse: 'You will read, in a quarter of an hour, the poem of Paris [...] The history of France, its last pages mainly, are written on the boulevards.'[20]

The sketch thus points to the presence of history as a mainly visual metropolitan experience, crucially dependent on fast, live observation. Not only can older layers be felt through the surface and new ones be anticipated by the attentive observer, but past, present and future come together through linear

---

18 'Maintenant prenons notre vol comme si nous étions en omnibus, et suivons ce fleuve, cette seconde Seine sèche, étudions-en la physionomie...' Balzac (note 17), p. 94.
19 '[...] vous atteignez au cœur du Paris actuel, qui palpite entre la rue de la Chaussée-d'Antin et la rue du Faubourg-Montmartre.' Ibid., p. 95. 'Ses [the Boulevards'] trois mille boutiques scintillent, et le grand poëme de l'étalage chante ses strophes de couleurs depuis la Madeleine jusqu'à la porte Saint-Denis.' Ibid., p. 91.
20 'Allez, au grand trot d'un cheval anglais, de la place de la Concorde et de la Madeleine au pont d'Austerlitz, vous lirez en un quart d'heure ce poëme de Paris [...] L'histoire de France, les dernières pages principalement, sont écrites sur les Boulevards.' Ibid., p. 104.

physiognomic 'reading' that is itself made possible by speedy motion. At the beginning of the journey one encounters some splendid buildings dating back to pre-revolutionary times, including that of the composer Lully, which will sooner or later be demolished; others express 'the astonishing revolutions of property in Paris'. These revolutions have, for example, enabled a tailor to finance the construction of the Maison Frascati, 'a sort of Colosseum-like *phalanstère*' at the corner of the Boulevard des Italiens and the rue Richelieu, from which the speculator is expected to make a million.[21] The building was erected on the site of the old Hôtel Frascati, a gambling-establishment, and the fact that the same spot is now occupied by a massive, extremely lucrative commercial and residential block is ironised in the reference to it as a *phalanstère*, Fourier's utopian concept of housing for a socialist community, a *phalange*.[22] The 'statement' this building makes through its sheer dimensions becomes clear from the illustration, especially in contrast to the much more modest-sized façades depicted previously. The views from the boulevard into side streets also illuminate the expected 'antagonism' between the exclusive rue Richelieu and the future centre of plebeian entertainment, the rue de la Paix (illustration 10, p. 68).

The journey has so far focused on buildings, and it is in this respect that the sketch corresponds to the moving panorama. In vogue particularly as scenery for theatrical pantomimes since the 1820s, moving panoramas of the 1840s normally simulated 'river or sea voyages' and occasionally journeys along 'well-known urban axes such as the Champs-Elysées and the rue de Rivoli or the Nevsky Prospekt in St Petersburg'.[23] The effect, as indicated earlier, was achieved by long painted strips being run across a proscenium. Balzac's reference to the boulevard as a river of stone paralleling the Seine might be explained through this context, as might his mention of other famous metropolitan thoroughfares including, amongst others, London's Regent Street and the Nevsky Prospekt ('la Perspective à Péters-

---

21 'Admirez les étonnantes révolutions de la propriété dans Paris! [...] un tailleur construit cette espèce de phalanstère *colyséen*, et il y gagnera, dit-on, un million [...].' Ibid., p. 97.
22 This reference very probably alludes to arcade-like, sheltered walkways inside the vast building. Benjamin quotes the following passage from Fourier in his *Arcades Project*: 'La Phalange n'a point de rue extérieure ou voie découverte exposée aux injures de l'air; tous les quartiers de l'édifice nominal peuvent être parcourus dans une large galerie.' Walter Benjamin, 'Das Passagen-Werk', in *Gesammelte Schriften*, ed. by Rolf Tiedemann and Hermann Schweppenhäuser, 7 vols (Frankfurt a. M.: 1991), V,1-2, (V,1, p. 95).
23 Comment (note 11), pp. 64-5; see also Altick (note 4), pp. 203-10.

gle de la rue. Ce sera démoli quelque jour, comme la maison de Lulli, située aussi à un angle, celui de la rue Neuve-des-Petits-Champs et de la rue Sainte-Anne, et où il a signé son nom par des sculptures parmi lesquelles se voit, sous forme de lyre, le violon qui fit sa fortune.

Maison de Lulli.

A la rue de la Paix, tout change, le passant abonde. Autrefois le Boulevard finissait réellement là. Tout Paris débouchait par la rue de la Paix pour aller aux Tuileries. La rue de la Paix est la future antagoniste de la rue Richelieu, ce sera la rue Saint-Denis moderne. Dès que vous avez passé ce point, vous atteignez au cœur du Paris actuel, qui palpite entre la rue de la Chaussée-d'Antin

Rue de la Paix.

Maison et café Frascati. — Rue Richelieu. — Café Cardinal.

Illustration 10
Bertrand, vignettes in [Honoré] de Balzac, 'Histoire et physiologie des Boulevards de Paris', in *Le Diable à Paris. Paris et les Parisiens. Mœurs et coutumes, caractères et portraits des habitants de Paris, tableau complet de leur vie privée, publique, politique, artistique, littéraire, industrielle, etc., etc.*, 2 vols (Paris: Hetzel, 1845-6), II (1846), 95 and 97.
Wood engravings by J. Quartley (p. 95) and Brugnot (p. 97).

bourg', described as an 'imitation' of the Parisian boulevards)[24] as well as Berlin's Unter den Linden.[25] In fact there is a fold-out panorama of 1846 entitled *Boulevards de Paris*, issued by the weekly *L'Illustration*, which shows just how much 'in the air' the representation of the boulevard was in terms of a continuous strip of illustration. Although the foldout is not run past the viewer like a moving panorama, its medial significance is very similar in that it makes the eye run along an uninterrupted sequence of images and thereby suggests movement along an urban axis, depicting both sides of the street in seemingly simultaneous vision. For example, the junction of the Rue Richelieu on the southern side of the Boulevard des Italiens, also shown in Balzac's sketch, can thus be studied with the opposite, northern side in view (illustration 11, p. 70).

However, this panoramic print does not in fact synchronise the views of both sides. The southern side of the Boulevard des Italiens is here shown opposite the northern side of the Boulevard Poissonnière, which lies further east. Rather than suggesting simultaneous lateral vision, which would be at odds with the flat, non-perspectival print, the foldout represents a journey from the Madeleine to the Bastille and back, with the viewer focusing on one side of the boulevard each time. The northern side is the one facing up when the foldout is opened and will therefore be studied first. Interestingly, all the omnibus coaches depicted on the northern side are going east, towards the Bastille, suggesting the viewer's 'outward' journey. When the back cover has been reached, the panorama is turned by 180 degrees and viewed backwards, with the southern side now on top (as in illustration 11) and omnibuses running westwards, back to the Madeleine. In the bottom half of the illustration, an omnibus can be seen on its 'outward' journey to the Bastille, having just passed the junction with the Rue du Faubourg-Montmartre on the northern side.

The affinity of Balzac's sketch as an illustrated medium with the popular printed panorama is obvious. Both attempt to capture the socio-architectural totality of a quintessentially Parisian line of avenues. The foldout could in fact be seen as a continuous visual representation of what is an accentuated

---

24 Balzac (note 17), p. 89.
25 Unter den Linden was the subject of a very early moving panorama, the so-called 'Lindenrolle', a four-meter long lithographed strip rolled up in a lacquered canister which was published in 1820. According to the printseller's advertisement, the strip, showing both sides of the 'Linden', could also be viewed in a small camera obscura. See H.-W. Klünner's commentary which accompanies the modern fold-out reproduction: *Panorama der Straße Unter den Linden vom Jahre 1820* (Berlin: Nicolai, 1991), p. 7.

Illustration 11
Boulevards de Paris. Section of foldout panorama published by *L'Illustration*, [1846]. Wood engraving from many blocks.

and necessarily selective verbal-visual depiction in the sketch. The sketch, however, transcends the two-dimensionality of the panorama, as well as the limitations it imposes on the visual imagination and the experience of speed and simultaneity, in various ways. Neither an 'histoire' nor a 'physiologie' of the boulevard could be offered by the visual panorama. The sketch achieves this, first of all by operating with text *and* images, thus *interpreting* the exterior of the boulevard while depicting it. The very fact that things seen are subsumed under the category of 'physiognomy', a surface disclosing meaning, is essential. This physiognomy consists of an ensemble between buildings and populations. The further observation proceeds, the more prominent the social face of the boulevard becomes. Towards the end, a long, shabby section is passed near the Porte Saint-Denis and Porte Saint-Martin, which ultimately becomes deserted in the vicinity of factories; – clearly the territory of the popular majority, the city's and the nation's revolutionary force:

> This is the only spot in Paris where you hear the *cris de Paris* and where you see the *peuple* milling about, and those rags apt to surprise a painter, and those looks fit to frighten a man of property![26]

The picture of the *peuple* thus drawn in words, with reference to the art of painting, and interpreted at the same time, immediately appears as a graphic image inserted into the text. This visual-verbal ensemble is 'framed' at the top and at the bottom of the page by pictures representing the architectural context. It shows the neighbourhood's astounding richness in establishments of popular entertainment. No fewer than seven theatres line the northern side of the Boulevard Saint-Martin: the Théâtre de la Porte-Saint-Martin, Théâtre de l'Ambigu-Comique, Cirque-Olympique, Folies-Dramatiques, Gaîeté, Funambules and Délassements-Comiques (illustration 12, p. 72).

Clearly the centre of the page depicts the drama of popular life acted out on the street, the same performance that is staged indoors night after night. This is an aspect the fold-out panorama, while faithfully reproducing the façades of the theatres and the appearances of the people, cannot emphasise. The sketch comments on the visual paradigm of popular spectacle, not only by suggesting the affinity between social acting and popular stage acting, but also by making explicit in words the interdependence between hunger for food and hunger for entertainment:

---

26 'C'est le seul point de Paris où l'on entende les cris de Paris, où l'on voie le peuple grouillant et ces guenilles à étonner un peintre, et ces regards à effrayer un propriétaire!' Balzac (note 17), p. 102. On the 'cris de Paris' and the genre of city 'Cries', see my Chapter 4, pp. 153-61.

pellent incessamment leurs spectateurs. Cinquante marchandes en plein vent y vendent des comestibles et fournissent la nourriture au peuple qui donne deux sous à son ventre et vingt sous à ses yeux. C'est le seul point de Paris où l'on entende les cris de Paris, où l'on voie le peuple grouillant et ces guenilles à étonner un peintre, et ces regards à effrayer un propriétaire!

Feu Bobèche était là, l'une des gloires de ce coin, et comme tant de gloires, sans successeurs. Son compère s'appelait Galimafrée. Martinville a écrit pour ces deux illustres saltimbanques les parades qui faisaient tant rire l'enfant, le soldat et la bonne, dont les costumes émaillent constamment la foule sur ce célèbre boulevard, que voici dans toute sa vérité.

Illustration 12
Vignettes by Bertall (centre of page) and Bertrand (bottom of page; engraver: Brugnot), in [Honoré] de Balzac, 'Histoire et physiologie des Boulevards de Paris', in *Le Diable à Paris*, 2 vols (Paris: Hetzel, 1845-6), II (1846), 102.

There, eight theatres[27] incessantly summon their spectators. Fifty women street vendors sell their goods, providing food for the people who will pay two *sous* for their stomach, and twenty for their eyes.[28]

Material need and the need for spectacle go hand in hand. The theatrical face of the boulevard in the evening, made up of teeming crowds who gather at the entrances of the theatres, the street sellers and their cries and the cheap plaster façades of the establishments themselves, speak of social dynamism. The sketch's final glimpse of the Column on the Place de la Bastille, erected in honour of those who lost their lives in the 1830 Revolution, and, across the river, of the Jardin des Plantes and the Salpétrière, associated with scientific and medical progress, are tokens of the forces that are inscribed in the physiognomy of the boulevard and that will continue to change it. The mode of acceleration, itself inseparable from the dynamism disclosed by this surface, seems to make 'history' available in a moment.

The simultaneous viewing and reading experience afforded by the sketch impacts on the understanding of 'history' in terms of 'physiology'. Through the interplay of text and images, an uninterrupted socio-historical voyage is enacted during which, from one side street to the next, the 'reading' eye meets new challenges. The reader's physical experience of reading, viewing and reflecting parallels that of the observer as a reader of a moving social panorama. For example, while this observer remarks on the stark contrast between the elegance and affluence at the boulevard's western end and the provinciality of its middle section, which blends into the proletarian appearance of the east, the reader experiences contrast from one page to the next, from the 'lions' parading on the pavement near the Opera to the petite bourgeoisie around the Bazar Bonne-Nouvelle and the Théâtre du Gymnase (illustration 13, p. 74).

Viewing these contrasting appearances as one single 'physiognomy', the observer/reader deciphers not so much the boulevard's actual history, as the title of the sketch seems to suggest, but rather becomes aware of 'histoire' as an energy forcing itself into presence through the social geography of the streets. How else are we to understand the assertion that in former times the

---

27 Balzac here presumably includes the Théâtre du Gymnase, situated slightly further to the west on the Boulevard Bonne-Nouvelle.

28 'Huit théâtres y appellent incessamment leurs spectateurs. Cinquante marchandes en plein vent y vendent des comestibles et fournissent la nourriture au peuple qui donne deux sous à son ventre et vingt sous à ses yeux.' Balzac (note 17), pp. 101-2.

Illustration 13 Bertall, vignettes in [Honoré] de Balzac, 'Histoire et physiologie des Boulevards de Paris', in *Le Diable à Paris*, 2 vols (Paris: Hetzel, 1845-6), II (1846), 98-9. Wood engravings by Verdeil, Tamisier and J. C[aqué].

boulevard finished at the corner of the rue de la Paix because this was where 'the whole of Paris' used to turn right to go to the Tuileries?[29] The boulevard certainly did not finish there, but the fact that it was not filled with public life beyond this point makes it *de facto* non-existent in terms of the 'historiography' of this sketch. What is meant by 'physiologie des boulevards' is the reading of their 'physiognomy' in such a way that 'history' becomes a life science, an understanding of socio-historical development happening before the eyes of the observer and, indeed, including the very act of mobile observation and simultaneous understanding. 'Physiologie' is thus an epistemological category, denoting the visual-cognitive process as well as the genre of the sketch itself. It is difficult to think of a closer correlation between subject matter and form.

Further, but significantly different evidence of how the observer's mobility relates to panoramic viewing is provided by German sketches. They are of particular interest in the political context referred to before, in other words, that of a country lacking a capital. Sketches of individual German cities were often written by liberal journalists in search of an 'ideal' *Hauptstadt* and therefore strike one in the first instance as travel writing. City portraitists of this kind would typically be North or West Germans inspired by the French revolution of 1830 and by the vague prospect of progress towards a national constitutional state at home. In the absence of significant political moves in this direction, attention was focused on signs of social development that would push forward the political agenda. 1830s sketches of German cities are therefore in fact exercises not so much in travel writing as in domestic sociopolitical observation, supporting the 'quest for the German citizen'.[30]

The cosmopolitan point of observation: Eduard Beurmann's panorama of Frankfurt and August Lewald's panorama of Munich

In 1835 the journalist Eduard Beurmann collaborated on the Frankfurt *Phönix* where some of his sketches first appeared. His *Frankfurter Bilder* (Pictures of Frankfurt) were published in book form in the same year. Applying a mode of rapid *al fresco* drawing, the author assembles around fifty short chapters into

---

29 'Autrefois le Boulevard finissait réellement là. Tout Paris débouchait par la rue de la Paix pour aller aux Tuileries.' Balzac (note 17), p. 95.
30 See my article 'The Quest for the German Citizen: Physiognomies of "Bürgerlichkeit" in Sketches of the Vormärz', in *Politics in Literature. Studies on a Germanic Preoccupation from Kleist to Améry*, ed. by Rüdiger Görner (Munich: iudicium, 2004), pp. 52-82, in which the regional dimensions of this sociological enterprise are explored.

a sequence (literally a 'row') of 'pictures' which is opened and closed – and thereby implicitly formed into a circular panorama – by his reflections on speed and change.[31] The fast transport provided by the new long-distance express coach service that has brought the observer from Lübeck to Frankfurt, a journey wittily described in the first chapter, 'Der Eilwagen', draws Germany's politically backward North closer to the more developed, liberal South-West. The shrinkage of time and space symbolised by the 'Eilwagen' fuels the expectation of political change as well as throwing into sharp relief the contrast between Frankfurt's political culture that seems to have moved with the times heralded by July 1830, and the time-resistant world of the German provinces such as the staid middle-class Protestantism of Northern merchant towns. The acceleration of transport becomes a metaphor for the rapid movement of the times, of the very 'Zeitgeist' itself that is bound to overthrow anything that is static:

> What brought me from the North to the South was little short of an act of magic. Today I was in old *Lübeck*, the ponderous old head of the Hanseatic League of yore, and five days later in the land where you drink your 'Schoppen' of wine, not far from the Rhine, in the ancient city of Frankfurt where the German Emperors were once elected [...]. What a sudden change when I got off the express coach in the Rahmhof at Frankfurt; the time that I had spent sleeping and dreaming in it lay, like one long night, between Lübeck and Frankfurt. [...] It is to the express coach alone that I owe this sudden, abrupt transfer from the phlegm of the North to the serene wine-induced humour of the South.
>
> High roads, express coaches, railways, steam carriages – our time is hurrying us on. Revolutions, Empires, Restorations, Reformations, – everything is meant to fly towards its destination in no time. Between the nineties of the previous century and the thirties of our own, the zeitgeist itself has become, I would not say a steam carriage, but at least an express coach. [...] Since the greatest events of world history [...] have, during the past few decades, been galloping over the earth *ventre à terre*, swirling mankind along in their wild chase, it would have been unjust if travellers

---

31 The first sentence of the postscript reads: 'Die Reihe meiner Bilder wäre somit geschlossen' ('The row of my pictures could thus be considered closed'). Eduard Beurmann, *Frankfurter Bilder* (Mainz: Kupferberg, 1835), p. 391.

alone had been left out, abandoned to the sleepy mail coach service of former times.³²

The connection thus made between the revolutionary movement of the times and accelerated modes of transport affects the mode of social observation in the form of 'pictures' in words. Beurmann's urban sign-reading bears the stamp of the 'modern', that is to say, of sketchy, rapid journalistic writing and has to be read as politically subversive. The result is not a moving linear street panorama like Balzac's, but an outline attempting a complete social and political view of the city, of its people, institutions, eating and drinking, Jews and gentiles, political groupings, newspapers, societies, localities and transport. Thus, for example, after asserting that the traveller's first business is to absorb the 'physical' nature of the place before gradually coming to grips with its 'moral' aspects, Beurmann unfolds a moral picture of Frankfurt's former Jewish ghetto, the *Judengasse*.³³ This reflects on the city's double face as a traditionally stratified merchant town, the social boundaries of which are becoming more permeable, as well as on its potential to champion the cause of Jewish emancipation purely on economic grounds. On the one hand, Jews were, until very recently, discriminated against in an almost medieval fashion by the city's ruling bourgeoisie and its senate; on the other hand, it is precisely in this climate that the Frankfurt Jewry was able to produce the Rothschilds and their world empire which, as Beurmann indicates with pre-

---

32 'Es war gewissermaßen ein Zauberschlag, der mich vom Norden nach dem Süden versetzte. Heute war ich in dem alten *Lübeck*, dem schwerfälligen alten Haupte der seligen Hansa, und über fünf Tage im Schoppenlande, unweit des Rheins, in der alten Kaiserwahlstadt *Frankfurt* [...]. Welche plötzliche Veränderung, als ich im Rahmhofe zu Frankfurt aus dem Eilwagen stieg; die Zeit, die ich in ihm verschlafen und verträumt, lag, wie eine lange Nacht, zwischen Lübeck und Frankfurt. [...] Diese plötzliche, jähe Übersiedelung aus dem Phlegma des Nordens in den heiteren Weinhumor des Südens verdankte ich lediglich dem Eilwagen. / Chausseen, Eilwagen, Eisenbahnen, Dampfwagen – unsere Zeit treibt zur Eile. Alles soll im Fluge zum Ziele eilen: Revolutionen, Kaiserreiche, Restaurationen, Reformationen. Seit den neunziger Jahren des vorigen Jahrhunderts bis zu den dreißiger Jahren des unsrigen ist der Zeitgeist selbst – ich will nicht sagen ein Dampfwagen – aber doch wenigstens ein Eilwagen geworden. [...] Da die größten Weltbegebenheiten [...] in den letzten Decennien *ventre à terre* über die Erde galopirt sind, und die Menschheit in ihrer wilden Galopade mit sich fortgerissen haben, so würde es unbillig gewesen seyn, die Reisenden allein dem schläfrigen Postzuge früherer Zeit zu überlassen.' Beurmann (note 31), pp. 3-5.
33 The chapter entitled 'Frankfurt im Innern' (Frankfurt seen from inside) culminates in the portrayal of the *Judengasse* (ibid., pp. 25-7).

Marxian optimism, is bound to break down medieval and provincial slavery of any kind. Having recourse to the current image of the journalistic observer straddling two historico-geographical worlds, Beurmann says that the *Judengasse* makes you 'stand in the middle ages with one foot, and in the most modern times with the other'.[34] The depiction of the house still inhabited by the mother of the Rothschild dynasty, amidst the old ghetto's squalor, brings home the dynamic tension of the zeitgeist. The puns in this passage also emphasise in gendered terms the tension between world-conquering finance (represented by Jehovah, Rothschild the elder, the worldly rulers and the Rothschild sons) and the sedentary piety of the mother:

> In the Judengasse at Frankfurt-am-Main there stands a modest house. It is the home of the old, time-weary, pious mother of the Rothschilds. She wants to close her eyes on the same spot that was once blessed by the Jehovah of her people, and where He showed His grace to her lord and husband before the lords of this world showed their grace to her sons. Before this could happen, however, these sons were obliged to serve as a golden shield[35] to some of these lords, in recognition of which they were raised to the level of 'your grace'. They all went out into the world and took the burden of all the world on their shoulders, acquiring many a medal *pour le mérite*. But the mother of the Rothschilds wants to die in the Judengasse.[36]

The blend of provinciality and cosmopolitanism, fostered by financial power, a sense of civic pride and a pro-Western outlook (still, one could remark, a characteristic of Frankfurt today), makes this city the locus of Beurmann's preferred prototype of the German citizen.[37] Unlike the real show panorama that is viewed from an elevated platform and simulates a bird's eye view, these 'Frankfurt pictures' present their objects from the distinctly involved

---

34 'Mit einem Fuße stehst du im Mittelalter, mit dem andern in der neuesten Zeit'; Beurmann (note 31), p. 26.
35 A pun on 'Rothschild' which literally means 'red shield'.
36 'In der Judengasse zu Frankfurt a. M. steht ein einfaches Haus. Hier wohnt die alte betagte fromme Mutter der R o t h s c h i l d . Sie will dort an der Stelle ihre Augen schließen, wo der Jehovah ihres Volks ihr Haus gesegnet, und wo die Gnade des Höchsten ihrem Eheherrn früher gnädig war, als die Gnade der Herren der Welt ihren Söhnen, die zuvor Manchem jener ein goldener Schild werden mußten. Man hat sie dafür zu gnädigen Herren gemacht, und sie sind alle in die Welt gegangen und haben alle Welt auf ihre Schultern geladen und sich manchen Orden *pour le mérite* erworben. Aber die Mutter der Rothschild will in der Judengasse sterben.' Beurmann (note 31), p. 27.
37 See his chapter 'Die Stände' (The Social Classes), ibid., pp. 90-113.

perspective of the traveller who approaches the city full of political hope and impatience. This is why Karl Gutzkow referred to them in a review as 'capriciously sketched rather than painted in the Dutch manner' and in this way opening up a perspective onto 'more noble, higher regions'.[38] This involved perspective is less noticeable in Beurmann's other panoramic depictions, for example, a later four-volume work, *Deutschland und die Deutschen* (1838-40), in which he attempts a representation of Germany and the Germans in terms of a circular painting. This (incomplete) national panorama was inspired by Bulwer's *England and the English* and partly based on Beurmann's own extensive sketches of northern merchant towns (Lübeck, Bremen and Hamburg) which had been published as *Skizzen aus den Hanse-Städten* (Sketches from the Hanseatic Cities) in 1836. Interestingly, his introductions to both works emphasise the observer's physical and/or intellectual distance from the objects observed as a precondition of the panorama's truth. This distance is once more inseparable from the observer's own mobility as a journalist with a critical eye for the regional limitations of German society, culture and politics.

Beurmann shares this view with another urban panorama sketcher, August Lewald, founder and editor of the important illustrated weekly *Europa*, whose *Panorama von München* (Panorama of Munich, 1835) brought out the semi-rural backwardness of this South German metropolis of art. The distance between the viewer and his object is visually imagined as the 'Standpunct' ('standpoint') or platform from which a panoramic overview is obtained. Lewald states in his eponymously titled first chapter:

> In order to conceive a panorama, you have to climb a considerable height from where things will present themselves to the eye in a wide circular view and in a picturesque, interesting manner. As regards Munich, connoisseurs suggest the spire of St. Peter's church for this purpose. From there you will see the houses, towers, and streets, the gardens, meadows, river banks of the Isar, the river, the hills and the distant mountains; it is a delightful view. People, too, can be seen, but they are small and unrecognisable; the picture remains mute, and whatever the changing light of the morning or evening may illuminate in it, it will basically remain unchanged. To record a panorama of this kind is the task of the painter in colour. The painter in words must choose a different kind of height than St.

---

38 '[...] aus allen diesen mehr capriciös skizzirten, als niederländisch ausgeführten Bildern zieht sich eine eigne Straße, welche [...] die Fernsicht eröffnet in edlere, höhere Regionen [...].' [Karl Gutzkow], 'Frankfurter Bilder', *Phönix*, 108 (7 May 1835), 431.

Peter's spire as his destination, from where to sketch his living, speaking circular painting. He will scarcely find the right point in Munich itself.[39]

The elevated viewing point from which to produce a 'living' and 'speaking' panorama, the very purpose of sketching in words, is thus pitted against the viewing point of a visual panorama which, even if it were to be enlivened by dioramic light effects, must remain silent and lacking in real life. Curiously enough, the platform for the socio-cultural, verbal panorama must be spatially removed from the actual place it depicts in order to achieve a true-to-life picture. Furthermore, the 'right perspective' ('recht[e] Gesichtspunct') from which Munich's many architectural and artistic attractions, results of the culturally ambitious and politically increasingly reactionary policy of Ludwig I, have to be viewed, will not be found in travel guides or regional authors' works. 'So-called "patriotic writers"' who observe things solely from the angle of their own domestic affairs, Lewald dryly remarks, will not normally produce 'works in the manner of Bulwer's "England and the English"'.[40] The destination he himself chooses as a suitable viewing point is a classic of travel literature as well as of contemporary dioramic media. His Munich panorama unfolds from the perspective of a romantically lonesome castle in the Alps with a commanding view of the River Adige: 'As I drink the clear mountain air, my view wanders beyond my surroundings, and the far distance opens itself up to it; I see Munich.'[41] *Panorama von München* thus invokes the visual paradigms of the panorama and the diorama only to state its own superi-

---

39 'Um ein Panorama zu entwerfen muß man eine bedeutende Höhe besteigen, wo sich die Gegenstände im weiten Rundblicke, malerisch und interessant dem Auge darstellen. Für München wird von Kennern der St. Petersthurm vorgeschlagen. Von dort sieht man die Häuser, Thürme, Straßen, die Gärten, Auen, die Isarufer, den Fluß, die Höhen und die fernen Berge; es ist ein reizender Anblick. Auch Menschen sieht man, aber sie sind klein und unkenntlich; das Bild bleibt stumm, und was auch der Morgen oder Abend darin wechselnd beleuchten mag, im Wesentlichen immer unverändert. Solch ein Panorama aufzunehmen ist Vorwurf des Farbenmalers. Der Maler mit Worten muß eine andere Höhe, als die des Petersthurmes sich zum Ziele wählen, von wo er sein lebendes, sprechendes Rundbild entwerfen will. In München selbst wird schwerlich der rechte Punct für ihn zu finden seyn.' August Lewald, *Panorama von München*, 2 vols (Stuttgart: Hallberger, 1835), I, 8-9.
40 'Gewöhnlich empfangen wir von sogenannten "vaterländischen Schriftstellern," die über ihre eigenen Angelegenheiten schreiben, keine Werke in der Art von Bulwer's "England und die Engländer."' Ibid., p. 6.
41 'Ich trinke die reine Luft der Höhe und über meine Umgebung hinweg schweift mein Blick; die Ferne öffnet sich ihm: ich sehe München.' Ibid., p. 13.

ority as a socio-cultural drawing based on, and appealing to, sharply outlining visual imagination ('Phantasie') which is in turn inseparable from the travelling observer's memory and reflection.[42] Beurmann, for his part, writes his panorama of the three northern Hanseatic cities from the loneliness of a little back room in Frankfurt's *Hochstraße*, referring to his memory ('Erinnerung') as the actual 'Standpunkt' from which the pictures are drawn.[43] In his case, it is the liberal, 'southern' viewpoint of the Frankfurt journal *Phönix* (hopefully subtitled *Frühlings-Zeitung für Deutschland*, 'Springtime Journal for Germany') that provides the critical platform from which northern civic life is viewed.

It seems that in the German context, panoramic imagination operates more effectively if the objects observed are not only out of sight, but absent, to be 'recalled' before the mind's eye and delineated in critically penetrating writing. This is not because the images of the cities are too overwhelming to be recorded from a closer distance, but because the writer needs to reassure himself of an extraneous, unparochial standpoint from which the living, 'speaking', socially analytical panorama (as opposed to a mimetic portrait) can be obtained. To characterise this surface-piercing view, nothing seems more suitable than microscopic imagery. Lewald's recourse to the metaphor of the magnifying glass makes possible social critique as an act of humorous visual imagination. In his chapter on Munich beer we find a passage on the heavy physiognomy of the drinker, the epitome of local narrow-mindedness in its contrast to the lean, wrinkled appearance of the mobile, 'foreign', northern German observer himself, and physio-sociological proof of the city's half-charming, half-exasperating immobility:

> His dark purple cheeks show an immensely delicate coral tissue. If you can gain permission to do so, viewing this section through a good magnifying lens will give you great pleasure. You marvel at the wonders of nature. – What is a forest of mould, what are water serpents and vinegar dragons, what is the world living in cheese [...], compared to my discoveries, with the help of a superior English magnifying glass, on the face of a 24-*Maaßer*? I beg the reader's permission to use this expression for a man

---

42 '[...] suchte ich meine Phantasie auf München zurückzulenken, und wunderlich klar gestaltete sich Alles vor meinen Blicken' ('I sought to redirect my imagination to Munich, and everything took shape miraculously clearly before my eyes'); ibid., p. 9.
43 See Eduard Beurmann, *Skizzen aus den Hanse-Städten* (Hanau: König, 1836), p. 7.

who absorbs 24 *Maaß* of beer a day; it is just as right and proper as '24-pounder' etc.[44]

The expression is particularly 'proper' because the 'measures' of beer (this is what 'Maaß', now spelled 'Maß', actually means) downed by the male population per day serve as a quantitative indicator of the missing political potential in regional German societies. (Frankfurt's wine-drinking bears the opposite connotation.) The reference to the English magnifying glass, on the other hand, constitutes a doubly compounded image. One has to bear in mind England's leading role in precision technology, especially with regard to navigational instruments, and its prominence in the early entertainment industry; two factors which were in fact brought together by sketch-writing.

Microscopic viewing

From the early nineteenth century, English sketches had alluded to clockmaking and optical technology, or more precisely, the entertainment media based on them, to advertise the acuteness of their own social portraits. For example, an encyclopaedic depiction of the British capital in individual sketches by William Combe (text) and Thomas Rowlandson (architectural plates) appeared from 1808-10 as *The Microcosm of London*, a reference to the eighteenth-century 'Microcosm' which was an automaton presenting moving figures and pictures while playing music, much in the manner of an allegorical clock.[45] Pierce Egan introduced his and the Cruikshanks' *Life in*

---

44 'Auf den dunkelvioletten Wangen zeigt sich ein überaus zartes Korallengeflechte. Wenn man die Erlaubniß dazu erhalten kann, so gewährt es einen großen Genuß, diese Partie durch eine gute Lupe anzusehen. Man erstaunt über die Wunder der Natur. – Was ist der Schimmelwald, was sind Wasserschlangen und Essigdrachen, was ist die Welt im Käse [...], gegen meine Entdeckungen mit Hülfe einer vortrefflichen englischen Lupe auf dem Gesichte eines vier und zwanzig Maaßers? Man erlaube mir diesen Ausdruck für einen Menschen, der täglich 24 Maaß Bier zu sich nimmt; er ist eben so richtig und bezeichnend, wie 24 Pfünder u. dergl.'. Lewald (note 39), I, 51.

45 See Altick (note 4), who makes a direct link between British seafaring technology and the development of public entertainment (p. 60): 'Christopher Pinchbeck [...] belonged equally to showbusiness and the clockmaking trade. As a clockmaker he participated in that remarkable surge of creativeness [...] which resulted in English astronomical clocks, chronometers, and other marine instruments being recognized as the best in the world and gave English seamen the accurate navigational tools they needed. Pinchbeck himself, however, was less interested in making such in-

London (1820-21) as 'A Camera Obscura View of the Metropolis', guaranteeing the clearest possible vision without the observer being seen. The title of Lady Blessington's sketches of metropolitan society published in 1822, *The Magic Lantern*, related to the projection apparatus whose mechanisms and scientific use formed a staple part in the education of 'enquiring minds'.[46] August Lewald's reference to the English magnifying glass, coupled with allusions to microscopic viewing and denoting the sharpness of his own satire, thus resounds with connotations of a sociological and generic kind. Moreover, it is very topical in evoking the visual trauma of the 1830s, in other words, the sight of animalcules swarming in a drop of ordinary drinking water. This is again associated with London, where in the 1830s institutions such as the Adelaide Gallery attracted crowds to projections of microscope images blown up to a very large scale without losing their precision. Projectors of this kind came into use after the invention of limelight, created by oxyhydrogen gas, and the first 'oxyhydrogen microscope' was displayed at Stanley's Rooms in Old Bond Street in 1833.[47] In 1830-31 Prince Pückler-Muskau had published his notorious travelogue based on letters written from England and Ireland, complete with a passage describing his horror at the 'disgusting water animalculæ [...] which we daily swallow', seen through a precursor of the oxyhydrogen instrument, an 'achromatic microscope', at 24 Regent Street.[48] In the image of microscopic worlds revealed under the skin of a Munich beer-drinker with the help of a powerful English lens, Lewald thus also indirectly refers to the model of Pückler, the unorthodox, aristocratic dandy traveller, and to himself as the mobile, cosmopolitan German observer-cum-journalist.

By making the observer's own mobility part of the mode of observation, sketches indicate their superiority to the viewing media that had dynamised static surfaces, or disclosed life beneath surfaces, in the first place. The dynamic present with which sketches thus engage as a meta-medium extends to their epistemological foundations. The history of living mores that they record involves the act of seeing, writing and reading, and also of their own production and reproduction, as the previous chapter has shown. With regard to their cognitive orientation, exemplified by Balzac's 'Histoire et

---

    struments than in producing barrel organs for country churches and musical automatons such as singing birds.'
46 David Robinson, *The Lantern Image. Iconography of the Magic Lantern 1420-1880* (London, Nutley: The Magic Lantern Society, 1993), p. 9.
47 See Altick (note 4), p. 370.
48 See ibid., pp. 369-70. The passage is found in Pückler's letter of 2 August, 1827.

physiologie des Boulevards', they practise social 'life science'. At the same time, of course, and true to their medial function, they entertain their readers while enlightening them. One central aspect of their balance between amusement and analysis is their focus on 'type'.

3
Physiology, Zoology and the Constitution of Social Types

What made the sketch industry flourish on a European scale was the transnationality of developments in publishing and of the social type reproducible as printed type. Sketches were able to draw on various aspects of an iconographic tradition of printed types, for example, the 'city Cries' which will be dealt with in my next chapter, and it is important to bear the existence of such a tradition in mind for a discussion of the *physiological type* developed by sketches. The precision of their observation, much though it may have in common with photographic accuracy, derives from an artistic view of 'type' which is a cartoon-like abstraction. 'Draughtsmanship' therefore plays a particular 'informative role' in sketches, a role which is eventually 'undercut', according to Judith Wechsler, by the introduction of photogravure in the 1870s.[1] The cognitive function of the sketch is that of developing 'typical' physiognomies, interpreted in the light of physiology and through an interplay with written portraits. This function lives off the impetus to capture 'the impress of the present age' (Douglas Jerrold) in graphic images so that, according to Jules Janin's introduction to *Les Français*, posterity will possess a complete visual record of contemporary mores.[2] Another driving force is the need to expose the age's invisible face, 'its virtues, its follies, its moral contradictions, and its crying wrongs', to quote Jerrold once more.[3]

Can this dual aim to capture and to expose be achieved in the way that Kenny Meadows suggests in his humorous self-portrait? It shows the artist as a phrenologist, measuring with his fingers the skull of his bawling infant sit-

---

1 Judith Wechsler, *A Human Comedy. Physiognomy and Caricature in Nineteenth-Century Paris* (London: Thames & Hudson, 1982), p. 14.
2 See Douglas Jerrold, 'Preface', in *Heads of the People*, 2 vols (London: Tyas, 1840-1), I (1840), iii-vi (p. iii), and Jules Janin, 'Introduction', in *Les Français peints par eux-mêmes*, 8 vols (Paris: Curmer, 1840-2), I (1840), iii-xvi (p. xvi).
3 Jerrold (note 2), p. iii.

ter. Phrenology, a kind of sub-discipline of physiognomy, attempted to divine particular faculties from the shape of cranial bones.

Illustration 14 Kenny Meadows, frontispiece in *Heads of the People: or, Portraits of the English. Drawn by Kenny Meadows. With Original Essays by Distinguished Writers*, 2 vols (London: Tyas, 1840-1), I (1840). Wood engraving by Orrin Smith.

The artist-phrenologist is certainly popular; the child's parents are watching the progress of his drawing with excitement as the width of their child's forehead seems a particularly telling sign of character. A whole crowd is waiting to be portrayed in the same way. The illustration itself actually depicts much more than the phrenologically precise 'heads' produced by the fashionable artist. Although focusing on physiognomic expression in a number of faces, suggesting a wide spectrum of characters and moods, it shows full-length figures, and not in isolation, but as a social body. The individuals discernible apart from the parents include a burly man in a cocked hat, ladies in bonnets, a man peering forth under his top hat, a blackened little figure and a man in profile with aquiline features. These are in fact all portraits appearing in *Heads of the People*: 'The Spoilt Child', 'The Beadle of the Parish', 'The Landlady' (of a tavern), 'The Farmer's Daughter', 'The Sentimental Singer' (another 'Tavern Head'), 'The Chimney-Sweep' and 'The Fashionable Physician'. The individual portraits in Meadows's collective sketch are thus abstractions representing professions or types. Jerrold calls them 'Popular Portraits', their 'aim [...] being to concentrate in individual peculiarity the characteristics of a class'.[4] The composite picture of types assembled behind the portraitist's back is comparable to the whole of the collected serial, while the artist-phrenologist plays the role of the individual contributor to the collection. He is aware of, but cannot see the whole of which he draws component parts. Although Meadows, the self-reflective draughtsman, does depict this whole and enables the viewer to see the artist as part of it, even he cannot make visible the connections between the parts of the social body. The arched doorway framing the picture points to the common purpose of the crowd, including the artist, in other words, to portray and to be portrayed, but it is impossible to see what motivates 'the' popular sketcher to engage in breathless serial production, drawing type after type, nor what motivates 'the' landlady of a tavern and 'the' beadle of a parish to have their heads sketched. The unseen bond pulling the types together can only be imagined. On the part of the artist, it may be financial need, as he does not seem to possess an easel, but uses the back of his chair instead. On the part of the people it may be fashion, dictating that one must have one's portrait sketched by an artist with phrenological expertise. It may also be a deeply felt need to have one's physiognomy captured quickly, accurately and relatively inexpensively, 'daguerreotyped', so to speak, before life moves on. The wish of the proud parents for a precise record of their insufferable child's head seems to imply this. The artist may likewise be driven by the desire to serve his age and posterity as a quasi-scientific, precise (one needs to note his glasses) sketcher of common people of whom otherwise no records would survive. Seen from this angle, the characters in the picture are united by a 'typical' attitude produced by conditions that cannot be depicted.

---

4   Douglas Jerrold, 'Preface', in *Heads of the People* (note 2), II (1841), iii-iv (p. iii).

What Meadows is following here, placing typical physiognomies and the fashionable concern with phrenology into an unseen social context, is the cognitive model of physiology. Transferred from the human to the social body, it allows the intimation, and also the exposure, of invisible connections in a functional totality of social interaction,[5] and it applies to all collective serials like *Heads of the People*. The unseen world of social conditions connects the assembled 'popular portraits', and these portraits are in turn determined by the notion of a social whole shaping types. Although physiognomy, the cognitive model associated with the notion of 'character', remains crucial to sketches in their focus on surface appearances and their meaning (as was seen in Balzac's portrait of the Boulevards), the distinctly sociological viewpoint of sketches, reading 'character' as professional or avocational 'type', relates them more strongly to the model of physiology, which provides a meta-physiognomic paradigm. *'Physiologies'*, as Judith Wechsler remarks, 'are descriptions of *mœurs* rather than of bodily features'; the roles they study are 'described primarily by social behaviour and interactions rather than by visual characteristics of the individual'.[6] It therefore makes sense to subsume all sociological sketches under the broad heading of 'physiology', even if their generic titles do not explicitly refer to medical or biological models.

Social types such as the 'young upwardly mobile couple', the 'ageing hippie' or the 'anorak' belong to our quotidian knowledge just as much as they are, in less flippant terminology, indispensable to sociological enquiry. The humorous typological grouping of whole sections of the population was the chief occupation of sketch-writers and draughtsmen during the infancy of sociology. Ruth Amossy has discussed the French sketch industry and its serial production of 'types' in relation to 'stereotyping'. She refers to Larousse's *Grand Dictionnaire Universel du XIXe siècle*, according to which a 'type' signifies an object uniting within itself the main characteristics of all objects of the same kind and hence contributes to our knowledge. By contrast, a 'stereotype' – the term was not introduced into social science until the 1920s – obstructs knowledge. It represents a prefabricated generalisation, an abstraction which is not based on first-hand observation and which is, above all, selective and fixed. It focuses on certain collectively recognised characteristics and ignores any evidence not fitting the picture. Any relativity or flexibility in the categories used for stereotyping would, in Amossy's argument, mark the end of the stereotype. Although she concedes that the distinc-

---

5 Karlheinz Stierle has called the totality suggested by physiological sketches a 'Funktionszusammenhang': *Der Mythos von Paris. Zeichen und Bewußtsein der Stadt* (Munich, Vienna: Hanser, 1993), p. 181.
6 Wechsler (note 1), p. 16 and p. 34.

tion between type and stereotype is 'problematic', she sees Balzac's famous 'types', but above all the Parisian *Physiologies*, as a massive exercise in stereotyping.[7] Her verdict is not, however, based on detailed analysis. For example, the crucial relationship between text and image is ignored, and so is the textual structure of these sketches which often take a received or common view as their point of departure, only to replace it by an analytical, 'scientific' view of the type. True, scientific discourse may be a prime vehicle to reinforce stereotypes with the aim of keeping control, particularly of women, as my interpretation will show. However, the experience of social development which de-individualises characters and produces types is an authentic one. Its reflection and discursive treatment in sketches cannot therefore altogether be dismissed as trading in second-hand images and *déjà-vus*. The precision, authenticity and reliability of the observation can be measured by the degree of a sketch-writer's awareness that the criteria constituting a type are themselves subject to social factors and to change. In graphic sketches, the line between type and stereotype seems to separate what Jerrold calls the 'popular portrait' from generalising caricature.

By evolving types, sketches make their own characteristic contribution to sociology. They have, of course, to be set in the context of contemporary sociological theory (and, related to this, also of biological science) so that the originality of their analysis becomes evident. In the following, an attempt is therefore made to consider the theoretical and scientific background of sketches within their national cultures; a background to which they often refer themselves.

Two founding figures of sociology, Fourier and Saint-Simon, formulated the idea of a science concerned with the earthly well-being of humankind in opposition to the 'imprecise' disciplines of theology, philosophy and political theory. Fourier claimed that in basing this new science on natural laws, above all on the classification of human passions and their mutual attraction, he had made a discovery like Columbus's. Mathematics, music, physics and botany are his paradigms when he conceives the society of the future as an order of analogies, balances and harmonies.[8] Saint-Simon, on the other hand, based social science on a science of animate life, that is to say, on physiology. In

---

7 See Ruth Amossy, *Les idées reçues. Sémiologie du stéréotype* (Paris: Nathan, 1991), particularly pp. 49-64.
8 It has been pointed out that Fourier nevertheless dynamises 'balanced and static' concepts of the Enlightenment according to a set of 'increasingly complex and sophisticated [...] social situations': I.D. Lloyd Jones, 'Charles Fourier: the Faithful Pupil of the Enlightenment', in *Philosophers of the Enlightenment*, ed. by P. Gilmour (Edinburgh: Edinburgh University Press, 1989), pp. 151-78 (p. 155).

'Mémoire sur la science de l'homme' (Paper on the Science of Man, 1813) he declared this to be the only positive human science to date, and thus the model for all branches of knowledge concerning humanity.[9] In 'De la Physiologie appliquée à l'amélioration des institutions sociales' (On Physiology as Applied to the Improvement of Social Institutions, 1812) he gave full expression to the concept of society based on the physiological model:

> [...] physiology [...] looks at individuals from a higher plane, as no more than organs of the social body, the organic functions of which it must study [...].
>
> For society is by no means a simple conglomeration of living beings whose actions, independent of any final goal, are caused by nothing but the arbitrariness of individual will, and produce nothing but unimportant, incidental results. On the contrary, society is primarily an organised machine whose every part contributes to the functioning of the whole in a different way.
>
> Collectively, human beings constitute a genuine *being* with a more or less vigorous or faltering existence, depending on the regularity with which its organs carry out the functions assigned to them.[10]

Today's reader, mindful of vitalist ideologies claiming a union between individuals and the popular body, may feel uneasy about this concept of society as an organic whole. In the first part of the nineteenth century, however, these notions were not irrational. Nathalie Preiss's chapter 'La Physiologie scientifique appliquée à l'étude de la société: naissance d'une nouvelle science sociale' (Scientific Physiology Applied to the Study of Society: the Birth of a

---

9 See Pierre Ansart, *Saint-Simon* (Paris: Presses Universitaires de France, 1969), pp. 75-6.

10 '[...] la physiologie [...] plane au-dessus des individus qui ne sont plus pour elle que des organes du corps social dont elle doit étudier les fonctions organiques [...]. / Car la société n'est point une simple agglomération d'êtres vivants, dont les actions indépendantes de tout but final n'ont d'autre cause que l'arbitraire des volontés individuelles, ni d'autre résultat que des accidents éphémères ou sans importance; la société, au contraire, est surtout une véritable machine organisée, dont toutes les parties contribuent d'une manière différente à la marche de l'ensemble. / La réunion des hommes constitue un véritable ÊTRE, dont l'existence est plus ou moins vigoureuse ou chancelante, suivant que ses organes s'acquittent plus ou moins régulièrement des fonctions qui leur sont confiées.' Saint-Simon, 'De la physiologie appliquée à l'amélioration des institutions sociales', in *Œuvres de Saint-Simon et d'Enfantin*, 47 vols (Paris: Dentu, 1865-78), XXXIX; extract printed in Ansart (note 9), p. 79.

New Social Science) illuminates exactly in what respect biological paradigms became keys to the notion of 'society'; they made it possible to conceive interaction.[11] As Karlheinz Stierle has remarked, when transferred to the study of society, the concept of an ensemble of vital functions becomes one of functional totality to which the individual type or phenomenon, empirically observed, is linked via signifiers.[12] It is perhaps not surprising that this conceptual interlinking of abstraction and observation made Hyacinthe Azaïs, in *Physiologie du bien et du mal, de la vie et de la mort, du passé, du présent, de l'avenir* (Physiology of Good and Bad, Life and Death, the Past, Present and Future; 1836) think of physiology not merely as a social science, but as the science of sciences.[13] Saint-Simon himself had stressed the importance of physiology as a positive science which has moved away from speculation. The general theory of physiology as an empirical discipline will, he argued, emerge from a combination of the most advanced science of man, rigorously based on observation, which has hitherto been produced.[14] Three of his four model scientists were medics: Félix Vicq-d'-Azur (1748-94), a comparative anatomist; Xavier Bichat (1771-1802), whose work on body tissues revolutionised anatomy and physiology, the Marquis de Condorcet (1743-94), mathematician, philosopher, economist and politician, *Encyclopédiste*, from whom Saint-Simon derived his view of history in terms of 'organic' and 'critical' epochs; and Georges Cabanis (1757-1808), who established a link between the physical and the moral human condition and can be seen as one of the earliest social physiologists.[15]

---

11 See Nathalie Preiss, *Les Physiologies en France au XIXe siècle: étude historique, littéraire et stylistique* (Mont-de-Marsan: Éditions InterUniversitaires, 1999), pp. 238-42.

12 'Die Idee eines Ganzen des Lebenszusammenhangs [...] wird [...] zur Vorstellung eines Funktionszusammenhangs, auf den das einzelne immer schon zeichenhaft verweist.' Stierle (note 5), p. 181.

13 See Preiss (note 11), p. 238.

14 Saint-Simon, 'Mémoire sur la science de l'homme', in *Œuvres de Saint-Simon et d'Enfantin*, 47 vols (Paris: Dentu, 1865-78), XL; extract printed in Ansart (note 9), pp. 75-6.

15 Cabanis belonged to the group of liberal philosophers known as the 'idéologues' assembled around Destutt de Tracy, who developed a 'science of ideas' on the basis of human sensual faculties and the ideas about them, shaped by social interaction. Cabanis's friend and 'medical ally' ('medizinischer Mitstreiter') Jean-Louis-Marc Alibert, a dermatologist, established a direct connection between the condition of the human body and the political environment in his article of 1795, 'De l'influence des causes publiques sur les maladies et la constitution physique de l'homme'; he was also the author of a two-volume medico-moral 'Physiologie', *Physiologie des*

The school of Saint-Simon consolidated social science on the model of physiology, culminating in the foundation of sociology as a discipline by a former secretary of the master, Auguste Comte. Saint-Simonianism, embracing sociological and socialist thought (the practical use of physiology for the improvement of institutions having been Saint-Simon's concern right from the beginning), is the main intellectual context in which the French journalistic physiologies have to be seen, heralded by Brillat-Savarin's *Physiologie du goût* (Physiology of Taste, 1826) and Balzac's *Physiologie du mariage* (Physiology of Marriage, 1829).[16] Balzac in particular was steeped in contemporary social theory. For example, his collaborators on the *Feuilleton des journaux politiques*, founded in March 1830, included supporters of the (former) Saint-Simonian P.J.B. Buchez who, following Comte, had examined the 'terms of transition from individual to social physiology'.[17] Balzac shared the passionate commitment of these young men to social and historical analysis and to publishing, without feeling attracted to their theoretical 'megalomania'.[18] When, in February 1830, he announced a series of social studies from his pen in terms of a 'natural history of a completely new kind' ('cette histoire

---

passions, ou nouvelle doctrine des sentiments moraux, which appeared in 1825. See Günter Oesterle, 'Das Komischwerden der Philosophie in der Poesie. Literatur-, philosophie- und gesellschaftsgeschichtliche Konsequenzen der "voie physiologique" in Georg Büchners *Woyzeck'*, in *Georg Büchner Jahrbuch*, 3 (Frankfurt a. M.: Europäische Verlagsanstalt, 1983), 200-39 (pp. 231-2). The relationship between medical science and the genre of fashionable *Physiologies* becomes evident, for example, in the introduction of the doctor Morel de Rubempré to *Physiologie de la première nuit des noces*; see Hans-Rüdiger van Biesbrock, *Die literarische Mode der Physiologien in Frankreich (1840-1842)* (Frankfurt a. M.: Lang, 1978), p. 121. Morel de Rubempré also authored several works which adapted Lavater's physiognomics to broader typological and social study: *Le Lavater des tempéramens et des constitutions* (1829) as well as *Le Nouveau Lavater complet*, divided into a *Réunion de tous les systèmes pour étudier et juger les hommes et les jeunes gens* and a *Réunion de tous les systèmes pour juger les dames ou les demoiselles* (1838).

16 While Brillat-Savarin, in his witty anecdotal treatise on 'Taste', still poses as a truly scientific physiologist ('il se pose en véritable physiologiste scientifique'), Balzac and, in 1833, Sophie Gay in her *Physiologie du ridicule*, clearly move away from the understanding of *Physiologie* in purely scientific terms. See Preiss (note 11), pp. 214-15.

17 '[L]es "termes de passage de la physiologie individuelle à la physiologie sociale"'. The reference is an article published by Buchez in *Le Producteur*. See editors' notes in Balzac, *Œuvres diverses*, ed. by Pierre-Georges Castex (Paris: Gallimard, 1990–), II (1996), ed. by Roland Chollet and René Guise, in collaboration with Christiane Guise, p. 1529.

18 See ibid., p. 1472.

naturelle toute neuve'),[19] he certainly used current sociological terminology. What is more, in the same essay he refers to two medical scientists also claimed as models by Saint-Simon, namely Cabanis and Bichat, to support his argument for a philosophy based on facts and analysis.[20] Balzac's call for empiricism has a polemical aspect. He attacks the influence of German Idealism to which contemporary French thought has, as he sees it, succumbed. What he has in mind in particular is the eclectic system of Victor Cousin, an attempt to synthesise the thought of Hegel, Schelling and the Scottish philosopher Reid. But Cousin is only one example of a new thirst for the absolute, a craving for all-embracing systems. A kind of Northern 'methodism' has seized the intelligentsia,[21] a fierce, dogmatic pursuit of truth. Affecting the arts (in the guise of Romantic aesthetics) as well as the philosophical disciplines (ironically Saint-Simonianism itself, having constituted itself as a religion), it shuts out empirical reality and paralyses the scientific drive. What is sold as the latest philosophical innovation is in fact nothing but retrograde metaphysics. Nobody nowadays, Balzac maintains, has the courage of a Cabanis or a Bichat, those beacons of French physiological science, to base analysis solely on observation. The metaphysical bug has in fact spread particularly vehemently to Saint-Simon's physiological 'science de l'homme', and it has done so with no little help from the master's own ideas laid down in *Le Nouveau Christianisme*. What Balzac finds particularly intolerable about the new 'methodism' is the complete loss of wit and irony it has generated in social as well as sociological discourse; something he sees as profoundly un-French. His sketches are meant to present an alternative, while following, in their physiological analysis, *the* paradigm of Saint-Simon's social science. Medical physiology, as (probably) Balzac himself explains in an anonymous review of his own *Physiologie du mariage*, is 'the art of knowing the purpose of the organs, of finding it out if necessary, according to the system within which nature has constructed them',[22] and thus social physiology

---

19 Honoré de Balzac, 'Complaintes satiriques sur les mœurs du temps présent' (first published in *La Mode*, 20 February, 1830), in *Œuvres diverses*, II (note 17), 739-48 (p. 748).
20 See ibid., p. 741.
21 Ibid., p. 743.
22 'Ce mot de physiologie [...] n'est pas si terrible qu'il le paraît. Il ne signifie en médecine, que l'art de connaître la destination des organes, de la deviner au besoin, d'après le système dans lequel la nature les a construits.' [Anon.], 'Physiologie du mariage [...] Deux vol. in-8°. Paris, Levavasseur et Urbain Canel. 14 F. 12 F net', in Balzac, *Œuvres diverses*, II (note 17), 673-5 (p. 673). This review, published in the *Feuilleton des journaux politiques* on 17 March, 1830, is attributed to Balzac.

is 'the art of finding out, on the basis of external appearances', the invisible goals of human action. These need to be divined, for example, from even the slightest, hardly perceptible moves in people's marriages.[23] The relationship between appearances and invisible functions is something science can only describe as a causal and linear process. Sketches can depict the dynamic interplay between surface and depth; in fact they thrive on shifts between signifiers and the signified. Balzac's portrait of the grocer, 'L'Épicier', published in *La Silhouette* in April 1830, is a prototype of physiological sketch-writing. Focusing on one phenomenon, it unfolds a whole social spectrum at the same time, including contemporary philosophy, and illuminates its subject in the varying light of all these unseen connections. This sketch can be considered as a deliberate development on Balzac's part, as he now applies the concept of moral physiology, tested out in the two-volume *Physiologie du mariage* (published in December 1829), to the brief study of a professional type. In *La Silhouette*, 'L'Épicier' appeared in the section 'Galerie physiologique', and it was reproduced three days later in *Le Voleur*, quite possibly with Balzac's consent since he was involved in this journal, as 'Physiologie de l'épicier'. It is perhaps the first journalistic study of a profession ever to bear this generic heading. The physiological method is here developed with conceptual force and technical virtuosity, exposing the type as the focal point of unseen connections. It must be borne in mind that the 1830 version of 'L'Épicier' had no illustrations; wood engraving had not yet seen its breakthrough in periodic publications. Only nine years later, in the first instalment of *Les Français peints par eux-mêmes*, did the heavily revised sketch appear with Gavarni's 'type' (illustration 15).

Honoré de Balzac, 'L'Épicier' (*La Silhouette*)

The physiology is introduced by a comic, quasi-religious invocation of the grocer:

> Sublime being! Incomprehensible being, source of sweetness and life, light and pleasure, model of resignation![24]

---

23 'La physiologie du mariage sera donc l'art de deviner le but secret des actions des maris [...] d'après leurs apparences extérieures, [et] d'appliquer un résultat à leurs moindres démarches [...].' Review of 'Physiologie du mariage' (note 22), p. 673.

24 'Être sublime! Être incompréhensible, source de douceur et de vie, de lumière et de plaisir, modèle de résignation!' Honoré de Balzac, 'L'Épicier', in *Œuvres diverses*, II (note 17), p. 723.

Illustration 15
Gavarni, 'type' for [Honoré] de Balzac, 'L'Épicier', in *Les Français peints par eux-mêmes*. [From vol. 4:] *Encyclopédie morale du dix-neuvième siècle*, 8 vols (Paris: Curmer, 1840-2), I (1840), opposite p. 1. Wood engraving by Lavieille.

This is then contrasted with the stereotypical view of the figure commonly held in the higher circles of society. Here the word 'épicier' is used as an almost proverbial expression of contempt, covering anything from lack of taste to philistinism and plebeian presumption. It is not those using 'épicier' in *this* sense that the sketch hopes to convert to the 'faith of grocerism' or the 'religion épicéenne',[25] but those who are better disposed towards the profession and therefore willing to read the following 'analyse physiologique'. It begins with a humorous description of clothes: a reddish-brown pair of trousers, blue socks, broad shoes, a cap of false otter-skin decorated with blackened coins, and a triangular apron bib pointing towards its wearer's solar plexus. People, the text implies, should not be despised because of the way they dress. Does the grocer never think, as prejudice has it? He reads Voltaire, hangs patriotic engravings after Horace Vernet in his living room, cries when he sees a melodrama and understands Victor Hugo's *Hernani*, the play signalling the aggressive modernist turn of Romanticism.[26] How many French citizens could claim such a high level of education? On top of all these cultural achievements, the countless books which have passed through the grocer's hands, leaf by leaf, have given him the knowledge of a bibliographer.

A satirical portrait has thus been drawn which already includes more social detail than could be visually depicted. Although played off against his common image, the grocer is ironically cast as the stereotype. The examples given of his education only confirm the lack of it; everything he knows or likes is commonplace. The assertion that he understands *Hernani* is a brilliant dig at the conventionality for which Balzac criticises Hugo (as well as at the hype surrounding the play). The grocer reads Voltaire probably for the same reasons he adorns his lounge with patriotic engravings – a good French citizen has to be seen to do it. As to his bibliographical knowledge, it stems from books ending up as paper cones in his shop. This allusion to the fate of unsold publications is itself a suitably unoriginal joke, a 'plaisanterie traditionnelle', on Balzac's part.[27]

---

25 Balzac (note 24), p. 723.
26 Its premiere, two months before Balzac's sketch, had been a carefully orchestrated *éclat*.
27 See editors' note in *Œuvres diverses*, II (note 17), p. 1530. In the 'Préface' to the French edition of his *Lutezia* (May 1855), Heine, expressing his fears of a communist future without poetry, had recourse to the same joke: '[...] hélas! mon *Livre des Chants* servira à l'épicier pour en faire des cornets où il versera du café ou du tabac à priser pour les vieilles femmes de l'avenir.' Heinrich Heine, *Historisch-kritische Gesamtausgabe der Werke*, ed. by Manfred Windfuhr, 16 vols (Hamburg: Hoffmann und Campe, 1973-97) XIII,1 (1988), 163-9 (p. 167).

What follows is a physiological examination of social contexts. Could it be that the real reason why the grocer is despised lies in the simple fact that he *works*? If this is so, we may as well revert to the state of savages because all civilisation is built on '*le travail*' (emphasis in the original).[28] The latter categorical statement is what Balzac, in other physiological essays, calls an 'axiome'[29] – a first principle from which certain deductions are to be made. In this case the principle smacks very much of the Saint-Simonian doctrine of utility, assigning to the productive or 'industrial' class the first rank in society because it supports itself as well as all the other classes. The industrial class, according to Saint-Simon, 'works in order to produce, or to make accessible to the different members of society, one or several material means to satisfy their needs or their palates'.[30] This class divides into three groups: agrarian producers ('les cultivateurs'), manufacturers ('les fabricants') and merchants ('les négociants').[31] In this scheme, the grocer is a prime example of the working, industrial class. This glorification of the useful type feeding the social body produces its own negative cliché of parasitic idlers,[32] a cliché which Balzac satirises consistently. The 'analyse physiologique' to which the grocer is subjected therefore starts from an ironically twisted axiom, placing work and the supply of society with material goods at the centre of human civilisation. This premise will not be entirely disproved, but its emphasis will change as a result of further observation.

The analytical centrepiece of the physiology is a 'synoptic picture' ('tableau synoptique') exposing the ensemble of connections that make the grocer the heart of the social organism. What if a new village or quarter were put up, provided with everything necessary to civilised life, – except a grocer's shop? The community would quite simply lack its 'most powerful social link' ('le plus puissant de tous les liens sociaux'),

---

28 Balzac (note 24), p. 724.
29 See, for example, *Physiologie de l'employé* (first published with Aubert and Lavigne in 1841) and 'Monographie de la presse parisienne' (first published in Paul de Kock's collection *La Grande ville* in January and February 1843); both in Honoré de Balzac, *Œuvres complètes illustrées*, 26 vols, ed. by Jean A. Ducourneau (Paris: Les Bibliophiles de l'originale, 1964-76), xxvi (1976), 190-233 and 234-94.
30 'Un industriel est un homme qui travaille à produire ou à mettre à la portée des différents membres de la société, un ou plusieurs moyens matériels de satisfaire leurs besoins ou leurs goûts physiques [...].' Saint-Simon, 'Catéchisme des industriels', in *Œuvres de Saint-Simon et d'Enfantin*, 47 vols (Paris: Dentu, 1865-78), xxxvii; extracts printed in Ansart (note 9), p. 93.
31 Ibid.
32 See Saint-Simon, 'Du système industriel', in *Œuvres de Saint-Simon et d'Enfantin*, 47 vols (Paris: Dentu, 1865-78), xxii; extracts in Ansart (note 9), pp. 94-95.

A grocer! If you delayed planting a grocer in the middle of the main street, just as you have planted a cross in the heart of the town, the place would be deserted. [...] the grocer has to be there, stay there, day and night and at all hours.

From his shop emerges an admirable 'phenomenal triplicity', as Monsieur Victor Cousin would say, or a celestial trilogy, if we have to speak the language of the New School; and this trilogy, this triplicity, this triangle, this delta consists of the following: tea, coffee and chocolate, the triple essence of modern breakfasts, source of all pre-dinner pleasures.

From his shop flows the source of brightness, another phenomenal triplicity: lamp oil, candles and tallow lights.

From here one carries salt, pepper and paprika, another trilogy.

Sugar, liquorice and honey, another triplicity.

Since grocery, responding to a general need, represents a true unity of three angles, it would be like an exercise in splitting hairs to demonstrate that in this domain, everything is deduced in triplicate. In literary terms, the grocer is a trilogy; in religious terms, an image of the trinity; in philosophical terms, a perpetual phenomenal triplicity; in political terms, he embodies the three powers. Above all, he is unity.

Just as memory is the essence of the arts, the grocer is the uniting link of all our needs, bound up with every detail in the life of a human being.[33]

This analysis mainly satirises fashionable pseudo-religion, and it develops the social function of the grocer by comic contrast. Contemporary thought aspires

---

33 'Un épicier! Si vous tardiez à planter un épicier au milieu de la rue principale, comme vous avez planté une croix au sein de la cité, tout déserterait. [...] il faut que l'épicier soit là, reste là, jour et nuit, à toute heure. / De cette boutique procède une admirable *triplicité phénoménale*, dirait M. V. Cousin, ou une trilogie céleste, s'il faut parler le langage de la nouvelle école; et cette trilogie, cette triplicité, ce triangle, ce delta, c'est: le thé, le café, le chocolat, triple essence des déjeuners modernes, source de toutes les jouissances antédinatoires. / De là procèdent l'huile à brûler, la bougie et la chandelle, autre triplicité phénoménale, source de lumière. / De là procèdent le sel, le poivre et le piment, autre trilogie. / Le sucre, la réglisse et le miel, autre triplicité. / Ce serait chose fastidieuse que de vous démontrer que, véritable unité à trois angles, tout se déduit, en épicerie, par une triple production, en réponse à un besoin; ainsi, littérairement parlant, l'épicier est une trilogie; religieusement parlant, c'est une image de la trinité; philosophiquement, c'est une triplicité phénoménale perpétuelle; politiquement, il représente les trois pouvoirs, et devant tous, c'est l'unité. / L'épicier est le lien commun de tous nos besoins, et se rattache nécessairement à tous les détails d'une vie humaine, de même que la mémoire est l'essence de tous les arts.' Balzac (note 24), pp. 724-5.

to totality by means of triadic schemes, whether they be those of Cousin received from German Idealism or those of the Saint-Simonians which classify the social universe (three groups of the industrial class; three types of future education: artistic, learned and industrial; three types of social activity, and so on).[34] Like all intellectual vogues, the present one has its jargon. Cousin's expression, 'triplicité phénoménale', is placed at the centre of a dazzling variety of phenomena revolving around the figure of three. Balzac's central analytical category, that of material need or 'besoin', undermines this system of triple deductions. Need or social necessity is what all the fashionable 'celestial trinities' come down to. The grocer, the embodied 'delta' (one remembers his triangular bib), satisfies the demand for triadic schemes in every conceivable material respect. The frugal modern breakfast, which to Balzac is the culinary symbol of intellectual 'methodism' − not a meal, but an abstraction,[35] − duly breaks up its pure essence in triple form; but even this condensates into the materiality of stimulating liquids; tea, coffee and chocolate. Without them, the modern metaphysicians would not be able to rise to their heights. Other abstractions, such as light or sweetness, can ultimately be reduced to the matter that feeds them. This witty juxtaposition of the ideal and the material sphere makes the 'incomprehensible being' of the grocer, the 'source of sweetness and life, light and pleasure', look less mysterious. He provides the secret basis for the systems that contemporaries construct in the realm of ideas. If the triadic schemes of German Idealism can be seen as a secularised version of the Christian dogma of the Trinity, Balzac's 'épicier' represents the ultimate stage of secularisation. In a mildly blasphemic reversal of this notion, the grocer, the epitome of the material world, is presented as the meta-triangle, the delta of God's eye, 'l'alpha et l'oméga',[36] absorbing triadic principles of order (trinity, triplicity, trilogy, the three powers) from major

---

34 See E.M. Butler, *The Saint-Simonian Religion in Germany* (Cambridge: Cambridge University Press, 1926), p. 40 and p. 44.

35 In 'Nouvelle théorie du déjeuner', first published in *La Mode* on 29 May 1830, Balzac observes that the trend-setting young generation has practically abolished the 'déjeuner' and reduced the number of meals to just one big 'dîner' in the evening. He interprets this as a sign of the times. Ambition, knowledge and romantic sentiment, the three main 'classes' of the modern mind, are all equally opposed to obesity. The ideal French cuisine would now consist of pure essence, in other words, liquidised food (observing, it is to be noted, the French art of packaging substance in light forms): 'il s'agira pour [la cuisine française] de mettre le plus de substance possible sous la plus petite forme, de déguiser l'aliment, [...] de fluidifier les filets de boeuf, de concentrer le principe nutritif dans une cuillerée de soupe [...]'. *Œuvres diverses* (note 17), II, 768.

36 Balzac, 'L'Épicier' (note 24), p. 726.

branches of philosophical knowledge (theology, philosophy, literature and politics). The sublime being, the absolute to which modern theory aspires, has been effectively brought down to earth. It is the grocer. The central link of all modern needs, attached to every detail of human life and uniting within himself, unconsciously, the orders of philosophical knowledge, he turns out to be *religio* translated into purely material bonds. The 'religion épicéenne' is therefore something of a pleonasm, the *reductio ad absurdum* of the Saint-Simonian idea that the religion of the new, 'organic' age will be the sum total of its knowledge and find its leaders in the intelligentsia.[37]

Balzac's physiology has taken an about-turn and replaced the stereotype of the grocer by a sacred monument to materialism. But the 'synoptic picture' exploring his role is not yet finished. Moving on from the satire on metaphysics, a miniature portrait of society is now painted in the form of brief imaginary dialogues consisting of question and answer. The questions always express a need or a demand, while the answers invariably point to 'l'épicier' as the provider. Whether a poet needs pen and ink, a smoker is dying for a Havanna, a lover wants to surprise his beloved with an unfashionably deluxe breakfast (and finds himself short of stain remover afterwards), whether an insomniac is in need of a sleeping drug or whether a losing gambler wants gunpowder and bullets to blow his brains out, – 'l'épicier' will provide it. An amusing panorama of society is thus unfolded from the supplier's point of view. The needs and desires of all professions, age groups, ranks and classes are met by the grocer. Quite simply, all human acts and deeds depend on him (and it is important to read this passage in the original):

> Vous ne pouvez pas faire une lieue, un crime, une bonne action, un repas, une œuvre d'art, une orgie, une maîtresse, sans avoir recours à la toute-puissance de l'épicier.
> (You cannot travel a league, commit a crime, do a good deed, cook a meal, produce a work of art, hold an orgy or acquire a mistress without having recourse to the omnipotence of the grocer.)[38]

The universal application of the verb 'faire', impossible to translate as 'make' or 'do' in every instance, seems to confirm the Saint-Simonian axiom that all

---

37 For a concise and amusing overview of Saint-Simon's philosophy and of the main tenets of Saint-Simonianism see Butler (note 34), pp. 4-50; the role of the 'utopians' in the emergence of the French intellectual is lucidly discussed by Theodore Zeldin, *France 1848-1945*, 2 vols (Oxford: Clarendon Press, 1973-7), in his chapter 'The Genius in Politics', I (1973), 428-66.
38 Balzac (note 24), p. 726.

civilisation is based on work. However, 'faire', used as a kind of auxiliary, is meaningless in itself. Balzac exploits its semantic neutrality to show that doing and making are not virtues per se, but that their moral value depends on their object. What the grocer satisfies is the basic need enabling human action, irrespective of its moral ends, in other words, 'faire' without an object. By selling all sorts of commodities, he facilitates good, bad or simply necessary acts. In his shop, moral value and utility value are converted into exchange value. Civilisation is not based on work, but on money; the 'axiome' is thus implicitly, although significantly, modified. Civilisation begins and ends with the grocer who has 'sold himself to the public like a soul to Satan'.[39] This immorality is, however, neither satanic nor divine. It simply expresses the function of the type within the social body.

Balzac's analysis eventually deals with the grocer not in mock-religious or moral, but in cultural terms. Grocery provides a perfect source for the arts if memory is their essence, as was asserted earlier in this sketch. The grocer and his cultural archive, the shop, are inseparable; one defines the other, as Gavarni's sketch at the top of the 1839 version (illustration 44, p. 278) also suggests. The grocer is

civilisation in the form of a shop, society in a paper cone, necessity armed from tip to toe. He is encyclopaedia in action, life itself split up in drawers, bottles, bags and jars.[40]

At its profoundest level of analysis, the physiology suggests that understanding civilisation means understanding the grocer, and understanding the grocer means understanding civilisation. The triangular shapes of the apron bib and paper cones are a witty cipher of social totality, associated emblematically by Gavarni's 'delta' in the form of a Roman D at the beginning of the 1839 sketch. These mundane signifiers are infinitely more meaningful than the 'triplicité phénoménale' and to be studied by anyone wanting to know what things are (the grocer is an encyclopaedia) and why they are as they are (he is necessity). His function can only be described in metaphors of concentration and centrality such as the 'knot' ('nœud'), and the 'pivot'. How, then, can this 'cogwheel' ('rouage') of the social machine be so drastically misjudged and

---

39 'Il s'est vendu lui-même au public comme une âme à Satan.' Ibid.
40 'C'est la civilisation en boutique, la société en cornet, la nécessité armée de pied en cap. C'est l'encyclopédie en action, c'est la vie elle-même distribuée en tiroirs, en bouteilles, en sachets, en bocaux.' Ibid.

underestimated?[41] When will those who govern, think or create, stop despising what is useful and valuing only what is idle, decaying and useless?

Balzac's sketch is now again touching on the negative image of 'l'épicier' from which it started, but the physiognomic details pertaining to the type have acquired a completely different significance. Whilst before they simply indicated the stereotype, they now point to pivotal social function. Recognised as the embodiment of money-based civilisation, the grocer is shown in action by means of a concluding *mise en scène*, where he functions as a civil, because perfectly materialist, individual. An image of politeness, he gives directions to a stranger who asks the way, taking a few steps outside the shelter of his canopy even when it rains and keeping an eye on his protégé as he walks away, as Dedalus did on Icarus. He never refuses a glass of wine or a piece of sugar to a woman taken ill on the pavement. His courteous smile, captured by Gavarni's full-size figurine in the later version, is the most genuine in the whole of society because – irony of ironies – it is based on interest. A society ruled by self-interest must produce a false physiognomy of urbane, good and charitable manners to make interest work. In that sense the grocer's civility is eminently 'true' ('vraie').

This physiology analyses not only its main type, but also his educated image-makers who (as the 1839 version makes explicit) rule the *feuilletons* with their verbal and pictorial satire. They never miss an opportunity to poke fun at the grocer. They have to do so because of the gulf between appearances and meaning, or between the negative stereotype and the eminence of the type as a social signifier. The falseness of surfaces is something Balzac, anticipating Marx, identifies as characteristic of a society ruled by interest.[42] The grocer as the epitome of the philistine is a necessary creation of the intelligentsia. However utilitarian their theoretical absolutism may claim to be, it only reinforces the separation of the material from the ideal world or, in semiotic terms, of signifiers from the signified. A Saint-Simonian of the Latin Quarter would probably not recognise the useful if he saw it and would look down on the grocer no less than a student of Cousin. What Balzac's physiology presents as the 'true' picture of the grocer arises precisely from the identification of the type with the principle of utility, necessity and interest, but it is stripped of the idealist pretension that turns the image into a negative stereotype. A real to-

---

41 Balzac (note 24), p. 724 and p. 727.
42 See also Balzac's comments on French society under the Restoration in 'Complaintes satiriques sur les mœurs du temps présent' (note 19). Under the surface of the old monarchic order, the worst excesses of the modern age happen, driven by self-interest and money (p. 744).

tality based on material needs and interest finds its true representative in the grocer and only its false reflection in totalising theories. Physiological analysis even extends to the perspective from which the physiology is written. The analytical voice includes itself, by the first person plural, in the incorrigible class of those who despise things that are useful ('ce qui est utile') and value everything idle, decayed and useless ('ce qui est oisif, pourri, inutile'). For someone of this ilk to acknowledge the material principle on which modern civilisation is built, an act of self-denial is required which borders on masochism. The final satire wallows in descriptions of the bad taste displayed by the hero of modern civilisation. The grocer goes to his country garden in a wicker cart, keeps a glass-domed clock in his living room, representing a cupid rising from an eggshell, and surrounds his bed with curtains of yellow calico. The 'résignation' described as a trait of the grocer who meets all of society's needs, whether for good or bad ends, is also the resignation of the 'physiologist' who paints modern *mœurs* regardless of their moral nature.

The structural density of this physiology is extraordinary. For *Les Français peints par eux-mêmes* Balzac produced a considerably more relaxed version. One senses that in the 1830 sketch he is making an effort to emulate or rather outdo the theorists he satirically attacks. His physiological explanation of the social universe is no less ambitious than Cousin's project of a universal philosophical system, or that of the Saint-Simonians of universal social philosophy and reform. By 1839/40, at the onset of the great vogue of *Physiologies*, the journalistic genre had found its identity, so to speak, vis-a-vis sociological theory. As a hybrid between graphic and discursive representation, it was *the* form designed for the exploration of 'type'. By placing typical physiognomies in the context of contemporary developments, and by elucidating from the network of developments what is typical, sketches avoid the utopianism inherent in sociological thought, including Comte's, which suggests that a proper application of science will ultimately 'rule out the possibility of any irrational and subversive upheavals' like the French Revolution and produce a conflict-free state of human existence.[43] The contemporary type, analysed with the help of the physiological model, represents a pattern of cognition much more akin to the essayistic, perspicacious kind of sociology of an Alexis de Tocqueville or an Edward Lytton Bulwer.[44] They accept the long-

---

43 J.H. Abraham, *The Origins and Growth of Sociology* (Harmondsworth: Penguin, 1973), p. 92.
44 Bulwer's *England and the English*, 'inhabit[ing] a borderland between disciplines', notably sociology and history, is compared to Tocqueville's *De la démocratie en*

lasting effects of the Revolution, that 'cornerstone on which the new science of sociology was founded',[45] and attempt to detect the direction of these effects from the analysis of observed phenomena. Bulwer's sociological work, *England and the English*, is, of course, also a book of character sketches. This publication of 1833 throws into sharp relief the philosophical background against which its own sociological analysis has to be understood, in other words, the utilitarianism of the Benthamite school. The reception of French positivism was only just beginning to make itself felt in the England of the early 1830s,[46] and physiology is therefore not referred to explicitly as a model for sketch-writing until the early 1840s when 'Natural Histories' and 'Physiologies' appeared in *Punch*.[47] Bulwer, this much is certain, points to the one great lack within Benthamism, which is the development of a science of society:

> Such a philosophy [as Bentham's] will be most apt to fail in the consideration of the greater social questions – the theory of organic institutions and general forms of polity; for those [...] to be duly estimated, must be viewed as the great instruments of forming the national character; of carrying forward the members of the community towards perfection, or preserving them from degeneracy.[48]

Obviously this criticism of Bentham is informed by an understanding of society in physiological terms, namely as an organism. The English philosopher's blind spot, it is argued, stems from his definition of human action almost solely in terms of interest and result without considering the wider context. While Bentham has placed legislation on a solid scientific basis, he has failed to perceive, and indeed to give a scientific foundation to, the knowledge that links human action to 'dispositions, and habits of mind and heart'.[49] The physiological slant of this critique then becomes even clearer, as it is argued that a different kind of 'moralist' from Bentham is required to discover 'the relation of an act to a certain state of mind as its cause, and its connexion

---

Amérique by Standish Meacham. See his 'Editor's Introduction' to *England and the English* (Chicago: University of Chicago Press, 1970), pp. ix-xxv (p. ix).
45 Abraham (note 43), p. 92.
46 Meacham (note 44) points to J.S. Mill's series of articles in *The Examiner*, 'The Spirit of the Age' (Spring 1831): p. xvi.
47 These English 'Physiologies', however, were probably influenced far more by French sketches than by French social theory.
48 Edward Lytton Bulwer, *England and the English* (Paris: Baudry, 1833), p. 474.
49 Ibid., pp. 471-2.

through that common cause with large classes and groups of actions apparently very little resembling itself'.[50] French sociological thought has very probably been absorbed by the writer of these lines. This is almost certainly not Bulwer himself, but John Stuart Mill. The latter's 'considerable' assistance in the critique of Bentham, included in the appendices of *England and the English*, is acknowledged at the beginning of the work, even if Mill's name is not mentioned.[51] At any rate, Bulwer himself contributes his substantial share to a sociological understanding of England in the 1830s, and his analysis works, crucially, with the notions of visibility and character. The physiognomic paradigm is also prominent in Dickens's sketches and very obvious in *Heads of the People*. It is interesting to note how English sketches, without referring to the pattern of physiology, nevertheless 'physiologise' physiognomy in the sketching of social types. They do so, for example, by exploiting the relationship between a graphic sketch and the text, and this method surely accounts for the immediate success of *Heads of the People* in France and its adaptation in the great illustrated project of *Les Français peints par eux-mêmes*. It is equally interesting to find that British medical physiology of the time discovered its social applicability, if Alexander Walker, a former 'Lecturer on Anatomy and Physiology at Edinburgh'[52] and a populariser of medicine, can be seen as representative. His *Physiognomy Founded on Physiology* (1834) offers a fascinating parallel to *Heads of the People*, and a brief comparison between these two forms of social physiology is instructive.

Walker analyses, for example, the impact of professional environments on the body, and reads physiognomies as expressions of the social world. 'Physiognomists have erred', he writes, 'in considering the head alone as the subject of their science. That science applies to the whole body'.[53] Physiognomic surface-reading must look to the physiological whole of which the head is the most important part. This 'whole' comprises not only the body itself, but its function in society. Walker seeks to demonstrate, for example, that certain professional habits inscribe themselves in the face of the individual. In exactly the same terms the French physiologist Moreau de la Sarthe had 'extended' Lavater's physiognomics about twenty-five years before, arguing that this science had defined the 'general varieties' of mankind sufficiently and the new challenge was now 'to study the detailed varieties [...]

---

50 Ibid., p. 473.
51 See also Meacham (note 44), p. xviii, who states that Mill wrote the appendix on Bentham for Bulwer. I have not been able to substantiate this.
52 Information on the title page of *Physiognomy Founded on Physiology* (note 53).
53 Alexander Walker, *Physiognomy Founded on Physiology, and Applied to Various Countries, Professions, and Individuals* (London: Smith, Elder, 1834), p. 7.

which derive from the diversity of conditions of life among civilised peoples. Each métier, each profession, should [...] be regarded as a particular education, continued through life, which develops, exercises, strengthens certain organs, and establishes a specific relationship between the individual and his environment'.[54] While Moreau then mentions the example of a surgeon who, having to face pain and suffering every day, develops (literally) a 'stiff upper lip', Walker points, among others, to the physiognomy of the schoolteacher:

> The teacher, especially of the young and troublesome, has so perpetually the smile of approbation and the frown of displeasure alternating in his face, that both become to [a] certain extent fixed, and an arrangement of features is finally acquired, which may almost be supposed to serve both purposes at once, so as to save him all trouble of changing [...].[55]

The combination of a smiling and a frowning countenance here does not offer a key to passions and character, as in traditional physiognomic reading, but to an environment that produces such expressions and eternalises them in the face of the professional. As part of a socio-physiological concept, physiognomy defines the characteristics of a social type. Walker's argument is illustrated by a picture which can be seen as a scientific equivalent to Meadows's sketch of the 'Country Schoolmaster' in *Heads of the People* (illustrations 16a and b).

However, despite the affinity between the medical and the journalistic depiction of a type, there is a crucial difference. In the medical publication, the image serves the text. The 'type' illustrates the physiological concept of physiognomy, being subordinate to both social factors and scientific discourse. In the journalistic publication, the image is the text's point of departure; text and image illuminate each other. Meadows's drawing represents the 'physiognomy' which prompts the 'physiological' reasoning of William Howitt's sketch, which in turn colours one's reading of the graphic portrait. The text-image correlation allows for a dialectic in the definition of 'type' which scientific determinism lacks. As has been shown in the interpretation of

---

54 L.J. Moreau de la Sarthe, 'Observations sur les signes physionomiques des professions', in volume six of Lavater's *L'Art de connoître les hommes par la physionomie*, pp. 222-47; quoted and translated by Wechsler (note 1), p. 25.
55 Walker (note 53), p. 196.

Physiology, Zoology and the Constitution of Social Types 107

THE SCHOOLMASTER.

Illustration 16a 'Plate XIII. The Schoolmaster', in Alexander Walker, *Physiognomy Founded on Physiology, and Applied to Various Countries, Professions, and Individuals* (London: Smith, Elder, 1834), p. 195. Etching.

THE COUNTRY SCHOOLMASTER.

The village all declared how much he knew:
'Twas certain he could write—and cipher too.
GOLDSMITH.

Illustration 16b Kenny Meadows, 'The Country Schoolmaster', in *Heads of the People, or: Portraits of the English*, 2 vols (London: 1840-1), II (1841), opposite p. 65. Wood engraving by Orrin Smith.

'L'Épicier', journalistic physiologies can create a relationship between appearances, unseen factors and their own reasoning which is not linear or unilateral. They can also evoke an emotional response that has no place in science, particularly not where the construction of 'types' is involved, that is to say, sympathy with a whole class of contemporaries. The author of the sketch 'The Country Schoolmaster', Howitt, was a contributor to and then proprietor of *The People's Journal* in 1846 and took a keen interest in country populations and in education. Besides, he shared the cosmopolitan outlook of the period. He wrote a two-volume *Rural Life of England* (1838), and a German counterpart, *Rural and Domestic Life of Germany*, published in 1842, during a prolonged stay in Heidelberg where he and his family had moved 'to advance the education of the older children'.[56] The type depicted here is distinct from the metropolitan types preferred by social physiologists, and the sentiment inspiring his portrait could not contrast more with that of Balzac's 'L'Épicier'. This highlights the variety of moral energies feeding European sketch production. How, then, does physiological analysis work in a text-image relationship?

Kenny Meadows / William Howitt, 'The Country Schoolmaster' (*Heads of the People*)

First of all, the text offers an explanation of the teacher's appearance which is not dissimilar from physiological determinism. Facial expression reveals professional habit. The country schoolmaster shows an 'air of pedagogue pomp', but also of half scholarly, half clerical benevolence. Together with his 'penmanship' and 'an antiquely amusing [...] school costume',[57] this exterior points to humble rural surroundings. In an uneducated environment, this often self-educated man of letters is much in demand. The sketch then mentions circumstances which will not be detectable from appearances. To generations of country schoolmasters, who 'have gone on their way like little unnoticed books', villages and hamlets owe their 'little glimmering of morals and manners, and a passable shape of humanity'.[58] Moreover, it is made clear that this type will be ousted from the very society he has helped to humanise, by an act of parliament which is to introduce a government-controlled school system.

---

56 'Howitt, William' in *Oxford Dictionary of National Biography*, ed. by H.C.G. Matthew and Brian Harrison, 60 vols (Oxford: Oxford University Press, 2004), XXVIII, 530-2 (p. 531).
57 William Howitt, 'The Country Schoolmaster', in *Heads of the People* (note 2), II (1841), 69.
58 Ibid., p. 71.

'The railroad of national education is about to run through' the 'ancient patrimony' of the country schoolmaster and to make this 'picturesque, if somewhat dogmatic' type, who has, for centuries, carried out his profession as an amateur, fall by the wayside.[59]

The written sketch thus sets Meadows's drawing in a multi-layered social context, pointing to a discrepancy between social reality and the common perceptions of the type. These associate him with old-world stability on the one hand, and provincial insignificance on the other. Yet country schoolmasters, those 'little unnoticed books', have not only brought manners and morals to rural backwaters, but have actually left reflections in English literature and had a far greater impact on the world of letters than the literature itself suggests. Oliver Goldsmith, whose couplet on the schoolmaster ('The village all declared how much he knew: / 'Twas certain he could write – and cipher too') forms a kind of caption to the drawing, is a prominent, but relatively rare example of a writer recognising his debt to a country pedagogue. Meadows's sketch of an eighteenth-century physique, complete with eighteenth-century verse, thus represents 'one of the most marked characters of the country',[60] an image sadly contrasting with the profession's actual impending doom. Ironically, Goldsmith's elegy 'The Deserted Village' from which the couplet is taken, already speaks of the 'village master' as someone whose 'fame' is 'pass'd', anticipating the urbanisation of the country on a grand scale to which Howitt, seventy years later, refers as a reality. 'Steam and railroads' now require 'a steam and railroad system of education'.[61] Even if one accepts that modernisation is needed, it should not happen by decree, making a whole class of provincial teachers redundant overnight. The text explicitly calls for 'generous sympathy' to mitigate the lot of an 'old man' who will soon be replaced by modern professionals, and casts a nostalgic light over the physiognomy depicted opposite its opening page.[62] This physiognomy must be looked at from the point of view of transitoriness, which also unites the written and the graphic sketch: '[I]f we are to preserve a portrait of the Country Schoolmaster, we must sketch it now or never.'[63] Meadows's sketch, for its part, is drawn with a written and a serial context in mind and not intended as a lasting work of art in its own right. This is true of all his 'heads of the people' and must be the reason why they were thought to 'possess little power of at-

---

59 Howitt (note 57), p. 67.
60 Ibid., p. 65.
61 Ibid.
62 Ibid., p. 72.
63 Ibid., p. 68.

traction' in themselves.[64] Yet, as wood engravings appearing outside the text, they have a certain autonomy and dignity, constituting a catalogue of vernacular types to which the text offers a commentary. John Orrin Smith who was a sought-after engraver on wood, having already worked in commission for the Paris publisher Léon Curmer, helps to lend these 'popular portraits' their particular ambiguity between portraiture and typifying abstraction. We find him also among the engravers of *Les Français peints par eux-mêmes*.

Stereotype or typological portrait?

One reason for the success of *Les Anglais peints par eux-mêmes*, the translation of *Heads of the People* which prompted Curmer to launch *Les Français*, must have been the serialisation of visual-verbal 'types'. The English expertise in capturing the 'typical' was already admired by Balzac in his praise of the 'Englishman' amongst French caricaturists, Henry Monnier, whom he advertised in the prospectus for *La Caricature* as an exemplary contributor to the new journal.[65] Balzac sees in him the French Hogarth, a sketcher of society with a penetrating intelligence, able at the same time to 'copy' ('copier'), 'capture' ('saisir') and 'create' (créer') what forms the social body – 'le type'.[66] Words would take up many pages in an almost futile attempt to do the same thing. 'Based on the shrewdest observation *of classes*',[67] one graphic type by Monnier therefore bears the 'stamp' ('cachet') of the class in its entirety.[68]

This is the language of classification. Caricature provides the graphic model of the social type thus classified, while the scientific paradigm is supplied by zoology. Balzac himself makes the connection between social typology and zoology in the 'Avant-propos' of his *Comédie humaine* (1842):

> Does not society transform man, according to the kind of environment in which he acts, into as many different men as there are varieties in zoology?

---

64 Graham Everitt, *English Caricaturists and Graphic Humourists of the Nineteenth Century*, 2nd edn (London: Swan Sonnenschein, 1893), p. 356.
65 See Balzac, *Œuvres diverses* (note 17), II, 795 and 798. Equally talented as a sketcher in words and in pictures, Monnier was instrumental in founding both *La Silhouette* and *La Caricature*; see also pp. 39-42 of this study.
66 In the article on Gavarni. See Balzac, *Œuvres diverses* (note 17), II, 777-82 (p. 778 and p. 781).
67 Monnier's talent 'a eu pour base l'observation la plus sagace *des classes*'; ibid., p. 778.
68 Ibid., p. 779.

[...] There have thus existed, and there will always exist, social species just as there are zoological species.⁶⁹

Zoological patterns of classification are much in evidence in the *Physiologies*. 'What is a Lorette?' A Lorette defies definition. 'You don't explain her, you analyse and you classify her.'⁷⁰ This kind of opening is as typical as the types themselves, analysed in terms of 'species'. Wood-engraved vignettes are, also typically, 'stamped' into the text, sometimes as emblems by which the type is to be recognised. The original meaning of the French 'cliché' (printing block or plate), suggests an analogy between the visual types presented here and stereotypes.⁷¹ Do the graphic images of *Physiologies* indeed produce types in the form of stereotyping caricatures? Amossy's assertion that *Physiologies* trade in prefabricated, fixed images focuses particularly on the image of the women of loose morals including the Lorette and the Grisette, both favoured types in physiological literature.

In *Physiologie de la Lorette*, the image of the type faces the page on which the actual classification (under the heading 'Classement des spécialités') begins. Gavarni's Lorette points her little telescope, not at the theatrical stage below, but at a possible suitor in the audience, as she is ostensibly wont to do (illustration 17, p. 112). This satirical image of the loose woman on the lookout is intended to 'sum up' the Lorette. Gavarni draws an ambiguous physique. One eye sharply gazing through the opera glass, the 'lorgnette-Derepas', the other closed behind a heavily made-up lid, the huntress seems to have espied her prey. But a faintly mocking smile and a relaxed posture seem to indicate that she is not that keen on a catch; she rather has the air of an observer. The near blacking-out of her right eye is also enigmatic. Does it suggest blindness to the world outside her own pursuits or a need to hide part of herself?

---

69 'La Société ne fait-elle pas de l'homme, suivant les milieux où son action se déploie, autant d'hommes différents qu'il y a de variétés en zoologie? [...] Il a donc existé, il existera donc de tout temps des Espèces Sociales comme il y a des Espèces Zoologiques.' Honoré de Balzac, 'Avant-propos', in *La Comédie humaine*, ed. by Pierre-Georges Castex, 12 vols (Paris: Gallimard, 1976-81), I (1976), 7-20 (p. 8).
70 Maurice Alhoy, *Physiologie de la Lorette* (Paris: Aubert, Lavigne, [1841]), p. 11 (reproduced in illustration 17, p. 112).
71 In fact, both the expression 'type' and 'stereotype' also derive from printing. See Ségolène Le Men, 'Peints par eux-mêmes', in *Les Français peints par eux-mêmes* (Paris: Éditions de la Réunion des musées nationaux, 1993), pp. 4-46 (p. 45-6), and Amossy (note 7), pp. 25-6.

112 *Sketches of the Nineteenth Century*

10

O Lorettes, que d'ovations vous attendent!
braquez donc sur votre poète vos lorgnettes
Derepas, et dites-vous:
  Voilà celui qui a donné le premier coup de
  trompe de notre marche triomphale!

11

Classement des spécialités.

cette demande: qu'est-ce qu'une Lorette? Voici la réponse: — La Lorette échappe à la définition. On ne l'explique pas, on l'analyse, on la classe.
C'est à tort qu'on a cherché à établir quelques rapprochements entre la Lorette et la grisette.
La grisette est un être qui tend à disparaître comme le quartier qu'elle habite. Le pays latin est appelé à devenir une contrefaçon des steppes de Pologne, une parodie des landes de Gascogne, le bassin du Luxembourg sera frère du bassin d'Arcachon, la rue Saint-Jac-

Illustration 17   Gavarni, vignettes in Maurice Alhoy, *Physiologie de la Lorette* (Paris: Aubert, Lavigne, [1841]), pp. 10-11. Wood engraving of Lorette by [Mme] H. Surbled.

The emblematic first letter of the text, an A intertwined with a rosary and surrounded by scattered playing cards, a half-open book and a burnt-down candle, suggests a life between virtue and debauchery. This, according to Amossy, is precisely the stereotype – the fallen woman who, despite her low life, has preserved her piety and a heart of gold. The stereotype, if this is indeed what it can be called, here assumes the authority of an emblem. If the source of this 'idée reçue' about the Lorette is, as Amossy suggests, Parent-Duchâtelet's report on prostitution of 1836, the *Physiologie de la Lorette*, published five years later, could just about be regarded as a work turning a sociologically established type into a stereotype. In only a brief reference to the visual medium of the *Physiologie*, Amossy emphasizes that Gavarni's types possess the character of 'visual formulae' supporting the textual stereotype and rather vaguely describes them as 'bordering on caricature' while displaying 'charm and humour'.[72] I would argue that caricature, the visual medium which expresses a stereotypical view most adequately, is not the one by which *Physiologies* depict types, and Gavarni's portrait of the Lorette is a case in point. Read together with the eulogy preceding it, which ends

---

72 See Amossy (note 7), pp. 52 and 60.

with the author's invitation of the Lorettes to point their opera glasses at him, the first singer of their glory, the features of the Lorette seem to express amused disbelief. Likewise, the Lorette depicted at the end of the *Physiologie* is ready to crown whoever comes up with a tune for the song written about her. The difference between the text classifying the Lorette and the living woman is thus kept in the reader's mind, and the graphic portraits are vital in this respect. Unlike the emblematic, ornamental letter types, the portraits counterbalance the classifying physiological discourse. Gavarni's 'type', the Lorette with the lorgnette, exemplifies superbly what Graham Everitt, writing at the end of the nineteenth century, described as the momentous change in graphic satire from traditional 'caricature' to 'sketches' or 'cartoons' in the 1830s.[73] The 'coarseness' and 'suggestiveness' of the old school (such as Rowlandson, Gillray and George Cruikshank in his beginnings) yields to portraiture seizing the typical in an amusing way without over-exaggerating it. Specifically with regard to the *Physiologies*, Günter Oesterle has observed the same process: Enlightenment caricature with its emphasis on 'foregrounds' gives way to 'modern' caricature which takes in 'backgrounds', circumstances and unconscious factors.[74] It cannot be denied that cartoons, that is to say, 'modern' caricature in Oesterle's understanding, have to operate with techniques of selecting and simplifying. In order to 'sketch', however, they also need to bear the mark of authenticity, the 'impress of the present'. This balance between first-hand observation and typification is the hallmark of the generation of artists creating 'popular portraits' in the 1830s and 40s. And how does Gavarni create a type that is not a caricature, viz. stereotype? According to the brothers Goncourt (who, four years after the artist's death, pointed out that he was not a caricaturist), by providing the type with the features of an individual: 'Gavarni is a portraitist of types...'. He draws from the 'memories of humanity' stored in his mind, which are like 'masses of superimposed plates (clichés)', to produce portraits which strike you as completely authentic and unexaggerated, even if they are not drawn from life.[75] The ambiguous physiognomy of the Lorette is thus not a handed-down 'cli-

---

73 See Everitt (note 64), p. 5.
74 '[S]tatt des vordergründig Typischen der aufklärerischen Karikatur wird das Hintergründige, Nebenbeihersprechende, Unbewußte der modernen Karikatur wichtig.' Oesterle (note 15), p. 233.
75 'Gavarni est un portraitiste de types ... '; 'Dans la création de ces hommes et de ces femmes, le crayon de Gavarni travaille [...] avec les souvenirs d'humanité emmagasinés dans sa mémoire, et pareils à des amas de clichés superposés.' Edmond and Jules Goncourt, *Gavarni. L'Homme et l'œovre* (Paris: Fasquelle, 1925; first edn 1870), pp. 91-2.

ché', but a vision derived from superimposing many mental sketches – daguerreotyped images, so to speak – so that the sharp outlines of each stored plate or 'cliché' melt into one. It is a summing-up of momentary portraits in a remembered 'typical' portrait.

The text of the *Physiologie* also has to sum up individual lives, and this is done by means of classification. The emblematic A introducing the 'classement des spécialités' is echoed by an O, in the form of garlands of laurel held by a 'retired' Lorette, at the end. Between the alpha and the omega, the type is classified according to divisions (such as the Lorette who lives under the control of her parents versus the emancipated Lorette) and their genera and species (for example, the plebeian Lorette, the Lorette with ancestors, the Lorette with anonymous parents, and the exotic Lorette), before particular aspects of milieu and habit are considered. How did the writers of *Physiologies* arrive at this extraordinary way of categorising social groups in zoological terms? The answer lies, again, in the methodological significance of biological or 'life' science for the emerging science of society.

The paradigm of Life Science

Physiology, the science of the human body, is linked to zoology, the science of the animal kingdom, through anatomy, the knowledge of parts of the body and their structures. More precisely, this link is provided by comparative anatomy, the discipline inferring functions of parts of the body through comparison and analogy. By 1833, when the first volume of the *Penny Cyclopædia* appeared, comparative anatomy had been established for about half a century. In the relevant entry the results of this discipline were judged as follows:

> It has [...] made sufficient progress, not only to have furnished the most important aids to the study of human anatomy and physiology, but to have supplied a secure and broad foundation for all zoological knowledge, both as regards existing and extinct races. As the basis of modern zoology, comparative anatomy presents a subject of the highest interest.[76]

The force of this statement will be readily appreciated if one bears in mind that in 1837, Charles Darwin, having returned from his travels around the world, was beginning to write his *Note Books*, collecting all the data that

---

76 'Anatomy, comparative', in *The Penny Cyclopædia of the Society for the Diffusion of Useful Knowledge*, 27 vols (London: Knight, 1833-43), I (1833), 500-3 (p. 500, col. 2).

would support his theory of evolution by selection. Conceiving species not only in terms of precisely defined types, but in terms of development was very much a contemporary concern, and comparative anatomy offered the key to both. The controversy between France's leading naturalist, Georges Cuvier, and his colleague Geoffroy de Saint-Hilaire, which erupted in a public *éclat* in 1830, was, as Goethe noted, of European significance because it set the analytical, defining principle in zoology against its synthetic, genetic counterpart.[77] Yet both together, he argues, form the basis of the science, as one cannot exist without the other. Characteristics of a type cannot be defined, and a type cannot be classified, unless the functions of bones and organs are understood with regard to habitat; the functions of parts of the body, the diversification of species and the functional whole of the environment and its inhabitants cannot be grasped without an accurate knowledge of types. Geoffroy's evolutionist model, presuming a functional unity of the natural system or 'l'unité de composition', was, one could argue, 'physiological', and for this reason it appealed much to Balzac. In the 'Avant-propos' of the *Comédie*, he pays homage to both Cuvier and Geoffroy as paradigms of his own scientific approach to society, and, like Goethe, expresses his preference for the latter because of his unitary model.[78]

By about 1830, physiology and zoology, especially of the French school, were clearly established as *the* lead sciences in Europe, attracting the greatest public interest, and their impact on social knowledge was immense. Biographies of men who started out as students of natural history or medicine and ended up (or at least, developed equally) as sociologists, activists, politicians and/or socially committed writers are a sign of the times. P.J.B. Buchez, for example, Christian socialist and president of the Assemblée Nationale in 1848, studied natural history at the Jardin des Plantes where Lamarck, Cuvier, Geoffroy and many other of France's famous 'naturalists' researched and lectured. He qualified as a doctor, co-founded the French Carbonari and the Saint-Simonian 'Club des Amis du Peuple', fell out with Saint-Simonianism and supported Neo-Catholicism, became, in 1831, the editor of the *Journal des sciences morales et politiques* and later wrote a 46-volume *Histoire parlementaire de la Révolution*. Albert Smith, the writer of sketches called *Natural Histories*, as well as of novels and stage extravaganzas, later one of the century's great multi-media entertainers, had studied medicine at London's Middlesex Hospital and, from 1838, at the Sorbonne. He was about to set up a

---

77 See Johann Wolfgang von Goethe, 'Principes de philosophie zoologique', in *Goethes Werke*, ed. by Erich Trunz, 14 vols (Munich: Beck; Hamburg: Wegner, 1973-6), XIII (1975), 219-50.
78 See Balzac, 'Avant-propos' (note 69), pp. 7-8.

practice in London in 1841, but his talent as a social observer got the better of him. Smith was in fact only one of a 'medical trio' amongst the early *Punch* collaborators;[79] the other two were the cartoonist John Leech, who 'attained at St. Bartholomew's that practical knowledge of anatomical drawing which did him good service in his artistic career';[80] the other was Percival Leigh (pseudonym: Paul Prendergast) whose diagnostic powers as a doctor remained remarkable even after he had 'abandoned [...] the lancet for the pen'.[81] Georg Büchner, one of Germany's foremost social dramatists, revolutionary, translator of Victor Hugo and signed-up contributor to Gutzkow's *Deutsche Revue* (repressed before even its first number was able to appear), studied natural history and medicine at Gießen and Strasbourg, where one of his teachers was a disciple of Cuvier, and where, in student circles, he also encountered French socialist theory. Having co-authored a pamphlet inciting the paupers of Hesse to rise against their exploiters, he escaped imprisonment by fleeing to France. In 1837 he died of typhoid, contracted probably through the dissection of fresh fishes, just after taking up a lectureship in natural history at Zurich. The first rector of this newly founded university, Lorenz Oken, is another example of a socially committed natural philosopher and zoologist. A generation older than Büchner, he, too, had left Germany for political reasons. A most inspiring teacher by all accounts, he believed that natural history should be the foundation of public education, just as Saint-Simon believed that physiology should become a staple of school curricula. Between 1833 and 1841 he published his popular *Allgemeine Naturgeschichte für alle Stände* (Natural History for Readers of All Classes) in seven volumes and thirteen sections, probably the last comprehensive work on this subject to be written by a single author.[82] It is not the concern of my study to discuss the validity of Oken's or any other scientist's contribution to biology or medicine, but only to indicate ways in which these branches of knowledge are paradigmatic for the study of society during the period in question.

How, then, does the model of zoological classification help sociological sketch writers in their constitution of 'types'? First of all, they have the option of referring to the popularity of natural history as part of their analysis (this also applies to the paradigm of anatomy which will be discussed in Chapter 5). Secondly, they show the difference between common perception and analytical categorisation, defining the type by means of implicit or

---

79 M.H. Spielmann, *The History of 'Punch'* (London: Cassell, 1895), p. 303.
80 Everitt (note 64), p. 289.
81 Spielmann (note 79), p. 299.
82 See 'Oken', in *Allgemeine Deutsche Biographie*, 56 vols (first edn 1887, repr. Berlin: Duncker & Humblot, 1970), XXIV, 216-26 (p. 220).

explicit comparison (following the model of comparative anatomy) and explaining the function or genesis of particular characteristics socially (as zoology would explain them through their natural function, environment and/or genesis). However, there is one crucial point where social typology differs from zoology. While the classification of species will not change the animal kingdom, only human knowledge of it, social classification is eminently linked to the dynamic of the social body it analyses. Those who classify are themselves subject to their science, and the analysis of conditions producing types constitutes an instrument for social change. This means that social knowledge may change the type or even help to make it 'extinct'. Whether or not a sketch, particularly of the classifying kind, implies the relativity of its categories and findings is an acid test, scientifically speaking, of its sociological quality. The concluding two examples will illustrate this.

Under the title 'Naturgeschichte der deutschen Kameele' ('Natural History of German Camels'), a public lecture was given in 1835 before Frankfurt's Museum, a society devoted to the arts and sciences and comparable, perhaps, to the Philosophical and Literary Societies of British towns. The lecturer was Karl Gutzkow, then writer of the literary review section (*Literatur-Blatt*) of the Frankfurt journal *Phönix*, which also printed his paper (and which, in the same month, featured the last instalments of Beurmann's 'Skizzen aus den Hansestädten').[83] The title indicates that it is a satire in the style of traditional fable, with the animal standing for a human quality; in this case for philistinism, as in German, 'Kamel' is an idiom for stupidity and pedantry. Gutzkow's 'natural history' therefore does not classify a profession, but a mental disposition. The circumstances generating philistinism are to be sought in the milieu of German academia. Since the vast majority of professionals and civil servants, that part of the middle class which creates the moral physiognomy of the nation, were brought up in the narrow world of the university system, the classification of the philistine according to habitat and habits attacks the state of the polity head-on.

Significantly, one German professor, even if he deals with human and real camels all the time, is excepted from the genus – Lorenz Oken. Elsewhere, Gutzkow praises his *Naturgeschichte* (which, targeting readers of all classes, appeared in affordable monthly parts), for the educative effect it was having on a wide audience. Its serial publication initiated even complete non-specialists to ever more complex scientific trains of thought. 'We barely notice', Gutzkow says, 'how we have turned from laymen into people who are

---

83 See Chapter 2, p. 79.

in the know, and that we are right in the middle of the system'.[84] The popularity and popular style of this great biological publication no doubt prompted Gutzkow to present his lecture as a 'natural history', and to describe it wittily as a 'significant contribution' ('einen wesentlichen Beitrag') to Oken's serial enterprise.[85] But from where could he have received the idea of applying the zoological 'system' to moral analysis? There were no sociological forerunners in German philosophy; the system that held the young generation under its spell, Hegel's, had potential in this respect, but to Gutzkow it seemed like the apotheosis of theology in the guise of the philosophy of history. To give the 'Philosophie der Geschichte' a more scientific foundation, Gutzkow developed his own concept of a 'comparative anatomy of events' ('vergleichende Anatomie der Ereignisse').[86] This, he declares, he owes to the English tradition of 'anatomising' history rather than 'constructing' it. Yet these reflections, written down in prison a year after the lecture to the Museum, still offer no clue as to the theoretical provenance of Gutzkow's moral zoology. The answer lies most probably in his excellent familiarity with European journalism; the 'natural histories' and 'physiologies' of the Parisian school will have been a staple part of his reading. His friend Glaßbrenner, also no stranger to the French press, had already come up with a humorous stratification of society in 1832, redefining in social terms the racial division of the human species according to the German physiologist Johann Friedrich Blumenbach.[87] At the back of Gutzkow's mind there must, however, also have been one famous piece of German social satire, presented in the mode of natural history. Its author was Ludwig Börne, originally student of medicine, then of political science, journalist and revered fig-

---

84 '[W]ir fühlen kaum, daß wir aus Laien Kundige geworden sind, daß wir uns mitten in dem Systeme selbst befinden.' [Karl Gutzkow], 'Werke der Industrie', *Phönix*, 138. *Literatur-Blatt*, 23 (13 June 1835), 549-51 (p. 550).

85 Karl Gutzkow, 'Naturgeschichte der deutschen Kameele', *Phönix*, 49 (26 February 1835), 193-5 (p. 195). See also reference to internet edition of *Gutzkows Werke und Briefe* in the Bibliography.

86 See Karl Gutzkow, 'Zur Philosophie der Geschichte', in *Schriften*, ed. by Adrian Hummel, 2 vols plus one vol. of materials (Frankfurt a. M.: Zweitausendeins, 1998), I, 553-728 (p. 594). On Gutzkow's criticism of Hegel and on his own concept of an 'anatomy' of history see my own articles, 'Englische "Anatomie" gegen deutsche "Konstruktion" der Geschichte', *Chroniques allemandes*, 7 (Grenoble: Université Stendhal-Grenoble III, 1999), 57-68, and 'Anatomie und Enzyklopädie als Muster literarischer Verfahrensweisen im Werk Karl Gutzkows', in *Zeitdiskurse. Reflexionen zum 19. und 20. Jahrhundert*, ed. by Roland Berbig, M. Lauster and Rolf Parr (Heidelberg: Synchron, 2004), pp. 43-54.

87 See 'Der Mensch und seine Vorzüge. Humoristisch-satyrische Betrachtung von Ad. Brennglas', *Berliner Don Quixote*, 25 (12 May 1832), [1-3], esp. p. 2.

urehead of the 'young' school of writing in the 1830s. He had written a mock-zoological tale (ostensibly to fool the censor) on the slowness of the German public transport system, entitled 'Monographie der deutschen Postschnecke. Beitrag zur Naturgeschichte der Mollusken und Testaceen' (Monograph of the German Postal Snail. Contribution to the Natural History of Molluscs and Testacea). It had first been published in his own journal, *Die Wage*, in 1821. As a Francophile and superb translator from the French, Börne was no doubt *au fait* with socio-physiological writing. The exceedingly cumbersome German transport system, the very image of the nation's backwardness, is analysed, aptly by a French governess, in what is referred to as a 'physiology of mail carriages' ('Physiologie der Postwägen'),[88] and the piece still echoes through Beurmann's satirical eulogy on the 'Eilwagen' of 1835.[89] A German social physiologist in Parisian exile from 1830, Börne delighted the young generation back home by his *Briefe aus Paris* (Letters from Paris), appearing with Hoffmann & Campe from 1832, where he voices his exasperation at the Juste Milieu, scarcely an advance on the repressive system in the fatherland, and refers to his own lonely republican wisdom as that of a believer in 'God, nature, anatomy and physiology'.[90]

His own affinity with Börne would no doubt have played on Gutzkow's mind for one particular reason. Börne's legendary 1825 commemorative speech on Jean Paul, the great humorist, had been commissioned by and delivered to the same society Gutzkow was now lecturing to a decade later, the Frankfurt Museum. While Börne's *Denkrede* marks a decisive step in building a progressive German literary counter-canon, revolving around the public word and witty subversion, Gutzkow's *Naturgeschichte* has to be seen as an attempt to establish allusive, emancipatory public discourse further as *the* paradigm of modern German letters.

Karl Gutzkow, 'Naturgeschichte der deutschen Kameele' (*Phönix*)

The common perception, Gutzkow indicates, is that there is no such thing as an indigenous German camel. There may not be any evidence of a pre-historic

---

88 Ludwig Börne, 'Monographie der deutschen Postschnecke', in *Sämtliche Schriften*, ed. by Inge and Peter Rippmann, 5 vols (Düsseldorf [from vol. 4 Darmstadt]: Melzer, 1964-8), I (1964), 639-67 (p. 650).
89 See pp. 75-7 of this study.
90 'Weil ich an Gott glaube, und an die Natur, und an die Anatomie, und an die Physiologie [...].' Ludwig Börne, 'Briefe aus Paris', in *Sämtliche Schriften* (note 88), III (1964), 3-867 ('Zweiundvierzigster Brief, Paris, Dienstag, den 15. März 1831', p. 230).

species (although fossil finds point to the one-time existence of whales, mammoths and lions in Swabia and Hesse), but there can be no doubt that the camel is now thriving everywhere in Germany. The speaker's own experience is cited in support of the allegation. As a student in Heidelberg a couple of years ago, he went through the usual rites of passage, making his first encounters with the world inside and, more importantly, outside the lecture hall; – the great big world of Heidelberg and the Mannheim opera. Such was the youthful enthusiasm of those years following in the wake of the July Revolution (1832/33 being indeed a time of political excitement in the German South-West) that Heidelberg seemed the navel of the world and one's own friends the representatives of humanity. If anyone dared to object that there were other ravishing places such as the Lüneburg Heath or the soft meanderings of the river Spree, that creature was immediately put down as a 'Kameel'. And, lo and behold, a metamorphosis used to occur:

> [T]he animal bulged out and stretched itself, growing increasingly big and humpy, projecting its neck right out in the air; callouses emerged on its chest, its hooves split in two, its head became flatter and flatter at the top and longer and longer at the bottom, until it ended in a goat-like beard flopping around its chin.[91]

The speaker here creates something like a physiognomic and performative illustration. Anticipating techniques later exploited by Kafka, his prose sketch translates the figurative understanding of a zoological term into narrated reality. Gutzkow alludes to a now obscure slang usage of 'Kame(e)l' by which students ridiculed someone who was not a member of the fraternity or not a good sport, in other words, a 'swot', 'boor' or 'philistine'.[92] The transformation of the student into a zoological genus wittily indicates the stultifying and dehumanising effect of German provincial education. The friends of the Lüneburg Heath and of the Spree who cannot warm to the politicised humanism of 'young Heidelberg' are the worst camels, but the self-irony in Gutzkow's description of those who see Heidelberg as the centre of humanity indicates that their enthusiasm is no less provincial. In fact, the delusion that

---

91 'Und siehe, das Thier blähte sich und dehnte sich aus, und wurde immer größer und buckliger, und streckte seinen Hals weithin in die Luft, und Schwielen legten sich ihm an die Brust, und seine Hufe spalteten sich, und der Kopf wurde oben immer flacher – und unten immer länger, bis zu einem Barte, der ihm ziegenhaft am Kinne wackelte.' Gutzkow, 'Naturgeschichte der deutschen Kameele' (note 85), p. 193.
92 See 'Kamel', in Jacob and Wilhelm Grimm, *Deutsches Wörterbuch*, 33 vols (Munich: Deutscher Taschenbuch Verlag, 1984), XI, 95-96 (col. 96).

they have understood the world, so that they can classify as camels those who have not, makes them prime examples of Gutzkow's first sub-category of the family, the species of the dominant 'public camel'. What is certain is that a place like Heidelberg breeds the *genus camelus*, lacking the very basics of urban observation and urbane manners. Once its individuals have left their formative environment, they will easily fulfil their functions in an oppressed society. In other words, the various types of camel are the perfect organs for the German body politic.

Taking the liberty to correct 'some of Buffon's assertions',[93] Gutzkow subdivides the genus into public, moral and social camels (zoologically incorrect, as there are only two species of *camelus*). The public camels are dromedaries, adorned with only one hump of fat which is heavier than the two of the Bactrian camel. Being a resilient and agile species, they control the German public sphere, ensuring that nothing innovative, imaginative, enlightening, liberating or revolutionary will ever crop up in the sciences and in the arts, in philosophy and theology or in publishing and public discourse. Not because they are reactionaries – they simply have no enthusiasm for the polity as a whole and are thus insensitive to its inherent dynamism. They claim to have deep insight into processes of circulation ('tiefe Einsicht in den Kreislauf der Begebenheiten'), but have not the faintest idea of what connects with what. In short, they are not social physiologists and therefore useless for the liberal cause. Gutzkow's moral camels are lamas; although zoologically not camels, they are all the more prominent in the social genus. This is where the comparative method of classification comes into its own. Sociologically, Buffon needs to be corrected because the 'lama' shows characteristics that are clearly also present in the 'dromedary' and in the 'Bactrian camel'. The views of this type are also blinkered, and, as in the other two species, this is what makes it all the more self-assured and righteous. Being a distinct species, it differs from the other two in its pity-inspiring sadness. Moral camels are head-drooping representatives of the philistine mindset. Protestant morality makes them shrink from the *élan vital* with which nature has endowed the human species. This does not, of course, prevent them from being judgmental and censorious: 'These camels do not read Goethe because they think he will spoil their morals, and they call frivolous everything that is solely the exercise of a force with which nature has endowed us.'[94] Exerting moral censorship on what they read, they will also be offended by rich and full characters whom

---

93 Gutzkow (note 85), p. 194.
94 'Diese Kameele lesen Goethe nicht, weil sie glauben, er werde ihre Sitten verderben, und nennen Alles frivol, was nichts ist, als der Gebrauch einer Kraft, welche die Natur uns spendet.' Ibid.

they are completely unable to judge since they cannot understand *any* character in context, 'im Zusammenhange'. If a failure to read appearances and to see connections is a common feature of the *Philister* in his public and in his moral variant, then this shortcoming must be most painful where social signreading and signalling matter most – in the modes and manners of social intercourse. Gutzkow's 'social' camel should be, as he says, 'a light, gazellelike class' ('ein leichtes, gazellenartiges Geschlecht'), moving in society with ease and grace, but alas, no such type has been produced by the German social milieu. Instead, we find a true camel, something akin to the heavy, double-humped species which in German is aptly named 'Trampeltier'. Its social skills, less than nil, prompt the speaker's exasperated question, 'When will this species become extinct?' ('Wann wird diese Thiergattung aussterben?').

The reference to the un-philistine Oken and his *Naturgeschichte*, designed precisely to support the formation of an enlightened public, concludes this humorous, but biting exercise in social classification. The *Philister* is certainly not an invention of Gutzkow, having been a favourite butt of German Romantic satire. Clemens Brentano had even come up with a 'physiological' attack entitled 'Der Philister vor, in und nach der Geschichte' (The Philistine before, in and after History) which incidentally was also presented as an address, in this case to the patriotic *Christlich-deutsche Tischgesellschaft* (Christian-German Dining Society), in 1811. It was styled as a witty 'scientific' list of 'symptoms' of philistinism which could contribute to a 'physiology and zoology of philistines'.[95] However, the critical impetus of this Romantic satire, as Günter Oesterle has argued, is philosophical, not sociological.[96] Gutzkow's zoological analysis of German middle-class blinkeredness, delivered a quarter of a century later, is sociological in that it refrains from reproducing the negative stereotype of the philistine. Instead, the reader or listener is confronted with an imaginative metamorphosis of the proverbial cliché into a real animal, in other words, into a physically existing social type whose life depends on the system supporting him and whose existence makes the system work. Nor does this physiological satire originate from a sense of superiority over the philistine. A former student at Heidelberg, Gutzkow includes himself in the social body analysed and also signals that anyone in his

---

95 Brentano declares it impossible to offer an exhaustive 'Physiologie und Zoologie der Philister', but promises to present 'eine Reihe von Symptomen des Philistertums, als einen Beitrag zur Wissenschaft'. Clemens Brentano, 'Der Philister vor, in und nach der Geschichte', in *Werke*, 4 vols, ed. by Wolfgang Frühwald, Bernhard Gajek and Friedhelm Kemp, 2nd edn (Munich: Hanser, 1973-8), II (1973), 959-1016 (p. 986).
96 See Oesterle (note 15), p. 228.

audience must feel that the analysis could well apply to him, too. Not to 'her': women, allowed to attend the events of the Museum, are not included amongst Gutzkow's camels; they are only shown to suffer, particularly under the 'social' species of the animal:

How unfortunate the girl with whom such a fusspot falls in love! She dances too much for his liking, and yet he is the only one she will dance with. She talks too kindly to people, and yet she does it only to prove that she is not in a bad mood because of him. Such a camel in love is the plague of humanity. He promises his fiancée the most abhorrent things, such as their own family tomb and shares in the Gotha life assurance company; in short, it is easy to imagine what sort of life lies in store *after* marriage.[97]

Is it the women in his audience that Gutzkow mainly addresses his lecture to? He concludes it by expressing the ironic hope that none of his listeners, when leaving the venue, will whisper to their companion, 'You, too, are such a camel'. If those who utter these words are imagined as wives or fiancées, women are indeed addressed as the agents of social change, encouraged to use the typology of philistinism as an instrument of liberation. At any rate, the sketch clearly indicates that classification does not ossify types; that, on the contrary, it is designed to transform mentalities, and that maybe one day not only the 'social' species of the camel, but also its 'moral' and 'public' variants will have ceased to exist.

The female half of the population fares less favourably in the following zoological exercise, published in 1837: *Sketches of Young Ladies: In Which These Interesting Members of the Animal Kingdom are Classified, According to their Several Instincts, Habits, and General Characteristics.* Thus the title of a physiology by 'Quiz', in real life Edward Caswall, then graduate of Brasenose College, later divine and author of many well-known hymns who converted to Catholicism under the influence of Cardinal Newman. Perhaps it was Caswall's success as a humorous author, 'Scriblerus Redivivus', of *Pluck Examination Papers for Candidates at Oxford and Cambridge* (three editions, 1836) that

---

97 'Wie unglücklich das Mädchen, in das sich ein solcher Umstandsprinz verliebt! Sie tanzt ihm zu viel; und sie tanzt doch nur mit ihm. Sie spricht zu freundlich mit den Leuten; und sie thut es doch nur, um zu zeigen, daß er ihr keine böse Laune macht! Ein solches verliebtes Kameel ist eine Plage der Menschheit. Es verspricht seiner Braut die abscheulichsten Dinge: ein eigenes Familienbegräbniß, eine Aktie in der Gothaer Lebensversicherungs-Anstalt; kurz, man kann sich denken, was erst kommen wird nach der Hochzeit.' Gutzkow (note 85), p. 195.

drew the attention of Chapman & Hall to the 23 year-old? His *Sketches*, published under the Boz-like pseudonym Quiz, with Dickens's Phiz as illustrator, and appearing at the height of the *Pickwick* fashion, did not fail to sell (by 1838 a seventh edition had to be printed). Caswall seemed to have found a successful formula not only as a social zoologist, but also in publishing terms, as the length and presentation of his *Sketches* echoed Dickens's serial parts without being a serial. Individually published, this 80-page monograph of a 'type', illustrated by six steel plates and sold at three shillings, provided the format for Dickens's own *Sketches of Young Gentlemen* (1838), a retort to Caswall, and *Sketches of Young Couples* (1840). It was also the pattern to be adopted by the (cheaper and more richly illustrated) Parisian *Physiologies* and Albert Smith's English adaptations of them as *Natural Histories*.

'Quiz' / 'Phiz', *Sketches of Young Ladies*

In the preface the author refers to his innovation, that of applying 'the Linnæan system' to the classification of young ladies, as an achievement he had in vain been expecting of a famous specialist like Cuvier or at least of scientists associated with the March of Intellect such as 'Dr. Lardner or Mrs. Somerville'. Dionysius Lardner, holder of the Chair of Natural Philosophy and Astronomy at University College London since 1828, was well-known in the 1830s for his popularising *Cabinet Cyclopædia* and *Cabinet Library*, while Mary Somerville, apart from epitomising the progress in education as an eminent woman scientist, had earned her recognition through a work commissioned on behalf of the Society for the Diffusion of Useful Knowledge, *The Mechanism of the Heavens* (1831). Lardner's and Somerville's failure to undertake a classification of young ladies seems particularly regrettable to Quiz because these two could have corrected some recently published findings of a certain Dr. Buckland. Here the ironic twists of the facetious argument become difficult to follow, as it turns out that, despite his exercise in seemingly 'progressive' social zoology, Quiz's sympathies do not lie with the advance of knowledge at the expense of traditional gender roles, but with Buckland's religious conservatism. William Buckland, Reader in Geology and Mineralogy at Oxford whose work was quoted at length in the *Penny Cyclopædia*, was also Canon of Christ Church (later Dean of Westminster) and professed a 'natural theology', aiming to prove that science supported faith. In *Reliquiæ Diluvianæ* (1823), he had interpreted the fossil finds from caves and fissures as evidence of the Mosaic Deluge. His geological contribution to the 'Bridgewater Treatises': *Geology and Mineralogy Considered with Reference to Natural Theology* (1836) created great public attention. A student of divinity like Caswall would have engaged with Buckland's scientific publications almost by necessity.

The criterion for classification in *Sketches of Young Ladies* turns out not to be social, as the characteristics of the 'genus' merely consist of being young and female. Nor do the categories defining 'species' leave much room for sociological reasoning, focusing as they do on aspects of character and physiognomy rather than social circumstances. The table of contents thus lists the distinctions of types normally by just an adjective, such as the 'busy' young lady, the 'romantic', 'evangelical' and 'matter-of-fact' young lady, to which are added the 'plain', 'stupid' or 'clever' young lady. The suspicion that classification here serves as an outlet for misogyny is hardened by the author's statement in the preface that, according to Dr. Buckland's system, young ladies would be classified as 'Ichthyosauri', the extinct, highly voracious, cave-inhabiting creatures dealt with at length in *Reliquiæ Diluvianæ*. Quite wrong, the author remarks; under the Linnæan system they need to be classed as 'Troglodites'. *Troglodytes, Linn.*, as readers even with zoological expertise would probably not immediately have guessed, is a sub-class of the wren family. The chivalrous Quiz thus superficially defends the fair sex while dealing it a blow. Troglodytes are much more readily understood to be human cave-dwellers, and not even extinct in that capacity.[98] Young Ladies having thus been assigned to the lowest stage of civilisation, it is no wonder that they are then classified by the degree to which they are uncivilised. One of the worst species is presented right at the beginning of the *Sketches*, 'The Young Lady Who Sings'. This type abuses her cultural accomplishments, in other words, being able to perform arias and songs, even in German, Italian and French, and to accompany herself on the piano, in order to dominate every party she and her mother are invited to, and, worse, to prevent the poor young male she will inevitably engage as her page-turner from having fun with the other young females. Phiz cannot help reverting to straight caricature in the portrayal of the singer, while the other women, engaged in gossiping and flirting, and yearningly ogled by the man standing by the piano, are depicted as a jolly bunch (illustration 18, p. 126).

The male gaze is overtly at work here, directed away from the songstress and towards the beauties in the centre, one of whom is casting her eyes

---

98 The *Damen Conversations Lexikon* glosses 'Troglodyten' as 'Höhlenbewohner' (inhabitants of caves), adding that formerly, the term was used with particular reference to the population of the east coast of Ethiopia and that in natural history, chimpanzees are also known as troglodytes. See 'Troglodyten' in *Damen Conversations Lexikon*, ed. by Carl Herloßsohn, 10 vols (Leipzig: Volckmar, Adorf, 1834-8), X (1838), 202, and *Digitale Bibliothek* edition (Berlin: Directmedia, 2005), entry no. 10945.

Illustration 18 'Phiz' [Hablot Knight Browne], 'The Young Lady Who Sings'. Frontispiece in 'Quiz' [Edward Caswall], *Sketches of Young Ladies: In Which These Interesting Members of the Animal Kingdom Are Classified According to their Several Instincts, Habits, and General Characteristics* (London: Chapman & Hall, 1837). Steel plate.

cheekily at the beholder. *Sketches of Young Ladies* is clearly written as a guide for Englishmen, either implicitly addressed by the first person plural or explicitly as 'sir', looking for a wife: 'If we are ever to fall in love, in this late season of our existence, preserve us from falling in love with the extremely natural young lady.'[99] Such is the kind of advice. This pragmatic interest is appealingly veiled in chic 'scientific' observation ('the naturalist may lay down three principal eras in the romantic young lady's life'),[100] an exclusively male business, as the reader is unmistakeably given to understand. A young lady aspiring to be a 'naturalist' is the horror of horrors, even if she genuinely classifies animals and not men:

> [T]he natural historian young lady is always a most surprisingly humane person; accordingly, to her infinite honour, she always contrives to kill [...] insects in the manner most agreeable to their feelings. Sometimes she drives a heated needle bolt through the head of a beetle, taking a humane caution to sever the spine; because, as she says, that is the seat of sensation. Sometimes she deluges a spoonful of oil over some other equally fortunate animal, which, she assures you, kills him directly; although to be sure his legs go on moving for five hours and upwards afterwards, owing, as she philosophically observes, merely to the muscular motion.[101]

The gendered reference to the insect drowned in oil betrays the author's fear of the scientifically-minded woman. If she applies her science to the male 'genus', the result will be catastrophic:

> [W]e are afraid that in case of our dying before her, she would cause us to be stuffed, and sent in a glass case to the British museum as a natural historic curiosity.[102]

In the case of a female mind, treating the other sex as a gallery of curious animals is obviously a transgression. For this reason the 'natural historian young lady' is classified as something little short of a monster.

---

99 'Quiz' [Edward Caswall], *Sketches of Young Ladies: In Which These Interesting Members of the Animal Kingdom Are Classified According to their Several Instincts, Habits, and General Characteristics. With Six Illustrations by 'Phiz'* [Hablot Knight Browne] (London: Chapman & Hall, 1837), p. 71.
100 Ibid., p. 11.
101 Ibid., p. 45.
102 Ibid., p. 48.

Sketches of Young Ladies exemplifies how power structures of a gendered kind are sought to be preserved through classification. The types appear to be constituted from personal observation, but this observation is not disinterested. It describes and judges women according to their likely matrimonial virtues, which, as does not need to be spelled out, are those of a patriarchal order. Without exception, Caswall's types are stereotypes; images that have to be rigid in order not to undermine the observer's own power over the observed. Not surprisingly, the position of the male 'naturalist' is not itself subject to analysis.

Yet scientific paradigms of sketches leave ample scope for them to thematise the analyst and the business of observation. The illustration of the Lorette pointing her telescope at the opening of the text which classifies her shows the great self-reflective potential inherent in the genre. This Chapter has shown that the constitution of social types by sketches cannot be subsumed under stereotyping, however much the classification method and the mass production of this kind of literature may suggest this to be the case. The continued interest of these sketches to historians and sociologists could hardly be explained if they were nothing more than recycled clichés. Only detailed interpretation of an individual sketch will show whether a stereotype is reproduced or whether a type is constituted. This happens through more or less explicit deviation from a stereotyped notion, and through a dynamic relationship between text and image. In unillustrated texts, such as the 1830 version of Balzac's 'L'Épicier', this dynamic is created by a heightened tension between surface appearances and analysis or, as Gutzkow's example has shown, by the literal enactment of a proverbial cliché which draws attention to the difference between a seemingly harmless common signifier and the astonishingly baneful social effects of the signified. As Karlheinz Stierle has argued, the overarching scientific model of physiology which sociological sketches adhere to is fruitful in terms of semiological awareness,[103] which in turn lies at the heart of social cognition. This awareness attaches not only to the objects of analysis, but includes the business of social anatomy itself, as Chapter 5 will show. The anatomising eye has, of course, its own literary and iconographic provenance in the moralist tradition which sociological sketches very often allude to – the subject of my next Chapter. Apart from his many modern signifiers, Gavarni's dandified devil of observation (illustration 1, p. 7) refers to one of the figures that dominates this tradition.

---

103 See Stierle (note 5), p. 46 and p. 181.

4
The Devil in Europe: Sketches and the Moralist Tradition

> The general Purpose of this Paper, is to expose the false Arts of Life, to pull off the Disguises of Cunning, Vanity and Affectation, and to recommend a general Simplicity in our Dress, our Discourse, and our Behaviour.
>
> Richard Steele, *The Tatler*[1]

Some French thinkers of the sixteenth and seventeenth century, including Montaigne, La Rochefoucauld and La Bruyère, are dubbed 'moralists' because they considered, in a more or less essayistic form, actual human behaviour, that is to say, the 'disguises' and 'vanities' of their contemporaries, rather than measuring people's actions against absolute moral standards, as moral philosophers would. Reflecting on the mores of the age was, however, not a prerogative of these essayists. My discussion of the 'moralist tradition' therefore refers to the reflection on mores and their depiction in a more comprehensive sense and attempts to indicate the scale on which sketches adapted this heritage to new needs.

Asmodeus

The scene: Madrid. Night. A student, Don Cleophas Leandro Perez Zambullo, has just been transported in rapid flight to the tower of San Salvador's church by Asmodeus, a little devil whose limp and use of crutches make him less agile on the ground, and who now proves his gratitude to Don Cleophas for having freed him from a bottle:

---

1 Dedication of *The Tatler: By Isaac Bickerstaff, Esq.*, in [R. Steele], *The Lucubrations of Isaac Bickerstaff*, 4 vols (London: Nutt, Knapton, Sprint et al., 1733), I, before p. 1.

I am about [...] to take away the roofs from the houses of this great city; and notwithstanding the darkness of the night, to reveal to your eyes whatever is doing within them. As he spake, he extended his right arm, the roofs disappeared, and the Student's astonished sight penetrated the interior of the surrounding dwellings as plainly as if the noon-day sun shone over them. It was, says Luis Velez de Guevara, like looking into a pasty from which a set of greedy monks had just removed the crust.

The aspect of interiors laid bare in amazing confusion prompts an even more challenging act of *moral* exposure:

To unlock for you the secret chambers of the human heart, I will explain in what all these persons that you see are engaged. All shall be open to you; I will discover the hidden motives of their deeds, and reveal to you their unbidden thoughts.

These concealed springs of human action are, of course, greed and the sex drive, and they are revealed by almost literally dismantling human bodies. In a technique also observed by sketches, the reader's eye is guided through deictic visual description:

In the next house there are a pair of pictures worth remarking. One is an antiquated coquette who is retiring to rest, after depositing on her toilet [toilet-table], her hair, her eyebrows and her teeth; the other is a gallant sexagenarian, who has just returned from a love campaign. He has already closed one eye, and placed his whiskers and peruke on the dressing table. His valet is now easing him of an arm and one leg, to put him to bed with the rest.[2]

Alain René Le Sage's *Le Diable boiteux*, known in English usually as *Asmodeus* (*or The Devil Upon Two Sticks*), published in 1707, is based on the picaresque novel *El Diablo cojuelo* (1641) by Luis Vélez de Guevara, to whom the narrator's comment refers. Also drawing on character portraits in the manner of the French moralists, as in the description of the old lecher or the ageing coquette, and unfolding a multi-faceted picture of urban life including the interiors of a prison and a madhouse, Le Sage's novel set a pattern for panoramic urban depiction. Its characteristic is the combination of a coordi-

---

2 Alain René Le Sage, *Asmodeus; or, The Devil on Two Sticks. [...] With a Biographical Notice of the Author, by Jules Janin. Translated by Joseph Thomas; and Illustrated by Tony Johannot* (London: Thomas, 1841), pp. 20-3.

nating (in the terms of this study: physiological or synthetic) view from above with the penetrating (anatomical or analytic) view of interiors. I will refer to this momentous panoptic formula henceforth as 'Asmodean'. Le Sage's devil fuelled the idea of metropolitan vision that could traverse national boundaries. A visiting Asmodeus brought to light the vices, follies and injustices of one's own capital and nation. Thus the demon reappears in *The Devil upon Crutches in England, or Night Scenes in London*, written *upon the Plan of the Celebrated Diable boiteux* in a *Satirical Work* for which *a Gentleman of Oxford* claimed authorship (1755), or on stage in 1768, in a farce entitled *The Devil upon Two Sticks*, by the 'English Aristophanes', the actor and playwright Samuel Foote. Towards the end of the century, Le Sage's plot was continued in a London setting, in the novel *The Devil upon Two Sticks in England* (1790) by William Combe, better known as the author of verse to Rowlandson's plates in the satirical 'Dr Syntax' series, issued by Ackermann in the early decades of the nineteenth century. The same publisher was responsible for Combe's and Rowlandson's *Microcosm of London*, an early example of encyclopaedic visual-verbal representation of the city, which has already been mentioned in connection with sketches alluding to optical media.[3] In Berlin, the limping devil featured in a journal founded in 1827 by a novelist and writer of comedies, Ferdinand von Biedenfeld, and co-edited by Moritz Saphir. 'In the form of satirical dialogue' and 'with constant reference to Vienna, London and Paris', *Der hinkende Teufel zu Berlin* subjected life in the Prussian capital to an entertaining review.[4] In Paris itself, the new edition of Le Sage's *Œuvres* in 1828 had been preceded by numerous reincarnations of Asmodeus in all shapes, from a two-volume 'philosophical and moral tableau' entitled *Le Nouveau Diable boiteux* by Publicola Chaussard, in which the devil and his companion fly to post-revolutionary Paris by balloon (1799), via a 'guide anecdotique' to the capital aimed at foreigners

---

3 See p. 82. The year in which the *Microcosm* started to appear, 1808, also saw the publication of 'a three-volume pastiche on contemporary manners' called *Asmodeus or The Devil in London. A Sketch* by Charles Sedley. See Michael Sadleir, *Bulwer and His Wife. A Panorama 1803-1836* (London: Constable, 1933), p. 299, note 1. Sadleir here curiously refers to the form in which the 'satirical commentary' is presented as 'dialogues between Asmodeus and the Devil'.

4 See Ursula E. Koch, *Der Teufel in Berlin* (Cologne: Informationspresse – Leske, 1991), p. 31 and note 22: 'Der Autor diente dem in Berlin zu Besuch weilenden "Teufel" als fiktiver Fremdenführer und beschrieb in Form satirischer Dialoge, unter stetigen Hinweisen auf Wien, London und Paris "alle Gegenstände und Erscheinungen des bürgerlichen Lebens, in bunter Reihe wie ein Maskenzug im Karneval"'. Koch here quotes a 'programmatic statement' relating to *Der hinkende Teufel*.

(1823),[5] a periodical created by Horace Raisson in the early 1820s which eventually became *Le Diable boiteux. Feuilleton littéraire. Journal des spectacles, des mœurs, des arts et des modes*,[6] to a forerunner of the modern department store, a 'magasin de nouveautés' called *Le Diable boiteux*, in Restoration Paris.[7] If there is a common denominator to all these diabolical references, it must be the claim to provide an all-embracing reflection of contemporary mores, be it in the form of observation and criticism, characters, or stocks of fashionable merchandise.

After 1830, Le Sage's devil became omnipresent in a dazzling array of city sketches. 'Asmodeus is everywhere; Asmodeus is no longer somebody in particular, but he is everybody', remarked Jules Janin in 'Asmodée', his essay introducing the *Livre des Cent-et-un*.[8] The enormous scale on which observers of mores operated after the July Revolution, as regards both subject matter and the range of their means of production and circulation, is indeed a distinguishing feature. Nothing of this magnitude had ever been achieved before, nor had such semiological shrewdness been displayed by writers who were also conscious of the fact that social anatomy was an industry. Thanks to these qualities, the art of reading physiognomies and of obtaining insight into the social body lost any pretence to exclusivity. The fashionable, dandified analyst of 'Society' during the Regency and the 1820s (epitomised by Pierce Egan whose *Life in London* bears a dedication to George IV), was succeeded by the 'popular portraitists' who came together in *Heads of the People* and *Punch*. In Germany and Austria, too, socio-physiognomic reading was perceived to be spreading on a considerable scale. A Viennese first-person observer of the early 1840s, publishing in *Wien und die Wiener*, takes it for granted that the reader will be a fellow 'Lavaterian', able to divine in a crowd

---

5 See Karlheinz Stierle, *Der Mythos von Paris* (Munich, Vienna: Hanser, 1993), pp. 143-4.

6 Balzac was a collaborator on the *Feuilleton littérarire*, which originated from *Le Diable boiteux* and then seems to have bought up its own progenitor to become *Le Diable boiteux. Feuilleton littéraire. Journal des Spectacles* etc.; see Balzac, *Œuvres diverses*, ed. by Pierre-Georges Castex (Paris: Gallimard, 1990–), II (1996), ed. by Roland Chollet and René Guise, editors' notes pp. 1297-8.

7 See Walter Benjamin, 'Das Passagen-Werk', in *Gesammelte Schriften*, ed. by Rolf Tiedemann and Hermann Schweppenhäuser, 7 vols (Frankfurt a. M.: Suhrkamp, 1991), V,1-2 (V,1, 87 and 103).

8 'Asmodée est partout; Asmodée n'est plus quelqu'un, Asmodée c'est tout le monde.' Jules Janin, 'Asmodée', in *Paris, ou Le Livre des Cent-et-un*, 15 vols (Paris: Ladvocat, 1831-4), I, 1-15 (p. 14).

madly waltzing past 'the physiognomies of individual professions and classes at first sight'.[9] The quantitative and qualitative leap in social sign-reading after 1830 was expressly reflected upon in France: 'The individual mocking observer does not exist any more'; instead, 'everybody is studying and commenting on the way we live', according to Janin in the *Livre des Cent-et-un*.[10] This first (and as yet unillustrated) collaborative series of Paris sketches was originally announced as *Le Diable boiteux à Paris*,[11] but the title it was eventually given proved much more appropriate. One hundred and one contributors or more – the list of signatories who had pledged their support includes over one hundred and fifty[12] – seemed to lend ample evidence to the assertion that penetrating the mores of the time was no longer the business of the lone moralist. Fifteen years before, in 1815, the first-person 'hermit' in Jouy's series boasted of a 'penetrating' and 'intrusive' eye able to discern the motives of people's actions and to decipher the habits, characters and professions of pedestrians from the way they moved in the streets of Paris.[13] The fact that by 1831 a whole generation of men (and women) of letters was apparently able to make this claim is given a methodological explanation in the *Livre*. The complexity of *mœurs* in the 1830s, we read in its address 'Au Public', has made wide-spread sign reading necessary, and to portray this complexity, a

---

9 'Da finden wir denn ohne Schwierigkeit – denn der Leser und ich sind ein Paar Lavaterianer – die Physiognomien der einzelnen Stände und Klassen gleich auf den ersten Blick aus der Gesamtmasse heraus.' C.F. Langer, 'Wiener Carnevals-Freuden. I. Oeffentliche Bälle und Redouten', in *Wien und die Wiener, in Bildern aus dem Leben* (Pesth: Heckenast, 1844), pp. 383-99 (p. 389).
10 'Il n'y a plus de railleur en particulier, en revanche tout le monde étudie et corrige les mœurs [...].' Janin, 'Asmodée' (note 8), p. 14.
11 See the publisher's note 'Au public', in *Paris, ou Le Livre des Cent-et-un* (note 8), I, v-xv (p. v).
12 See ibid., pp. xi-xv.
13 'Je pénètre ce que je regarde; je suis doué d'un coup-d'œil *intrusif* qui me montre les gens *intus et in cute*; je démêle jusque dans leur repos le mobile de leurs actions'; 'j'en suis venu au point de reconnaître, à la contenance, à la démarche d'un passant, sa profession, ses habitudes, et même son caractère'. Chapter 'XXVI. – 25 décembre 1815. Les Passans', in Etienne de Jouy, *L'Hermite de la Guiane, ou Obervations sur les mœurs et les usages français au commencement du XIXe siècle*, 3 vols (Paris: Pillet, 1816-17), I (1816), 325-37 (p. 325 and p. 326). See also Stierle, *Mythos* (note 5) where Jouy, and in particular his observation of pedestrians, is discussed as 'possibly the earliest representation of this specific experience of the big city' ('vielleicht die früheste Darstellung dieser spezifischen Erfahrung der großen Stadt'), pp. 173-4.

differentiated kind of observation is required, involving a big group of spectators and therefore resulting in a 'multiple painting' ('peinture multiple').[14] The *Livre* was remarkable also in exploiting a form of publication in serial volumes for its innovative 'encyclopaedia of contemporary ideas',[15] intended to save the publisher Ladvocat who, like many of his colleagues, was threatened by ruin because of the crisis in the book trade, aggravated by the competition of journals.[16] The vignette on the title page, designed by Henry Monnier and engraved by Charles Thompson, showed Asmodeus wielding his stick, seated on Diogenes's barrel, and a writer taking notes from observation – no doubt Addison, one of the fathers of journalism (illustration 26, p. 168).[17] Ten years later, the recipe of publishing an *Encyclopédie morale du dix-neuvième siècle* in the instalments of *Les Français peints par eux-mêmes* had triumphed.

The shockwaves of July 1830, the Cholera, the Reform Bill, the penny periodicals and their international network, the increasing literacy of lower social strata, the awareness of a 'young', in other words, politically radical generation rising to power through journalism in the cities of Europe, the first signs of poverty on an industrial scale, the shrinkage of space and time effected by the railway and the telegraph, – all these factors came together in the idea of a supranational spirit of the times whose incarnation was Asmodeus, the figure representing overviewing and penetrating vision and an acute ability to diagnose the state of the contemporary European body. It is impossible to determine whether Bulwer's series 'Asmodeus at Large' in the *New Monthly Magazine*, appearing at the time of the Reform Bill, where the devil and the first-person observer unfold a parallel vision of London and Paris, was inspired particularly by the *Livre des Cent-et-un* which started in 1831 or whether it drew on the Asmodean tradition in more general ways. It seems equally open to speculation whether the short-lived satirical journal of 1832, *Asmodeus, or the Devil in London*, which started as *The Devil in London* and was illustrated by Kenny Meadows and Isaac Robert Cruikshank, has to be seen as a response to Bulwer's series or whether, like *Figaro in London* and later *Punch*, it took its inspiration from Parisian publishing.[18] 1833, when a

---

14 'Au public', in *Paris, ou Le Livre des Cent-et-un* (note 11), p. vii.
15 '[U]ne espèce d'encyclopédie des idées contemporaines'; ibid., p. ix.
16 See ibid., pp. ix-x and Roland Chollet, *Balzac journaliste. Le tournant de 1830* (Paris: Klincksieck, 1983), pp. 514-15.
17 Addison's name is included amongst those inscribed on a stone table in the background of the picture.
18 See Sadleir (note 3), p. 299, n. 1; also Graham Everitt, *English Caricaturists and Graphic Humourists of the Nineteenth Century*, 2nd edn (London: Swan Sonnen-

German translation of the *Livre des Cent-et-un* reached volumes five and six, was also the year in which Gutzkow published a sketch of Berlin glee clubs, 'Die Singekränzchen', in Cotta's *Morgenblatt für gebildete Stände*, but it had possibly been intended for the German counterpart to the *Livre* which never materialised.[19] In it the author pays homage to contemporary Parisian and London journalism and to Le Sage through the figure of Asmodi, the narrator's limping friend, who has introduced him to the secret world of European high politics. Asmodi also makes the vocally untalented narrator join an amateur choir, thus get involved with a perky shop assistant, and gain insight into the leisure activities of Berlin's (lower) middle class – the actual subject of the sketch. The activity of Asmodi as a matchmaker, harking back to Asmodeus's task of arranging marriages that are morally slightly 'off', therefore remains in the background. To the initiated reader, however, the liaison between the educated middle-class narrator and the uneducated, sharp-witted working woman is flagged up as an issue of contemporary mores.[20]

It may be worth mentioning that, apart from the Asmodean fashion, Le Sage himself was in vogue during the period, the 1828 edition of his *Œuvres*, already mentioned, being a case in point. In 1833, in the *Novelist's Library* which featured mainly British and foreign eighteenth-century classics, *Gil Blas* appeared with illustrations by George Cruikshank and a frontispiece by Meadows.[21] The English translation of *Le Diable boiteux* quoted at the beginning of this Chapter is that of the 1841 edition published by Joseph Thomas, who translated the work himself after discovering the shortcomings of the hitherto current eighteenth-century translation. His *Asmodeus* also contained a biographical note of Le Sage by the celebrated Jules Janin and many vignettes by Tony Johannot, one of the leading Parisian illustrators who was also, around the same time, contributing to *Les Français peints par eux-mêmes*. This English edition therefore presented Le Sage's lesser known novel in absolutely up-to-date shape.

The culmination point of sketch production alluding to Asmodeus must be the serial *Le Diable à Paris*, in the twelfth and thirteenth instalment of which

---

schein, 1893), p. 357; Celina Fox, *Graphic Satire in England during the 1830s and 1840s* (New York: Garland, 1988), p. 82.

19 See p. 47 and note 52.

20 On 'Die Singekränzchen' as an Asmodean sketch see my own essay, 'Physiologien aus der unsichtbaren Hauptstadt', in *Karl Gutzkow. Liberalismus – Europäertum – Modernität*, ed. by Roger Jones and M. Lauster (Bielefeld: Aisthesis, 2000), pp. 217-54 (pp. 240-5).

21 See Robert L. Patten, *George Cruikshank's Life, Times, and Art*, 2 vols (New Brunswick: Rutgers University Press, 1992), I, 353-4.

Balzac's 'Histoire et physiologie des boulevards de Paris'[22] appeared in 1846. Gavarni's frontispiece (illustration 1, p. 7) epitomises the tradition of Asmodean viewing, but also its fundamental innovation, in representing the devil on the one hand as a colossal, matchstick-legged figure with an overview as well as a close-up perspective on the city, and on the other, as a composite modern figure, a 'colporteur' or hawker of cheap literature, a magic lantern performer, and above all, a man of fashion with monocle and walking stick. In other words, this devil represents the multiplicity of contemporary media in the shape of a city stroller. The printed map under his feet corresponds to the printed sheets in his basket and to the printed image that depicts him. The present-day observation of metropolitan mores is shown to be very much a matter of reproductive media.

By comparison, the burly devil dressed in Renaissance costume, cock feathers on his hat and scourge in hand, whose image adorns the 1848 satirical *Satan. Berliner Charivari*, seems extremely conventional:

Illustration 19 Title illustration of *Satan. Berliner Charivari*, 6 (1848). Wood engraving by 'Gl.'. From: Ursula E. Koch, *Der Teufel in Berlin. [...] Illustrierte politische Witzblätter einer Metropole 1848-1890* (Cologne: Informationspresse – Leske, 1991), p. 72.

---

22 Discussed on pp. 65-75 of this study.

However, despite the rather heavily Germanic Mephistophelian imagery, more cosmopolitan and Asmodean connotations are evident from the way in which the devil figure here echoes that of Gavarni. The Berlin Satan is also of superhuman dimensions and straddles a wide open space in the city's recreational Tiergarten from which tiny pedestrians are seeking to escape. The Revolution of 1848 had brought about a short spell of unrestricted freedom of the press in most German states and rekindled the cosmopolitan sentiment that was already in evidence after 1830, but was oppressed together with any stirrings of radicalism from 1832. When the political climate was heating up again in 1847, Albert Hopf, a democrat, launched a *Berliner Charivari* which soon got into difficulty with the censors, changed its name after the Revolution to the even more conspicuously radical *Satan*, and acquired the new eye-catching title vignette which remained in use when the journal became *Der Teufel in Berlin*.[23] Interestingly, *Satan* constituted a link with Parisian graphic journalism not only in its title, but in its witty use of little human figures forming letters of the alphabet (a practice also common in *Punch*). For example, the S of 'Satan' takes the form of a crouching scribbler (with devil's horns and tail) whose telltale scratching pen is under (aural) observation by an eavesdropping policeman. As a camouflage, the huge quill on the journalist's head ends in a flag showing the Prussian eagle. A satirical tale of Berlin's public mores is thus told in the graphic letters of the title. In the Leipzig *Charivari*, which had rather more staying power than its Berlin namesake, the letters of the title consisted of nothing but little devils and the odd snake:

Illustration 20   Title vignette of *Charivari*, 129 (19 March 1845), [p. 2049]. Wood engraving.

---

23 See Koch, *Teufel in Berlin* (note 4), pp. 71-5, for this information, and also for reproductions of the title pages.

The implied identification of satirical journalism with a diabolical force is not unjustified, as rulers and censors were well aware and Philipon's notorious pears satirising Louis Philippe in the early years of the July Monarchy had borne out. But there is another side to the analogy between the devil and the satirist, particularly in his function as a painter of mores. A creator of human types, his activity may verge on satanic hubris. The gigantic Frenchmen, presumably representing the producers of sketches and their publisher, who handle the puppet-size people in the illustrations of the contents table in *Les Français peints par eux-mêmes* (vol. 1), give pause for thought:

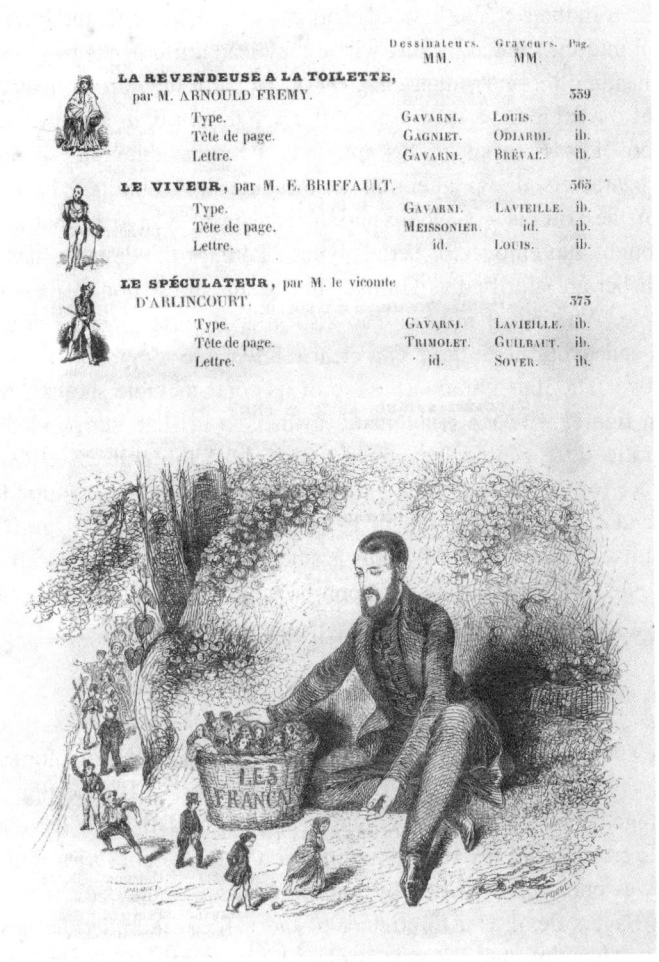

Illustration 21 [Hippolyte] Pauquet, vignettes for first and last page of contents table in *Les Français peints par eux-mêmes*. [From vol. 4:] *Encyclopédie morale du dix-neuvième siècle*, 8 vols (Paris: Curmer, 1840-2), I [381 and 388]. Wood engravings by Porret.

Are the painters in pictures and words (the head piece presumably showing the draughtsman on the left and the writer on the right) faithfully representing their own people in a national self-portrait, as the title of the serial promises, or are they creating homunculi after their own image? The arrangement of the contents table leaves this question open and thereby supplies further evidence of the potentially self-critical ambiguity that characterises the medium of sketches. From their creators' hands and contemplative gaze, the little figures slip down into the contents table, where they lead a life of their own as illustrations heading the individual chapters. Eventually they are collected at the bottom of the table by a man who will carry them off in a basket with the inscription 'Les Français'. This interplay between miniature people and graphic characters draws attention to the sketches contained between the boards of the volume – a whole nation reduced to octavo format and marketed, bought and enjoyed as serial 'types'. Perhaps the draughtsman, writer and publisher are glorified as Gulliver-like giants in relation to their Lilliputian people. Whether or not one can also infer a sense, or even critique, of Faustian endeavour here, there is a clear reference to a diabolical heritage in volume two. The illustration at the top of its contents table shows a Mephistophelian figure, with the emblematic feather on his hat, surrounded by the idiosyncratic little people that are a hallmark of the collection. Gavarni's frontispiece for the second volume depicts an angelic-demonic figure looking into a hand mirror and writing in front of a wall covered in 'graffiti', on which a bill advertising *Les Français* has been stuck. This allegorically represented contemporary moralist sits appropriately on a pile of books (illustration 22).

La Bruyère and the *histoire des mœurs*

The only author whose name is legible on the spines of these volumes is La Bruyère, the great moralist of France's 'siècle d'or'.[24] His portrait is also shown, together with that of Theophrastus, on a medallion in the elaborate arabesque created by Émy for the introduction to the whole series. This introduction was once more written by Janin. While in 'Asmodée' he had eulogised Le Sage's devil as a forerunner of the modern moralist, he now pays homage to Theophrastus' *Charakteres* and La Bruyère's *Caractères*. Le Men has suggested that the apparent obsession with their own moralist pedigree reveals a desire in mid-nineteenth-century sketch-writers, and particularly in Janin, 'the pasha of *feuilleton*', to ennoble their own business.[25] Be that as it

---

24 The stylistic significance of La Bruyère and other seventeenth- and eighteenth-century French moralists for the *Physiologies* has been examined in detail by Nathalie Preiss: *Les Physiologies en France au XIXe siècle: étude historique, littéraire et stylistique* (Mont-de-Marsan: Éditions InterUniversitaires, 1999), pp. 13-43.

25 'A vrai dire, toute cette ardeur généalogique n'est là que pour redorer le blason d'une littérature issue du journal [...]'. Ségolène Le Men, 'Peints par eux-mêmes...', in *Les Français peints par eux-mêmes. Panorama du XIXe siècle* (Paris: Éditions de la Réunion des musées nationaux, 1993), pp. 4-46 (p. 32).

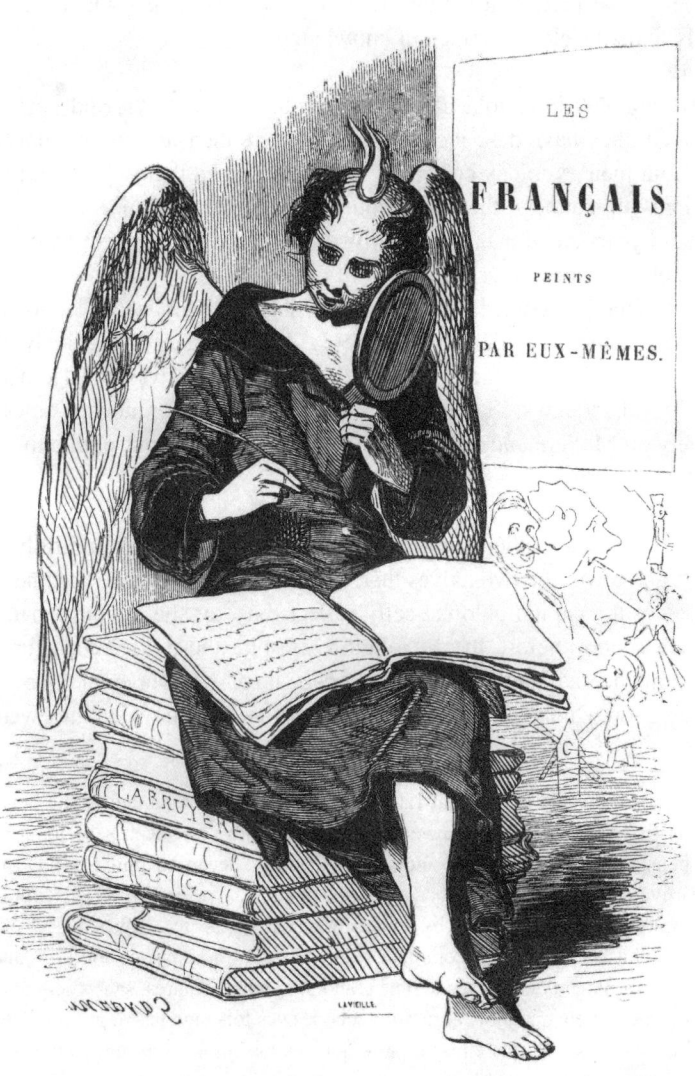

Illustration 22 Gavarni, frontispiece for vol. 2 of *Les Français peints par eux-mêmes* (Paris: Curmer, 1840). Wood engraving by Lavieille.

may, Janin's comments on the status of the historiography of mores draw attention to the fact that this whole discipline is in need of proper recognition. What the *Caractères* have in common with a work such as *Les Français*, he says, is the writing of history not in terms of battles and sieges, but in terms of people's quotidian existence. Official *histoire*, treacherous, violent and full of lies, has a corrective in the unofficial *histoire des mœurs* which is, to date, a sadly underdeveloped branch of knowledge:

> [Historians] have told us how men fought each other, and not how they lived; they have described with utmost care their armour and not bothered about their everyday coats; they have concerned themselves with laws and not with manners; they have done so much that the miserable seven thousand years since mankind has lived in society have almost been a net loss to observation and to the history of *mœurs*.[26]
>
> In fact, just consider how few moralists have condescended to enter into the simple details of everyday life! [...] With regard to the lively depiction of a people's characters and mores, Antiquity lives off Homer, Theophrastus, Plautus, Terence and scarcely anyone else; modern times have to rely on Molière and La Bruyère, two portraitists of our public life who are at once serious and humorous [...].[27]

La Bruyère and Molière split their observation neatly and faithfully between court and town, the two halves that, according to Janin (who assumes that the mores of the capital automatically reflect those of the nation), characterised French society before the Revolution. Despite the outmoded nature of this division, he maintains, there are constants of 'serious-humorous' moralist observation which will be true regardless of the age in which they were made,

---

26 This is an ironic reversal of La Bruyère's apodictic statement at the beginning of the first chapter of *Les Caractères* that everything has been said about the seven thousand years and more since human beings began to think; see [Jean de] La Bruyère, *Les Caractères de Théophraste traduits du grec avec Les Caractères ou les Mœurs de ce siècle*, ed. by R. Garapon (Paris: Garnier, 1990), p. 67.

27 '[Les historiens] ont dit comment se battaient les hommes et non pas comment ils vivaient; ils ont décrit avec le plus grand soin leurs armures, sans s'inquiéter de leur manteau de chaque jour; ils se sont occupés des lois, non pas des mœurs, ils ont tant fait, que c'est presque en pure perte que ces misérables sept mille années que nous comptons depuis qu'il y a des hommes en société ont été dépensées pour l'observation et pour l'histoire des mœurs. / En effet, comptez donc combien peu de moralistes ont daigné entrer dans ces simples détails de la vie de chaque jour! [...] Dans cette représentation animée des mœurs et des caractères d'un peuple, l'antiquité ne vit guère que sur Homère et sur Théophraste, sur Plaute et sur Térence; les temps modernes s'appuient sur Molière et sur La Bruyère, deux représentants sérieux et gais à la fois de notre vie publique [...].' Jules Janin, 'Introduction', in *Les Français peints par eux-mêmes*, 8 vols (Paris: Curmer, 1840-2), I (1840), iii-xvi (p. iv).

fashion being one of the obvious subjects. An example of the kind of timelessness Janin probably had in mind is La Bruyère's urban character portrait, 'le fleuriste': Owning a garden in one of the 'faubourgs', this man will not for 'mille écus' part with his precious *Solitaire* or *Orientale* tulips because they are to him the most beautiful things on earth; once the fashion has faded, however, he will consider them tasteless, give away the bulbs for nothing and stock his garden with whatever the mode dictates.[28]

These universally applicable classics of moralist observation aside, however, the Revolution and social developments in the nineteenth century – not least the changes since 1830 – have, in Janin's view, so thoroughly transformed the face of society that the moralist's entire navigation kit has had to be changed. Not only have the types of La Bruyère's and Molière's time disappeared or are now found in far less ridiculous incarnations, but whole systems of interaction have vanished like submerged islands whose location can no longer be identified by the navigators of the next generation.[29] Correspondingly, if faced with aspects of modern Paris, the moralists of the seventeenth century would be clueless. A whole host of types has emerged that were unknown at their time, such as the man of money (replacing the aristocratic 'grand seigneur'), the street urchin ('le gamin de Paris'), or all those new females, including the 'grisette', the 'comédienne', the 'young woman who is mad about her body' ('la fille folle de son corps'), and the 'woman who is free in the whole freedom of the word' ('la femme qui est libre dans toute la liberté du mot').[30] As to interactive systems, Janin asks what La Bruyère would have to say about the literary practices of today when, for example, he doubts the possibility of several writers together producing a masterpiece.[31]

The point made here about the division of labour in the contemporary *histoire des mœurs*, which needs to do justice to a multitude of social environments, resembles the programme of a 'peinture multiple' devised by the *Livre des Cent-et-un* almost ten years before. The huge variety of manners, life-

---

28 See La Bruyère, *Les Caractères* (note 26), pp. 393-4.
29 'Mais voici bien une autre révolution dans les mœurs et dans l'étude des mœurs! Tout un hémisphère qui disparaît! Un monde entier qui s'abîme comme font ces îles de la mer, signalées par les voyageurs de la veille, et que les navigateurs du lendemain ne retrouvent plus à la place indiquée par les hydrographes contemporains.' Janin, 'Introduction' (note 27), p. vii.
30 Ibid., p. xii and pp. vi-vii.
31 See ibid., pp. ix-x. La Bruyère writes: 'L'on n'a guère vu jusques à present un chef-d'œuvre d'esprit qui soit l'ouvrage de plusieurs: Homère a fait l'*Iliade*, Virgile l'*Énéide*, Tite-Live ses *Décades*, et l'Orateur romain [Cicéron] ses *Oraisons*.' *Les Caractères* (note 26), p. 69.

styles and modes of communication now existing have divided the 'kingdom' of France into numerous little 'republics' and make the tradition of moral observation come into its own, according it the status of a science. Every tiny social territory now needs its own 'historian in his proper place', an expert who will 'speak of what he has seen and heard in the country he inhabits'.[32] What seems surprising in the light of this argument, however, is the scant regard Janin has for Louis Sébastien Mercier who seminally transformed the moralists' 'serious-humorous', aphoristic essay genre, if not into a multi-authored city portrait, then into something paving the way for it.

'Tableaux de Paris'

Consisting of hundreds of 'pictures', Mercier's *Tableau de Paris* (1776-88) marks the inception of verbal drawing as a discursive form capturing contemporary metropolitan mores, in other words, the birth of city sketches.[33] Although Janin cannot fail to register the visual quality of Mercier's writing, he judges it in the condescending tone of the *Livre des Cent-et-un* where these pre-Revolution 'tableaux' had been referred to as 'written on the kerb' ('écrits sur la borne') and therefore stylistically no longer suitable for the refined taste of 1830s Paris.[34] Janin does not quite count Mercier among the gutter class, but among the 'valets' in the historiography of mores who have left behind 'silhouettes drawn on a kitchen wall with a trembling hand'.[35] The contrast with today's view of the *Tableau de Paris* could not be greater. Far from being deemed a Cinderella of noble moralist cousins, it is seen as the great ma-

---

32 'Ce grand royaume a été tranché en autant de petites républiques, dont chacune a ses lois, ses usages, ses jargons, ses héros, ses opinions politiques […] Il est donc nécessaire […] que chacune de ces régions lointaines choisisse un historien dans son propre lieu, que chacun parle de ce qu'il a vu et entendu dans le pays qu'il habite.' Janin, 'Introduction' (note 27), p. ix.

33 It first appeared as a serial in the *Journal des dames* and, from 1781, in book form (2 vols, Hamburg and Neuchatel, 1781; as well as London, 1781; augmented edition in 12 vols, Amsterdam, 1782-8). See Kai Kauffmann, *"Es ist nur ein Wien!" Stadtbeschreibungen von Wien 1700 bis 1873* (Vienna, Cologne, Weimar: Böhlau, 1994), pp. 210-11 and note 33.

34 See 'Au public', in *Paris, ou Le Livre des Cent-et-un* (note 14), p. ii. The expression 'écrits sur la borne' with regard to Mercier's portraits is not original; the accusation of having written his sketches on the kerb was first made against Mercier by Rivarol; see Stierle, *Mythos von Paris* (note 5), p. 233.

35 '[C]es valets de chambre de l'histoire'; 'ces faiseurs de silhouettes crayonnées d'une main tremblante sur le mur d'une cuisine'; Janin, 'Introduction' (note 27), p. iv.

trix of modern urban depiction up to and including Baudelaire's *Tableaux Parisiens*.[36] Moreover, since the cognitive model of physiognomy, developed in the late eighteenth century, enabled Mercier to formulate his portraits in terms of deciphering an urban face, in other words, in terms of a 'skill' that could be acquired, he helped to shape the tools that individual sketch-writers were learning to use in Europe's cities in the late eighteenth and in the early part of the nineteenth century. The *Tableau de Paris* is therefore discussed as a key work at the beginning of Stierle's voluminous study of eighteenth and nineteenth-century depictions of Paris, and at important junctures of Kauffmann's hardly less comprehensive survey of descriptions of Vienna in which the socio-physiognomic 'Skizze' or sketch, the equivalent of the 'tableau', emerges in the 1780s.[37] The explosion in sketch production after 1830, including the partnership between text and image, would be impossible without the serial openness and visual semiotics that characterize all 'tableaux' (or corresponding urban depictions), a genre which goes back to Mercier's enormous collection made of individual verbal pictures.

Together with the Asmodean, 'panoptic' view, Mercier's 'kaleidoscopic' view of the city – the use of inverted commas is meant to indicate that in both these cases, the epithets are anachronistic – provided another powerful model for the totalising visions which sketch collections constructed in analogy with popular media.[38] It has been suggested that the 'General view' ('Coup d'œil général') and the 'Physiognomy of the big city' ('Physionomie de la grande ville') with which the *Tableau de Paris* opens,[39] might owe something to the overview from on high at the beginning of *Le Diable boiteux*.[40] Mercier's 'Physionomie' indeed takes the spectator to the top of Notre-Dame:

> The city is round like a pumpkin; the plaster which forms two thirds of its material, and which is white and black at the same time, announces that the city is built of chalk and founded on chalk. The eternal smoke rising from those countless chimneys veils the tips of the spires; you see a kind of

---

36 See Stierle's influential article 'Baudelaires Tableaux Parisiens und die Tradition des "tableau de Paris"', *Poetica*, 6 (1974), 285-322. An English version appeared under the title 'Baudelaire and the Tradition of the *Tableaux de Paris*' in *New Literary History*, 11 (1979-80), 345-61.
37 See Stierle, *Mythos* (note 5), pp. 105-28; Kauffmann (note 33), esp. pp. 210-15 and 219-24.
38 See my Chapters 2 and 6.
39 See headings of chapters 1 and 4 in: Louis Sébastien Mercier, *Tableau de Paris. Nouvelle édition*, 12 vols (Amsterdam, 1782-8; repr. Genève: Slatkine, 1979), I, 1 and 17.
40 See Kauffmann (note 33), p. 214, n. 50.

cloud forming above so many houses, and the perspiration of this city is, so to speak, perceptible.

Yet what is to be painted in words is what the eye *cannot* see:

> I will pass over in silence Paris's topographical situation, as well as the description of its buildings, monuments and curiosities of all kinds, because I value more highly a picture of the spirit and the character of its inhabitants than all those lists one will find in the *Etrennes mignonnes*.[41] It is the moral state of the city that I have devoted myself to; to see the rest, all it takes is a pair of eyes.[42]

Whereas Le Sage's Asmodeus makes visible interiors and explains them, down to the last secrets hiding behind the bodily appearances of their inhabitants, Mercier's observation stops at the veil of smoke above the roofs. No act of magic can expose what goes on underneath; instead, the physiognomist's interpretation is required. A topography surpassing that of the *Etrennes mignonnes*, in other words, a moral map of Paris is to be unfolded by the mind that can 'read' the emissions of countless chimneys as 'perspiration', a sign of life from the city's huge social body. Physiological thought is already in evidence in Mercier, albeit not conceptually, when the sole purpose of the city's contrasting trades and professions is described as one of self- and mutual support, like the function of organs in a body:

> Looking out of the window, you contemplate the man who makes shoes in order to have bread, and the man who makes clothes in order to have shoes, and the man who has both clothes and shoes but still toils away in

---

41 *Etrennes mignonnes, curieuses et utiles*, appearing under this title since 1728, were almanachs which often contained topographical materials.

42 'La ville est ronde comme une citrouille; le plâtre qui forme les deux tiers matériels de la ville, & qui est tout à la fois blanc & noir, annonce qu'elle est bâtie de craie, & qu'elle repose sur la craie. La fume éternelle, qui s'élève de ces cheminées innombrables, dérobe à l'œil le sommet pointu des clochers; on voit comme un nuage qui se forme au-dessus de tant de maisons, & la transpiration de cette ville est pour ainsi dire sensible. / […] / Je passerai sous silence sa position topographique, ainsi que la description de ses édifices, de ses monumens, de ses curiosités en tout genre; parce que je fais plus de cas du tableau de l'esprit & du caractere de ses habitans, que de toutes ces nomenclatures qu'on trouvera dans les *Etrennes mignonnes*. C'est au moral que je me suis attaché; il ne faut que des yeux pour voir le reste.' Mercier (note 39), I, 17-18.

order to raise enough to buy a painting. Your eyes catch the baker and the apothecary, the obstetrician and the undertaker, the blacksmith and the jeweller, who all work in order to go, one after the other, to the baker, the apothecary, the obstetrician, and the wine merchant.[43]

The eye that is particularly privileged to connect the visible world to an invisible social organism and its malfunctions is that of the garret-dweller. Not only does he look down on the city below, but his place in the urban body is that of the brain. As 'in the human machine, the summit encloses the noblest part', so do the city's highest floors afford vital accommodation to those who think, write and paint; they will in fact lose their inspiration when deprived of the sight of chimneys.[44] For example, painters of *mœurs* such as Greuze and Vernet could not have formed their unmistakable genre style anywhere but in a *grenier* under the roofs of Paris; not only because of their overview afforded there, but because of their physical closeness to those parts of the population whom poverty forces to live on the sixth floor. At this point, Mercier employs his contrastive technique to particularly great effect: When the poor man rises in the morning to continue his punishing and fruitless labour, he can hear his neighbour, a gambler, returning from a night of debauchery. This individual, spatially so close to the unfortunate, but with a heart 'a thousand *lieues* distant', may have gained or lost on one single card a sum big enough to support a whole family. The thought of knocking on his neighbour's door will never cross his blunted mind. Yet there is also one whose entire sensibility is formed by the shocking diversity of fortunes that hides beneath the roofs of the city:

> The writer is often placed between these striking contrasts, and this is the reason why he becomes vehement and sensitive; he has seen from a close distance the misery of the most numerous section of the population in a

---

43 'En mettant la tête à la fenêtre, on considere l'homme qui fait des souliers pour avoir du pain, & l'homme qui fait un habit pour avoir des souliers, & l'homme qui ayant des habits & des souliers, se tourmente encore pour avoir de quoi acheter un tableau. On voit le boulanger & l'apothicaire, l'accoucheur & celui qui enterre, le forgeron & le joaillier, qui travaillent pour aller successivement chez le boulanger, l'apothicaire, l'accoucheur & le marchand de vin.' Ibid., p. 9.

44 'Comme dans la machine humaine le sommet renferme la plus noble partie de l'homme, l'organe pensant, ainsi dans cette capitale le génie, l'industrie, l'application, la vertu occupent la région la plus élevée. [...] Lorsqu'ils en descendent, les écrivains perdent souvent tout leur feu; ils regrettent les idées qui les maîtrisoient lorsqu'ils n'avoient que le haut des cheminées pour perspective.' Ibid., pp. 10-11.

city that is called rich and splendid, and this is a profound impression he will retain.[45]

For this moralist, being a painter of *mœurs* is tantamount to being an 'orateur du plus grand nombre', in other words, to speaking for those who are not fortunate, which indicates a possible relationship between *tableaux* and the rhetoric of legal defence. This, at any rate, has been suggested with regard to later descendents of the genre, the *Physiologies*.[46] His overt advocacy of the cause of the poor, apart from being an offence against the moralist's traditional impartiality, may also explain the lack of favour Mercier found in the opening note for the *Livre des Cent-et-un*. From the perspective of many intellectuals in 1831 the impoverished sections of the Parisian populace constituted a potential for republican violence one was not going to rouse again so soon after the creation of the Juste Milieu. But before long, portraitists of mores were to act resolutely as advocates of the deprived, especially in the 1840s, and it is not surprising that one of the politically more radical Parisian sketch collections should have offered a 'coup d'œil général' that was strongly reminiscent of Mercier's empathy. This was George Sand's opening contribution to *Le Diable à Paris* of 1844.[47]

In its provision of an initial overview, the 'tableau' thus links up with the older Asmodean tradition. To convey the idea of knowing, penetrating and all-embracing vision, a moralist did not, however, have to adopt a bird's eye perspective. Comprehensive and intrusive perception was also associated with the man of the world, a kind of Asmodeus on the ground, roaming the streets of the capital, not missing a bit of news in his favourite haunts, the coffee-houses, and, significantly, pioneering the very medium in which sketches were to thrive, that is to say, journalism. In Monnier's title vignette for the *Livre des Cent-et-un* (illustration 26, p. 168), Asmodeus seated on high actually seems to make an encouraging gesture to Addison who is taking notes on the ground.[48]

---

45 'L'écrivain est souvent placé entre ces contrastes frappans, & voilà pourquoi il devient véhément & sensible; il a vu de près la misère de la portion la plus nombreuse d'une ville qu'on appelle opulente & superbe; il en conserve le sentiment profond.' Mercier (note 39), p. 13.
46 See Christoph Strosetzki, *Balzacs Rhetorik und die Literatur der Physiologien* (Mainz: Akademie der Wissenschaften und der Literatur; Stuttgart: Steiner, 1985).
47 Discussed on pp. 204-8.
48 This title vignette gives great prominence to the English ancestry of contemporary moral observation. Apart from Addison's name, the commemorative stone in the background features those of Sterne, Fielding and Goldsmith.

'Mr. Spectator'

I have passed my latter years in this city, where I am frequently seen in most public places, though there are not above half a dozen of my select friends that know me [...]. There is no place of general resort wherein I do not often make my appearance: sometimes I am seen thrusting my head into a round of politicians at Will's, and listening with great attention to the narratives that are made in those little circular audiences; sometimes I smoke a pipe at Child's, and, while I seem attentive to nothing but the Postman, overhear the conversation of every table in the room. I appear on Sunday nights at St. James's coffee-house, and sometimes join the little committee of politics in the inner room, as one who comes there to hear and improve. My face is likewise well known at the Grecian, the Cocoa Tree, and in the theatres both of Drury Lane and the Haymarket. I have been taken for a merchant upon the exchange for above these ten years, and sometimes pass for a Jew in the assembly of stock-jobbers at Jonathan's. In short, wherever I see a cluster of people, I always mix with them, though I never open my lips but in my own club.

Thus I live in the world rather as a Spectator of mankind, than as one of the species; by which means I have made myself a speculative statesman, soldier, merchant, and artisan, without ever meddling with any practical part in life. I am very well versed in the theory of a husband or a father, and can discern the errors in the economy, business, and diversion of others, better than those who are engaged in them; as standers-by discover blots which are apt to escape those who are in the game. I never espoused any party with violence, and am resolved to observe an exact neutrality between the Whigs and Tories [...]. In short, I have acted in all the parts of my life as a looker-on, which is the character I intend to preserve in this paper.[49]

It is necessary to quote Addison's mock-autobiographical essay which formed the first number of *The Spectator* (1 March, 1711) at such length in order to illustrate the comprehensiveness that characterizes this anonymous observer. Despite his self-description as an uninvolved 'Spectator', his knowing position relies more on hearing than on vision; his face is a familiar sight about town, yet he does not seem to make that much of seeing others; his is an altogether more intellectual kind of insight than that conveyed by Le Sage's contemporaneous devil. The medium of journalism, and what is more, of moral

---

49 *The Spectator*, 4 vols (London, New York: Routledge, Warne & Routledge, 1860), I, 2-3.

observations issued on a daily basis in his 'paper', is also significantly different from that of picaresque fiction. The journal thus announced by the Spectator is designed to 'improve' the very mores that are observed in its pages, and this is to be achieved by impartial judgement based on knowledge. We learn that an 'insatiable thirst' for such knowledge, nourished by familiarity with just about all 'celebrated books, either in the learned or the modern tongues', made him travel to 'all countries of Europe' and even to Egypt before settling in London.[50] The observations he now makes as a city stroller and frequenter of public places are informed by an encyclopaedic education, which also accounts for the versatility with which he moves between the various social and political 'circles' of the metropolis, possessing inside knowledge of every one but belonging to none except his own 'club'. These 'select friends' in turn represent a spectrum of social types (the country gentleman, the lawyer of the Temple, the merchant, the military man, and the gallant) and are introduced as a kind of editorial team whose reasoning and common sense informs the articles in *The Spectator.*

But who is the 'Spectator' himself? His muteness ('I [...] do not remember that I ever spoke three sentences together in my whole life')[51] matches his namelessness and lack of a social role; neither statesman, soldier, merchant nor artisan, he mentally embraces all these professions. It is interesting that, at the Exchange and in its vicinity, others should take him for a merchant or a Jewish stock-jobber – both associated with the international dynamism of money. In fact, if the Spectator embodies anything, it is a currency and a value, the currency being the news from all the political, social and cultural quarters he frequents, the sum total of contemporary modes of thought and behaviour; the value being the literary gold standard forged from European letters of all ages against which the currency is measured. His presence at all places in the city where there is something to be heard or seen, the familiar sight of his figure, his seemingly aristocratic idleness which disguises an 'insatiable thirst' for news,[52] his freedom from family ties, as well as his own facelessness and anonymity, mark him out as the prototype of both the journalist and the *flâneur*. More specifically, he is the ancestor of the English man

---

50 *The Spectator* (note 49), I, 2.
51 Ibid.
52 The fact that looking out for the 'Postman' may serve as a pretence for eavesdropping on conversations in the coffee-house is due to the reliance of the developing postal service on places such as Will's, from which patrons would collect their mail. See John and Linda Pelzer, 'Coffee Houses in Augustan London', *History Today*, 32 (October 1982), 40-7 (p. 41); Jenny Uglow, *Hogarth. A Life and a World* (London: Faber & Faber, 1998), p. 22.

of letters who, in the early 1830s, narrates his adventures as a radical journalist accompanied by a present-day devil in Bulwer's 'Asmodeus at Large' (*New Monthly Magazine*, 1832-33). Different professional discourses correspond to different coffee-houses: the conversation will be political at Will's, and, with a Whig or Tory slant respectively, also at St. James's and the Cocoa Tree; theological at Child's; learned at the Graecian; and at Jonathan's, it will be business talk.[53] The names of coffee houses were indeed used as shorthand for the branches of knowledge associated with them, so that they could serve Steele as subject headings in his *Tatler*:

> All Accounts of *Gallantry, Pleasure* and *Entertainment*, shall be under the Article of *White's Chocolate-House*; *Poetry*, under that of *Will's Coffee-House*; *Learning*, under the Title of *Grecian*; *Foreign* and *Domestick News*, you will have from *St. James's Coffee-House*, and what else I have to offer on any other Subject shall be dated from my own Apartment.[54]

Thus places of sociability became, literally and figuratively, topoi of knowledge. This classification of the social body according to areas of cognition, and the corresponding socio-topographical division of journal text, indicate where the *Spectator's* and *Tatler's* legacy would be most fruitful for sketch production, namely in 'encyclopaedic' arrangements, such as Bulwer's *England and the English* and Gutzkow's *Die Zeitgenossen*.[55] Equally, an individual sketch such as Albert Smith's 'The Casino' (published in *Gavarni in London*, 1849),[56] where scientific education and public entertainment are intricately associated with a certain locality, can be seen to look back on precisely this tradition. Specific coffee houses, such as The Graecian in which Fellows

---

53 See Pelzer (note 52), p. 44.
54 *The Tatler*, 1 (12 April, 1709), in [R. Steele], *The Lucubrations of Isaac Bickerstaff* (note 1), I, 2.
55 See pp. 260-8. For explicit references to Addison and Steele, see Edward Lytton Bulwer, *England and the English* (Paris: Baudry, 1833), pp. 283-4, where the *Tatler* and *Spectator* are mentioned as the origins of the 'revolution that has been effected by Periodical Literature', and Karl Gutzkow, *Die Zeitgenossen*, 2 vols (Stuttgart: Verlag der Classiker, 1837), I, xxii-xxiii, where the periodical form of moral observation introduced by these two journals is praised as a model, even if their moralistic tone is criticised. Bulwer and Gutzkow show their indebtedness to Steele and Addison even more clearly in creative works set in the London of Queen Anne; Bulwer in his novel *Devereux* (1829) and Gutzkow in his play *Richard Savage* (1839).
56 Discussed on pp. 243-8.

of the Royal Society socialised, were affiliated with, if not the seats of, scientific education.

Apart from the coffee house, Addison's 'Spectator' regularly visits the Drury Lane and Haymarket theatres. The history of London life, according to Peter Ackroyd in his 'biography' of the city, was shaped by all forms of theatre.[57] It then seems only logical that both Steele and Addison, observers of an 'improving' kind, should also have been active as playwrights, and that plays should have served them in their journals as a main source of reflection on real-life modes and manners. There was a close correlation between the moralist agenda and the respectable stage, and significantly the prestigious Haymarket Theatre was, from 1747, in the hands of Samuel Foote – the same man who wrote and acted in the farce *The Devil upon Two Sticks*. Foote's first success, *Taste*, featuring David Garrick as the 'shady auctioneer' Puff, in fact 'dramatized' the 'arguments' of the age's most eminent moralist in the visual medium, Hogarth, who had publicly exposed the conceitedness of self-professed connoisseurs gullibly buying fake Rembrandt etchings.[58] Hogarth's painting of Garrick and his wife shows the actor with the prologue to *Taste*, written by himself,[59] and thus draws attention to the stage as a moral institution. Drama also occupies a central space in Janin's survey of *histoire des mœurs* introducing *Les Français* where Molière is represented as a historiographer of modern mores through the medium of 'serious-humorous' plays. The 'high' moralist art of witty and satirical typification certainly fed into nineteenth-century sketch production, and out of it grew, for example, the *Comédie humaine*, the century's great narrative tableau of mores which significantly alludes to the stage. However, just as sketches have a closer relative in Mercier's *Tableau* than in La Bruyère's *Caractères*, in the field of dramatic expression their more immediate cognates have to be sought in mundane forms rather than in seventeenth or eighteenth-century moral comedy or farce, and what is more, in forms that are hybrids between crafts and art, such as puppet shows, magic lantern performances and street pantomime.

One profane genre of this kind, occupying a liminal position between vocal street performance and graphic art, was satirized by Steele's alter ego Isaac Bickerstaff: '[T]he *London Cries*', he purports, have recently been subjected to profound analysis by a 'great Critick' of opera who has found reasons as to 'why Oysters are cried, Card-Matches sung, and Turneps and all other Vege-

---

57 See Peter Ackroyd, *London. A Biography* (London: Chatto & Windus, 2000), chapter 'London as theatre', pp. 147-98.
58 See Uglow (note 52), pp. 510-12 and 529-30.
59 See ibid., pp. 529-30 and 588 as well as plate xi.

tables neither cried, sung, nor said, but sold, with an Accent and Tone neither natural to Man or Beast'.[60]

City Cries, the world as a stage and the magic lantern

Street vendors, and their custom of audibly drawing attention to their wares, were a subject of European woodcuts from the early days of the printed image. Popular images of urban occupations, referred to as 'Cries', were displayed in the windows of print sellers, and thus they constitute a graphic tradition that is distinct from caricature and represents possibly the single most important visual arts influence on sketch production. Sean Shesgreen has drawn attention to the fact that the genre was a kind of theatrical text-image hybrid from the start, in that the pictures of hawkers were 'animated by poetry or prose recording their shouts or naming their trades' and hence called 'Cries':

> Spelled with a capital 'C' to distinguish vendors' likenesses from their yells, the metaphorical term 'Cries' identifies storied images that represent sounds silently, sounds and voices that, in life, were common, vulgar, transgressive, even threatening, socially and politically.[61]

Their implied taming of transgressive vulgarity apart, 'Cries', according to Shesgreen, acknowledged the urban poor as citizens and were created 'by faceless continental and English engravers', in other words, craftsmen with an affinity to the street sellers they portrayed. The earliest known set of prints of this kind, sold in Paris around 1500, marks the beginning of 'a tradition of images depicting peddlers, not as clowns or louts, but as dignified city labourers'. In the late seventeenth century, the early form of single-sheet prints of Cries, representing 'as many as thirty-six figures in visual lists of lookalike ciphers', gave way to individual prints on different leaves which were arranged as sequences or 'ensembles':

> Casting hawkers as single characters, these ensembles underscored but also promoted, after Cromwell, the new visibility of commoners and, below them, 'necessary people', the somebodies – or, in the case of Cries, the

---

60 *The Tatler*, 4 (18 April, 1709), in *The Lucubrations of Isaac Bickerstaff* (note 1), I, 20.
61 Sean Shesgreen, *Images of the Outcast. The Urban Poor in the Cries of London* (New Brunswick: Rutgers University Press; Manchester: Manchester University Press, 2002), p. 2.

nobodies – in the portrait. Introduced into England by Dutch and Italian artists, ensembles offered as few as two or as many as a hundred genre portraits, the former to be framed and hung, the latter to be bound and shelved. [...] As well as bearing one general title, ensembles carry, on individual leaves, particular captions that encouraged dismemberment for framing or reselling.[62]

The seventeenth century thus sees the emergence of the 'typical portrait' both in painting (as 'genre') and in print (as single-character 'Cries' assembled into groups), while it also marks the birth of the 'sketch' as an extempore or preliminary drawing in fine art.[63] An interest in the humble aspects of life and art, as well as the commercial dimension of reproduction, therefore inform an utterly secular, intermedial form of representation revolving around drawn and printed types, their body language and their aural presence in urban space, a tradition which nineteenth-century graphic and written sketches heavily draw on. The genre of Cries was still vigorous in the 1830s and well beyond;[64] for example, the young Gavarni published three plates (still signed with his real name, Chevalier) entitled *Cris de Paris*.[65] The fourth volume (1841) of *Les Français peints par eux-mêmes* contains a whole sequence of wood-engraved street Cries, designed by Hippolyte Pauquet – portraits of, for example, the milkwoman, the water seller or the vendor of umbrellas –, but accompanied, of course, by substantial written sketches which transform the hitherto mainly graphic tradition into proto-sociology. As Le Men and Shesgreen have emphasised,[66] the pictorial 'cris de la ville' were by definition a reproducible and also a collectable serial genre, which relates them very closely indeed to nineteenth-century sketch compilations. One could add that, by virtue of their pantomimic iconography, presenting types as actors, they relate to the 'scenes' observed by sketchers of the nineteenth-century metropolis.

According to Peter Ackroyd, London's streets owed their specific theatricality to an intense interrelationship between civic and thespian pantomime. This ancient theatre of public life produced a range of stock characters of

---

62 Shesgreen (note 61), p. 2.
63 See p. 2 of my study.
64 See French and English examples in Shesgreen (note 61); according to information on pp. 149 and 172, the last London 'Cries' appeared in 1861.
65 The young artist chose to spell his name Chevallier with a single 'l', before eventually adopting 'Gavarni' as his pseudonym. See Edmond and Jules Goncourt, *Gavarni. L'Homme et l'œuvre* (Paris: Fasquelle, 1925), p. 41.
66 See Le Men (note 25), pp. 36-46; Shesgreen (note 61), pp. 24-5 and passim.

whom many were directly or indirectly linked with acting. The Cries of London thus occupy an important place at the interface between the stage and the street. The poorer the people whose income relied on outdoor sales, the more they depended on their vocal and mimic talents, and the more likely they were to be captured as Cries. Ackroyd points to an early and well-known example of the genre, Marcellus Laroon's *The Cryes of the City of London Drawne after the Life*, published in 1687 and 'reissued by various booksellers until 1821',[67] a series that influenced Hogarth to the point of critical parody.[68] It is interesting to note that Steele satirises the *London Cries* as a semi-musical genre to be analysed in operatic terms; a demand which was actually fulfilled in characteristic 'serious-humorous' fashion about one hundred and thirty years later by the composer, music pedagogue and collaborator on the *Revue des Deux Mondes*, Joseph Mainzer. He contributed the written sketches to the 'cris de Paris' in *Les Français* which, complete with notation, must be a pioneering example of musical sociography.[69] The cries of the women street vendors in Balzac's sketch,[70] apart from being portrayed as an essential feature of the boulevard's quotidian drama, have as their backdrop a scenery of popular theatres (see illustration 12, p. 72). It seems that the close iconographic connection of Cries with the stage applies to Paris as much as it does to London. Street sellers were turned into pantomimic icons supporting a trade in parodied, copied and pirated images well before the age of industrial print, as Shesgreen's study amply testifies. Not only that, but real-life characters were able to fashion themselves after such pre-existing images of lower-class types.

---

67 Shesgreen (note 61), p. 43. His study contains a detailed interpretation of Laroon's series (pp. 45-89).
68 See Ackroyd (note 57), p. 153; Uglow (note 52), pp. 53 and 409; Shesgreen (note 61), esp. pp. 104-16.
69 Born in Trier, Germany, the *Abbé* Mainzer started his profession as a music teacher in a seminary, but in the early 1830s turned from Catholicism towards democratic liberalism. His career epitomises the Europeanness of the period, as in 1833 he left Germany for Paris where he must have had contacts with the big community of radical compatriots gathered in artisans' associations, and ended up as a highly influential music pedagogue in England. His publications in English, running to many editions, include *Singing for the Million. A Practical Course of Musical Instruction* (1841), *Music and Education* (1848) and a periodical in four volumes, *The Musical Athenæum; or Nature and Art, Music and Musicians in Germany, France, Italy, England, and Other Parts of Europe* (1842).
70 'Histoire et physiologie des Boulevards de Paris', discussed on pp. 65-75 of this study.

Not surprisingly, a city of theatre such as Vienna produced a wealth of stock characters whose provenance is an inextricable medley of moralist depiction, stage representation, visual art and reality. They include, for example, the fashionable, seductive chamber maid ('Stubenmädchen') who appears far too richly dressed and made up for her subordinate station and represents a threat to the moral order. This type emerged in an amazing interchange between late eighteenth-century satirical brochures, engraved images (including a series of 'Cries'),[71] popular comedy and real-life travesty, with prostitutes appearing on the streets and respectable ladies at balls both in the guise of chamber maids.[72] Interestingly, the late eighteenth-century satirical descriptions of Vienna first drawing attention to the type grew out of 'moral weeklies' (*Moralische Wochenschriften*) modelled on the *Tatler* and *Spectator*.[73]

Sketches were able to draw on the legacy of Cries in a highly reflective form, conscious of the process that was gradually ousting from street life many familiar types of poor men and women selling their goods or services, and of the lasting appeal that the iconography of Cries possessed. Joseph Mainzer's series in *Les Français* illustrates change within continuity, juxtaposing the present-day types with their appearance a few centuries ago while emphasising the timelessness of the respective vocal 'cry' itself. Gavarni's portrait of the 'Orange-Girl', on the other hand – a sight once common in the vicinity of London theatres –, seems to be tinged with nostalgia (illustration 23). The written sketch accompanying this plate in *Gavarni in London*, by an anonymous 'Old Playgoer' who is as perceptive of characters on the real-life stage, explicitly refers to the discrepancy between the drawn type, which follows a graphic tradition of its own, and the actual sellers of oranges now. Thirty years ago, 'fine buxom young women, with a sharp answer always ready for those who tried to banter them', were 'features in the entertainment' of the (male) spectator, and their role model – known at least to the 'Old Playgoer' – goes right back to the seventeenth century, to the days of Marcellus Laroon. In other words, female orange-vendors 'appeared to consider themselves as descendants of Nell Gwynne, and as such, bound to keep up their characters for smart repartee'. Apart from being the mistress of Charles II, Nell Gwyn(ne) was an orange-seller and

---

71 Forty copper plates of Christian Brand's *Zeichnungen nach dem gemeinen Volke besonders Der Kaufruf in Wien* (Drawings after the Common People, especially The Cries of Vienna) appeared in 1775-76. See Kauffmann (note 33), p. 491, and his plate no. 5 of the 'Stubenmädchen'.
72 See Kauffmann (note 33), pp. 178-82, esp. p. 180.
73 See ibid., pp. 133-62.

The Devil in Europe: Sketches and the Moralist Tradition 157

Illustration 23
Gavarni, 'The Orange-Girl', in *Gavarni in London*, ed. by Albert Smith (London: Bogue, 1849), opposite p. 45. Tinted wood engraving by Henry Vizetelly.

actress in one person and thus the archetypal 'Cry'. The text suggests that, since oranges are now sold by 'children and old women' who are obviously no longer acting the part, the 'Orange-Girl' will soon join the historical 'woodcuts' of 'the "cries" of London' kept 'in the British Museum'. Implicitly, the sketch's own illustration is thus shown to be of an outmoded genre.[74] Interestingly, too, the first publication to refer to Cries as a genre with a distinct history was by the keeper of prints and drawings at the British Museum, the engraver John T. Smith. His *Cries of London: Exhibiting Several of the Itinerant Traders of Antient and Modern Times* (1839) 'is a book about books. Thirteen of its thirty illustrations reproduce not hawkers, but old prints of hawkers'.[75] The 1830s therefore have to be seen as a decade in which the cognitive value of Cries as a printed form was first recognised, and the sketch industry has much to do with this recognition.

A Berlin stock character, famous for his plebeian wit and heavy drinking, was known as 'Eckensteher' or 'lingerer at corners', a class of man that could be hired to carry heavy loads, but which lost its subsistence as cabs were becoming available more cheaply for the same purpose. In 1843 Adolf Glaßbrenner published an obituary on the 'Eckensteher', significantly in the form of a satirical *dramatic* sketch, in which the character, 'Nante', who had become a staple of popular drama and caricature, and who had ironically been 'created' in a series of 1832 sketches by Glaßbrenner himself, dies as the last of his kind, having lost the battle against the chorus of cab drivers. His death, however, coincides with the birth of an allegorical genius embodying 'North German poetry of the people' ('norddeutsche Volkspoesie').[76] Theodor Hosemann's coloured copper plate satirically emphasises the Romantic transfiguration of the 'Eckensteher', full of alcoholic spirit as usual, by the spirit of the 'Rose-Girl', another type of the 'Cries' genre (illustration 24). The demise of popular stock characters who, as printed icons and stage types, have set a precedent for 'people's art', is seen as a precondition for the rise of a new, democratic form of poetic imagination, one perhaps that leaves behind the

---

74 An Old Playgoer, 'The Orange-Girl', in *Gavarni in London*, ed. by Albert Smith (London: Bogue, 1849), pp. 46-7. See also my discussion of this sketch in Chapter 6, p. 243.
75 Shesgreen (note 61), p. 170.
76 See A. Brennglas [Adolf Glaßbrenner], 'Nante Nantino, der letzte Sonnenbruder, oder: Die Entstehung der norddeutschen Volkspoesie', in *Berlin wie es ist und – trinkt*, part 19 (2nd enlarged edn Leipzig: Jackowitz, 1848; 1st edn 1843). The series *Berlin wie es ist und – trinkt* had opened with Glaßbrenner's sketch 'Eckensteher' in 1832.

humble genre of sketches. The punster Glaßbrenner inevitably exploits the connotation of reactionary immobility in the denomination 'Eckensteher'.

Illustration 24   Theodor Hosemann, frontispiece for A. Brennglas [Adolf Glaßbrenner], 'Nante Nantino, der letzte Sonnenbruder, oder: Die Entstehung der norddeutschen Volkspoesie', in *Berlin wie es ist und – trinkt*, part 19 (1843, second, enlarged edition 1848). Coloured copper plate.
From: Adolf Glaßbrenner, *Berlin wie es ist und – trinkt. Vollständiger Nachdruck der Ausgaben 1835-1850*, ed. by Paul Thiel, 2 vols (Leipzig: Zentralantiquariat der Deutschen Demokratischen Republik, 1987), II (no pagination).

A Parisian sketch of 1834 dealing with 'Cries' that advertised democratic periodicals in the early 1830s emphasises their politically subversive nature. The fact that these voices have now been silenced is not due to social change, but to oppressive legislation banning 'les crieurs publics' – little wonder since the journals *Le Populaire* and *Le Bon Sens* employed a small army of criers helping to popularise their programme of political education of the working class. This version of the March of Intellect included journalism that was actually produced by the 'ouvriers' themselves; a section in *Le Bon Sens* entitled 'Tribune des prolétaires' was written by workers for their own class.[77] The vendors of these papers were an uncomfortable vocal and visual reminder of the republican forces that had helped the 1830 Revolution to succeed:

> Before the law against the public criers you could see, amongst those serving as organs of Democracy, men in large tricolore hats and blue workingmen's smocks with scarlet edgings who would announce gravely and emphatically:
> *Le Populaire, in the interest of the French People written by Monsieur Cabet, member of the Chamber of Deputies* […].
> Close to the criers of the *Populaire* those of the *Bon Sens* would walk about tirelessly, recognisable by their red smocks, which earned them, on the part of a parliamentarian and magistrate much given to hyperbole, the strange epithet 'Satan's emissaries'.[78]

The collection *Nouveau Tableau de Paris au XIXe siècle* (7 volumes, 1834-35), in which this sketch, 'Les Cris de Paris' by Henry Martin, appeared, was a kind of radical response to the *Livre des Cent-et-un* which had explicitly distanced itself from the style of Mercier.[79] The *Nouveau Tableau* takes up the eighteenth-century *Tableau's* technique of pitting against the bright world of Parisian culture and luxury the lots of those who are shut away in misery and poverty, such as prisoners, patients in a mental asylum or the paupers

---

77 See Raymond Manevy, *La Presse française de Renaudot à Rochefort* (Paris: Foret, 1958), p. 157.

78 'Avant la loi contre les crieurs publics on remarquait, parmi ceux qui servaient d'organes à la démocratie, les hommes au large chapeau tricolore, à la blouse bleue lisérée d'écarlate, annonçant d'une voix grave et accentuée: / *Le Populaire, journal rédigé dans l'intérêt du peuple français par M. Cabet, député*, aujourd'hui exilé, par suite d'une rigoureuse condamnation. / Près des crieurs du *Populaire* circulaient incessamment ceux du journal *le Bon Sens*, reconnaissables à leurs blouses rouges, qui leur valurent de la part d'un député-magistrat très enclin à l'hyperbole, l'étrange épithète d'émissaires *de Satan*.' Henry Martin, 'Les Cris de Paris', in *Nouveau Tableau de Paris au XIXe siècle*, 7 vols (Paris: Madame Charles-Béchet, 1834-5), III (1834), 157-72 (pp. 168-9).

79 On the *Nouveau Tableau de Paris* and its differences from the *Livre des Cent-et-un* see Stierle, *Mythos von Paris* (note 5), pp. 241-50.

who have to clean subterranean sewers at night.[80] In this context, the 'cries' that have fallen victim to the ban on vocal advertising seem like a token of the collection's own commitment to what is 'banished', be it from the actual face of the city or from the pages of its recent, hugely successful 'painting', the *Livre des Cent-et-un*. The seemingly incidental reference to a middle-class politician demonising the criers of *Le Bon Sens* as 'Satan's emissaries' is therefore loaded; the assertively proletarian *cris de Paris* – a 'far cry' from the traditional ragged street vendors – are indeed a modern reminiscence of the old moralist, the devil, who now points to the deceptiveness of polite Juste-Milieu surfaces.

Apart from 'Cries', which *enact types*, the theatrical elements of the moralist heritage are also much in evidence where the *interplay* between types, classes and milieus is concerned, that is to say, in the proper domain of sketches as physiological studies. The pronounced moralist direction taken by late eighteenth-century French drama theory, for example, made it possible to conceive of the ways in which characters 'affect' each other in terms of a painting. Stierle has shown that the roots of Mercier's *Tableau de Paris* lie in Diderot's concept of 'drame' (a genre between comedy and tragedy), according to which moral depths are disclosed at certain points where the play stands still in a quasi-painterly 'tableau' capturing the emotional high-point of a scene and making characters step out of their individual selves to reveal insights into the human condition.[81] This idea of the dramatic 'tableau' was developed in analogy with the 'peinture morale' of Greuze. An obvious English parallel would be Hogarth's paintings of just such 'moments' from Gay's *Beggar's Opera*, which translate moral drama into visual art. Mercier took Diderot's anti-classicist programme further in relating the 'tableau' not so much to the human condition, but to the specific moral physiognomy of the age. Drama should paint a 'tableau of our present *mœurs*', revealing 'the interior of our houses, that interior which is to an empire what entrails are to the human body'.[82] The fact that such a revelation of the moral organism eventually took the form of Mercier's own 'tableau' of discursive sketches, not of drama, does not diminish the importance of the dramatic paradigm. More than sixty years after the first periodical instalments of the *Tableau de Paris*, *Les Français peints par eux-mêmes* was introduced as a hybrid painted drama, a

---

80 Stierle points out that the *Livre des Cent-et-un* did not neglect the dark sides of Parisian life, but tended to underplay their disturbing aspects; see ibid., p. 244.
81 See Stierle, 'Baudelaires *Tableaux parisiens*' (note 36), particularly pp. 268-88.
82 '[L]e tableau de nos mœurs actuelles, l'intérieur de nos maisons, cet intérieur qui est à un empire ce que les entrailles sont au corps humain': Mercier in *Du Théâtre ou Nouvel essai sur l'art dramatique*, Amsterdam 1773, quoted ibid., p. 287.

'comedy in one hundred varied acts', in which seriousness and wit, observation and irony, sangfroid and mischievousness are united through the combined efforts of prose writers and draughtsmen. Never before, says Janin, echoing himself and the *Livre des Cent-et-un*, has moralist observation operated collaboratively, as it does today;[83] and never before has the 'science of comedy' proved so fruitful outside the theatre, more precisely, in narrative and, above all, in the visual arts. 'The painter and the draughtsman have asserted themselves as true moralists', and the drama thus unfolding will be a gigantic 'tableau' in which the whole nation participates as actors 'forced to pose' in front of the collective of literary and graphic painters of mores.[84] In fact it is not certain, in this multi-medial and multi-authored play, who are the actors, who the dramatists, and who the spectators. The actors – 'les Français' – paint themselves, according to the collection's title, which means they are also their own observers or spectators and presumably their own dramatic inventors.

This is, in a new guise, the classic moralist view of the world as a stage, a proscenium which human beings enter to play their parts and from which they will eventually exit. This ancient formula with its overtones of *vanitas* – all earthly endeavour being but a show of puppets on the strings of Death – was in fact highly productive for sketches. It allowed an utterly secular grasp of human life in terms of acting out roles that are created by 'fortune' and 'vanity', in other words, by historically relative factors such as class, wealth, education, manners and modes, whilst also permitting an understanding of social interaction in terms of a performance happening here and now, on the actually existing stage of society that can be empirically observed.[85] Interestingly,

---

83 'Du temps de La Bruyère, on n'avait jamais vu un chef-d'œuvre *qui fût l'ouvrage de plusieurs*; nous ne voyons que cela de nos jours.' Janin, 'Introduction' (note 27), p. ix.
84 'De nos jours, cette science de la comédie, trop négligée au théâtre, s'est portée [...] dans les histoires, dans les romans, [...] dans les tableaux surtout. Le peintre et le dessinateur sont devenus, à toute force, de véritables moralistes, qui surprenaient sur le fait toute cette nation si vivante, et qui la forçaient de poser devant eux. Pendant longtemps, le peintre allait ainsi de son côté, pendant que l'écrivain marchait aussi de son côté; ils n'avaient pas encore songé l'un l'autre à se réunir, afin de mettre en commun leur observation, leur ironie, leur sang-froid et leur malice. [...] De cette association charmante il devait résulter le livre que voici: une comédie en cent actes divers [...].' Ibid., p. xv.
85 Nathalie Preiss (note 24), p. 241, has drawn attention to a three-volume *Physiologie du théâtre* by Hippolyte Auger, disciple of Saint-Simon and, with Buchez, founder of the journal *Le Gymnase* in 1828. Auger refers to modern theatre not only as a

The Devil in Europe: Sketches and the Moralist Tradition 163

Thackeray's *Vanity Fair*, probably the most prominent example of a moralist nineteenth-century title apart from *La Comédie humaine*, originally bore the subtitle *Pen and Pencil Sketches of English Society* when it appeared in twenty monthly parts (1847-48) with the author's own illustrations. In the introduction to the book edition, Thackeray refers to himself as the 'Manager' of the 'Show' that is about to start again, having (in its serial instalments) already toured 'all the principal towns of England'. Thus compared to a mobile spectacle, the narrative assigns to the narrator the position of a puppeteer who manages his 'dolls' and 'figures' in the same way as life is played out on the fairground around him, by a medley of spectator-actors. The fair of human action is both timeless and immediately present:

> As the manager of the Performance sits before the curtain on the boards, and looks into the Fair, a feeling of profound melancholy comes over him in his survey of the bustling place. There is a great quantity of eating and drinking, making love and jilting, laughing and the contrary, smoking, cheating, fighting, dancing and fiddling: there are bullies pushing about, bucks ogling the women, knaves picking pockets [...]. Yes, this is VANITY FAIR; not a moral place certainly; nor a merry one, though very noisy.[86]

This sketch-like present-tense depiction connects to a worldly theatre, to the *theatrum mundi* of the Baroque stage as well as Bunyan's *Pilgrim's Progress* and Christian morality plays with their comprehensive casts from the beggar to the rich man and from Heaven to Hell, but without sharing their religious framework or ahistorical view of humankind. The notion of social interaction as role play received probably even stronger support from the *commedia dell'arte* tradition, above all, from its pantomimic stage language adopted so brilliantly by the graphic sketches of the July Monarchy, as Wechsler has shown.[87] Pantomime is translated into the body language of the metropolitan population who recognise each other and communicate in a shifting social universe by a flexible kinetic sign system. In all these respects, the dramatic aspects of the moralist tradition, understood here in a comprehensive sense, harmonise with, or are indeed indispensable to, the specific visual-verbal 'life

---

successor of the temples of Antiquity, replacing them in their sacerdotal and regenerative functions, but as a living social organism.
86 William Makepeace Thackeray, 'Before the Curtain'. Prologue of *Vanity Fair. A Novel Without a Hero*, in *The Works of William Makepeace Thackeray [...]*, 26 vols (London: Smith, Elder, 1910-11), I (1910), lii-lv (pp. lii-liv).
87 See Judith Wechsler, *A Human Comedy. Physiognomy and Caricature in Nineteenth-Century Paris* (London: Thames & Hudson, 1982).

science', the physiology of society, that sketches develop. But, as usual, they will themselves refer to more trivial forms than morality plays or Italian comedy in order to signal their affinity with the 'theatre of the world'. One such form is the Punch and Judy show, a kind of puppet version of the *commedia dell'arte*, 'Punch' actually deriving from 'Pulcinella', one of the genre's stock masks. A form of entertainment absolutely inseparable from street life and fairgrounds in Britain, its nature changed, as Patten has observed, from potentially mildly erotic to literally hard-hitting when the traditional marionettes, still used in the eighteenth century, were replaced by glove-puppets: 'The reborn Punch was [...] a combatant, beating up his friend, baby, wife, and doctor, the constable, [the hangman] Jack Ketch (whom he tricks into hanging himself), and the devil.'[88] It therefore seems little surprising that this popular hero and rogue should have found his way into political satire and have been selected as the title figure for London's *Charivari*.[89] The title and subtitle of *Punch, or the London Charivari* actually form a powerful union of associations with the theatre of the street. 'Charivari' stems from the Greek 'karebaria', meaning 'headache', and denotes the victim's physical reaction to what is meant by a 'charivari', namely, a caterwaul (or 'Katzenmusik' in German) performed outside houses of old men when they married young women, but also of widows who married young men (in other words, cases of exactly the 'ridiculous' kind of matrimony that Asmodeus arranges as part of his devilish tasks). The instruments used for this cacophonous serenade, a European custom going back to the Middle Ages, included pots and pans, rattles, cracked bells, hunting horns and the like, and the incident that was behind Philipon's choice of name for *Le Charivari* was a celebrated racket which, in 1832, punished an unpopular politician who had abandoned his radical leanings in favour of the Juste Milieu.[90]

The aggressive aspects of spectacle connoted with 'Punch' and 'charivari' are less noticeable, and certainly not of a physical nature, in Pulcinella's fellow mask, Arlecchino or Harlequin, and numerous related characters such as the clown, the jester, the fool and the 'Hanswurst' of older German popular comedy. Their particular spikiness consists in making the world laugh at its often uncomfortable mirror image. Some of the early cover illustrations for

---

88 Patten (note 21), I, 320.
89 Titles of other satirical magazines also alluded to the moralist tradition: *Le Figaro* and its European imitations to Beaumarchais' Barber of Seville, or Glaßbrenner's *Berliner Don-Quixote* to Cervantes' Knight of the Sorrowful Countenance.
90 See Ursula Koch and Pierre-Paul Sagave, *Le Charivari. Die Geschichte einer Pariser Tageszeitung im Kampf um die Republik (1832-1882)* (Cologne: Informationspresse – Leske, 1984), pp. 16-17.

Punch and the wrapper for *Wien und die Wiener* show that the iconography of all these stock comic characters was conflated into one of popular spectacle – a universal theatre where the street or fairground is the stage, and where the distinctions between fools, mimes, comic actors, stock characters and audiences become as fluid as that between live performance and graphic or written depiction.

Illustration 25a A.S. Henning, cover for first volume of *Punch* (1841). From: M.H. Spielmann, *The History of 'Punch'* (London, Paris, Melbourne: Cassell, 1895), p. 27.

In A.S. Henning's illustration, the puppets are sitting still while the comic action goes on outside their booth, around the fairground barker who is drumming up the audience, and the little pickpocket relieving the enormous gentleman of his wallet displays the dead-pan physiognomy and nimbleness of a mime.[91] Kenny Meadows's Punch is scarcely a puppet, but a grotesquely threatening mask who performs a balancing act on the shoulders of the figures below and, by staring the viewer straight in the face, makes him or her part of

---

91 The painter Benjamin Haydon depicted a very similar scene in *Punch or May Day* (Tate Gallery), a detail of which is reproduced as the cover illustration of Dennis Walder's edition of *Sketches by Boz* in the Penguin Classics series.

166 Sketches of the Nineteenth Century

Illustration 25b Kenny Meadows, cover for fifth volume of *Punch* (1843). From: M.H. Spielmann, *The History of 'Punch'* (London, Paris, Melbourne: Cassell, 1895), p. 46.

the world of fairground spectator-actors. Portrayed as acrobats, the writer and the draughtsman are part of the show, supporting the weight of the Punch pyramid, and the barker has changed into a charivari orchestra of percussion and wind instruments, wailing his trumpet at the viewer.

Wilhelm Böhm's fool on the cover design for *Wien und die Wiener* shows an image of Vienna, a daguerreotype of 1842 as one can assume, to a group of slightly incredulous-looking Viennese people whose trades or professions make them stock characters and comic actors (illustration 25c). The fool frames the scene together with the chimney-sweep, an indication of the special status this trade enjoys in the nineteenth-century comedy of mores.[92] It is

---

92 See pp. 198-200 of this study. Brian Maidment's work on representations of the dustman in nineteenth-century graphic art reveals a related role of this figure, one at the bottom of the hierarchy of trades whose association with household rubbish and

The Devil in Europe: Sketches and the Moralist Tradition 167

Illustration 25c [Wilhelm Böhm], wrapper design for serial parts of *Wien und die Wiener, in Bildern aus dem Leben*.

the sweep's sooty figure that allows an association with the devil of satire, and interestingly, his ladder leads up to the comic masks on the wall, including jester's bells that are also found on the fool's cap.

The imagery of the devil and the fool is actually united in Henry Monnier's title vignette of the *Livre des Cent-et-un*. Here Asmodeus shows his tradi-

---

ashes gives him the status of an outsider who acts at once as an observer and as a 'memento mori' character. See Brian Maidment, *Dusty Bob. A Cultural History of Dustmen 1790-1870* (Manchester: Manchester University Press, 2007).

tional signifiers, namely, a small body, a wooden leg and a stick, while also being provided with a fool's cap and ruff:

Illustration 26 Henry Monnier, title vignette in *Paris, ou Le Livre des Cent-et-un*, 15 vols (Paris: Ladvocat, 1831-4). Wood engraving by Charles Thompson.

This ensemble of signs conveys what sketches are about in synthesising dramatic aspects of the moralist heritage, – they construct ciphers of spectacle and penetrating observation that are free from suggesting any particular viewing subject.

In this respect they are again well-placed to exploit their affinity with contemporary media shows. Who else but Janin would have pointed this out? To highlight the topical, realistic and humorous quality of *Les Français*, he connects its performative aspect with a particular kind of visual-verbal entertainment. Before the reader, he says, 'we will display ourselves not just as bust portraits,[93] but from tip to toe and in as ridiculous a fashion as we can possibly muster. In that magic lantern where we shall pass in review one after the

---

93 This is a reference to the model of *Les Français peints par eux-mêmes*, in other words, the French translation of *Heads of the People* as *Les Anglais peints par eux-mêmes*, which, like its English original, contained Meadows's bust portraits of types.

other, nothing shall be forgotten, not even lighting the lantern'.[94] The projection of image after image in review-type fashion, suggesting a linear continuity of the visual experience, was indeed a characteristic of magic lantern shows, the main precursors of modern cinema.[95] Oxy-hydrogen light, which also made it possible for microscope views to be projected sharply onto big screens, turned the *laterna magica* into *the* instrument of mass instruction and entertainment of the mid- to late nineteenth century. Shown with the help of 'sliders', very much like slides in a modern projector, the coloured glass plates depicted everything from foreign sights, the wonders of nature and science, political events, and episodes taken from well-known works of literature, to melodramatic scenes, cartoons and lewd character sketches. Since illustrations from books or periodicals could also be transferred to slides,[96] Janin's comparison of the wood-engraved plates of *Les Français*, which were also available in a coloured version, to pictures of a magic lantern show is therefore not purely metaphorical. Moreover, the proximity of these shows to the variety programmes of the popular stage, 'in which everything from the clown via Hamlet to Nelson's battle is assembled, in relatively autonomous scenes, on the same plane', has been pointed out by Ulrike Hick with reference to the performances of the itinerant lantern showman Timothy Toddle.[97] This lends further evidence to sketches embracing the 'theatre-of-the-world' aspect of certain forms of popular spectacle. These include the world seen through a peep-hole. In Glaßbrenner's serial *Berlin, wie es ist und – trinkt*, for example, the peepshow man ('Guckkästner') and his programme of scenes from contemporary history which are shown and wittily 'explained' to metropolitan audiences, serves as a recurring self-referential feature.

Yet perhaps the most interesting detail, with regard to the moralist tradition, pertains to the 'magic' of the lantern. Spectres and apparitions of all kinds

---

94 '[N]ous nous montrerons [...] non pas seulement peints en buste, mais des pieds à la tête et aussi ridicules que nous pourrons nous faire. Dans cette lanterne magique, où nous nous passons en revue les uns et les autres, rien ne sera oublié, pas même d'allumer la lanterne [...]'. Janin, 'Introduction' (note 27), p. xvi. The allusion is to a French proverb ('He had forgotten nothing – except to light the lamp') which derived from popular depictions of the magic lantern, showing an ape as its operator. See David Robinson, *The Lantern Image. Iconography of the Magic Lantern 1420-1880* (London, Nutley: The Magic Lantern Society, 1993), p. 10.
95 See Ulrike Hick, *Geschichte der optischen Medien* (Munich: Fink, 1999), p. 171.
96 See ibid., p. 161.
97 'Auch in seiner Dramaturgie korrespondiert das Programm der des Varieté-Theaters [...]. Hier wird gewissermaßen vom Clown über Hamlet bis zur Schlacht unter Nelson in relativ autonomen Szenen alles auf gleicher Ebene versammelt und allein durch den äußeren Rahmen der Vorführung zusammengehalten.' Ibid., p. 179.

were a speciality of phantasmagoria shows satisfying the taste for Gothic thrill, in which the lantern image was projected on a diaphanous screen from behind, and these shows are connected to the original purpose of the lantern as an instrument of seventeenth-century Jesuit pedagogy. The Devil appearing on the wall of a dark room, with the mechanical source of his appearance well hidden, was one of the ways in which anti-Reformation tenets could be propagated.[98] While the admonition, 'memento mori', is also behind the Baroque notion of the world as a stage, a notion that – *malgré soi* – potentially supported the process of secularisation, the Devil as a mechanically controlled image, a painted shadow depending on the light from a lantern, acted as a secret agent of enlightenment. Thus, the magic lantern occupies a special place in the history of mores, serving the need for superstition on the one hand, and offering a sense of superiority over the world of magic on the other. The showman became the 'magician-engineer',[99] in charge of a miraculous *theatrum mundi* that was created, as all spectators were aware, by human craft. A sketch by Robert Seymour brings out this dialectic beautifully (illustration 27).

Responding to an objection by a female spectator against the picture which shows a baker chasing the Devil, the roguish Cockney lanternist says, 'Yes, Marm, I knows the Old'un used to get the better of the Baker, but the Gemman vot does our slides always makes the Baker get the better of the Old'un.' Sketches share with the magic lantern their involvement in the Enlightenment Project in making the mundane triumph over the mysterious, and in drawing attention to the fact that the real mysteries are everyday-people such as the female spectator herself. Why should she be disappointed by a baker 'getting the better of the Old'un'? The luminous eye of the *laterna magica*, as Gavarni's frontispiece for *Le Diable à Paris* suggests (illustration 1, p. 7), is one of the instruments of vision in the worldly universe of signifiers.

This vision owes much to the tradition of associating moralist insight with the Devil. As the next Chapter will show, however, the fact that the penetrating gaze which produces an anatomy of mores loses any connotations of demonic transgression is due to discursive processes engineered to a large extent by the sketch industry. Part of this industry is the portrait which Tony Johannot draws of Asmodeus for the 1841 edition of *Le Diable boiteux*. Here Le Sage's devil becomes yet another cipher of observation, an eccentric little physiognomy situated between fairground spectacle and street-strolling (illustration 28, p. 172).

---

98 See Hick (note 95), pp. 131-2 and 146-7.
99 Jonathan Crary, *Suspensions of Perception. Attention, Spectacle and Modern Culture* (Cambridge, MA: MIT Press, 2000), p. 274.

The Devil in Europe: Sketches and the Moralist Tradition 171

Illustration 27   Robert Seymour, cover illustration for *Sketches by Seymour*, vol. 4 (London: G.S. Tregear, 1838 [?]). Steel etching by Henry Wallis (?).

Illustration 28
Tony Johannot, frontispiece in Alain René Le Sage, *Asmodeus; or, The Devil on Two Sticks. With a Biographical Note of the Author*, by Jules Janin. Translated by Joseph Thomas (London: Thomas, 1841).
Wood engraving by Brevière.

5
Turning Insides Out: An Anatomy of Observation

The claim of sketches to offer penetrating insight into nineteenth-century mores needs to be understood against the background of scientific developments. The fact that physiognomy enjoyed a high respect as a science would be unthinkable, as Caroline Warman has argued, if the discipline had not been appropriated by the lead science of medicine. The second, new French edition of Lavater's *Physiognomische Fragmente*, under the title *L'Art de connoître les hommes par la physionomie*, was undertaken from 1806 by the doctor Moreau de la Sarthe, a representative of the 'vitalist' school which maintained 'that it required a dedicated science of "life" to understand the body properly'.[1] Moreau's annotations of Lavater's work are intended to fill 'all the gaps' the Swiss author had left 'relating to the links between physiognomy and the anatomical and physiological sciences'. The new French edition of *Physiognomische Fragmente* therefore marks the point of entry of physiognomy into medicine.[2] Moreau also edited the collected works of the comparative anatomist Vicq d'Azyr, from whom he eventually took over the editorship of the medical section of the *Encyclopédie méthodique*. Having been pooh-poohed by the original *Encyclopédie*, physiognomy hence features as a serious science in the *Encyclopédie méthodique*, its later version. In other words, from about 1800 French physiologists gave physiognomy its place in

---

1 See Caroline Warman, 'What's behind a face? Lavater and the Anatomists', in *Physiognomy in Profile. Lavater's Impact on European Culture*, ed. by Melissa Percival and Graeme Tytler (Newark: University of Delaware Press, 2005), pp. 94-108 (p. 98).
2 I have quoted Warman's translation of Moreau. The original reads: 'Nous avons pensé [...] agir d'après ses [Lavater's] principes, et nous conformer à ses intentions en remplissant toutes les lacunes qui se trouvaient dans son ouvrage, relativement à ces rapports de la physionomie avec les sciences anatomiques et physiologiques.' Ibid., p. 97.

the study of the human body. This was necessary because those keen to establish medical life science had to rely on the observation of functions in the living body.[3] Comparative anatomy, crucial though it was to the understanding of the organism, could only be carried out on corpses and skeletons. Physiognomy, the interpretation of body surfaces, thus became a kind of anatomy without dissection.[4]

By analogy with this, social life science attempted to gain knowledge of the social body by describing and analysing surface phenomena and thereby performing an anatomy of mores. Sociological sketches thus often claimed medical precision for their insights. Pierce Egan in his *Life in London* (1821), for example, expressed the hope that his 'palpitating efforts' to portray the metropolis would pass muster before the 'microscopic eyes' of the 'Professors of the Royal Academy'.[5] Bulwer, for his part, argued in 1833 that the 'light sketches' of 1820s novels (including, notably, his own *Pelham or The Adventures of a Gentleman*) had so successfully 'dissected' the fashionable exclusivity of London life that the 'public mind' had seen through the oligarchical constitution of England; it had 'pierced from the surface to the depth', had '*probed* the wound' and was now ready to '*cure*' it through reform.[6] Balzac, in 'Théorie de la démarche' ('Theory of bearing', 1833), saw the 'moral microscope' as the proper tool of the social observer,[7] while Janin in 1839 referred to the 'scalpel' as his instrument.[8] In the same year Gutzkow's *Zeitgenossen* was praised as a work of surgical perfection whose author had 'severed', 'with the meticulousness of the anatomist', 'the muscles from the mechanism of time' so that 'the most delicate nerve fibres and the arteries in which the blood flows' were exposed, 'undisturbed and unharmed'.[9] Gutzkow

---

3   See Warman (note 1), pp. 98-9.

4   Anecdotally, the *Punch* collaborator and doctor Percival Leigh had such penetrating physiognomic vision that he diagnosed a friend who seemed perfectly healthy as mortally ill by just looking at him and asking a few questions. The friend, who was not told of this prognosis, was dead within a month. See M.H. Spielmann, *The History of 'Punch'* (London, Paris, Melbourne: Cassell, 1895), pp. 299-300.

5   Pierce Egan, *Life in London; or, the Day and Night Scenes of Jerry Hawthorn, Esq. and His Elegant Friend Corinthian Tom [...]* (London: Sherwood, Jones, 1823), p. 9.

6   Edward Lytton Bulwer, *England and the English* (Paris: Baudry, 1833), pp. 315-17.

7   See Honoré de Balzac, 'Théorie de la démarche', in *La Comédie humaine*, ed. by Pierre-Georges Castex, 12 vols (Paris: Gallimard, 1976-81), XII (1981), 259-302 (p. 277).

8   Jules Janin, 'Introduction', in *Les Français peints par eux-mêmes*, 8 vols (Paris: Curmer, 1840-2), I (1840), iii-xvi (p. xv).

9   'Mit anatomischer Feinheit sind die Muskeln von dem Zeitgetriebe abgelöset und unverwirrt, unzerrissen liegen die feinsten Nervenfädchen und die blutdurchström-

himself, in 1835, praised Balzac's 'anatomy' of money.[10] By 1840 one of the contributors to *Heads of the People*, F.G. Tomlins, was able to call himself, as a matter of course, an 'anatomist' whose 'business' it was 'not to trace the history of the heads we dissect, but to characterise their peculiarities'.[11] The journalistic revolution of the 1830s entailed a democratisation of the penetrating moralist view. At the same time, the process of anatomising mores – laying-bare hidden social mechanisms – lost all associations with sinful behaviour which the opening-up of bodies used to imply. This paralleled the efforts made in Britain, for example, to make medical dissection socially acceptable. Jeremy Bentham's will in which he donated his body to anatomical study, and its spectacular autopsy in 1832, are significant in this respect. It is in this context that a discussion of the *flâneur* as a sign-reading observer has to be set. Unlike Benjamin's accepted interpretation of the type, he constitutes another figure of observation that turns insides out rather than making the the streets homely.

The *flâneur* re-examined

Like the other collections following in its wake, the *Livre des Cent-et-un* presents the *flâneur* as a new type whose existence is defined by externality, by abandoning private space and moving in the streets as well as by extroverting meaning which used to be hidden so that it becomes accessible in urban physiognomies. The *flâneur* is a cipher for the deciphering view which thrives in its proper environment, the urban crowd. This crowd is not to be understood as an object which the *flâneur* and the reader of a physiological sketch need in order to reassure themselves of their diabolical superiority as decipherers. Nor are they, from an ostensibly secure, static, unseen position, able to laugh about the Other, as Richard Sieburth argues, following Baude-

---

ten Arterien vor uns.' [Heinrich] Albert Oppermann, 'Ueber die sogenannten Bulwerschen Zeitgenossen', in *Jahrbuch der Literatur. Erster Jahrgang. 1839* (Hamburg: Hoffmann & Campe, 1839), pp. 257-310 (p. 266).

10 In his review of *Père Goriot*: [Anon.], 'Vater Goriot, Familiengemälde aus der höheren Pariser Welt. Nach dem Französischen des Balzac. […]', *Phönix*, 156. *Literatur-Blatt*, 26 (4 July 1835), 623-4 (p. 624). In this context Gutzkow's reference to 'autopsy' as the specific strength of the social dramatist Büchner is also of interest. See Gutzkow's letter to Büchner of 10 June 1836, in Georg Büchner, *Sämtliche Werke, Briefe und Dokumente*, ed. by Henri Poschmann, 2 vols (Frankfurt a. M.: Insel, 2002), II, 440-1 (p. 441).

11 F.G. Tomlins, 'The Capitalist', in *Heads of the People*, 2 vols (London: Tyas, 1840-1), II (1841), 208-15 (p. 208).

laire's theory of laughter and indirectly Benjamin's of the *flâneur* here.[12] The fantasy of seeing without being seen is exactly that of the 1820s 'swell' observing the city from the 'snugness' of a camera-obscura viewer as in Pierce Egan's *Life in London*.[13] Contrary to this perspective, the 1830s observer is included in the crowd as its reflective viewing device, and the same technique of 'reading externality' that he applies to the city needs to be applied to him as a type. Social anatomy, in other words, has passed to collective ownership.

The sketch portraying the *flâneur* in the sixth volume of the *Livre* says that it is unnecessary to lift a roof, in Asmodean fashion, to view the domestic secrets of the professional stroller. Why? Because he has none. His ambiance is the public sphere, and in order to understand him you need to watch him move about the streets. The type whose definition it is to be outside reading surfaces is himself crying out to be deciphered as a meaningful external phenomenon, and the author of the sketch is significantly named 'un flâneur'. 'Nothing', we learn, 'escapes his investigative gaze' as he moves forward 'in the middle of the crowd of which he is the centre' – not an unseen centre of power, but a recognisable type in whose reflections the seen world centres. This type, himself subject to analysis, is presented as an integral part of the general 'movement' on which his vision vitally depends. From the latest display of luxury and lithographs in shop windows to the progress of a building forever under construction, or an unfamiliar face, 'everything is to him a text of observation'.[14] This compulsive sign-reading is further described as a phe-

---

12 'Le succès de cette "littérature panorama" de l'époque a sans doute quelque rapport avec l'assurance de pouvoir voir sans être vu. Un rêve semblable d'invulnérabilité ou d'immobilité est sous-jacent au mécanisme réconfortant de la satire dans les *physiologies*, car il rend leurs lecteurs capables de jouir de la supériorité (diabolique, comme le dirait Baudelaire) du rire sans être eux-mêmes impliqués comme cibles du ridicule.' Richard Sieburth, 'Une idélologie du lisible: le phénomène des "Physiologies"', *Romantisme*, 47 (1985:1), 39-60 (p. 58).

13 '[...] safety [...] should be the primary object of the traveller. The curious, likewise, in their anxiety to behold delightful prospects or interesting views, ought to be equally careful to prevent the recurrence of accidents. The author, in consequence, has chosen for his readers a *Camera Obscura* View of London, not only from its safety, but because it is so *snug*, and also possessing the invaluable advantages of SEEING and not being *seen*.' Egan (note 5), p. 18.

14 'Le voyez-vous mon flâneur, [...] comme il s'avance librement au milieu de cette foule dont il est le centre [...]! Tout, autour de lui, ne paraît marcher, courir, se croiser, que pour occuper ses yeux, provoquer ses réflexions, animer son existence de ce mouvement loin duquel sa pensée languit. Rien n'échappe à son regard investigateur: une nouvelle disposition dans l'étalage de ce magasin somptueux, une lithographie qui se produit pour la première fois en public, les progrès d'une construc-

nomenon and actually a 'need' ('besoin') of civilisation at an advanced, 'aged' ('vieillie') stage. Because of specialisation and the division of labour, the *flâneur* has a single occupation, which is to see, and to see everything like his ancestor, the serpent of Paradise.[15] This Satanic drive towards knowing and exposing becomes 'useful' ('utile') in modern society because the observer is himself part of the crowd culture he observes. Far from enjoying the privilege of diabolical insight, he shares it with anyone who is interested and by virtue of having his portrait, written by another nameless stroller, published in a collective volume. 'Innocuous' this type may be, as Benjamin remarks with regard to all the types analysed by physiological sketches;[16] but this is beside the point. What matters centrally is the fact that observation now has no privileges attached to it, not even those of 'great literature'. Thus, the *flâneur* of the *Livre des Cent-et-un*, this heir of Satanic vision, is, typically, 'a retired general, an emeritus professor, a former merchant' or 'a diplomat temporarily off duty'.[17] As he hardly ever leaves his own *quartier* he knows 'every inhabitant and every regular' ('chaque habitant et chaque habitué') of the boulevard, and he is himself known to the staff in all the restaurants of the area. By the mid-1840s the suggestion of personal acquaintance between the *flâneur* and his environment will have gone, as we shall see in the interpretation of Ernst Dronke's *Berlin*. However, even the earlier representation of the *flâneur* as being in his element on the street is not important in terms of making a threatening environment look familiar, but in terms of demystifying the penetration of surfaces.

With this process of secularisation and democratisation in mind, I want to discuss various examples of writers observing mores in an 'anatomising' manner, and the kinds of observer figure represented in their work. It will be shown that sketches perform a moral anatomy of the anatomising eye. In doing so, they raise two issues. First, does the observer's penetrating gaze threaten to destroy its object, or can it be conducive to empathy? Secondly, how adequate is a purely physiognomic reading of the signs when it comes to social ills such as poverty and exploitation?

---

tion qu'on croyait interminable, un visage inaccoutumé [...], tout est pour lui un texte d'observations.' Un flâneur, 'Le flâneur à Paris', in *Paris, ou Le Livre des Cent-et-un*, 15 vols (Paris: Ladvocat, 1831-4), VI (1832), 95-110 (p. 101).
15 See ibid., pp. 96-8.
16 See Walter Benjamin, 'The Paris of the Second Empire in Baudelaire', in *Charles Baudelaire, a Lyric Poet in the Era of High Capitalism* (London: Verso, 1983), 11-101 (p. 36).
17 '[U]n général en retraite, un professeur émérite, un ancien négociant, un diplomate en disponibilité'; 'Le flâneur à Paris' (note 14), p. 100.

In Bulwer's 'Asmodeus at Large' the world-weary observer clearly continues the tradition of 1820s dandyism and the knowing gaze of *Pelham*. He belongs to the class with the 'cold, grey, scrutinizing eye' so memorably described by Ellen Moers in her book on the Dandy.[18] Although hardened by *ennui*, observation here is sympathetic to social change and critical of its own penetrating destructiveness. The constructive force Bulwer's criticism achieves in *England and the English* is unthinkable without this previous self-dissection of the analytical eye. 'Asmodeus at Large' is, generically, situated between novel and criticism, consisting of a series of mostly dialogical sketches and a final narrative episode. It was published in the *New Monthly Magazine*, which Bulwer was editing at the time, between January 1832 and February 1833, and its journalistic context serves as a reminder of the fact that social science received a considerable impulse from the Cholera epidemic ravaging Europe between 1830 and 1832. The same issue that contains part five of *Asmodeus* (July 1832) also has a review of J.J. Kay's *The Moral and Physical Condition of the Working Classes Employed in the Cotton Manufacture in Manchester*, in which attention is drawn to the link between the disease and enquiries into the living conditions of the working classes.[19] The appalling state, for example, of the sanitary system in the poor districts of Manchester made their populations particularly vulnerable to infection. The section *Monthly Commentary* in the April issue had already, under the heading 'The State of the Metropolis', spoken of the epidemic as a force of 'exposure', making visible to the whole of society 'the starvation, penury, and destitution which enormous masses of the people of London are hourly suffering from'.[20] The temporal conjunction between the Cholera, exposing the intolerable material situation of vast parts of the population, and the endless parliamentary dealings over the Reform Bill, indicative of the toughness of the old oligarchical system, brought home the relationship between the physical and the moral condition of society. As if this was not enough, the minds of British contemporaries were excited by 'horrors of the dissecting-room',[21] in other words, news of exhumed bodies and murdered persons being sold to schools of anatomy. A society which was badly in need of political and social reform, and the savvy to analyse and to address its ills, had not even found a civilised

---

18 Ellen Moers, *The Dandy. Brummell to Beerbohm* (New York: Viking Press, 1960), p. 37 and p. 74.
19 See 'The State of the Poor in a Manufacturing Town', *New Monthly Magazine*, 35 (July-December 1832), 53-7.
20 'The State of the Metropolis', *New Monthly Magazine*, 34 (January-June 1832), 396-7 (p. 396).
21 'The New Year', *New Monthly Magazine*, 34 (January-June 1832), p. 1.

way to foster *medical* anatomy by a guaranteed supply of bodies (which makes palpable the moral force of a post-mortem on a public figure and reformist like Bentham). What is more, the poor were the most likely victims not only of the Cholera epidemic but also of the so-called 'burkers' who sold bodies to surgeons.

Bulwer's first-person narrator-observer has all these topical socio-medical simultaneities at his fingertips. His vision is 'Asmodean' in that it penetrates the moral face of society *as a whole*, offering an overview of developments under the surface and their interconnections on a European scale. This totalising view feeds partly on the man of letters' enormous store of knowledge (hence the densely intertextual quality of the series), partly on the man of fashion's streetwise gaze and scintillating wit. Nothing, to be sure, surprises him.

Edward Lytton Bulwer, 'Asmodeus at Large' (*New Monthly Magazine*)

Like his ancestor in Le Sage's novel, Bulwer's Asmodeus is a spirit imprisoned in a bottle. Significantly, the lotion is kept in the waiting room of the quack consulted by the first-person narrator who thinks he is suffering from 'consumption' and is musing about the benefits of leaving his 'poor remains to the surgeons at once', as this will at least ensure 'newspaper credit' of his 'generosity' before he dies. The other hope he has is of quick death either from the Cholera (although the higher classes are usually not affected by it) or at the hands of the quack, 'that illegitimate sportsman of human lives, who kills us without a qualification'.[22] The ensuing conversation with the unseen demon in his bottle then gives these aphoristic thoughts a different turn. Once released, Asmodeus awaits the narrator in his own home. When the latter enters his library, expecting to meet the limping *diablotin* from *Le Diable boiteux*, he finds a respectable, well-rounded nineteenth-century middle-class gentleman. He could be taken to be a 'lawyer or professional man' as he is in possession of 'a high forehead, a sharp face, and a pair of spectacles on his nose'. This distinctly undemonic physiognomy of the Devil is all of a piece with his reading of the latest three-volume novel which the 'I', editor of the *New Monthly Magazine*, has lying on his desk (*The Usurer's Daughter. By a contributor to "Blackwood's Magazine"*, which is William Pitt Scargill, London 1832).[23] Asmodeus later admits that he has in fact looked through 'six

---

22 'Asmodeus at Large', *New Monthly Magazine*, 34 (January-June 1832), 38. For individual instalments of the series, see Bibliography.
23 See ibid., p. 41.

volumes in a quarter of an hour', reading them 'as attentively as a reviewer'.[24] The 'library' is the appropriate place (and the *New Monthly Magazine* the appropriate outlet) for the men-of-letters dialogue that develops between the narrator and the Devil, over dinners in London and Paris, in clubs, on rooftops and after theatre performances, and which sustains the knowing gaze of 'Asmodeus at Large'. By way of explaining his 'unlikely' gentlemanly exterior, Asmodeus launches into a penetrating critique of English society which focuses on the importance of surfaces:

"[...] in England men go by appearances more than they do abroad; one is forced to look respectable and portly; the Devil himself could not cheat your countrymen with a shabby exterior. Doubtless you observe that all the swindlers, whose adventures enliven your journals, are dressed 'in the height of fashion', and enjoy 'a mild prepossessing demeanour.' Even the Cholera does not menace 'a gentleman of the better ranks;' and no bodies are burked with a decent suit of clothes on their backs. Wealth in all the countries is the highest possible morality; but you carry the doctrine to such great an excess, that you scarcely suffer the poor man to exist at all. If he walk in the country, there's a Vagrant Act; and if he has not a penny to hire a cellar in town, he's snapped up by a Burker, and sent off to the surgeons in a sack. It must be owned that no country affords such warnings to the spendthrift. You are one great moral against the getting rid of one's money."[25]

These comments are trenchant because they take a step beyond dissecting fashionable society. A good decade before Carlyle's *Past and Present* and the social novels following in its wake, Bulwer here exposes a value system in which being poor counts as an offence potentially punished by death. In a society where wealth signifies morality, lawfulness and health, and poverty means crime and disease, it is an existential matter what clothes you wear. If you are too poor to pretend, your body is claimed, either by the law, by sickness or by criminals administering to the 'respectable' business of medical progress. The sarcastic remarks about those who make the codes, the higher classes, being untouchable 'even' by the Cholera, and about their moral standards being so dictatorially efficient that 'even' the Devil has to abide by them if his deceitful ways are to work, must have been hard-hitting however radical the general climate was during the years of the Reform Bill.

---

24 Ibid., p. 45.
25 Ibid., pp. 41-2.

In keeping with the medical paradigm, Bulwer's Asmodeus applies a 'salve of penetration' to the narrator's eyes to enable him to see through surfaces. In an instant his gaze pierces 'a certain palace', that of Westminster, the Houses of Parliament, but the vision vouchsafed to him here is deemed unpublishable. Inside the building, a debate about the Reform Bill is in its usual dull progress, represented in the text by three rows of asterisks. Parliamentary reports were, of course, published (Dickens was one of their writers), but Bulwer, himself an MP, observes diplomatic silence, at the same time indicating satirically that the speeches are not worth reporting. The Devil has meanwhile taken the narrator off on a flight to Paris to dine at one of its choice restaurants, the Rocher de Cancale. We do not learn *how* they fly until they have reached the French coast. Asmodeus proves a genuinely up-to-date spirit in utilising *the latest ideas* as his means of transport. Over Boulogne, a refuge of English bankrupts and therefore a microcosm of England's dire social state (complete with a 'smuggler's vessel' carrying 'a chest of human corpses for the surgeons'),[26] they avail themselves of high-flying socialist theorems as a vehicle, hoping these might transport them quickly to the French capital, the centre of progressive thought:

> We had mounted on a couple of schemes for Saint Simonizing Paris, which the Devil caught out of the soul of a French waiter, and we were up in the clouds in an instant.
> "Damn it!" quoth the Devil, very profanely, "we shall be in the moon presently. When a Frenchman does speculate, he takes good care to do it in right earnest: Earth's lost sight of before you can say Jack Robinson."[27]

This allusion to the lack of empirical observation in Saint-Simonianism, a social doctrine which loses sight of society,[28] is then followed by an application of penetrating vision to the state of France, diagnosed as being in universal transition:

---

26 Ibid., p. 44.
27 Ibid., p. 46.
28 This point was made almost verbatim two years before Bulwer's publication by Balzac: 'However dear bread may be in Paris, they will praise to you the maize harvests which the year 1840 will yield. They soar so high that they lose everything from sight [...].' ('Que le pain soit cher à Paris, ils vous vantent les récoltes que le maïs nous donnera en 1840. Ils s'élèvent si haut qu'ils ne voient plus rien [...].' Honoré de Balzac, 'Complaintes satiriques sur les mœurs du temps présent', in *Œuvres diverses*, ed. by Pierre-Georges Castex (Paris: Gallimard, 1990–), II (1996), 739-48 (p. 741).

"There is a change," said Asmodeus, as we sat perched on the dome of the *Invalids*, "there is a change in Paris since you were last here. Observe how serious the *salons* have become; the champagne of society has lost its sparkle."

I looked into the old remembered houses: Asmodeus said right – people were gambling, and talking, and making love as before, but not with the same gaiety; the dark spirit of change worked vividly beneath the surface of manners; circles were more mixed and motley than they had been; men without the *"De"* mixed familiarly with those who boasted the blood of princes; a tone of insolence seemed substituted for the tone of intrigue; and men appeared resolved rather to command the attainment of their wishes than to wheedle themselves into it.

"Fit subjects!" quoth the Devil, lighting his cigar, "for a king who rides bodkin in an omnibus!"[29]

The cigar-puffing Devil, we learn, is at heart a Tory, hence the sneering remark about the Citizen King literally rubbing shoulders with the common people on the crowded omnibus. The narrator's sympathies, however, lie with the 'dark spirit of change' that can be read from the 'surface of manners', a force which has replaced the closed aristocratic circles and the scheming and dealing of the Restoration by a mixed elite in which status and etiquette matter little. Interestingly, the physiognomic observation of lightness, grace and gaiety having yielded to an unusual bluntness, earnestness and heaviness in French manners concurs precisely with Balzac's lament about the Northern 'méthodisme' of the young 'doctrinaires' having killed 'la gaieté française'.[30] The next insight into the city's architecture includes pictures of the Home Department, of a meeting of the Saint-Simonian 'Club des Amis du Peuple' and of the interior of the Tuileries palace, home of the royal family. The eyes of a spy are required for such politically indiscreet glimpses; therefore, after their Saint-Simonian high-flying, Asmodeus and the narrator have recourse to a new intellectual vehicle which consists of 'a couple of notions of travelling from the mind of a German Prince'.[31] This is Prince Hermann Pückler-Muskau, who had visited the British Isles in the late 1820s and, in 1830 and 1831, published his revealing letters about English and Irish society. His observations largely target the distinguished circles in which he had moved as part of his very private (and unsuccessful) mission, that of seeking a marriageable, rich

---

29 Bulwer (note 22), p. 47.
30 See Balzac (note 28), pp. 743-4.
31 Bulwer (note 22), p. 113.

English heiress for himself. The mode of spying thus adopted by Bulwer's narrator indeed pertains to the observed object, the French Home Department, where the secretary-general of Casimir Périer and the Prefect of Police are studying a denunciation against the 'Amis du Peuple' and articles in the left-wing *Le Mouvement* in order to discover and invent socialist conspiracies.

Back in London, the Devil discovers that 'some one' has 'been putting our adventures into a Magazine'.[32] This self-reference to Bulwer's *New Monthly* then leads to some central comments on referentiality. In the world of letters there is never anything new; literature generates literature.[33] Thus Asmodeus himself is, of course, a 'reappearance', and by no means the first one, of Le Sage's devil; likewise, the *New Monthly Magazine* is but 'an old friend with a new face':

> It proposes to fill up a certain vacuum in English literature, and aims at the design of the Encyclopedists of France, leaving out their infidelity and so forth – to keep up philosophically with the *mouvement*, and to fight the old opinions with the new.[34]

The radicalism of the editor, much in keeping with the politics and the spirit of the French left wing, *le mouvement*, is thus shown to bear the clear signature of the changing world of the present while it also evokes the old antimetaphysical spirit and the universalism of the *Encyclopédie*. The one level of reference left out here, probably because it is too close to home, is the Byronic one. The narrator's politically progressive attitude is inseparable from *ennui*. Craving for 'novelty' because there is nothing new to divert him, he finds some relief in the latest mode: 'you appear after a new fashion', he says to Asmodeus, 'surely that is novelty enough in the world'.[35] The narrator-observer is thus himself firmly cast in the 'fashion' of a dandy to whom even the Devil and panoramic observation only offer temporary distraction. The series of dialogical socio-political sketches then turns into a sustained self-analysis of the frustrations and sufferings of the *enfant du siècle*. His disease is caused by the microscopical gaze.

In what has to be seen as a Faustian reference (and clearly anticipating some of Bulwer's science fiction, for example, *The Coming Race* of 1871),

---

32 Ibid., p. 117.
33 See also 'A Defence of Plagiarism' in the section 'The Lion's Mouth', *New Monthly Magazine*, 34 (January-June 1832), 301-2.
34 Bulwer (note 22), p. 117.
35 Ibid.

the inner secrets of nature, 'the germ and cause of things'[36] are revealed to the eyes of the observer who has progressed to a realm in the centre of the earth. Here he is privileged to *see* the invisible links which physiology and zoology can only *infer* from observation:

> Wherever I cast my eye, life upon life was visible. Every blade of grass swarmed with worlds invisible to the naked eye – but performing with mimic regularity all the courses of the human race; every grain of dust, every drop of water, was an universe [...].[37]

The gaze is at once scientific, that is to say microscopic, and speculative, seeing what cannot be seen even through a microscope. By linking microscopic imagery with vast 'imaginative conjecture' about the unity of creation (presented here as nature's 'mimicry' of humanity), Bulwer offers an early example of a nexus discussed by Kate Flint: that between the ever more minute optical vision of the century and its 'exercise of the speculative power'.[38] The narrator's vision of unity is, however, shown to be extremely relative; the same pair of eyes that can see life vibrating in everything may also in the next minute reduce everything to death and decay. The 'I', it turns out, is fated to call this destructive mode of anatomising his own. In a final narrative episode he is helped by Asmodeus, whose task since *Le Diable boiteux* has been to arrange liaisons, to enter into an affair. He falls in love with a young woman slightly below his station, only to drive her and himself to despair by his own doubt and analysis. She eventually drowns herself in the Thames. The series does not, however, end in melodrama, but in a characteristic narrator's *resumé* explaining how his problematic self ought to be viewed:

> In the narrator is embodied SATIETY which is of the world; in Asmodeus is the principle of vague EXCITEMENT in which Satiety always seeks for relief. The extravagant adventures, – the rambling from the ideal to the commonplace – from the flights of the imagination to the trite affairs and

---

36 'Asmodeus at Large', *New Monthly Magazine*, 35 (July-December 1832), 107.
37 Ibid., p. 111.
38 Quotation from John Tyndall, *Essays on the Use and Limit of the Imagination in Science*, 1870, in Kate Flint's chapter on 'dust' ('The mote within the eye'): *The Victorians and the Visual Imagination* (Cambridge: Cambridge University Press, 2002), pp. 40-63 (p. 63).

petty pleasures of the day – are the natural results of Excitement without an object.[39]

As in the affair between Goethe's Faust and Gretchen, 'PASSION' can only provide a temporary object of excitement and yields catastrophic results. The inevitable death of the woman exposes the destructive force of the analytical male gaze. Having dissected himself in this way, Bulwer's narrator reaches a gloomy verdict: 'No flowers can live long on a soil thoroughly exhausted. The doom of Satiety is to hate self, yet ever to be alone.'[40]

What 'Asmodeus at Large' presents is thus, at one level, a socio-political panorama of Europe in 1832, presented in dialogical sketches, and at another, an anatomy of anatomising vision, presented in a kaleidoscope of various forms, including straight fictional narrative. This diagnosis of the *mal du siècle* is echoed by the 'superfluous young men' in Russian, French and German literature, for example, by Gutzkow's protagonist Cäsar, 'a man capable of taking in' whatever he sees 'in an instant', and of 'isolating' components 'in such a way as to let his personality process them all and grind them into particles'.[41] This dandy whose head is a 'cemetery of dead thoughts'[42] significantly also ruins his beloved, the aristocratic Wally, through relentless analysis. Before she takes her own life, her mental health already succumbs to Cäsar's probing, knowing gaze. Since this novel can be regarded as a highly experimental piece of writing, consisting to a substantial extent of discursive, non-fictional text, it seems legitimate to discuss its most striking self-critique of penetrating vision at this juncture of my argument. In an extraordinary passage the narrative voice, doubling Cäsar's intrusive view, performs a vivisection of the heroine's brain as her consciousness has lost control:

> Wally's thoughts were exposed; the roof was wide open for every eye to see into that burning brain and to follow the entanglement of ideas. There they were all lying bare, [...] naked bodies stripped of their colourful gar-

---

39 'Asmodeaus at Large', *New Monthly Magazine*, 36 (January-June 1833), 168.
40 Ibid.
41 'Am Wege schritt [...] Cäsar, ein Mann, der imstande war, eine solche Gruppe wie die vorbeisprengende im Nu zu übersehen und jede darin waltende Figur so zu isolieren, daß er sie alle verarbeitete und an seiner eigenen Individualität zerrieb.' Karl Gutzkow, *Wally, die Zweiflerin*, ed. by Günter Heinz (Stuttgart: Reclam, 1979), p. 5.
42 'Er hatte einen ganzen Friedhof toter Gedanken'. Ibid., p. 6.

ments of speech; embryos of ideas as hideous to look at as the animalcules you detect in a glass of water when looking trough a magnifying lens.[43]

The imagery of dissection and microscopic vision, in combination with the 'embryonic' thoughts laid bare, here emphasises the gendered nature of the penetrating gaze. Autopsy was in fact often performed on corpses of female suicides. The female body thus opened up and exposed metaphorically in Gutzkow's text is a living corpse and will end up literally dead. This is merciless, anatomising vision in its most horrifically destructive form. Just as microscopic vision is here shown to be most unsettling (indicated by the topical reference to the drop of water revealing a horror cabinet of organic life),[44] anatomy is depicted as indeed transgressive. Yet Gutzkow's dandy figure, as well as Bulwer's, are almost free from demonic connotations. Their critical portrayal also means that they are diametrically opposed to Baudelaire's conception of the Dandy as the embodiment of heroic transgression.[45] As the 'principle of vague excitement', Bulwer's Asmodeus is also conceivably remote from Satan. This demon of penetrating vision experiences so many re-appearances in the nineteenth century precisely be-

---

43 'Die Gedanken Wallys waren freigegeben, das Dach stand offen, jedes Auge konnte in das glühende Hirn hineinsehen und die Verwirrung der Ideen mit seinen Blicken verfolgen. Da lagen sie alle, [...] nackte Leiber, die des bunten Gewandes der Rede ermangelten, Ideenembryone, so gräulich anzusehen wie die Infusorien, die man durch Vergrößerungsgläser in einem Wasserglase unterscheidet.' Gutzkow (note 41), p. 70.

44 Gerard Curtis's contention that 'the commodification of observation' through instruments such as the microscope 'was not unsettling', but that it simply reassured the nineteenth-century public (with the help of advertisements for optical products) 'that there exists an observable and real world beyond their standard field of observation', is therefore questionable. Microscopic observation as part of public lectures in the 1830s, for example, had a deeply shocking effect, as has already been pointed out in Chapter 2 (p. 83) and will become evident once more from Albert Smith's sketch 'The Casino' discussed in Chapter 6 (p. 245). It seems unlikely that those shocked by what they saw would have rushed out to buy themselves a microscope. See G. Curtis, 'Dickens in the visual market', in *Literature in the Marketplace*, ed. by John O. Jordan and Robert L. Patten (Cambridge: Cambridge University Press, 1998), pp. 213-49 (p. 217).

45 See the section 'De l'héroisme de la vie moderne' in 'Salon de 1846' and the section 'Le dandy' in 'Le Peintre de la vie moderne': Charles Baudelaire, *Œuvres complètes*, ed. by Claude Pichois, 2 vols (Paris: Gallimard, 1975-6), II (1976), 493-6 and 709-12.

cause the Satanic connotations of knowledge are seriously on the wane. One of the contributing factors is the sketch industry. This is not to say that sketch production makes available the unknown by imposing a layer of familiar signifiers on a world undergoing bewildering change. Nothing could in fact be further from what anatomising sketches are doing. Even if the penetrating gaze works empathetically rather than destructively, the effect can be anything but reassuring. One of Dickens's earliest sketches, 'Shops and their Tenants' (first published on 10 October, 1834, in the *Morning Chronicle*, under the section 'Street Sketches'), sympathetically extroverts the inner life of a house and ends in an extremely bleak vision. This sketch also seems to make a point of declaring that observation is no longer the privilege of the dandified man-about-town by setting the first-person observer against the 'race' of elegant idlers in stiff black neckcloths and light waistcoats, armed with the predictable 'jet canes', who spend all their time wandering along 'the leading thoroughfares' with the listless air of 'a policeman on duty'.[46] Nothing impresses them. As in 'Asmodeus at Large', a critical distance is thus created to 'satiety' with its mode of 'cold' viewing, but while Bulwer's observer is himself caught up in this mode, Dickens's develops an alternative. The reader of his sketch, included in the observing 'we', is invited to reject the dispassionate outlook of the swell and to see London's streets as 'inexhaustible food for speculation'.[47] This involves, crucially, a move from the fashionable and 'smart' to the shabby and neglected. Kathryn Chittick has noted the change of social focus that accompanies Dickens's switch from the 'Tales' he wrote for the review-type *Monthly Magazine* – witty, caricaturing narratives set in middle-class suburban environments and eventually forming the closing section in *Sketches by Boz* – to the 'Street Sketches' published in the daily *Morning Chronicle* with their emphasis on lower-class milieus and their development of 'acute' and empathetic viewing in 'succinct thumbnail narratives'.[48] The 'Street Sketches' were eventually placed in the centre of *Sketches by Boz*, in the sections 'Scenes' and 'Characters'. Even the empathetic observer, however, had to learn how to preserve a certain degree of dispassionate viewing in order to perform moral anatomy.

---

46 Charles Dickens, *Sketches by Boz. Illustrative of Every-Day Life and Every-Day People. With Forty Illustrations by George Cruikshank* (London: Chapman & Hall, 1839), p. 67.
47 Ibid.
48 See Kate Chittick, *Dickens and the 1830s* (Cambridge: Cambridge University Press, 1990), pp. 48-52.

Charles Dickens, 'Shops and their Tenants' (*Sketches by Boz*)

The subject of the sketch is the changing exterior and interior of certain metropolitan shops. This seems worthy of the taxman's attention as it is indicative of a general high fluctuation of retail traders; a considerable number of shops almost certainly 'have paid no taxes for the last six years'.[49] The tenants inhabited their premises for a maximum of two months each and were gone before the authorities could catch up with them. The fact that this irregularity seems to have escaped even the eye of the law could indicate not only lack of vision, but also lack of care for the functioning of the social body. Dickens's observing persona learns (and thereby teaches) precisely this – how to 'speculate' about social malfunctions on the basis of strict physiognomic observation. One shop is singled out as a 'sample of the rest' because it has been known to the observer ever since it was turned from a private dwelling into commercial premises.

The private house, deserted, offers the most desolate picture when one day someone removes its front-door knocker. By the disappearance of this distinctive piece of metal, the last clue to the character of the one-time inhabitants has gone. A 'theory' or 'physiognomy of street-door knockers', humorously expounded in another of Boz's *Sketches* ('Our Next-Door Neighbour'),[50] relates different types of knocker to the varying degrees of hospitality or formality which house-owners display on their front doors. The main entrance deprived of its knocker therefore renders completely faceless the already effaced house. However, the observer's sympathy with the house, referred to as 'our friend', lends it a human trait even in this state. It then undergoes a radical change of exterior and function. The observer registers this as the start of a totally new existence: one day the house has disappeared, and 'in its place' is found 'a handsome shop'. The new façade and premises seal its fate; it will never again be the 'substantial, good-looking private house' that it once was.[51]

In moves a linen draper whose eye-catching 'large bills', and particularly the 'gilt letters' spelling the name of the proprietor, have to be read as warning signs. Complete with an extraordinary display of 'ribbons and shawls' and the two 'elegant young men behind the counter, each in a clean collar and white neckcloth, like the lover in a farce',[52] this 'dazzling' theatrical exterior disguises (and thereby discloses) a lack of solidity: 'We saw all this with sor-

---

49 Dickens (note 46), p. 68.
50 Ibid., p. 45.
51 Ibid., p. 68.
52 Ibid.

row; we felt a fatal presentiment that the shop was doomed [...].'[53] Its decay can be inferred from symptoms that are familiar even today, beginning with the ticketing of sale items in the window and the placing of special bargains on the pavement, and ending with staff loss and dirty premises. Once the linen draper has gone, a chain of hapless shopkeepers follows in a downward spiral as bankruptcies accelerate. The next tenant, by all signs a widower who works elsewhere, does not disguise his lack of capital. His eldest daughter keeps the shop which is now much more plainly decorated, but still 'neat'. She tries to sell her own handmade fancy stationery. But poverty, apparent from the threadbare clothing of her siblings, will not be fended off in this way. One morning a pawnbroker is seen picking up the few pieces of furniture. Neither poverty nor the girl's consumptive state could move the landlord when payment was outstanding on Quarter Day.

To the observing 'we' it is 'perfectly clear' that the shop has 'no chance of succeeding now'.[54] Its decline is a foregone conclusion since no decent proprietor will move into a place where two predecessors have folded in quick succession. Even the most feverish 'conjecture' is at a loss as to what sort of trade will move in next. The house itself offers no clue, apart from the fact that some interior alterations are being made. It does not take a detective's intelligence to predict their outcome, but Dickens's observer modestly admits that 'we' failed to guess the obvious. Of course, the shop is being divided up. To follow the ever-varying combinations of businesses now operating side by side in such constricted space is initially amusing. The tobacconist who also sells walking sticks and Sunday papers has the greatest staying power; his opposite number behind the 'thin partition, covered with tawdry striped paper', is first a bonnet-shape maker and then a greengrocer, while he himself is succeeded by a 'theatrical hair-dresser, who ornamented the window with a great variety of "characters", and terrific combats', and then a tailor.[55] Shops opening in such seedy premises tend to be slightly suspicious, very specialised or downright exotic, and significantly, they tend to deal in modish accessories and appearances like the first tenant, even surpassing his theatrical window-dressing. The empathetic eye notices how, behind this loud and miserable façade, the physiognomy of 'our old friend' has begun to show, 'by almost imperceptible degrees', signs of a different kind of compartmentalisation. These indicate in equal measure the social class system, poverty and anonymity. The rooms other than the two businesses themselves have gradually been abandoned by the shopkeepers who now live in the little parlours

---

53 Ibid., p. 69.
54 Ibid., p. 70.
55 Ibid.

behind their shops. Nobody inhabits the upper rooms. One day a brass plate saying 'Ladies' School', mounted next to the former private door and soon joined by a second one with a different inscription, confirm the impression that living space on the upper floors has been converted into office space. To access these posher establishments, one needs to ring a bell – a different one for each. The eventual replacement of the house's front door knocker by side door bells tells a whole social history which has happened, over a few years, before the eyes of the observer. But the *pointe* is yet to come. Again, reality beats all speculative intelligence. The expectation that 'the house had attained its lowest pitch of degradation' proves wrong. The ground floor is one day found empty, front and back door open, and instead of impoverished human beings, animals are occupying the scene. A 'dairy' has just established itself in the vicinity, 'and a party of melancholy-looking fowls were amusing themselves by running in at the front door, and out at the back one'.[56] Domestic life has once and for all retreated from the house, and it seems certain that the ground floor, too, will become an anonymous space. The 'friend' is dead; physiognomy has turned into autopsy of the open body to confirm the diagnosis, which the speculative reader will arrive at. In an urban society which forces more and more people to try their luck in self-employment, living space is increasingly split up into commercial units which, the smaller they get, are less likely to sustain either the shopkeepers or their premises and accommodation. In the end, the badly needed space will be left uninhabited and underused because this is more profitable.

This sketch exemplifies the 'blackness' of Dickens's realism derived from his sketching technique. The description relies on one single example, and the observation is itself highly selective. Against the assertion that 'the rise *or* fall' of shops furnishes one of his 'principal amusements',[57] the observer focuses sharply on symptoms of decay so that the failure of a great many shops appears as the more important and the more objectively verifiable phenomenon. On the other hand, observation is shown to be necessarily a process of selection. The observing 'we' is identified as someone (or anyone) being able to choose, on the basis of first-hand experience, a truly representative sample out of 'twenty at least'.[58] What is more, to grasp the full social impact of what is being observed, the human factor needs to be paradoxically curbed. The observation even of misfortune has to be so detached as to be 'amused'; sign-reading is an entertaining, but also a seri-

---

56 Dickens (note 46), p. 71.
57 Ibid., p. 67.
58 Ibid., p. 68.

ously 'instructive' and dispassionate business.⁵⁹ However, blocking out human misery to such a degree is achieved almost against the grain. This becomes particularly clear at the point where the observer has just expressed his hope that death will now have relieved the consumptive girl of her suffering. He then immediately resumes his thread by stating his burning interest in the future of the shop: 'We were somewhat curious to ascertain what would be the next stage – for that the place had no chance of succeeding now, was perfectly clear.'⁶⁰ The abrupt turn to the main subject which does not even allow the thought of death to linger, combined with the self-ironic tone in the understatement of the observer's own curiosity, creates a kind of black humour inviting the reader to sense the underlying pathos. The pessimistic accentuation of the sketch thus not only discloses a dismal material reality, but also the passionate human interest of the observer. The more strictly he focuses on the inanimate object, the shop, the greater the scope for empathy with the human interior becomes. The penetrating gaze here works compassionately; and this is also why the house is invested with the physiognomy of a 'friend'. Far from being itself forcefully analytical, the gaze registers sympathetically the cutting-up of the space into ever smaller units. It is also truly a 'speculative', not a 'knowing' gaze, since the observer is sometimes clueless and in the end his most pessimistic prediction is surpassed by reality. All these qualities of observation contrast with the microscopical dandy eye. It is significant that the only point where this sketch applies an intrusive and knowing gaze is in the description of the snobs:

> Nothing seems to make an impression on their minds: nothing short of being knocked down by a porter, or run over by a cab, will disturb their equanimity. You will meet them on a fine day in any of the leading thoroughfares: peep through the window of a west-end cigar shop in the evening, if you can manage to get a glimpse between the blue curtains which intercept the vulgar gaze, and you can see them in their only enjoyment of existence. There they are lounging about, on round tubs and pipe-boxes, in all the dignity of whiskers, and gilt watch-guards; whispering soft nothings to the young lady in amber, with the large earrings, who, as she sits behind the counter in a blaze of adoration and gas-light, is the

---

59 '[W]e have not the slightest commiseration for the man who can take up his hat and stick, and walk from Covent-garden to St. Paul's churchyard, and back into the bargain, without deriving some amusement – we had almost said instruction – from his perambulation.' Ibid., p. 67.
60 Ibid., p. 70.

admiration of all the female servants in the neighbourhood, and the envy of every milliner's apprentice within two miles around.[61]

Those who will not be surprised by anything they see because they have already seen through and 'finished' it, find their only pleasure in fashionable and disreputable West End exclusiveness, away from the 'vulgar gaze'.[62] But they are unaware of the penetrating eye of an outsider who does not even need to 'peer' through the curtains in order to know what is going on inside. The gaze of Dickens's observer here outstrips the analytical gaze of the man of fashion by turning inside out what is not supposed to be seen. The only pleasure of this class gives the lie to its 'dignity', as it is distinctly vulgar. The gas-lit, amber queen of the cigar shop with her industrially produced jewellery, idol of all the lower-class, working young women in the neighbourhood, produces the sort of artificial thrill that can 'excite' the tired imagination of 'satiety'. Here not only the mode of observation, but the very prose style differs from that of the central part of the sketch. While this is cast in the form of past-tense narrative, more amenable perhaps to the process of empathetic observation, the passage dealing with the dandies is an analytical present-tense description with the occasional future expressing predictability ('you will meet them'). In other words, it exemplifies the 'cold' gaze that is the subject of the critique. Thus, how things are observed and the style in which this is rendered, differ according to the objects of observation. This is socially significant as it suggests a nexus between the knowing gaze, dispassionate discourse and the (would-be) aristocratic stroller on the one hand, and the speculative gaze, involved narrative and the plebeian stroller on the other. Most strikingly, empathetic viewing strongly focuses on women. We get glimpses of the consumptive girl 'as her pale face looked more sad and pensive in the dim candle-light', reflections on the fate of those like her who often end up as prostitutes in order to survive, and critical remarks about the 'charitable' ladies who 'interfere' with the lives of such women without having the faintest idea of their 'misery'. All these threaten almost to distract the observer from his business: 'But we are forgetting the shop.'[63] Chittick has pointed to the parallel between this passage and the glimpse of the fallen woman, the 'young lady in amber', through the window of the West End cigar shop. The girl unable to eke out a living by selling fancy stationery might one day end up like that, and thus a sympathetic light falls even on the female

---

61 Dickens (note 46), p. 67.
62 Chittick (note 48), p. 50, points to the fact that 'cigar shops' were 'euphemistically named places'.
63 Dickens (note 46), p. 69.

flaunting her attractions to the snobs in the passage written in the mode of the cold, intrusive gaze.[64] Perhaps Dickens's 'sentimentality' in representing certain female characters should be seen as a counter-statement to the analytical view which predominantly makes women its victims. By taking away the exclusive right to penetrating observation from the dandy class, and by exposing this class itself to such a view, Dickens's sketch democratises sign-reading. As an inclusive plural persona, his observer could be anyone with eyes to see and a mind to speculate. The past-tense narrative democratises observation by framing the subject as a simple, yet entertaining and instructive 'thumb-nail' story any perceptive city stroller could have told from personal experience. The present-tense and performative style of sketches, observed in the dialogical mode of 'Asmodeus at Large' even if its framework is cast as a past-tense narrative, is here adapted by Dickens to a first-person narrative of recollection. Passing by the same place over a period of time allows the viewer to sketch the 'biography' of the locality with hindsight in a series of physiognomic readings. Conjuring up lost presence, they turn the 'every-day life' that has disappeared from interiors into an imagined very recent past. 'Shops and their Tenants' thus empowers any observer-reader to view the city sympathetically as an archaeological site – a mode of viewing Dickens was to employ to great effect a decade later in his Italian sketches.[65]

This inclusion of 'any' stroller in the observing eye is, as has been shown, also a hallmark of the contemporaneous Parisian *Livre des Cent-et-un* where the *flâneur* is emerging as a type signifying the extroversion of interiors. Read critically, this extroversion may itself indicate a 'growing bourgeois predilection for "le dehors"', a wish of the middle class to 'appropriate, even to colonize [...] the streets and pavements of the city' after the 1830 Revolution in order to 'display itself and its own wealth to greater advantage and, above all, in conditions of complete security', as Richard Burton argues.[66] He goes on to state that this process of extroversion is fully accomplished by Haussmann's creation of the new face of Paris from the early 1850s onwards:

> The structure of houses becomes extroverted, geared [...] towards impressing the passer-by [...]; cafés, restaurants and shops are likewise conceived in relation to the boulevard, and in every aspect of existence the principle of *étalage* – with its concomitant divorce of form from substance,

---

64 See Chittick (note 48), pp. 49-50.
65 See pp. 60-4 of this study.
66 Richard Burton, *The Flâneur and his City. Patterns of Daily Life in Paris 1815-1851* (Durham: University of Durham, 1994), p. 63.

of signifiers from their signifieds – supplants the earlier norms of inwardness and concealment.[67]

If this is indeed the case, outward display becomes form devoid of substance, or rather, a surface which does not need to be penetrated any more because it is itself substantial. Viewers even of the 1830s and 40s, and by no means only of Parisian life, registered this extroversion of meaning. In 1846 Ernst Dronke, studying Berlin's street scenes, spoke of 'outward appearances' ('Aeußerlichkeit', literally 'outwardness') as 'the best characterisation' ('die beste Charakteristik').[68] However, by the mid-1840s when the potential for revolutionary class conflict arising from the progress of industrialisation was felt much more acutely than in the 1830s, and when metropolitan poverty became a serious challenge to moralist interpretation, the legibility of surfaces proved no longer sufficient as a tool for social understanding.

Ernst Dronke, *Berlin*

Dronke's book opens with a sketch entitled 'Auf den Straßen' (On the streets), a celebration of the *flâneur*: 'It is instructive for the quiet observer to stroll along the pavements and to study physiognomies'.[69] Observing Berlin's street life leads to a diagnosis of the 'unnatural state' of society, backed by statistical information. What Dronke analyses is a process of dissolution. Inequality, pauperism and crime are on the increase day by day and are undermining the three pillars of social order, in other words, the state, the family and morality. These symptoms suggest that Germany is 'on the eve of a great social crisis'; the 'movements' ('Bewegungen'; a code word for the 'left-wing' forces of change in Germany, too) will receive their decisive impetus from Prussia, and Prussia will receive it from Berlin.[70] Although in the event, the 1848

---

67 Burton (note 66), p. 68. Jonathan Crary makes similar observations in his interpretation of Manet's painting *Le Balcon* of 1868, seeing it as a manifestation of 'externality' or self-presentation without the suggestion of an interior, which requires a new technique of viewing. He also links this phenomenon to the designs of buildings along Haussmann's boulevards: *Suspensions of Perception. Attention, Spectacle and Modern Culture* (Cambridge, MA: MIT Press, 2000), pp. 83-4.

68 Ernst Dronke, *Berlin*, 2 vols (Frankfurt a. M.: Literarische Anstalt [J. Rütten], 1846), I, 13.

69 'Es ist für den ruhigen Beobachter belehrend, über die Trottoirs zu schlendern und Physiognomien zu studiren.' Ibid.

70 '[U]nläugbar [ist] aber auch, daß diese gesellschaftliche Verwirrung mit ihrer Unnatur von Ungleichheit, Pauperismus und Verbrechen, welche täglich weiter um sich greifen und alle Bande des Staates, der Familie und der Moral lösen, nicht län-

Revolution spread from Paris via the German South-West, reaching Berlin only relatively late in mid-March, Dronke's observations are acute in focusing on the social basis of revolutionary change.[71] What is interesting about this depiction of Berlin is the application of Parisian patterns of cognition. This relates not only to socio-physiognomic observation and the figure of the *flâneur*, but also to the types of the 'Grisette' and the 'Gamin' and to the two 'Physiologies' included ('Physiologie des Philisters', 'Physiologie des Korrespondenten'). With the help of such categories and methods, Dronke destroys the received idea of Berlin's plebeian character. The popular base ('Volkselement') supposedly distinguished by its stock characters that are gifted with famous Berlin wit (such as the 'Eckensteher', already declared dead by Glaßbrenner three years before),[72] is a fiction. Instead, there is a very varied population which is nevertheless united by pleasure-seeking and moral dissolution. The middle classes are obviously emulating their Parisian counterparts in not missing an opportunity to display luxury and a hedonistic lifestyle. The atmosphere of abundance and *laissez-faire* created by them affects all walks of life. In the streets one can move about incognito; hence everybody, 'from the highest to the lowest, rich and poor, religious and worldly people', succumbs to the lure of anonymous pleasure in the public space.[73] The overtness of extramarital relationships, for example, indicates a complete loss of etiquette and a levelling-out of class distinctions. This is where the 'Grisette', the unmarried young working-class woman, and her middle-class man have their place. Or the 'Berliner Köchin', the badly paid and maltreated, so-called 'cook' who is actually the maid-of-all-work of bourgeois households, and who proudly displays herself in public on her fortnightly free Sunday, arm in arm with her military lover. Clad in an astonishingly luxurious robe, a sign of 'false' appearances displaying rather than hiding her social status

---

ger fortbestehen kann und daß die Bewegungen auf diesem Gebiete den Vorabend einer großen gesellschaftlichen Krisis bezeugen. Diese Bewegungen aber werden für Deutschland in Preußen ihren Anstoß erhalten. Preußen ist Deutschland, und Berlin Preußen.' Dronke (note 68), dedication to Georg Herwegh, I, before p. 1.

71 The book was banned in Prussia immediately after publication, and Dronke, as a Prussian subject, sentenced, after a five-month period of arrest, to two more years' arrest. He was able to escape early in 1848 and flee to Brussels, where, as a member of the Communist League, he worked together with Marx and Engels. From June 1848 he was a collaborator on Marx's *Neue Rheinische Zeitung*.

72 See pp. 158-9 of this study.

73 '[D]as Leben reizt mit allen Verlockungen zum Genuß und so treten dann Alle, vom Höchsten bis zum Niedrigsten, Reiche und Arme, Fromme und Weltliche [...] aus ihren Verhältnissen heraus.' Dronke (note 68), I, 12.

196 *Sketches of the Nineteenth Century*

Illustration 29 'Berliner Köchinnen (Am Sonntag.)'. Frontispiece for A. Brennglas [Adolf Glaßbrenner], 'Köchinnen', in *Berlin wie es ist und – trinkt*, part 4 (sixth edition, 1845). Coloured copper plate.
From: Adolf Glaßbrenner, *Berlin wie es ist und – trinkt. Vollständiger Nachdruck der Ausgaben 1835-1850*, ed. by Paul Thiel, 2 vols (Leipzig: Zentralantiquariat der Deutschen Demokratischen Republik, 1987), I, n.p.

as well as testifying to the carnivalesque, levelling effect of the culture of pleasure, she is portrayed in Glaßbrenner's Berlin sketch above.

Amongst the uninhibited crowd populating the streets and pleasure grounds, individualities as well as moral considerations are cancelled out:

> The city's most prominent characteristic is the disappearance of the individual in the totality of people; hence the casualness, the autonomy of the

individual who does not have to guard himself or herself against small-town, philistine prejudice.[74]

This also means that family ties are in rapid decline. The collapse of patriarchal structures and the concomitant shift from domestic to public life, from an internal sphere ruled by moral restrictions to an anonymous external sphere is obvious in the streets:

> Since domestic life is scarcely to be found any more and everybody is out to seek pleasure, life in general no longer expresses itself in hearth and home, but outside, in the uncontrolled, frenzied activity of the streets, and out there, outward appearances are again the best characterisation.[75]

For the observer, physiognomies scarcely need to be deciphered any more. The internal life which they used to conceal has been extroverted, and the loss of people's attachment to 'hearth and home' expresses itself differently in the various pleasure-seeking types of the city. The easiest ones to spot are in fact those from the provinces, the young men squandering fortunes on their elegant appearance and spending their time doing nothing. 'Their stereotypical faces' ('ihre stereotypen Gesichter')[76] can be found in any place associated with Berlin's big pleasure industry. This represents both the surface and the essence of a society in which moral bonds are continually and tacitly being loosened.

The hedonistic physiognomy of the inner city contrasts sharply with that of the outer quarters. The one beyond the *Hamburger Tor*, the so-called *Voigtland*, is particularly 'dingy and eerie' ('düster und unheimlich'), as it is here that the 'shacks of misery and despair' ('Hütten des Elends und der Verzweiflung') are found.[77] The paupers struggling for survival out here present the

---

74 'Das Verschwinden des Einzelnen in die Gesammtheit ist der vorzüglichste Charakterzug der Stadt; daher die Ungezwungenheit, die Selbstständigkeit des Einzelnen, der nicht nöthig hat, sich vor kleinstädtischen, philisterhaften Vorurtheilen in Acht zu nehmen [...]'. Dronke (note 68), I, 41.
75 'Da ein häusliches Leben selten mehr zu finden ist, und Alles nur nach Vergnügungen jagt, so findet man den Ausdruck des Lebens nicht mehr am häuslichen Heerde, sondern außer dem Hause, in dem wilden, wirren Durcheinandertreiben der Oeffentlichkeit und die Aeußerlichkeit ist hier wieder die beste Charakteristik. Es ist für den ruhigen Beobachter belehrend, über die Trottoirs zu schlendern und Physiognomien zu studiren.' Ibid., p. 13.
76 Ibid., p. 57.
77 Ibid., p. 8.

reverse side of the world of pleasure. The loosening of moral ties which affects the whole of society means, in their case, utter demoralisation. In a semi-criminal milieu where no privacy exists, children grow up 'wild and without any education' ('wild und ohne Erziehung');[78] parents send them to work in factories, knowing and sometimes hoping that this will mean their death; prostitution and theft are the last resort for those desperate to pay their monthly rent, as without accommodation they will be sent to the workhouse and end their days under an inhuman police regime. The misery of those who need to work the whole day, prostitute themselves or steal in order to vegetate, and the good fortune of those who possess in order to enjoy are two aspects of the same society based on private property and exploitation. The face of demoralisation to be seen in the 'bad areas' of the city exposes as a sham the sensuous display of immorality in the world of luxury. It indicates that the liberated classless society simulated by that world can only become real when the state of exploitation, in other words, *the state*, ceases to exist. It will be interesting to see, the text implies, how the middle classes react to the view of abject misery in the remote quarters. The *Voigtland* is now being invaded by Berliners looking for new, bigger and presumably cheaper accommodation since the city is expanding.[79]

Spatial segregation between those who have and those who have not is decreasing. At the same time, some of the children of Berlin's poor who work in the city seem to possess the most amazing social insight. A far cry from the shrewd, cheeky Berlin plebs eternalized by Glaßbrenner, these 'Gamins' shock the unsuspecting pedestrian. They come in the form of crowds of chimney-sweeps, small enough to get into the modern flues which have been built in the 'barbarous' style necessitating the exploitation of children. London portraits of the chimney-sweep (Boz's sketch 'The First of May' and a portrait in *Heads of the People*) inform us that machines operated by master sweeps were available in the 1830s and 40s, but that the conservatism of the profession, lethargic house-owners and the peculiarities of older houses kept forcing children to do the same job by climbing up flues, often suffering lethal injuries or irreversible malformations of the body.[80] In the absence of illustrations from Dronke's book, Kenny Meadows's London chimney-sweep will have to do duty for his Berlin equivalent (illustration 30).

---

78 See the chapter 'Das Proletariat', in Dronke (note 68), II, 29-69 (p. 51).
79 See Dronke (note 68), I, 8-9.
80 See Dickens (note 46), p. 185; John Ogden, 'The Chimney-Sweep', in *Heads of the People* (note 11), I, 233-40 (pp. 239-40). On London chimney sweeps, see also Peter Ackroyd, *London. The Biography* (London: Chatto & Windus, 2000), pp. 650-1.

Turning Insides Out: An Anatomy of Observation 199

THE CHIMNEY-SWEEP.

I reverence these young Africans of our own growth—who from their little pulpits (the tops of chimneys) in the nipping air of a December morning preach a lesson of patience to mankind.

ESSAYS OF ELIA.

Illustration 30 Kenny Meadows, 'The Chimney-Sweep', in *Heads of the People: or, Portraits of the English*, 2 vols (London: Tyas, 1840-1), I (1840), opposite p. 233. Wood engraving by Orrin Smith.

'Having enjoyed no education' whatsoever, says Dronke of his Berlin sweeps, these boys 'become completely degenerate in this sort of occupation'.[81] People walking in the streets, particularly women, give them a wide berth because 'the boisterousness of these little rascals defies description.' Their misbehaviour presumably consists in deliberately blacking pedestrians through physical contact (easily achieved on Berlin's pavements which are not quite wide enough for two persons, but only 'for three legs' to walk side by side).[82] Invariably, however, these boys will 'shower' anyone, regardless of gender or class, with their 'crude jokes which really often hit home', the last resort of the city's celebrated popular wit if it ever existed.[83] Dronke does not spell out in what sense these jokes 'hit home', but one can imagine that they, too, expose what is already obvious to the observer, namely, that respectability is non-existent. Deprivation explains the lack of childlike naivety in these boys, but also the fact that they literally know the city inside out, from its streets as well as from the privacy of its interiors. As streetwise victims of exploitation, these children epitomise the moral anatomy of the metropolis, a place where domestic order is yielding to the uncontrolled dynamism of public life and capitalist growth. Basing his socialist commitment on a reading of physiognomies, Dronke recognises, in the figure of the sweep, the overlap between society's loosened mores and its economic immorality.

Iconographically, the insolent, stunted sweeps who are as familiar with private spaces, the rooms and guts of houses, as with the whole geography of the city seen from rooftops and streets, are connected with the little limping devil Asmodeus and his knowing gaze. Dickens's observer attaches a mythical, heathen quality to the sweep, connected to the celebrations of the first of May.[84] Even in Dronke's analysis of urban physiognomies, which is devoid of any demonising, the provenance of the sooty rascal with his disrespectful wit from the Devil and the jester in the moralist theatre of the world can be felt, as can the analogy of the type with the penetrating view of the observer. Dronke himself, a Prussian subject, but from the notoriously radical Rhine-

---

81 'Die barbarische Sitte der neueren Zeit, schmale und enge Schornsteine zu bauen, in die man nur Kinder hineinschicken kann, hat diesem Gewerb einen großen Zuschuß von armen Kleinen verschafft, welche ohnedies keine Erziehung genossen und in diesem Beruf vollends ausarten.' Dronke (note 68), I, 16.
82 '[D]aß nicht ganz zwei Menschen, sondern nur drei Beine nebeneinander darauf gehen können'. Ibid., p. 65.
83 'die Ausgelassenheit dieser kleinen Bengel überschreitet alle Begriffe'; 'die wirklich oft treffenden und derben Witze [...], mit denen sie ohne Unterschied der Person alle Vorübergehenden überschütten'. Ibid., pp. 16-17.
84 See 'The First of May', *Sketches by Boz* (note 46), pp. 181-8.

land, exercises the view of the naming and shaming fool in his exposure of the spying methods used by the Prussian police. Referring to Berlin's *Polizeidirektor* and other officials, he reveals how proletarians, who have the status of rightless criminals anyway, are provoked into breaking the law by paid *vigilantes* of the police so that their criminality is 'proved'.[85] The authorities reacted to the publication of *Berlin* as if it were indeed a work of the Devil, and the prosecutor's five-hour reading from it during Dronke's trial not only served to confirm the gravity of the transgression, but revealed, as aggravating evidence, the popularity of the style in which it was written.[86] The penetrating eye had become a force to reckon with.

Even if meaning now lies on the surface and the 'melting into air' of class distinctions seems palpable,[87] this only applies to the world of pleasure and luxury. To analyse the state of society as a whole, Dronke has to abandon his sketching of observations and to reason extensively about the structural inequality inherent in capitalism and about developments that are particular to a semi-feudal police state. His book presents a survey of Prussian society which extends well beyond what can be seen on the streets, in public spaces or, for that matter, in the districts of the poor who have nothing to hide. One could therefore argue that the 'principle of *étalage*' referred to by Burton hides one big aporia. The less the significance of people's social existence is concealed in domestic spaces and the more it is displayed to the public view, the less reliable the visual sense becomes as a guide to social understanding. A world of telling surfaces satisfies the eye more and more easily while it is becoming increasingly difficult to see connections. Physiognomy as a means of social anatomy will therefore not be sufficient. This is why the physiological model of grasping an ensemble which cannot physically be seen is paramount.

A superb example of how, somewhat paradoxically, the visual medium can lay bare to inspection the pathological state of the social organism is Bertall's sketch 'Paris, le 1er Janvier 1845. Cinq étages du monde parisien' ('Paris,

---

85 See Dronke (note 68), II, 179-80.
86 See Rainer Nitsche, 'Nachwort', in Ernst Dronke, *Berlin* (Darmstadt, Neuwied: Luchterhand, 1987), pp. 202-11 (p. 204).
87 See Dronke's pun in *Berlin* (note 68), I, 14, about the disappearance of the 'Eckensteher', which is reminiscent of Glaßbrenner's obituary on this type of 1843 (see pp. 158-9 of this study): 'ihr Stand ist verschwunden, wie bald überhaupt alle Stände verschwinden werden' ('their standing trade has gone, as traditional ranks of any kind are soon to go'), which anticipates Marx's and Engels's famous dictum, using the same pun, in the *Communist Manifesto*: 'alles Stehende und Ständische verdampft' (impossible to convey adequately in English, but commonly rendered as 'all that's solid is melting into air').

First of January, 1845. Five Levels of the Parisian World') in the serial *Le Diable à Paris*. The Asmodean view to which the title of the collection already alludes is transformed into a complete lateral view, achieved by a cross-section of the house. Bertall's pencil has here worked as a scalpel, so to speak; the interior of the five floors is exposed directly rather than being disclosed indirectly through a telling façade. The impressive exterior (seen in profile as the right-hand outside wall), the *étalage*, exposes bourgeois dominance and affluence which is 'true' enough, but what cannot be seen from outside is the social cost at which this wealth comes. This can only be revealed through an exposure of the whole building's inner life (illustration 31).

The sight revealed is uncomfortable. It indicates that, on this first day of the new year, the wealthy may 'own' the street, but that this situation could change. The luxurious first floor, connected to the street by the interface of the ornate balcony, houses the rich, bored bourgeois couple. Their *bel étage* perspective, signalled to the outside world, is, however, by no means dominant or in control. Little do husband and wife know of the social microcosm under the same roof. The New Year visitors, too, have limited insight. The higher up they climb, the lower they descend in the social strata, but nobody except a cat visits the top floor. What if the destitute living in the *mansardes*, the worker whose wife and children are crying for bread and the bohemian artists next door who are dancing to keep warm, join forces on the barricades one day? The old man whose bed is a shabby mattress on the floor and who, in the company of half a dozen mice, is sheltering under an umbrella from a leak in the roof, seems a less likely candidate for revolution. But what about the debtor on the third floor who has already pawned all his furniture and is now receiving an ultimatum from the usurer? Except for the concierge and his wife who have been given their New Year's gratuities (or 'étrennes'), nobody seems to greet 1845 in a happy mood. The visitors on the stairs look solemn, and even the young parents on the second floor appear little cheered by child number four in their cramped living room which also serves as their bedroom and the children's playroom. The five levels of the Parisian world show the viewer a stratified and unhappy social body. The danger inherent in these class distinctions would not be deciphered from the 'extrovert' façade of the house, seemingly eloquent though it may be with its splendour decreasing in proportion to the height of the floors the nearer one gets to the roof.

Except for the fact that it was illustrated, *Le Diable à Paris* followed in the tradition of the *Livre des Cent-et-un*. It varies the theme of the observing Devil imaginatively in that a demon called Flammèche is sent to Paris by Satan in order to send back his observations. In this task, Flammèche enlists the help of contemporary writers. The first contribution to arrive in his box, and the one that actually opens the collection, is a moralist survey in the best Asmodean

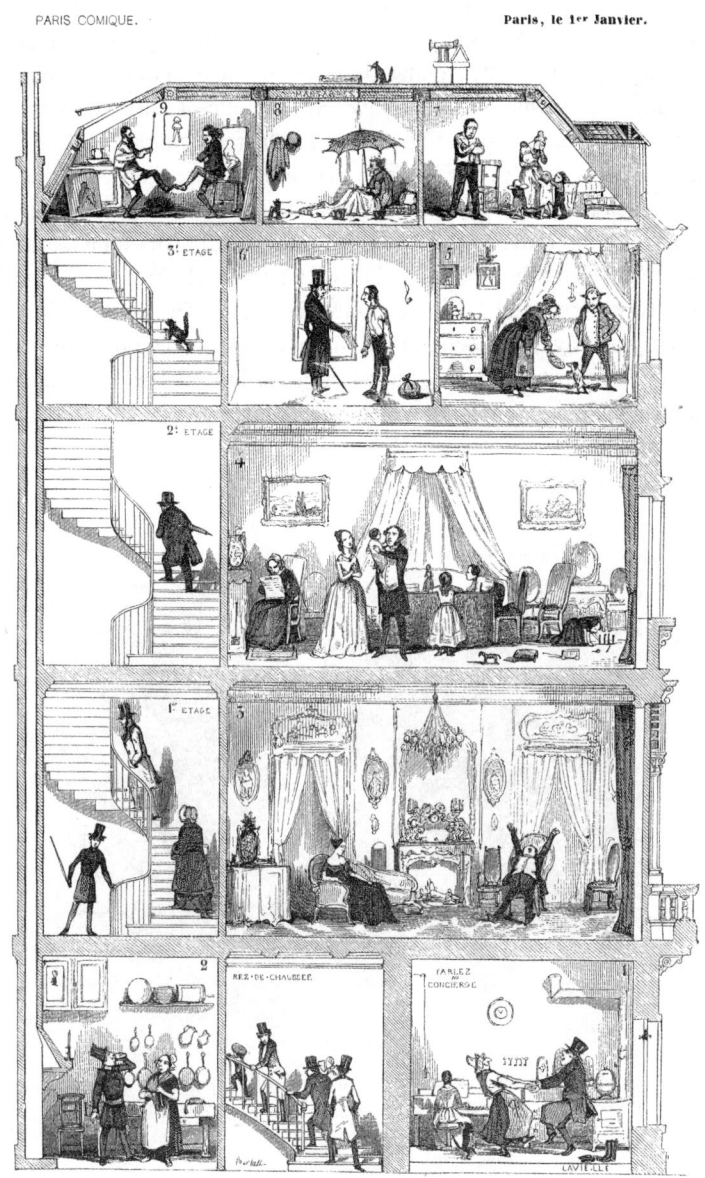

Illustration 31 Bertall, 'Paris, le 1er Janvier. Coupe d'une maison parisienne le 1er Janvier 1845. Cinq étages du monde parisien', in *Le Diable à Paris*, 2 vols (Paris: Hetzel, 1845-6), II (1846), 27. Wood engraving by Lavieille.

fashion – or so it seems. It is entitled 'Coup d'œuil général sur Paris' ('A general look at Paris') and is written by George Sand. Her resolutely socialist perspective creates an overview which could hardly be more condemning or depressing. It is presented under the sign of Melancholy – a vignette of a statuesque woman sunk in gloom over a silhouette of Paris (illustration 32a). This image sets an interpretative pattern for the rest of the collection. The way to look at Paris, it suggests, is from above, an impression confirmed by the illustration at the end of the sketch, depicting the woman writer at her window high up over the roofs of the city (illustration 32b). This female observer is, however, not actually looking at Paris. Her melancholy gesture implies that she has seen enough and is in deep thought over it. George Sand's text bears this out by positively refusing to *see*. In that respect it could be read, if not as a statement against the male penetrating gaze, then at least as a document of female viewing in a context which is distinctly marked by the male, Asmodean mode.

COUP D'OEIL GÉNÉRAL SUR PARIS.

Tu m'as fait promettre, honnête Flammèche, de te dire aussi mon mot sur Paris ; et, comme un diable candide et bénin que tu es, tu as insisté au point de rendre un refus impossible. Prends garde de te repentir de ta politesse; car, en vérité, tu ne pouvais t'adresser plus mal. Personne ne con-

Illustrations 32a and b Français, vignettes in George Sand, 'Coup d'œil général sur Paris', in *Le Diable à Paris*, 2 vols (note 88), I (1845), 33 and 40. Wood engravings.

George Sand, 'Coup d'œil général sur Paris' (*Le Diable à Paris*)

The devil Flammèche, who is addressed by the informal 'tu', could not have chosen a worse guide, the observer says, because she feels compelled to close her eyes to precisely the overwhelming visual world that everybody thinks is Paris. She even claims that she does not know 'the city of luxury and misery' ('la ville du luxe et de la misère')[88] because she hates it and will not look at it. The equation of viewing and knowing, however, is what is at stake in this sketch. To prove that viewing Paris is pointless, a picture is painted of all one would see:

> Anyone not made affected by presumptuousness or rendered stupid by preoccupation with material gain, looks as gloomy as *l'ennui* or as hideous as misfortune itself. Anyone not grimacing is crying, and anyone who by chance is neither grimacing nor crying is effaced and numbed to such an

---

88 George Sand, 'Coup d'œil général sur Paris', *in Le Diable à Paris*, 2 vols (Paris: Hetzel, 1845-6), I (1845), 33-40 (p. 38).

extent that even the paving stones worn by the steps of the multitude have more of a physiognomy than those *triste* human faces.[89]

Parisian physiognomies are uninstructive because they are predictable and perverse. Their predictability consists in their belonging to either this group or that or a third; their perverseness means that they are, strictly speaking, not physiognomies at all but masks of presumption, crying distortions or literally erased faces. It is the predictable and perverse face of a class society about which conclusions cannot simply be drawn from surface-reading. However, the observer's refusal to engage with the visual world has yet another reason. Witnessing the side-by-side existence of luxurious abundance and abject poverty means that it is impossible to write about it objectively, unless one cuts one's links with humanity:

> Oh! to watch this spectacle with indifference you need to have forgotten that you are human and not feel within yourself the vibrations of that electric current, a current of grief, indignation and pity, which makes every truly human soul quiver and is felt right down to the last and humblest link in the chain, at the view, at the very thought of injury and insult.[90]

In 1834 Dickens's observer was able to train himself to this pitch of 'indifference' while keeping a sympathetic view of the observed. For George Sand, writing in 1844, this balance has become impossible. To view human misery is one thing, to write about it is another.

However, the review of the relationship between seeing, writing and knowing does not stop here. In a series of experimental 'views', Sand explores the possibilities open to a writer. It may still be worth the devil's while to enter the big salons and to exercise his piercing gaze in that part of society which takes itself to be Paris and indeed the world, 'le monde'. The sketch here speaks, as it were, on the Devil's behalf and with a male voice, reading what is hidden under the surface of luxury and glamour: '*ennui*, disgust, fear,

---

89 'Tout ce qui n'est pas maniéré par l'outrecuidance, ou stupide comme la préoccupation du gain, e[s]t triste comme l'ennui, ou affreux comme le malheur. Tout ce qui ne grimace pas pleure, et ce qui par hasard ne grimace ni ne pleure est tellement effacé ou hébété, que les pavés usés par les pas de la multitude ont plus de physionomie que ces tristes faces humaines.' Sand (note 88), p. 34.
90 'Oh! pour voir ce spectacle avec indifférence, il faut avoir oublié qu'on est homme, et ne plus sentir vibrer en soi ce courant électrique de douleur, d'indignation et de pitié qui fait tressaillir toute âme vraiment humaine, à la vue, à la seule pensée du dommage et de l'injure ressentis au dernier, au moindre anneau de la chaîne.' Ibid.

the sufferings of amour propre, rivalry, ambition, envy', and, significantly, 'all the apprehension of the future and fear of popular revenge that expiate the crime of being rich'.[91] But even this exposure of the upper class remains unsatisfactory because it reinforces the identification of Paris with 'le monde'. The sketch then presents a non-penetrating view of the world of luxury, in other words, the common view of Paris as the land of Cockaigne, in order to suggest a utopian state of existence. Mankind feasts itself on the fruits of technology, the arts and the sciences, which have reached a state of perfection: flowers in the middle of winter, artificial light which outshines the brightest day, parquet floors on which feet seem to fly rather than walk, beautifully temperate indoor conditions which shut out the inclemencies of the seasons, exquisite paintings, sculpture, orchestral music, jewellery...[92] This surface painting, representing what people see in Paris, is at once true and false. It is true because it portrays authentically the achievements of nineteenth-century civilisation; it is false because those benefiting from the products of human industry, far from representing mankind, only make up a tiny and corrupt part of the population. The question, not to be derived from this observation, of how the privileged minority known as 'le monde' can be extended to encompass *'tout le monde'* or *'l'Humanité'*, is the central one. What the eye cannot see and what can only be known by the social theorist is the fact that, in order to produce all these wonders, man exploits man, in other words, the capitalist robs both the producer and the consumer.[93] She also knows that all the attempts made so far to organise 'a practical transaction between the exploiter and the producer', for example, through charity, only prolong the state of inequality, and that 'a different kind of science' based on social doctrine is required to tackle the problem.[94] However, that science has yet to be found, and it is not within the intellectual scope of the observer to develop it. She is condemned to comprehensive knowledge, to insight into the sickness of society as a whole, without being able to remedy it, in other words, to a profound *tristesse* of which Melancholy is the emblem.

---

91 '[P]longer dans les cœurs, et d'y lire l'ennui, le dégoût, la crainte, les souffrances de l'amour-propre, les rivalités, l'ambition, l'envie, [...] toutes ces appréhensions de l'avenir, toute cette peur de la vengeance populaire, qui expient le crime de la richesse'. Ibid., p. 36.
92 See ibid., pp. 36-7.
93 '[L]'exploitation de l'homme par l'homme'; 'je me demandais [...] ce que le fournisseur avait volé au consommateur et au producteur pour produire toutes ces merveilles'. Ibid., pp. 38 and 39.
94 '[C]ertains essais de transaction pratique entre l'exploitateur et le producteur'; 'il faut une autre science, basée sur la doctrine'. Ibid., p. 38.

This 'coup d'œil général' is 'Asmodean' in that it presents an overview, but only in this respect. It is not based on penetrating surface-reading. The power of piercing vision is only partly applied, and characteristically as an imagined devil's, only to be shown as useless. The power of empathy with the exploited, on the other hand, rules out observation of metropolitan poverty and writing based on it. For the female writer, even confidence in social science does not open possibilities for social reportage in the style of Dronke. All she can do is to alert her contemporaries to the discrepancy between society's utopian potential and its actual state.

Her non-reliance on the power of vision is then partly corroborated, partly relativised by the devil Flammèche's own observation, written by the editor of *Le Diable à Paris*, Hetzel (under his *nom de plume* P.-J. Stahl). Rendered speechless by what he has just read, he takes a look at Paris himself. He gazes at the people in the street:

> In that crowd there were indeed rich and poor, weak and strong people, people in rags and others who were elegantly dressed. [...]
> What he did not see was anybody happy, anyone whose bearing did not speak of desire, covetousness or regret.
> Yet having looked a second time and more attentively, in a manner that made him see right to the bottom even of souls who were most locked in themselves, he began to recognise, in the same crowd where he had at first seen nothing but egoistic interest, rivalling passions, and conflicting appetites in people who were all each others' enemies, – in that crowd he began to recognise fathers and children, brothers and sisters, spouses and lovers, visible and invisible links. He finally saw that there was not a heart so depraved as not to retain, as an imperishable fund of goodness, a little love; in other words, a little of that power which makes it possible to forgive a lot; a little of that power which saves.[95]

---

[95] 'Dans cette foule, il y avait en effet des riches et des pauvres, des faibles et des forts, des hommes en haillons et d'autres élégamment vêtus. [...] / D'hommes heureux, et sur la figure desquels on ne pût lire l'expression d'un désir, d'une convoitise ou d'un regret, il n'en vit pas. / Mais ayant regardé une seconde fois et avec plus d'attention, de façon à lire jusqu'au fond des âmes les plus repliées sur elles-mêmes, il en vint à reconnaître dans cette même foule où il n'avait vu d'abord que des intérêts égoïstes, que des passions rivales, que des appétits contraires, dans ces hommes tous ennemis... des pères et des enfants, des frères et des sœurs, des époux et des amants, des liens visibles et des liens invisibles. Il vit enfin qu'il n'y avait pas

In an ironic reversal of roles, the piercing look of the Devil yields a conciliatory general view of society, based on the Christian ethic of love and forgiveness. George Sand's humanist stance, by contrast, suspends the observer's gaze in a gloomy, irreconcilable view of class society, until such time as the fruits of labour can be enjoyed by the labouring class. In the male observer's case, too, the visual sense is shown to be insufficient as his view depends on the divination of invisible human links between people who are socially divided. In a later sketch written by him, entitled 'Les Passants à Paris', P.-J. Stahl has his observer reveal the potential of the isolated anonymous pedestrians in the street who do not take any notice of one another, to unite into a revolutionary 'peuple' when the time comes. Stierle sees this sketch as the first sociological analysis of the pedestrian and as a premonition of the 1848 Revolution at the same time.[96] It is not surprising for the dedicated republican Stahl / Hetzel, who in 1848 became 'chef de cabinet' in the Foreign Ministry and later in the Naval Ministry and had to emigrate under Louis Napoléon,[97] to have chosen the radical Sand as his star author contributing the first sketch to *Le Diable à Paris*.

The great challenge to social interpretation relying on the visual is poverty. Its face will not simply disclose physical and mental deprivation, but reflect indirectly on the middle-class affluence aggressively displayed in the cities. *Étalage*, on the other hand, does not necessarily signify affluence, but can itself be another face of poverty and decline, as Dickens's portrait of 'theatrical' shop decorations makes clear. To further the cause of social reform or revolution, demonstrating the limits or the pointlessness of penetrating surface-reading and expressing hope for a scientific development and practical application of 'la doctrine' was one possibility; another was to attempt, as Dronke does, to link physiognomic observation in street sketches with a deductive critique of capitalism. In an age geared towards visual signs, the writer needs to find a stance between interpreting those signs and 'speculating' about the wider social context. He and she are forced to see and to 'see through', even if they know that their gaze is useless or even destructive. The quasi-scientific precision of physiognomic observation and sketching are the starting-point; the moral 'scalpel' has to cut from the surface, regardless of its

---

de cœur si pervers qu'il n'y restât, comme un fonds impérissable de bien, – un peu d'amour, c'est-à-dire un peu de ce qui fait beaucoup pardonner, – un peu de ce qui sauve.' [P.-J.] St[ahl], 'Court monologue de Flammèche', in *Le Diable à Paris* (note 88), I, 41-2 (p. 41).

96 See Karlheinz Stierle, *Der Mythos von Paris. Zeichen und Bewußtsein der Stadt* (Munich, Vienna: Hanser, 1993), p. 272.

97 See ibid.

object, which can include the business of observation itself, and whatever the conclusions may be. It is significant that the great illustrated and collaborative sketch collections in which a physiological whole of unseen connections is suggested by text-image relationships (*Heads of the People, Les Français peints par eux-mêmes* and its international adaptations, *Wien und die Wiener, Le Diable à Paris* and others) appear from around 1840. Sand's 'anti-visual' sketch is thus part of a collection in which graphic sketches of the most varied kind appear as companions to texts or independently. The increasing importance of the unseen for understanding social interaction requires ever more complex multimedial, panoramic arrangements, besides opening new spaces for organising and publishing encyclopaedic knowledge.

6
The Panoramic Order: Piecing Together the City

The big sketch collections create order from an astonishing variety of components and perspectives. In other words, as bodies of knowledge they allow full scope for diversity within a cognitive superstructure that is always in evidence. Unlike sociology, however, they do not present knowledge of society in the form of empirical science. The forms in which they link observation and abstraction so that they become systems of cognition are, characteristically, hybrids between science, art and popular culture. The models of the panorama and of the encyclopaedia further support the paradigm of physiology which works as an epistemological vehicle, making possible the notion of interrelations in a living body. Wulf Wülfing has pointed to the analogy between panoramic and encyclopaedic orders in the sense that both aspire to cyclical completeness; be it a circular painting representing an overview or a printed work assembling a circle of knowledge, an *orbis doctrinae* (Quintilian's expression translating the Greek term *encyclopaedia*; the first encyclopaedias in book form date from the late sixteenth and early seventeenth century).[1] Both panoramas and encyclopaedias were, of course, important in their own right as media that popularised knowledge. But the aspect that matters to Wülfing and also concerns the present study is their status as models of (re)presentation. The encyclopaedic paradigm thus informs periodical publishing, especially the form of the review, whereas the panoramic one is frequently found in nineteenth-century travel literature.[2] Both represent orders constituted from a potentially infinite number of parts and aspects.

---

1 See 'Dictionary', in *The Penny Cyclopædia of the Society for the Diffusion of Useful Knowledge*, 27 vols (London: Knight, 1833-43), VIII (1837), 481-84 (pp. 483-4).
2 See Wulf Wülfing, 'Die telegraphischen Depeschen als "Chronik des Jahrhunderts". Karl Gutzkows "Ahnungen" von einem Medium der Moderne', in *Karl Gutzkow. Liberalismus – Europäertum – Modernität*, ed. by Roger Jones and M. Lauster (Bielefeld: Aisthesis, 2000), pp. 85-106 (pp. 86-8).

211

Building on my interpretation in Chapters 1 and 2, I will show in this and in the next Chapter how 'panoramic' and 'encyclopaedic' arrangements enable ephemeral sketches to participate in bodies of knowledge that are in themselves as dynamic as the processes observed by an individual sketch. The fundamental openness of these collections, thanks to their additive character which is distinct from serial fiction, lies at the bottom of this inherent dynamism.

The Asmodean view and the inverted traveller's view

The way in which vision and abstraction correlate in a panoramic mode is exemplified by Gavarni's frontispiece for *Le Diable à Paris* (illustration 1, p. 7). Following the tradition of the *tableau* and its overviewing 'coup d'œil général', the dandified devil, himself a cipher of Asmodean viewing, towers over an abstract representation of Paris in the form of a map. This depiction of the city as a whole transcends, but nevertheless guides vision. A grasp of the map conditions the view through the monocle; the precise, analytical perception of detail depends on the viewer's concept of the plan. This wood engraving seems like a visual translation of Balzac's description of the ideal 'observer' whose 'bird-of-prey vision' from on high is able to 'analyse' and to 'synthesise' in one single glance or 'coup d'œil'.[3] While there are scientists who have this gift, Balzac argues, such analytical-synthetic powers are extremely rare among observers of *mœurs*. When he formulated these thoughts in 1833, the serial projects which combined social analysis and synthesis on a grand collaborative scale were only just being pioneered by the *Livre des Cent-et-un*. The unity and completeness of vision that seemed unachievable for the individual moralist was to be attained by a collective, and this is what Gavarni's frontispiece of 1845 conveys. The analytical and synthetic principle structures the process of representation in hundreds of individual components. While Flammèche's basket full of scripts and his magic lantern point to the diversity of media, written and graphic, which serve the purpose of representing the 'whole' of the city, each written and graphic sketch feeding into the serial is a depiction of detail, created with the whole in mind. This whole is not only multimedial, but also multiperspectival. The magic lantern shows picture after picture in the manner of a slide show and the written sketches

---

3 '[...] ces sublimes oiseaux de proie qui, tout en s'élevant à de hautes régions, possèdent le don de voir clair dans les choses d'ici-bas, qui peuvent tout à la fois abstraire et spécialiser, faire d'exactes analyses et de justes synthèses'. Balzac, 'Théorie de la démarche', in *La Comédie humaine*, ed. by Pierre-Georges Castex, 12 vols (Paris: Gallimard, 1976-81), XII (1981), 259-302 (p. 276).

filling the basket are a random, not to say chaotic collection of viewpoints and subjects.

Even though *Le Diable à Paris* deliberately deviates from patterns of classification, the order arising from the jumble of its contributions is a physiological circular view, a panorama of unseen connections representing a social body in crisis. The collection *Wien und die Wiener*, although also presenting itself in terms of a panoramic view from above which co-ordinates knowledge of a spatial body, does not follow a physiological, but a geological lead model, as will be shown. But first of all, why did the panorama, identified but also devalued by Benjamin as the visual medium informing collaborative collections, provide such a powerful example of synthesis?

Panoramic superstructures for sketches, as indicated, originate from the eighteenth-century city *tableau* with its opening general view. Even if the comparison is partly anachronistic,[4] the *tableau* already resembles a panorama. It offers as complete a portrait of the city as possible in the form of a great number of individual sketches, which the reader assembles during the reading process, supplying the connections between the disparate observations associatively and by means of reflection.[5] The analogy with a panorama lies partly in the way big circular paintings were produced from numerous individual sketches taken on the spot, partly in what these paintings represented and in the way they were looked at. They offered a complete circular view, but could never be seen as a whole. What the viewer perceived was only a detail at a time while being conscious of the unseen surrounding totality. The individual sketch of a *tableau*, created (and read) as an aspect of a whole, thus represented the perception of a panorama viewer. Like the spectator in the middle of a circular painting who can focus on any aspect in no particular order, the reader of a *tableau* has the freedom to choose what to study, and in which order. The 'coup d'œil général' with which a panoramic arrangement opens is in itself panoramic and functions as a guide to the understanding of the city in terms of an imagined totality.

The principle of collaboration, introduced by the *Livre des Cent-et-un* in 1831, gives panoramic city portraits a new dimension. The individual creator of a *tableau* who puts together sketches on a broad canvas, so to speak, is superseded by the collective which produces, by division of labour (and this also applies to the production of visual panoramas), the great picture. Moreover, the collective of observer-sketchers corresponds to a de-individualised

---

4 Robert Barker's earliest public panorama opened in Leicester Square in 1793. See Bernard Comment, *The Panorama* (London: Reaktion Books, 1999), p. 161.
5 See Kai Kauffmann, *"Es ist nur ein Wien!" Stadtbeschreibungen von Wien 1700 bis 1873* (Vienna, Cologne, Weimar: Böhlau, 1994), p. 219.

observer-reader, one of the multitude who recognise in the anonymous *flâneur* of the *Livre* the figure of the time. Because of the more-than-one-observer principle, and also because of the well established position of panoramas as forms of spectacle by 1830, the analogy between collective city portraits and panoramas is even more compelling than it is in the case of single-authored *tableaux*. A further important aspect which Stephan Oettermann has noted is the 'new "democratic" perspective' of the visual panorama. This is generated by the absence of perspectival representation and therefore of the vantage point which distinguishes traditional painting. As a consequence, in a panorama there is no single viewpoint guaranteeing the only correct, undistorted perception of what is represented. This means that the circular painting allows for 'an infinite number of vantage points' and thereby 'theoretically' also enables an infinite number of viewers to see any part of it 'in an undistorted way'.[6] In collective sketch publications, as I have argued before, the traditional privileged view of the moralist (who produces a *'tableau'*) is democratised by the great number of moral observers. The collective painting they produce (in other words, a 'panorama' in the emphatic sense) has as many vantage points as there are contributions to the collection, and the contributors see their own participation in the multi-perspectival painting, the 'peinture multiple',[7] as a contemporary achievement.

Another reason why the analogy with panoramic representation works well for sociological sketch collections lies in the nature of the subject. Apart from battles, landscapes and foreign sights, the spectators of a panorama were able to see representations of their own city, viewed from an elevated point. The 1829 Panorama of London, for example, situated in the Regents Park Colosseum and 'one of the largest [...] hitherto attempted', according to the *Penny Cyclopædia* in 1840, showed a view 'from the top of St. Paul's, whose dome and western towers the spectator sees beneath and before him'.[8] This perspective from the top of a church not only represents a direct equivalent of the Asmodean view which is so prominent in sketch publications. The public in a panorama or the readership of sketches were also able to perceive their fa-

---

6 '[E]ine neue, "demokratische" Perspektive'; 'daß im Panorama, das über unendlich viele Augenpunkte verfügt, auch – theoretisch – unendlich viele Betrachter das sie umgebende Bild unverzerrt anschauen können'. Stephan Oettermann, *Das Panorama. Die Geschichte eines Massenmediums* (Frankfurt a. M.: Syndikat, 1980), pp. 25-6.
7 'Au public', in *Paris ou Le Livre des Cent-et-un*, 15 vols (Paris: Ladvocat, 1831-4), I (1831), v-xv (p. vii).
8 'Panorama', in *The Penny Cyclopædia* (note 1), XVII (1840), 191. A coloured aquatint representing an internal view of the panorama in the Colosseum, including the viewers' platform, is reproduced in Comment (note 4), p. 162.

miliar surroundings from the perspective of the visitor who wants a general impression or a plan before getting to grips with individual aspects. In other words, the panoramic order is akin to inverting the view of 'the other', the mode of travel literature, to become self-observing. Sketch collections containing a survey of the city, frequently in the form of a bird's eye view, therefore also often allude to a visiting observer. Panoramic orders may allow an approximation, if not an overlap, between the figure of the visitor, viewing places with a foreign eye, and that of the stroller (usually male) applying his gaze to 'his' familiar quarter. This will be shown particularly in the interpretation of *Gavarni in London*.

Sociological sketches can thus indeed be seen as a kind of travel literature.[9] They turn upon a home environment the inquisitve view inspecting foreign places.[10] Bulwer's *England and the English* carries a motto by Lady Mary Montagu:

> Every now and then we should examine ourselves: self-amendment is the offspring of self-knowledge. [...] Why should we print volumes upon other countries and be silent upon our own? Why traverse the world and neglect the phenomena around us? Why should the spirit of our researches be a lynx in Africa and a mole in England? Why, in one word, should a nation be never criticised by a native?[11]

The lynx eyes with which a colonising nation looks at Africa are to be turned on the state of the nation itself. The power of vision exercised on 'the other' must be inverted so as to become an instrument of self-inspection with the aim of 'self-amendment'. As Mary Louise Pratt has shown in her study of travel writing, panoramic depictions of, for example, African landscapes from elevated viewpoints were crucial for the self-enactment of the expansionist view. In a reference to Robinson Crusoe, she calls them 'the monarch-of-all-I-surveys'.[12] Such mapping out of overseas realms from above corresponds to the drawing of metropolitan maps from a surveying sociological perspective. The all-important question, however, is who will be empowered by panoramic representations of the city (for it is sketches of the metropolis that tend to be ordered in this way), and what self-knowledge or self-amendment imply in each case.

---

9 See also my Chapter 2.
10 On travel literature as a means of transculturation between the Western metropolis and (post-)colonial territories see Marie Louise Pratt, *Imperial Eyes. Travel Writing and Transculturation* (London, New York: Routledge, 1993).
11 Edward Lytton Bulwer, *England and the English* (Paris: Baudry, 1833), title page.
12 See Pratt (note 10), pp. 201-13.

Le Diable à Paris

Published in 106 instalments between February 1844 and December 1845,[13] *Le Diable à Paris* unfolds a panoramic spectrum which is set in an elaborate cognitive framework. Panoramas are, of course, not 'framed', and this is a difficulty of this collection which the editor addresses, as will be discussed.

One of the framing devices, woven through the whole collection, is of a self-reflective kind, telling the story of the imaginary visitor to Paris, the devil Flammèche. This variant of Asmodeus is, in the event, not normally active as an observer, but the sketches are written on his behalf. Flammèche is supposed to entertain the King of Hell, who is dying of *ennui*, by sending reports from the French capital. However, 'in his new guise as Parisian dandy' ('sous sa nouvelle forme de dandy parisien'),[14] the devil falls in love with the first *Parisienne* he encounters and finds himself incapacitated as an observer, so that the writers and draughtsmen of Paris have to rush to his aid. Their contributions, created playfully through the mask of demonic vision, reach the reader who is allocated the mask of Satan, as it is he to whom Flammèche communicates the sketches, his Parisian 'travelogue'. Hence the inversion of piercing 'diabolical', lynx-eyed observation in a self-scrutinising portrait of the metropolis is made transparent.

Another such device is George Sand's highly critical 'Coup d'œil général sur Paris',[15] presenting a case for unrelenting self-knowledge and cure of the social body beyond vision and observation. Hers is, however, not the only general view. The actual outer frame of the collection consists of topographical, historical and statistical information which, in each case, takes the form of a substantial survey. In other words, the trend to turn away from topography in favour of an observation of mores, heralded by Mercier's *Tableau de Paris*,[16] is now reversed, but only in order to lend support to the socially self-scrutinising panorama of sketches. The survey at the beginning of the first volume deals with the history of Paris, and it shows a 'coup d'œil général' straight away in the form of a vignette depicting a bird's eye view. This represents the city's historic heart, the *Île de la Cité*, two thousand years ago, and thanks to its position opposite Gavarni's frontispiece, it echoes the map of

---

13 See Stéphane Vachon, *Les Travaux et les jours d'Honoré de Balzac. Chronologie de la création balzacienne* (Paris: Presses du CNRS, Presses Universitaires de Vincennes, Les Presses de l'Université de Montréal, 1992), p. 233.
14 P.-J. Stahl [J. Hetzel], 'Prologue', in *Le Diable à Paris*, 2 vols (Paris: Hetzel, 1845-6), I (1845), 1-30 (p. 25).
15 See Chapter 5, pp. 205-8.
16 See pp. 144-8.

contemporary Paris beneath the devil's feet. Two thousand years of Parisian history are thus spatially condensed on paper, a 'survey' of an audacious kind which anticipates the way in which Balzac's 'Histoire et physiologie des Boulevards de Paris' (in volume two) links the past to living history:[17]

Illustration 33 Gavarni (engraver: Brugnot), frontispiece; Champin, head vignette, and Béart (?), ornamented letter on first page of *Le Diable à Paris*, 2 vols (Paris: Hetzel, 1845-6), I (1845). Wood engravings.

Although they offer an 'overview', Théophile Lavallée's historical and geographical sections at the beginning of the two volumes of *Le Diable à Paris* differ from the sketches contained in the main body, not only by describing Paris in the style of a guide, but also by being set in a smaller typeface. The cognitive frame of this panoramic collection is thus clearly marked by historical topography. Lavallée's texts and Champin's illustrations map out the city in a series of historical views, often from above, vignettes of buildings, areas

---

17 See pp. 65-75 of this study.

and streets and a perambulation of quarters, one by one. The function of this survey is, however, not to affirm a sense of locality, but, in keeping with the physiological paradigm, to dynamise the perception of space. Every corner of Paris is historically significant; revolutionary history is vibrating in everything one sees. The Place de la Concorde now counts among the most beautiful squares, but, having been the site of the guillotine during the Terror, it has seen almost as many dead bodies as the most famous battlefields.[18] One street evokes memories of such-and-such a momentous event, another of such-andsuch an outrage. These historical shock waves which communicated themselves to the rest of Europe and the world have made the place so significant. The city of dynamic time; the engine of European history – this is exactly the 'Paris discourse' of German travellers to which Ingrid Oesterle has devoted a number of intensive studies,[19] and which is borne out in every respect by this Parisian text. A visitor from across the Rhine could not have conceptualised Paris more clearly: it is not a topographical unit at all, not an assembly of stones and inhabitants, but the centre of a historical concept, 'la métropole de la civilisation moderne'.[20] This is why, the author claims in a concluding passage full of pathos, other nations are watching the city's every move: 'It is enough for three children running through the streets with a rag in the shades of the tricolour held high on a stick to make thrones shake, to put nations in a state of agitation, and to set armies in motion [...].'[21] Yet the text does not indulge in myth-making by conflating a foreign perception of Paris with a self-image. On the contrary, it alerts the reader to the fact that the threat of another revolutionary outbreak is indeed very real.

This is disclosed by a scrutinising reading of the city's *living* map. For example, the crowning achievement of science, the Jardin des Plantes with its world-famous Muséum d'histoire naturelle and its surrounding streets, all named after the great scientists, is in the immediate vicinity of one of the poorest quarters housing the industrial proletariat. Champin's bird's eye view illustrates this unmistakably:

---

18 See Théophile Lavallée, 'Histoire de Paris', in *Le Diable à Paris* (note 14), I, i-xxxii (p. xxix).
19 See Ingrid Oesterle's articles, 'Bewegung und Metropole', 'Metropole und Landschaft', 'Paris, die Mode und das Moderne', and 'Peripherie und Zentrum' listed in the Bibliography.
20 Lavallée, 'Histoire de Paris' (note 18), p. xxxii.
21 'Que trois enfants parcourent les rues en élevant un lambeau tricolore sur un bâton, les trônes tremblent, les peuples s'agitent, les armées se mettent en marche [...].' Ibid.

4° Le *Jardin des Plantes* a été fondé en 1633 par Guy de la Brosse, médecin de Louis XIII, qui acheta, à cet effet, les quatorze arpents avoisinant la butte des Copeaux, butte qui avait été formée par des dépôts d'immondices et avec laquelle on a construit le joli labyrinthe du jardin. Ce jardin, cinq fois moins étendu qu'il n'est aujourd'hui, était alors borné au nord par un vieux mur, au delà duquel coulait la Bièvre, et, jusqu'à la Seine, par des marais cultivés qui sont aujourd'hui compris dans l'enceinte de l'établissement. Guy de la Brosse y rassembla environ trois mille plantes et y fonda des cours de botanique, de chimie et d'astronomie. L'œuvre fut continuée successivement avec autant de zèle que de succès par Fagon, Tournefort, Jussieu, Buffon, etc. De nombreux cours furent créés, de nouveaux bâtiments

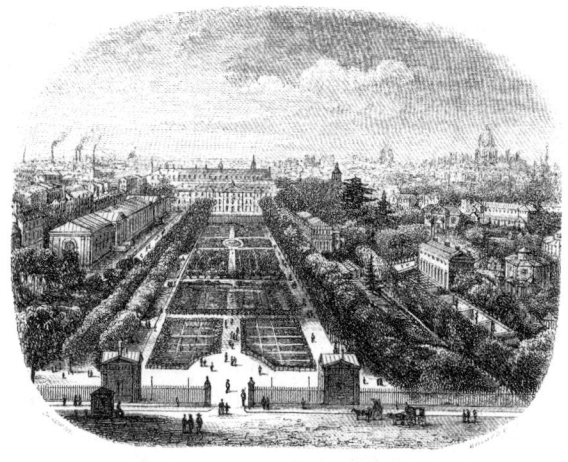

construits, et le jardin s'enrichit de collections données par l'académie des sciences, les missionnaires, les souverains étrangers. Un décret de la Convention organisa l'établissement en muséum d'histoire naturelle et y créa douze chaires ; Chaptal, sous l'empire, lui donna une

Illustration 34   Champin, vignette in Théophile Lavallée, 'Géographie de Paris', in *Le Diable à Paris*, II (1846), lix. Wood engraving by Brugnot.

Lavallée's text points out the moral and social implications of this spatial closeness:

> [...] finally Cuvier turned the Jardin and the Muséum into the world's most magnificent establishment of its kind. Its buildings, remarkable as much for their simplicity as for their elegance, – its rich collections and its picturesque garden attract an admiration which is perfectly legitimate. Yet when you arrive to see these wonders, having passed the quarter we are describing here, you cannot help thinking that there are perhaps one hundred thousand individuals in Paris vegetating in hovels without heat, air and bread, who would be happy to live in this place where such minute

care is lavished on stones, fossils, monkeys and giraffes; and you wonder whether so much luxury was necessary for the progress of science and for the benefit which the useful arts are able to draw from it.[22]

Parisian geography is here made socially readable. People are freezing and starving right next to the centre of world science. The proletariat is not profiting from the progress of mineralogy, physiology and zoology, although technology and commerce – the 'useful arts' – and indeed social science clearly have. 'La métropole de la civilisation moderne' has a fundamental flaw. Another revolution may put this right.

Thus, the diachronic and synchronic reading of the city's map as a panorama of constant, possibly violent socio-political change sets the parameter for an understanding of the extremely diverse contributions to *Le Diable à Paris*. George Sand's 'Coup d'œil général', with its emphasis on melancholic *stasis* rather than historical *dynamis*, offers an alternative panorama, which nevertheless concurs with Lavallées social sentiment. The decidedly republican and democratic slant that Lavallée and Sand give to their overviews seems particularly important since the individual contributors insist on total freedom of choice as to what they will offer. Under no circumstances, they agree with the devil, must the sketches follow a 'method' or 'classification' of any kind; on the contrary, a 'glorious jumble' ('beau désordre') is what should be aimed for.[23] The depiction of the scripts heaped in Flammèche's basket (illustrations 1, p. 7, and 33, p. 217) is therefore meaningful. In other words, the serial is intended to differ as sharply as possible from the regularity of the typological portraits in *Les Français peints par eux-mêmes* and from the classification patterns of the *Physiologies*. One glance at the contents tables, an ordering device which, amusingly, the devil insists on, convinces the reader that what is presented here is indeed 'un beau désordre'. Sketches of

---

22 '[...] enfin Cuvier a fait du jardin et du muséum le plus magnifique établissement de ce genre qui existe dans le monde. Ses bâtiments aussi simples qu'élégants, ses collections si riches, son jardin si pittoresque excitent une admiration bien légitime; mais quand on arrive pour visiter ces merveilles par le quartier que nous décrivons, on ne peut s'empêcher de penser qu'il y a peut-être dans Paris cent mille individus croupissant dans des taudis sans feu, sans air, sans pain, qui seraient heureux de loger là où sont entretenus avec une sollicitude si minutieuse les pierres, les fossiles, les singes, les girafes; et l'on se demande si tant de luxe était nécessaire aux progrès des sciences naturelles et au profit que peuvent en tirer les arts utiles.' Théophile Lavallée, 'Géographie de Paris', in *Le Diable à Paris* (note 14), II (1846), i-lxxx (p. lx).
23 See P.-J. Stahl, 'Prologue' (note 14), pp. 27-8.

people, places and institutions are found alongside aphoristic essays on this and that and short tales, interspersed with independent graphic series (in addition to the vignettes relating to the texts), depicting people and mores. This random collection is similar to the 'peinture multiple' presented by the prototype of collective serials, the unillustrated *Livre des Cent-et-un*. However, there clearly is a structural logic to the 'disorder' of sketches in *Le Diable* which can only be described as panoramic:

'Paris is a theatre with its curtain always up', said the illustrious writer who had pronounced against methods, 'and there are as many ways to consider the countless comedies that are played there as there are seats in its immense enclosure. Let everyone of us therefore see it as he can, one from the stalls, another from the boxes, and yet another from the gallery. [...]'[24]

The theatrical metaphor suggests an amphitheatre: seats arranged within the vast circle of the city's surrounding 'enceinte' and comedies played on the stage in the centre. This image translates into that of a panorama as soon as one considers that the stage is actually the city itself; its curtain is never lowered, and the acting takes place within the whole of its enclosure. There are not only as many viewpoints as there are seats, but there are as many comedies (the plural is important) as there are spectators. In this contemporary theatre of *mœurs*, the spectators are also the producers of the plays, transforming the real-life scenes they observe into 'sketches'. The 'enceinte' of Paris, whether understood literally as the city walls (a protective ring built in the 1780s to counteract tax fraud) or metaphorically as the vast urban expanse, is thus also an exhibition space for sketches. One could imagine them projected, in the manner of a magic lantern, on the surrounding walls which would then become a panoramic canvas. Since the stage and the panorama are both institutions of spectacle, the genre of the sketch comes into its own as a *theatrical* form particularly in panoramic superstructures. Balzac's various studies of Parisian types in the first volume, subtitled 'Les Comédies qu'on peut voir gratis à Paris' ('The comedies you can watch for free in Paris'), are a case in point, being largely conceived in the form of dialogue. Gavarni's series 'Les Gens de Paris', too, incorporates dialogue or at least captions that

---

24 '"Paris est un théâtre dont la toile est incessamment levée, dit l'illustre écrivain qui avait conclu contre les méthodes, et il y a autant de manières de considérer les innombrables comédies qui s'y jouent qu'il y a de places dans son immense enceinte. Que chacun de nous le voie donc comme il pourra, celui-ci du parterre, celui-là des loges, tel autre de l'amphithéâtre [...].' Ibid., pp. 27-8.

make the images speak, a technique quite different from the depiction of types in *Les Français peints par eux-mêmes* or the *Physiologies*:

— Tiens donc ça dans l'œil, innocent!... c'est mieux, et plus commode.
— Oui, mais je ne peux pas.

Illustration 35
Gavarni, 'Les Gens de Paris: Parisiens de Paris 4', in *Le Diable à Paris*, I (1845), after p. 228. Wood engraving by Leblanc.
'Tiens donc ça dans l'œil, innocent!... c'est mieux, et plus commode. – Oui, mais je ne peux pas.'
('Just hold that in your eye, simpleton!... It's better and more convenient. – Yes, but I can't.')

The group of men portrayed as 'Parisians of Paris', of which this pair is number four, represent metropolitan mindsets which can be as limited as those of country folk, and in fact, as with most cities, a great many 'Parisians' were originally denizens of the provinces. The square-faced, masculine dandy type whose tanned complexion seems to indicate not exactly a born and bred city man, lectures his pale young companion on how to wear a monocle, the object of fashion also sported by Flammèche on the collection's frontispiece. Squeezing it between brow and cheek is the done thing, even if this may not be 'more convenient' at all, as it strains facial muscles into a grimace. This does not stop the pale man trying very hard, but unsuccessfully, to be fashionable. By accusing him of being 'simple', the would-be swell betrays his own foolishness. Without its serial title and dialogue, this scene from the theatre of vanity would be incomprehensible, and the mini 'act' of which it forms part, 'Les Parisiens de Paris', a sequence of seven wood-engraved plates, has to be understood in the context of the 'drama' constituted by Gavarni's series 'Les Gens de Paris', with which the collection is interspersed and which is in turn illuminated by all the other diverse components of the serial, for example, by P.-J. Stahl's sketch 'Les Passants à Paris'[25] which immediately precedes 'Les Parisiens de Paris'.

Since every contribution adds another aspect and perspective, and since its subject is inexhaustible anyway, the collaborative city panorama is an infinite project. But it has to work in a finite medium. What in principle ought to be an open-ended serial needs to be concluded and appear in book form. In his editor's 'Conclusion', P.-J. Stahl therefore refers to the unfinished and interminable project of *Le Diable à Paris* as a 'circle which is forever vicious and without a way out, like all circles'.[26] But he also mentions what the work has achieved against the odds. Its graphic images, some of the finest available, present 'mercilessly' ('impitoyablement') everything one could possibly have put into such a collection, having had to use black much more often than white. Here the editor might be implying criticism of *Les Français peints par eux-mêmes* which was also available in a coloured version, and he resumes the dark, critical note of George Sand's opening general view. Through this echo, he is rounding off what is unfinishable. His 'Conclusion' ends appropriately with a vignette that constitutes another reminiscence, this time of the melancholic figure illustrating Sand's essay, and of the frontispiece showing the devil over Paris (illustrations 33 and 1). Like the woman sunk in gloom, Flammèche, the demon of observation, has now seen enough. The opposite of

---

25 See p. 209 of this study.
26 'Cercle à jamais vicieux, et sans issue, comme tous les cercles!' P.-J. Stahl [J. Hetzel], 'Conclusion', in *Le Diable à Paris* (note 14), II, 337-40 (p. 338).

his former self, the figure towering over the map, ready to conquer the city as a keen sign-reader, he is now depicted as a hermit. He is not even looking at the sketches on the walls of his hermitage, a house of cards – an allusion to the 'cris de Paris' which were often printed on cards.[27]

Illustration 36 Bertall, vignette at the end of P.-J. Stahl [J. Hetzel], 'Conclusion', in *Le Diable à Paris*, II (1846), p. 340. Wood engraving by Régnault.

All the world's a stage and everything visual is vain; the magic lantern has to abdicate its service. By means of this moralist image the reader is more than ever invited to rely on knowledge obtained from non-visual sources. A 'Statistique de la ville de Paris' therefore rounds off the collection. Compiled by Alfred Legoyt, it brings together, in seventeen densely printed pages, scat-

---

27 See Ségolène Le Men, 'Peints par eux-mêmes ...', in *Les Français peints par eux-mêmes. Panorama du XIXe siècle* (Paris: Éditions de la Réunion des musées nationaux, 1993), pp. 4-46 (pp. 36-41). The frontispiece of the second volume of *Le Diable à Paris* shows an artist at work, surrounded by an arched frame consisting of cards. Significantly, however, these depict modern types, not the traditional professions of the 'cris de Paris'.

tered statistical information about the population, consumption and the moral and intellectual state of the city, complete with data about its industry and commerce. This 'réunion' and 'coordination'[28] of figures concerning the development of the social body is in itself a considerable achievement. Typographically as well as in its style, it corresponds to the historical and geographical overviews at the beginning of each volume. Social science, or at least much of the knowledge feeding into it, therefore provides the solid frame between which the 'beau désordre' of the panorama unfolds.[29]

City panoramas presume a centrality of the place they are concerned with. Lavallée's historical survey states that the French metropolis is the centre not only of the country's civilisation, but of that of the modern world. Such a claim would have seemed extravagant if made by portraitists of German cities. In the case of Vienna, the only metropolis in the German Confederation that was the capital of a multinational state, a claim to supra-national centrality could be and was indeed made. This, as well as the oppressive Metternich régime which hampered liberal progress throughout the German states, made it difficult, especially for North German nationalists, to imagine Vienna as the capital of a unified *Großdeutschland*. Austrian liberals, on the other hand, whether they were in sympathy with German nationalism or not, could scarcely get their critical views printed at home because Austria's public sphere was even more restricted than that of the German states. Austrian oppositional authors usually had their works published in Germany and often 'emigrated' there.[30] Although depictions of Vienna had a long and rich tradition, including the enlightened *tableau*, portraitists of the city who wrote between 1820 and 1848 largely found themselves confined to the news sections of journals if they wanted to draw non-fictional pictures. In contrast to these discursive portraits, a narrative form of city portrait arose which Kai Kauffmann subsumes under the category of *Lebensbilder* (pictures from life). This

---

28 A[lfred] Legoyt, 'Statistique de la ville de Paris', in *Le Diable à Paris* (note 14), II, 341-57 (p. 341).

29 The *Nouveau Tableau de Paris au XIXe siècle* of 1834-35, which followed the *Livre des Cent-et-un* in its collaborative panoramic design, also included a comprehensive historical, geographical and statistical survey, but it was not arranged 'around' the sketches in the style of a scientific frame. As was already indicated in Chapter 4, however (pp. 159-61), this collection shares with the *Diable à Paris* a generally critical outlook which revises the Juste-Milieu image of Paris optimistically conveyed by the *Livre des Cent-et-un* at the beginning of the July Monarchy.

30 See Hubert Lengauer, *Ästhetik und liberale Opposition. Zur Rollenproblematik des Schriftstellers in der österreichischen Literatur um 1848* (Vienna, Cologne: Böhlau, 1989), pp. 59-64.

genre claimed a literary status of its own and offered a vehicle for conformist depictions of Vienna in accordance with the Habsburg myth.[31] The *Lebensbild* would portray the city as the centre of a world that differed from Western modernisation. Not entirely unjustly, since Vienna's signs of modernity developed under a strongly hierarchical and protectionist system which allowed no openly political forum anywhere, but plenty of non-political compensation in the public arena (such as theatre, music and dance). Under these conditions Austrian writers, unlike their German counterparts who only managed to produce single-authored city panoramas, created a collaborative panorama of Vienna, conservative in outlook and all the more remarkable for it.

Wien und die Wiener, in Bildern aus dem Leben (Vienna and the Viennese, in pictures from life) appeared in fifteen double instalments from 1841 and in book form in 1844.[32] Contributions from about a dozen named and unnamed authors were grouped around a series of steel plates by Wilhelm Böhm (draughtsman) and Carl Mahlknecht (engraver) depicting types in a manner very similar to *Heads of the People* and *Les Français peints par eux-mêmes*.[33] The collection was edited by Adalbert Stifter, Franz Stelzhamer and Carl Edmund Langer, and its panoramic design is one of its most striking characteristics.

Wien und die Wiener, in Bildern aus dem Leben

Stifter insisted that the planned collection should begin with an overview 'in which the *tableau* of the city' was to be 'rolled out for the reader'.[34] Consequently, his opening sketch, 'Aussicht und Betrachtungen von der Spitze des St. Stephansthurmes' ('View and contemplations from the top of St. Stephen's spire') unfolds a panorama in the form of a circular view. The perspective of the visiting observer is firmly assigned to the reader who is addressed in the second person, while the author of the panorama presents himself as a guide. He is in the know and therefore able to point things out, to roll out the picture, as has been indicated, '*for* the reader'. This is done in a grand deictic sketch in which the view is directed to the places described, which are then also interpreted by the first-person observer. The traveller/reader is thus involved in the panoramic view in a purely passive way, not allowed to make his own sense of what is seen/described. An inquisitive or critical external

---

31 See Kauffmann (note 5), pp. 351-2, 393 and 429.
32 See ibid., p. 388.
33 More on the subject in Chapter 7, p. 274.
34 '[...] wo dem Leser das Tableau der Stadt auseinander gerollt wird'. Stifter in a letter to his publisher Gustav Heckenast, quoted by Kauffmann (note 5), p. 389.

view is therefore ruled out from the start. After all, the newly arrived visitor is imagined as an unseasoned traveller, someone from the Austrian or German provinces who has completely lost his orientation in Vienna's bustle. He (for he will be male and is addressed as such in the text) depends on the guidance of the insider who will explain the city to him from above. Franz Stelzhamer's 'Wiener Stadt-Physiognomie und Wiener Volks-Charakter' ('City physiognomy and popular character of Vienna'), a sketch which was probably written as an introduction, but then placed near the middle of the collection, is also presented as a 'guide' ('Führer'), even as an 'interpreter of words and reader of signs' ('Wortausleger und Zeichendeuter') for the new arrival.[35] Far from being an exercise in social anatomy, it 'explains' to the incredulous reader, in an unmitigated eulogy, the thriving of Vienna's popular culture of pleasure under the patriarchal shield of its dynasty. What applies to Stifter's and Stelzhamer's overviewing sketches applies, by and large, to the collection as a whole. Vienna's social fabric is *presented* with comments for the reader rather than being *analysed* for the benefit of the social body itself.

Nevertheless, the 'pictures from life' promised by the title of the collection and listed in the table of contents create a highly varied impression and, in terms of diversity, are certainly not inferior to other panoramic collections. The preface points to the spectrum of types one is to encounter in the serial, from the lowest to the highest ranks (in that order),[36] without even mentioning the portraits of streets, places, institutions and manners which also feature prominently, including a study by Stifter of shop window displays.[37] Entirely in keeping with the principle of panoramic viewing, the city is described as a 'kaleidoscope' of 'scenes' which will gradually 'paint itself together' to a 'picture of life' during the process of reading.[38] Significantly, however, the reader is again imagined as passive in this process; the kaleidoscope will

---

35 See Franz Stelzhamer, 'Wiener Stadt-Physiognomie und Wiener Volks-Charakter', in *Wien und die Wiener, in Bildern aus dem Leben* (Pesth: Heckenast, 1844), pp. 157-64 (p. 164). Like Stifter, Stelzhamer was not from Vienna but had moved to the city from the provinces.
36 See [Adalbert Stifter], 'Vorrede', in *Wien und die Wiener* (note 35), pp. iii-iv (p. iii).
37 See Stifter, 'Waarenauslagen und Ankündigungen', in *Wien und die Wiener* (note 35), pp. 261-9.
38 'Es ist Zweck und Ziel dieser Blätter, [...] in ernsten und heitern Bildern, wie in einem Kaleidoskop Scenen dieser Hauptstadt vorüber zu führen, [...] so daß sich dem Leser nach und nach ein Bild des Lebens [...] dieser Residenz zusammen male [...].' [Stifter,] 'Vorrede' (note 36), p. iii. The image of the kaleidoscope is echoed by that of the mosaic in Stelzhamer's 'Wiener Stadt-Physiognomie und Wiener Volks-Charakter', to which I will refer below.

piece itself together for him, and he has no influence on the composition of the beautiful whole. His synthesising view is, of course, strongly guided by the general view at the beginning – and there lies the rub. To make the city their own, visitors/readers must internalise this view and experience its truth in all the various aspects of life, that is to say, by reading the individual sketches. The implication is that Vienna will not disclose itself to foreigners or quick visitors, only to those who have been initiated and conditioned by a long stay and have developed the *goût* to relish the place like the dessert after a meal.[39]

Statistical information is explicitly excluded from the collection;[40] presumably this would be considered unpoetic by the authors of *Lebensbilder*, and it would almost certainly be too close to the kind of critical scrutinising to which this collection presents an alternative. However, scientific aspects are not avoided. At first it seems as if Stifter's first-person observer in the introductory overview is applying the model of physiology. He refers to the city's heartbeat, which is the 'pulse of a great monarchy' ('Herzschlag einer großen Monarchie') and the precondition of the whole body's health, a body which the inhabitants of Vienna have helped to build, even if they are unaware of it.[41] There are also references to the blood running through the veins of the entire body and to Vienna as a 'gigantic stomach' ('ungeheure[r] Magen') fed daily by a million poor animals slaughtered during the night and by a forest of

---

39 'Diese Stadt muß wie ein kostbares Nachessen, langsam, Stückchen für Stückchen mit Prüfung ausgekostet werden, ja du mußt selbst ein solches Stückchen geworden sein, ehe der ganze Reichthum ihres Inhaltes und die Reize ihrer Umgebungen dein Eigenthum geworden sind. [...] harre nur, gehe immer aus, sei immer hier, werde gemach einer aus ihnen, und siehe, in geheimer Sympathie wirst du Alle auf der Gasse erkennen, ja so erkennen, daß du den Fremden sogleich herausfindest.' ('This city needs to be relished like an exquisite dessert, slowly, discerningly and bit by bit; in fact you have to have become one such bit yourself before its whole internal wealth and the charms of its surroundings become your own. [...] just persist, keep going out, stay in this place, become one of them gradually, and lo, a secret sympathetic bond will make you recognise *them all* in the street, even in such a way that you will spot a stranger immediately.' Adalbert Stifter, 'Aussicht und Betrachtungen von der Spitze des St. Stephansthurmes', in *Wien und die Wiener* (note 35), pp. v-xxi (p. xvi).

40 The first omission from the passage quoted in note 38, picked out in italics in the following, reads: 'Es ist Zweck und Ziel dieser Blätter, *nicht etwa eine Statistik Wiens zu bringen, sondern* [...]'. [Stifter], 'Vorrede' (note 36), p. iii.

41 See Stifter, 'Aussicht und Betrachtungen von der Spitze des St. Stephansthurmes' (note 39), p. v.

greenery mown down.[42] But physiology is not the dominant paradigm; indeed the physiological discourse, common in descriptions of London or Paris, only seems to have been taken up briefly in order to be replaced by a different one, setting up Vienna as a counter-image of the Western metropolis. From the great height of the *Stephansturm* the city shrinks to a geographical, or more precisely to a geological pattern, 'a disc' ('Scheibe') on which one discerns 'the jostling and thronging of roofs, gables, chimneys and towers, a jumble of prisms, cubes, pyramids, parallelopipeds and domes', and all this looks 'as if it had madly shot up and crystallised and was now jutting forth forever down below'.[43] The mineralogical metaphor hints at a scientific model that is indeed central to the collection. The city is to be read in relation to the longest imaginable time spans, the aeons of earth history crystallised in stone, indeed in relation to eternity – as Stifter's sketch of a visit to Vienna's catacombs makes explicit.[44] Accordingly, the surface seen from the top of the cathedral has to be understood in terms of natural history, for example, as a surging sea of houses, as a gigantic honeycomb of busy bees, as a heaving, bubbling, boiling expanse, or as a geological fold of jumbled layers. Read as such a surface, the city is firmly tied into the natural *orbis* surrounding it. Before focusing on the 'disc' of Vienna itself (the metaphor of a circular segment, suggesting a cutting from nature, is used repeatedly), the spectator is guided around the whole horizon in a huge cycle and made to focus on significant aspects of geography. The fact that the scene begins before daybreak and that the first ray of sunlight hits 'our spire' like a 'lightning flash' supports the presentation of order as a cosmological one.[45]

This is not the perspective of the devil of observation whose gaze is fixed on the city as a site of modern civilisation. Flammèche's map of Paris (illustrations 1 and 33), also unfolded beneath the observer, forms a layer of print imposed on a historical landscape (the windmills in the distance signifying Montmartre which was, at the time, not yet part of Paris). In other words, the

---

42 Ibid., p. viii; see also p. xvii: 'Eine Million Thiere ist heute Nachts gestorben, daß alle Diese unten zu essen haben; ein Wald von Pflanzen wurde abgemähet und hereingebracht [...].'
43 '[...] ein Gewimmel und Geschiebe von Dächern, Giebeln, Schornsteinen, Thürmen, ein Durcheinanderliegen von Prismen, Würfeln, Pyramiden, Parallelopipeden, Kuppeln, als sei das Alles in toller Kristallisation an einander geschossen, und starre nun da so fort.' Ibid., p. ix.
44 See Adalbert Stifter, 'Ein Gang durch die Katakomben', in *Wien und die Wiener* (note 35), pp. 49-62.
45 '[...] hui! ein Blitz fliegt an unsern Thurm: die Sonne ist herauf!!' Stifter, 'Aussicht und Betrachtungen' (note 39), p. viii.

invention of the printing press marks the beginning of modernity, a completely new sign system which obliterates the past and which is the city. The semantic function of Flammèche's map is therefore not topographical, but entirely historical, just as Lavallée's geographical survey of Paris reads the city's topography as a site of living history. The significance which Stifter's guiding observer gives to the panorama of Vienna is almost diametrically the opposite. The city is – granted – also interpreted as a site of human history, but human history *sub specie naturae*, if not *sub specie aeternitatis*:

> The people joyfully thronging in the streets, everyone serving their purpose which is usually one of pleasure, – this popular body is continually, industriously constructing, in its children and children of children of children, a building they do not know, after a plan they are ignorant of. They are tirelessly building away, and if one of them falls down, there is another one in his place immediately, hammer and trowel in hand and getting on with it, and when the building is finished, those few who happen to be on site are astonished. One of them will then go and tell the story, on many sheets of paper, of how it all came about, but he does not know either. There were wise men involved in the building, but even they were only able to see and direct parts of it. The one who commanded and surveyed *the whole* has never been seen by human eye.[46]

The city is built to God's plan which is communicated in parts to the representatives of God on earth, the 'wise men' at the top of the Habsburg state who keep a quasi-divine eye on the edifice, while the people who physically build the place over generations are merely driven by a constructive instinct and have no overview of any kind. However, this is precisely what Stifter's circular *tableau* proposes to unfold. Kauffmann has shown how the semantic system of his panorama works,[47] and my interpretation owes much to his.

---

46 'Das Volk, das hier jubelnd strömet, Jeder seinem Zwecke, meist dem der Freude dienend, dieses Volk bauet rastlos emsig in Kindern und Kindes-Kindes-Kindern an einem Baue, den es nicht kennt, nach einem Plane, den es nicht weiß – sie bauen unermüdlich fort, und stürzt Einer, so steht schon wieder ein Anderer mit Hammer und Kelle an seinem Platze und sputet sich – und wenn der Bau fertig ist, so erstaunen die Einigen, die eben zugegen sind! Dann geht einer hin, und erzählt in vielen Blättern, wie das Alles gekommen ist, aber auch er weiß es nicht. – Weise Lenker waren bei dem Baue, aber auch sie konnten nur Theile sehen und bestimmen. – Wer das G a n z e anbefahl und überwachte, den hat noch nie ein Auge gesehen!' Stifter, 'Aussicht und Betrachtungen' (note 39), pp. v-vi.
47 See Kauffmann (note 5), pp. 388-401.

Thus, the natural orbit with which the panorama starts (at the first-person observer's 'God-like' prompt)[48] can be seen as the *orbis* of Creation, in which the smaller ones of earth history, the history of mankind and of the city of Vienna are encapsulated, right to the present-day 'pictures from life' contained in the collection. The visitor's/reader's view is accordingly guided, from the horizon inwards right to the square down below, a movement of the eye which corresponds to the increasing light of day and the awakening of life in the city. This re-enactment of Creation, the locus of which is significantly the viewers' platform at the top of a cathedral, dramatically translates history as God's plan, and this plan is translated spatially in the topography of the city. Here the view moves from the centre to the periphery, that is to say, from the many other churches and the imperial palace, the 'Hofburg' – a 'little city in itself' ('selber eine kleine Stadt')[49] – to the 'Glacis', the green belt along the old ramparts, and from there to the suburbs. This order is politically significant; the Catholic monarchic centre keeps the modern city, rapidly growing beyond the 'Glacis', at bay. The view then takes in, amongst other things, the railway and the mint, both prime signifiers of dynamic time. However, they do not unsettle the topographical reading in terms of a divine plan. Just like the greedily expanding suburbs they are given a place in it as signifiers of human industry and ingenuity. These will lead the human race towards its destination. The subjugation of the power of steam indicates that mankind is on its way 'to become almighty in its own home, the earth' ('allmächtig werden in seinem Hause, der Erde').[50] Money, on the other hand, has an educative function. Its role must surely be to make human beings eventually reject its temptations, and to achieve moral freedom by controlling their desire for ever greater pleasure and gain.[51] Stifter is, of course, thinking in terms of thousands of years. 'In this way', Kauffmann observes, 'the spatial order of the city is (re)translated into a semantic order of human and universal history', a historical order or plan 'implanted by God in (human) nature'.[52]

This affirmation of a religious system of order in viewing the city has to be seen as a statement. It is made against the dominant reading of cityscapes as textbooks of modernity, which is the Western European way of reading them. Portraits of Vienna by Austrian writers of the period were, as has already

---

48 Ibid., p. 395.
49 Stifter, 'Aussicht und Betrachtungen' (note 39), p. ix.
50 Ibid., p. xi.
51 See ibid., pp. xii-xiii.
52 'Auf diese Weise wird die Raumordnung der Stadt in eine Bedeutungsordnung der Menschheits- und Weltgeschichte (zurück-)übersetzt, die ursprünglich von Gott in der Natur (des Menschen) angelegt ist.' Kauffmann (note 5), p. 396.

been indicated with reference to Kauffmann, split in two categories, a non-fictional, politically progressive kind and the largely fictional, conservative *Lebensbild*.[53] The serial *Wien und die Wiener, in Bildern aus dem Leben* represents a fascinating attempt to encroach on the territory of the modernisers by making extensive use of the discursive, non-fictional medium in order to reinforce the conservative view of the *Lebensbild*. And it is, of course, not the discursive medium alone that is exploited for the purpose. The collective mode of production, snappy typological and semiological sketches published as text-image productions in affordable instalments, a panoramic overview at the beginning and the self-referential design of the wrappers (illustration 25c, p. 167), alluding to the scenes of a comedy as well as to the daguerreotype, an even more modern medium for reproducing them than Flammèche's magic lantern, – all signalled the *dernier cri* in publishing.

The modern sophistication of the collection comes to the fore particularly in the 'daguerreotypical' sketching technique and in the scientific (as distinguished from the religious) frame supporting the panoramic order. It is the latter that interests us in the present context. The main purpose of Stifter's panoramic overview is to evoke a sense of topographical order, which the reader is supposed to reconstitute through the 'kaleidoscope' of sketches. The place is to be experienced in its uniqueness, as the centre of a Central European (in other words, neither Eastern nor Western) monarchy and as a modern city in every respect, except that its space has not been eroded by dynamic Western time. Vienna's time and space are to be perceived as emphatically localised. One fifth of the sketches deal with localities, sometimes during a particular time of day, and with excursions to the surrounding countryside. Daguerre's photographic apparatus provides just the right medium for such an authentic depiction of place and space. Using the most up-to-date reproductive technology of 1840, the timeless fool shows the Viennese of 1842 a view of their city as a daguerreotype, taken from a characteristic historical viewpoint under a gothic arch. *Wien und die Wiener* thus documents in its own way what Ingrid Oesterle, writing about the Paris travelogue of the artist and scientist Carl Gustav Carus, has termed the 'calling back of space consciousness' into modern perceptions of the city, dominated as they were by a consciousness of dynamic time.[54] In Carus's case it is Daguerre's diorama that

---

53 Kauffmann (note 5), p. 429.
54 See Ingrid Oesterle, 'Metropole und Landschaft, verzeitlichte Geschichte und geowissenschaftlicher Raum. Das Pariser Reisetagebuch von Carl Gustav Carus', in *Vormärzliteratur in europäischer Perspektive III: Zwischen Daguerreotyp und Idee*, ed. by M. Lauster (Bielefeld: Aisthesis, 2000), pp. 65-99 (p. 69).

provides a model for capturing space in its uniqueness, while geography, geology and meteorology are the sciences that inform the writer's observation. The same could be said about *Wien und die Wiener*. One particularly interesting contribution in this respect is Stifter's very funny sketch of Vienna's weather. The observing first person is introduced as an avid collector of curiosities, including metropolitan weather scenes, which has resulted in a comprehensive catalogue, divided into aspects of 'objective' and 'subjective' weather. Under the first category the observer (who is also a member of the Meteorological Society, organised in bureaucratic Austrian fashion so that he belongs to the bad weather department's subdivision for rain) 'proves' that the city has its own objective climate, very distinct from the rest of the country. Moreover, every district and every street of Vienna has its microclimate. The whole city's physiognomy changes dramatically between winter and summer in a way that could not be observed in the country. The study of 'subjective' climate, on the other hand, is a kind of socio-meteorology, registering the responses of various social types to varying degrees of atrocious city weather. At the end, the reader is tantalised by a glimpse of a baking Viennese summer which the author refuses to sketch in full:

I would love to finish by painting one of those indescribable waves of heat which burst into our houses like a desert storm and which are the scourge of fat gentlemen, yet I fear that the patience of our honoured readers would be tried all too severely, and that the tiredness I would have to depict would communicate itself to the reader rather than to the persons suffering from my painted heat.[55]

The reader is more or less invited to take up the brush and finish the meteorological picture in his or her imagination, fitting it into the city *tableau* or 'kaleidoscope'. The panorama of Vienna is that of a local climate, the details of which are entered in a collective 'table'. Stifter actually uses the expression 'Tafel' in its ambiguity between 'painting' and 'table', which corresponds to

---

55 'Ich möchte nun noch recht gerne eine unsägliche Hitze malen, die wie ein Samum in unsere Häuser fällt, und eine wahre Geißel der dicken Herren ist, allein ich befürchte, die Geduld unserer verehrten Leser auf eine gar zu harte Probe zu stellen, und die Ermattung, die ich schildern müßte, dürfte [s]ich eher dem Leser mittheilen, als den in meiner gemalten Hitze leidenden Personen.' Adalbert Stifter, 'Wiener-Wetter', in *Wien und die Wiener* (note 35), pp. 335-51 (p. 350).

the image of the city as a circular surface ('Scheibe' or disc) in which history has inscribed itself.[56]

As the scientific key to *Wien und die Wiener* is not physiology which seeks to understand the dynamics of the living organism, but the knowledge of earth life, the social types of *Wien und die Wiener* all have their topos, their place, in all senses of the expression. The social order is conceived as that of the traditional hierarchical *Ständeordnung* or order of estates. Those at its bottom are the rag-and-bone collectors and beggars; those at the top the aristocracy and the clergy. That top does not feature in a collection which aims to draw pictures from (popular) life, but neither do industrial workers, although manifestly existing, nor capitalists. They undermine the order of estates. The engraving of the bone man digging for objects in a rubbish heap just outside the city boundary, the 'Linie', illustrates this pre-industrial and localised understanding of 'type' very well. Unlike the title of the written sketch by Sylvester Wagner which is in high German, 'Der Knochensammler', the one underneath the picture shows the Viennese dialect expression, 'Beinelstierer' (illustration 37).

The 'Beinelstierer' represents the lowest of the 'honest' trades of Vienna and is now often found outside the 'Linie' because rubbish in the city is not as easily accessible as it used to be. He is gradually being moved to the outer margins of a place which is becoming an industrial metropolis, but he still has a place in it. Those higher up in the hierarchy of 'honest trades' are located around, but not within, the centre of power like concentric circles, either between the 'Linie' and the 'Glacis' or between the 'Glacis' and the inner city. The non built-up space around the ramparts, now no longer of military significance but functioning as the city's green belt, is still a clear buffer zone between the old central districts and the growing suburbs.

In a mineralogical image, Stelzhamer compares Vienna to 'a colourful deposit of mosaic stones, the actual city forming a modest centre of semi-precious cat's eye, framed by a garland of emerald [the Glacis] and then surrounded by a broad field of topazes, amethysts and jewels of all kinds [the suburbs], a most colourful mixture which eventually runs out into the less

---

56 See Stifter, 'Aussicht und Betrachtungen' (note 39): 'die ungeheure Tafel, auf der dieß Häusermeer hinauswogt'; 'die Tausende [...] ahnen es nicht, daß sie die Lettern sind, womit die Muse das furchtbare Drama der Weltgeschichte schreibt' (p. v); 'über dieser Riesenscheibe, die da wogt und wallt und kocht und sprüht' (p. vi), 'auf dieser dunklen Länderscheibe' (p. viii); 'Wir sehen sie, wie eine Scheibe um unsern Thurm herumliegen' (p. ix). The same metaphor in 'Wiener-Wetter' (note 55): 'daß die ganze Stadt nichts anderes ist, als eine große poröse Scheibe unter dem Netze der darauf niederfallenden Sonnenstrahlen' (p. 338); 'da sieht die Scheibe der Stadt nicht anders aus, als wie ein scheckiges, blumiges Tuch' (p. 341).

The Panoramic Order: Piecing Together the City 235

Illustration 37
Wilhelm Böhm, 'Beinelstierer', in *Wien und die Wiener, in Bildern aus dem Leben*, [ed. by Adalbert Stifter, Franz Stelzhamer and Carl Edmund Langer] (Pesth: Hekkenast, 1844), opposite p. 219. Steel plate engraved by Carl Mahlknecht.

precious and raw stone of the more distant surroundings'.[57] This suggestion of a flat, circular mosaic pattern links up with Stifter's imagery of the city as a geological 'table' or 'disc/segment' and, above all, with his reference to the collection as a 'kaleidoscope', a viewing instrument showing a circular, symmetrically mirrored, conglomeration of coloured glass particles. What, according to this imagery, creates unity out of disparate elements is the aesthetically appealing interplay of colour and shape ('kaleidoscope' meaning 'viewer of beautiful form'), the flatness of the display and the durability of the material into which the 'scenes' from life have been absorbed – all conceivably different from the imagery of the city as an amphitheatre or panorama of performed sketches, a space for the projection of ephemeral magic lantern pictures or sketches in which black prevails. The presentation of Vienna as a precious and, by implication, socially ordered circular mosaic also has implications for the way in which the city is seen to spread over its surrounding countryside. As Vienna's growth turns raw stone into jewels of suburbs, that of 'murky London' serves as an almost predictable contrast. The British capital expands 'like a gloomy face that only keeps extending its furrows and increasing their number'.[58] The dark sorrowful face also indicates that London time is modern industrial time. It is against this definition that *Wien und die Wiener*, making use of the most modern media and techniques, is set: 'Time's rapidly speeding wave breaks', according to Stelzhamer, when it reaches the 'earthy stuff' that Vienna and its people are made of in contrast to 'those airy-fairy Frogs'.[59] The centre of the Habsburg empire is thus also the antipode of Paris.[60] Not in terms of fashion, elegance and metropolitan glamour; the 'principle of *étalage*' was exceedingly well developed in Vienna, too, and Stifter's sketch of window displays offers a shrewd analysis of

---

57 '[...] so könnte er das Ganze vergleichen mit einem bunten Mosaiklager, wo dann die eigentliche Stadt mitten bescheiden daliegt, als das halbedle Katzenaug, zunächst eingefaßt von einem Smaragdkranz, und dann weit und breit umlagert von Topasen, Amethisten und Juwelen aller Art, die sich in buntester Mischung allmälig verlieren ins werthlosere und rohe Gestein der entfernteren Umgebung.' Stelzhamer, 'Wiener Stadt-Physiognomie' (note 35), p. 160.

58 'Wenn das düstere London in seiner Vermehrung einem finstern Angesichte gleicht, das nur immer und emsig seine Falten verlängert, und ihre Zahl erhöht [...].' Ibid.

59 'Es scheint, als habe unsere Nation mehr erdigen Stoff, als der luftige Franzmann [...] Aus Grund dieser Eigenschaft bricht sich an uns auch meistens die Rapidität der Zeitwelle [...].' Ibid., p. 162.

60 See also Kauffmann (note 5), who refers to the 1820-48 period as the one in which Viennese literary journals tend to consolidate the image of anti-modern Vienna as a 'counter-image to "dangerous Paris"' ('Gegenbild des "gefährlichen Paris"', p. 32).

it. It is the *reading* of this civilised surface that lies at the bottom of the anti-western presentation of Vienna. Earthly glitter, as a memento mori, is seen as essential to human existence. The baroque origins of the picture of mores are here most clearly in evidence, and maybe this is not surprising in a city where the public life of all classes was almost totally reduced to the sphere of spectacle and music. The typological portraits of *Wien und die Wiener* are thus often dramatic topoi. Many of them seem like stock characters in an everlasting Viennese *Volkskomödie* (in iconographic terms, like the pre-industrial city Cries)[61] rather than modern types or popular portraits. They are often presented as 'scenes' in dialect, and it is said about the type of the 'Stubenmädchen' (maid), one of the stock characters in any depiction of Viennese society, that she loves watching plays in which her double, a Viennese maid, is the playmaker.[62] Rarely do these representations of character roles reach the depth of analytical, physiological sketches, however informative and entertaining they are for the cultural historian. In this presentation, Vienna emerges as the capital not of world time, but of human and earth time. Only in this sense would *Wien und die Wiener* allow the reader to conceive of Vienna as the capital of the German nation, and it is precisely in this sense that the imaginary (North German) visitor whose orientation is towards London and Paris, is meant to view/read the sketches as 'painting themselves together'. It could be argued that this panorama resists a conquering North German overview.

German panoramic city portraits, as has been indicated, were not collaborative. The lack of a North or West German capital which could have focused energies in publishing, in a way censorship-ridden Vienna paradoxically managed to do, is certainly a major factor in this. The scale of single-authored panoramas is, of course, considerably smaller compared to collective works, but the principle of piecing sketches together from the perspective of an initial overview is essentially the same. Some of the most prominent examples, August Lewald's *Panorama von München* (Panorama of Munich), Eduard Beurmann's *Frankfurter Bilder* (Pictures of Frankfurt) and *Skizzen aus den deutschen Hansestädten* (Sketches from the German Hanseatic Towns), and Ernst Dronke's *Berlin* have been discussed elsewhere in this study.[63] Like most German sketch publications they were unillustrated – an indication of the fact that graphic artists working as cartoonists were comparatively scarce,

---

61 See pp. 153-61 of this study.
62 See [Anon.], 'Das Stubenmädchen', in *Wien und die Wiener* (note 35), pp. 10-15 (p. 14). See also p. 156 of this study.
63 See pp. 75-82 and 194-201.

but also of the fact that the infrastructure for wood-engraved illustrations was thin, at least until the boom in political satire from the late 1840s. Sketchers of London, even if they had no doubt about the national and world status of their capital, did not seem at all concerned with collaborative panoramas of it. *Heads of the People*, as we shall see, is not a panoramic work, partly because it does not focus on London only. There is one publication that does qualify, but it is produced on a modest scale compared to *Le Diable à Paris*, *Wien und die Wiener* or the unillustrated *Livre des Cent-et-un* and *Nouveau Tableau de Paris*. Nevertheless it certainly deserves to be discussed here. Its relation to travel writing is particularly prominent since the visiting observer is a real person, and one of the period's most celebrated draughtsmen too – Gavarni. He stayed in the British capital from the end of 1847 until 1851, and the collection *Gavarni in London*, edited by Albert Smith in 1849, presents twenty-three drawings on wood, engraved by Henry Vizetelly and accompanied by written sketches from a dozen London-based writers. Curiously, this publication focuses energies in English publishing that had not, since *Heads of the People* at the end of the 1830s, been brought together in a collective sketch project. In the course of the 1840s these energies were largely absorbed by the production of illustrated periodicals: *Punch* first, soon rivalled by *The Man in the Moon*, and on the 'serious' newspaper front, the *Illustrated London News* and the *Pictorial Times* which in turn provoked the foundation of the *Illuminated Magazine*.[64]

It does not seem to have taken Gavarni very long to familiarise himself with a society so different from that of Paris. According to his biographers, the Goncourts, he did not suffer the culture shock often experienced by French visitors to the smoke-filled English capital. On the contrary, he was fascinated by the difference that made him discover, 'at every instant, details, ways of being and characteristics that interested him'.[65] This experience also seems to have opened up new ways of representation. His portraits of metropolitan types became even more sophisticated in expressing 'the imperceptible nuances, those nothings which denote a lord in a crowd, those nothings which shape the silhouette of a "respectable man"!' He even, according to the Goncourts, captured a national physiognomy in the 'je ne

---

64 See Michael Slater, *Douglas Jerrold* (London: Duckworth, 2002), pp. 141-5.
65 '[...] il aimait le contraste de cette vie nouvelle, où sa curiosité surprenait, à tout moment, des détails, des manières d'être, des originalités qui l'intéressaient.' Edmond and Jules Goncourt, *Gavarni. L'Homme et l'œuvre* (Paris: Fasquelle, 1925; first edn 1870), p. 163.

sais quoi' that distinguishes English from French faces.⁶⁶ However, they see Gavarni's new management of light as the most remarkable artistic development brought about by his stay in Britain. His lithographs of rural Scotland are of a luminosity which none of his French plates had achieved.⁶⁷ It seems that Gavarni's engraved work, too, gained realistic depth by a differentiation of light. Unlike any of the plates in the 'Gens de Paris' series which he contributed to *Le Diable à Paris* about four years before, the London ones show semitones and nuances that almost create the effect of colour. They capture the diffuse (gas) light in London's foggy, smokey atmosphere.⁶⁸ It has to be said that the quality of English reproduction technology also had something to do with the excellence of these tinted wood engravings. Henry Vizetelly who executed them was a former apprentice of John Orrin Smith and one of two brothers in charge of a printing and engraving empire. Vizetelly & Co. were printers for David Bogue who published *Gavarni in London* as well as Albert Smith's *Natural Histories*, had a hand in the *Illustrated London News* and *Pictorial Times* and printed *Heads of the People*.⁶⁹ Not surprisingly, given these close connections, a number of Gavarni's London types also appeared in the *Illustrated London News* and its Parisian equivalent, *L'Illustration*.⁷⁰

Gavarni in London

Gavarni's stunningly produced, richly nuanced drawings of London life represent a panorama of the – from his point of view – 'other' metropolis across the Channel. There is no bird's eye view at the beginning, and this is probably deliberate. The French artist has 'pieced together' London by and for himself on his strolls, noting the differences within the similarities between the two world cities. The written sketches follow this process. In 'The Potato-Can', a

---

66 'Comme il a saisi et mis en saillie ce je ne sais quoi d'insaisissable et d'inexprimable qui distingue au premier abord une physionomie anglaise d'une physionomie française! [...] il a su encore mettre les nuances imperceptibles, les riens qui désignent un lord dans une foule, les riens qui profilent la silhouette d'un *respectable man*!' Goncourt (note 65), p. 160.

67 See ibid., pp. 167-8.

68 However, a new departure could already be seen in Gavarni's series of 1846-47 to which he himself referred as *Œuvres nouvelles*. See ibid., p. 137.

69 Albert Smith engaged Gavarni during his stay in London to illustrate some of his own *Natural Histories*. Gavarni was asked to contribute pictures of the Parisian Revolution of 1848 to the *Illustrated London News* which he had not even witnessed himself because he was already in London at the time.

70 See Goncourt (note 65), p. 152.

portrait of a street vendor who sells hot potatoes from a steam cooker (written by *Punch* co-founder Joseph Stirling Coyne), the first-person interlocutor shares the Parisian visitor's point of view. He plays Gavarni's and his own part together as a 'we'. This duo of strollers is keen to get the middle-class reader out of the shelter of his (undoubtedly *his*) home and onto the uninviting streets:

> "Kind or morose – urbane or surly reader! as the case may be, are you ready to accompany us in a stroll through the Strand?" [...]
> You thrust your face between the closely-drawn window-curtains of your luxuriously-appointed snuggery, and peeping out on a raw foggy November night, through which the gas-lamps shine with a sort of fuddled brilliancy upon the wet flagways, reply by a shake of the head, and an affectionate glance at the bright burning fire in your grate.
> "Pooh! never mind the night; light your cigar, and come with us: we are going character-hunting."[71]

What starts out as a 'hunt' for 'characters' from the perspective of an urban sportsman spotting interesting game, develops into uncomfortable observation. The written sketches thus reproduce the visiting observer's expeditions of discovery, focusing on 'characters' that his eyes have noted, and thereby turning his view into self-scrutiny. For example, the people buying cheap fare from the potato man at such a late hour give pause for thought, and middle-class 'benevolence' in the form of 'Charitable Societies' is sharply satirised when a 'thickly-coated, short, fat man, with fine purply-tinted features' – the chairman of one of these associations – appears on the scene to light his cigar on the potato stove:

> A rich odour of charity and roast venison diffuses itself around him, and words of the warmest sympathy for human sufferings seem to hang upon his moist lip, till a poor shivering woman, who has been anxiously watching the countenances of the passers-by, ventures, in a subdued voice, to ask for a penny.
> "Penny, be d—d! Go to the Workhouse if you're hungry," replies the benevolent Chairman, puffing the smoke of his cigar indignantly before him as he shuffles off.[72]

---

71 Joseph Stirling Coyne, 'The Potato-Can', in *Gavarni in London*, ed. by A. Smith (London: Bogue, 1849), pp. 101-6 (p. 101).
72 Ibid., pp. 105-6.

A penny is all the woman needs to buy herself a warming and satisfying meal from the potato man, a more charitable individual than the middle-class hypocrite. His is the class to which the cigar-smoking, 'luxuriously-appointed' reader who has been made to witness the scene, and the observer(s) also belong. Social observation and moral self-observation are rendered inseparable.

The perspective of this panorama is clearly one from the streets, and, socially speaking, from below. In lieu of a view from above or a topographical survey, there is in fact a characteristic kind of 'leader sketch', a written counterpart, provided by the editor Albert Smith, to Gavarni's frontispiece of London acrobats. It has to be borne in mind that Smith, not Gavarni, was probably responsible for the arrangement of the sketches in their particular sequence. The very opening of Smith's frontispiece sketch leads the reader into the maze of dingy, filthy alleyways:

> As you pass through one of those low, densely-populated districts of London where narrow dirty streets show the openings of noisome courts, narrower and dirtier still, and these again conduct to alleys, so dark and close, that sunlight never comes lower down the houses than the parapets of their roofs, you will be struck, above all things, by the swarms of children everywhere collected. [...] They form the great proportion of Mr. Punch's audience, when his scream is heard in the adjacent large thoroughfare.[73]

The Punch show goes on in real life. From its audience, the neglected children of the poor who have to amuse themselves in the streets, a performing profession is recruited – acrobats. Gavarni depicts a group of them changing clothes by a roadside, a smokey-grey silhouette of houses in the background, to get ready for a performance (illustration 38, p. 242). This image and its written sketch have leader status because throughout the collection the reader follows the performing arts careers of children of the poor. They become beggars (with more or less refined theatrical skills), street musicians, street vendors and crossing-sweepers (all having to rely on their performative talents), or thieves (another profession where thespian savvy is called for). This panorama, then, also presents a theatre of metropolitan life. Its main actors are the lowest classes who depend on pantomimic skills for their survival. However, their performative roles may be doomed in an increasingly industrialised society, as in the case of the crossing-sweeper.

---

73 Albert Smith, 'Acrobats', in *Gavarni in London* (note 71), [n.p.].

Illustration 38
Gavarni, 'Acrobats'. Frontispiece in *Gavarni in London. Sketches of Life and Character, with Illustrative Essays by Popular Writers*, ed. by Albert Smith (London: Bogue, 1849). Tinted wood engraving by Henry Vizetelly.

Cleaning machines and new surfacing materials (especially asphalt and granite) will render this type an 'extinct species' soon.[74] The 'Orange-girl', selling fruit from her basket, has almost certainly gone already but is still captured by the French artist, to the astonishment of the writer of the sketch: 'Your M. Gavarni may consider himself fortunate in having found an Orange-girl. [...] in a few years our illustration will be that of the same species with Hogarth's [...].'[75] Gavarni's highly sophisticated, almost three-dimensional portrait of the young orange vendor wrapped in her tartan cape on a gas-lit, foggy London winter afternoon (illustration 23, p. 157) – apparently a most up-to-date sketch – is here considered to be historical. The ultra-modern Monsieur Gavarni gives us a picture of the past. His 'Orange-girl' belongs to the class of 'Cries' and has already earned a place in the British Museum, or in the collector's scrap book, next to the extinct barrow-woman. The author's use of the term 'species' in a slightly garbled syntax could apply to both the type and the typological portrait; it, too, is of a certain kind and will soon belong to the gallery of historical London characters starting with Hogarth (or actually earlier with Laroon). Of course the sharpness of Gavarni's modern vision must have been precisely what made him spot the incongruity between the so-called 'Orange-girl' and her smoky industrial environment – one of those London curiosities.

The panorama of the metropolis also focuses on the upper classes, for example, in 'The Opera', 'A Sketch from the West-End', 'Marriage in High Life' or 'The Lounger in Regent Street'. It is, however, in crowd scenes that the panoramic character of the collection comes into its own. The picture of 'The Casino' is one of Gavarni's most nuanced (illustration 39, p. 244), accompanied by Smith's sketch which offers a comprehensive sociological and intercultural comment. The engraving shows a scene in a brightly-lit dance hall, 'The Casino'. The young couple in the foreground are sipping the fashionable 'sherry cobbler', in the latest frivolous fashion from the same glass, with the help of long straws. The straws on the table indicate that this is not their first glass. The man seems to be drinking thirstily (the fact that he has reached a sweaty state is betrayed by the taken-off top hat, a dripping lock of hair and a rather dishevelled cravat), while the woman is pausing, giving the viewer a mildly flirtatious look. The couples in the background, under the glare of the gas chandelier, are waltzing away. This nineteenth-century equivalent of a modern disco was housed in the same building that, only 'some time back' according to Smith (in the early to mid-1830s), used to be a

---

74 Albert Smith, 'The Crossing-Sweeper', in *Gavarni in London* (note 71), pp. 33-6 (p. 36).

75 An Old Playgoer, 'The Orange-Girl', in *Gavarni in London* (note 71), pp. 45-8 (p. 46 and p. 48). See also pp. 156-8 of this study.

Illustration 39
Gavarni, 'The Casino', in *Gavarni in London. Sketches of Life and Character, with Illustrative Essays by Popular Writers*, ed. by Albert Smith (London: Bogue, 1849), before p. 13.
Tinted wood engraving by Henry Vizetelly.

site of public instruction. The 'Casino' had started off as the 'Adelaide Gallery', an institution founded in about 1832 as 'The National Gallery of Practical Science, Blending Instruction with Amusement'. Co-founded by Thomas Telford, it represented, in Richard Altick's words, 'the first direct English progenitor of the modern science and technology museum'. The Adelaide Gallery was purpose-built and situated at the end of the new Lowther Arcade, 'a shop-lined passage leading from the Strand to Adelaide Street just east of St. Martin's-in-the-Fields'. It was 'a long, narrow room consisting of two levels, the lower of which had in the middle a seventy-foot-long tank, or miniature canal, holding 6,000 gallons of water. Arranged along the sides of this room and occupying the gallery as well were the machines, devices, and models sent in for display'.[76]

One of the most famous items was the Gallery's oxyhydrogen microscope 'with three sets of lenses which were said to magnify 16,000, 800,000, and 3,000,000 times, respectively.'[77] It was at the Adelaide that Albert Smith, then student of medicine, would have attended lectures, as he says, 'devoted to the diffusion of knowledge'. Within slots of 'twenty minutes', 'clever professors' used to teach 'elaborate sciences' there. These public lectures which abounded in 1830s London[78] were accompanied by demonstrations of steam engines and all sorts of machinery, diving bells, galvanic energy, and, most memorably, of microscope projections in especially darkened rooms. These seemed to have been created to shake 'the principles of teetotallers, by showing the wriggling abominations in a drop of water they were supposed daily to gulp down by pints'.[79] The trauma of the 1830s caused by the revelation through the microscope of vigorous animalcules, the tiniest zoological entities, swarming in every drop of drinking water, has been discussed at various points in this study. Smith's sociological sketch depicts it as just such a traumatic experience, especially for tee-totalling puritans. As was shown in Chapters 2 and 5, sociological observation analysed and appropriated the microscopical gaze, and so does Smith's sketch of the Casino, as will be seen.

---

76 Richard D. Altick, *The Shows of London* (Cambridge, MA: The Belknap Press of Harvard University Press, 1978), pp. 377-9. An illustration of the Adelaide's interior is found on p. 379.
77 Altick (note 76), p. 378.
78 See Iwan Morus, Simon Schaffer and Jim Secord, 'Scientific London', in *London – World City. 1800-1840*, ed. by Celina Fox (New Haven: Yale University Press, 1992), pp. 129-42. On the Adelaide Gallery specifically, see Altick (note 76), pp. 377-81.
79 Albert Smith, 'The Casino', in *Gavarni in London* (note 71), pp. 13-16 (p. 13).

The noble intention of popularising science through public lectures, we learn, was increasingly frustrated by a public hungry for pleasure. The organisers brought in entertainment, first by stealth and under the guise of disseminating useful knowledge. Smith refers to this 'transition stage' of the 'Adelaide' from a lecture hall and museum of technology to a dance hall as a time when the 'oxy-hydrogen light was slily applied to the comic magic-lantern; and laughing gas was made instead of carbonic acid'. Amusing magic lantern slides were projected, using the same lighting technology for pre-cinematic dissolving views that had been used for microscope shows,[80] to the accompaniment of an entertainer's comments. This sort of performance could still be passed off as an instructive lecture. But in the end all pretence had to be dropped. The magic lantern gave way to more sensual musical entertainment, and what had started as guest appearances of popular singers ended as a takeover by orchestras catering for the dance mania. In 1846 the Adelaide Gallery changed into 'Laurent's Casino', a dance hall 'on the model of the Salle Valentine in Paris'.[81] The only reminder of the building's original scientific purpose, Smith comments, are its great length and height and the 'rows of museum-like galleries running around the walls'. It is precisely from there, where the machines and instruments were once exhibited, that the observer of the dancing crowd unfolds a miniature social panorama:

> As you enter, a Polka is going on, and the *coup-d'œil* from the gallery is well worth the visit. At first the *salle* exhibits a scene of moving confusion similar to that which the drop of water formerly showed in the microscope. The dancers – and there may be sixty or eighty couples – are taking all directions, and in all styles, yet seldom coming into collison.[82]

The view through the microscope has been converted into social observation, a process which parallels the conversion of the building. Social microscopy (analysis) is also combined with a panoramic 'coup d'œil' (synthesis), representing Balzac's ideal of moralist observation.[83] Smith applies the Parisian panoramic technique in his own 'coup d'œil', while the French expression 'salle' indicates that the London dancing craze came from Paris.

---

80 It was in 1840 that the Adelaide Gallery introduced 'the Bicenascope, the improved oxyhydrogen dissolving view projector [...]. It [...] could be – and was – said to blend instruction with entertainment.' Altick (note 76), p. 380.
81 Ibid., p. 380.
82 Smith, 'The Casino' (note 79), p. 14.
83 Discussed in this Chapter on p. 212.

In other words, Gavarni has captured a scene that is most familiar to a Parisian viewer. The couples sipping their sherry cobbler from the same glass, however, is the London speciality which he focuses on. Smith is well aware of this, pointing out that even if the drink itself is not very alcoholic, the 'pneumatic and hydraulic principles' applied 'in its absorption' and the closeness of two pairs of eyes may lead to all kinds of results.[84] Drinking with a straw is also very convenient for the single observer, as it does not impede his vision. *His* vision? The young woman glancing at the viewer in Gavarni's drawing, although certainly not sitting by herself, is obviously making use of the freedom to observe others which this method of drinking allows. Is she observing the observer or is she trying to flirt? Gavarni, as usual, is portraying her expression as ambiguous. Smith's observer, on the other hand, realises the visitor's fascination with the sherry cobbler. He invites him to tear himself away from those frivolous crystal glasses and to take in the whole scene from the gallery. The 'moving confusion' down below is now made socially transparent as a 'droll kaleidoscope of London life'; an image which here suggests a constant movement of colourful particles rather than a beautifully ordered surface of stones. Focusing solely on men (which no Parisian or Viennese sketch of public dancing would), the observer points out that virtually all classes are present: the Earl, the 'Gents', in other words, would-be fashionable employees, men from the Guards, someone 'whose blood is as nearly royal as may well be, and voice the same', barristers, *littérateurs*, shop boys, provincial visitors, 'two university men, out on the loose', and a whole crowd of unidentifiable metropolitan faces. A 'singular mass' indeed, united by a desire for two hours' exertion in a hothouse amid the sounds of a 'capital band'.[85]

The museum of science and technology, turned into a dance hall, has become another place of study. It is a social panorama, and knowledge – not of natural history, but of the social body – is disseminated, not in lectures as before, but in a panorama of sketches. The crucial link between the two forms of cognition is the culture of entertainment. In contrast to *Wien und die Wiener*, *Gavarni in London* reveals a secret connection between science and the pleasure industry. It also analyses the compensatory function of dancing, which may be of special political significance in a society which has been spared an 1848 revolution:

> We really believe that the Casino is a wholesome institution [...]. Individuals who are cooped up all day, on high stools or behind counters, must

---

84 Smith, 'The Casino' (note 79), p. 15.
85 Ibid., pp. 15-16.

have some method of setting free their constrained energies. In France they despoil palaces and upset thrones [...]; in England, formerly they stole knockers and smashed lamps; and they also got wonderfully drunk.[86]

Letting off steam through rhythmical movement will keep the individual and social body in balance. Smith, the former medical student, understands the social need for a place like the Casino physiologically. He will therefore not 'anatomize the company' one meets there 'too minutely' (there are 'bad ingredients', no doubt)[87] as this would prejudice the middle-class reader against an institution that is so important for the social organism. Here speaks someone who is himself about to become one of the great nineteenth-century entertainers in the 'magic-lantern-and-laughing-gas' line. Gavarni has significantly focused on the performative and pantomimic aspects of the foreign metropolis and on the industrial half-light or artificial glare in which they appear. In the dance hall, industry and pantomime are harmonised in the interest of the social body, so to speak; the pantomime in the streets, however, performed by those at the low and lowest end of the social scale, often means an individual struggle for life in and against industrial reality.

* * *

Panoramic collaborative sketch productions empower a middle-class readership to synthesise the disparate aspects of the metropolis. The traveller's perspective acts as a mediator. Apparently familiar city environments are perceived in their fragmentation, particularity or 'foreignness'; a perception which engenders self-scrutiny. The critical look goes hand in hand with an analytical outlook and an overview which emphasises change and the need for social reform, 'self-improvement'. Such an outlook is much impeded, if not precluded, if the foreignness of the city is understood primarily as the visitor's problem, not as something inherent in the place itself. *Wien und die Wiener* attempts to keep familiar a metropolis which is becoming fragmented and unfamiliar, and it relies for this purpose on an imaginary provincial visitor who needs to be introduced to the city's unique topoi. Yet even this collection implicitly admits that Vienna's 'uniqueness' means fragmentation; a number of specialists need to be brought together to paint the parts of the panorama. Depending on how the viewer/reader is intended to approach the parts of the whole, whether critically or appreciatively, the cognitive models informing panoramic collections vary between the dynamic physiological,

---

86 Ibid., p. 16.
87 Ibid.

socio-geographical paradigm on the one hand and the static geological, physico-geographical one on the other. Society is either conceived as a living and changing organism, in other words, as an ensemble of performing actors, or as a body ultimately fitting into pre-existing space like stones into a mosaic or parts into a play. In all cases, however, panoramic superstructures are oriented towards a centre of perception even if no single central perspective is offered.

7
The Encyclopaedic Order: Reviewing the Nation and the Century

In the 1850s, Albert Smith sought to continue the tradition of combining amusement with instruction through his highly successful, pre-cinematic one-man shows. These were multi-media narratives of his journey from Suez to Cairo, presented at Willis's Rooms in 1850, of his ascent of Mont Blanc (1852-58, revived in 1859-60) and of his journey to China (1858-59), both performed at the Egyptian Hall in Piccadilly. 'His *Ascent of Mont Blanc* was the most popular entertainment of the whole decade, setting a standard and attracting a volume of box-office business which rivals could only envy', writes Altick.[1] The speaker would deliver fast-paced accounts, peppered with impersonations (in other words, performed character sketches), songs which often contained topical political allusions, and 'anecdotes having mostly to do with the eccentricities and affectations of English travelers and people met along the way'.[2] Smith's podium stood in front of ambitiously authentic Alpine or Chinese stage settings, and the 'cinematic' effects were achieved by dioramic views or, for the 'ascent' part of the Mont Blanc show, by a vertically moving panorama.[3] In other words, Smith skilfully selected, in the period marking 'the coming of the music hall', precisely those elements of entertainment 'that had hitherto been imported to rescue establishments which had started out as exemplary shrines of rational amusement but had found the going too rough without the aid of musical acts, dissolving views, comic routines, and conjurors'.[4] Significantly, however, these shows were still billed as

---

1 Richard D. Altick, *The Shows of London* (Cambridge, MA: The Belknap Press of Harvard University Press, 1978), p. 473.
2 Ibid., p. 474.
3 See Raymond Fitzsimons, *The Baron of Piccadilly. The Travels and Entertainments of Albert Smith (1816-1860)* (London: Bles, 1967), pp. 123-5, 181-2.
4 Altick (note 1), p. 473.

'lectures', as the third-last line of the programme cover for the *Ascent of Mont Blanc* shows:

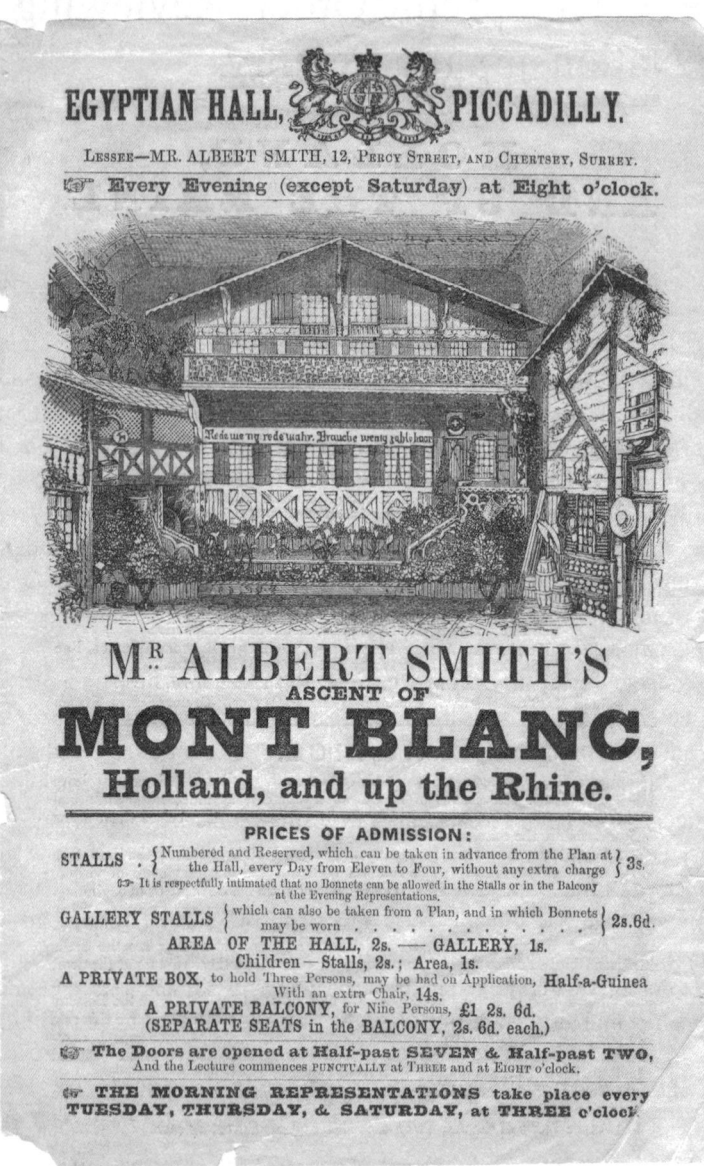

Illustration 40   Mr *Albert Smith's Ascent of Mont Blanc, Holland, and up the Rhine.* Programme cover.

Variations of the classifying view: museums, reviews and encyclopaedias

The building in which Smith performed from 1852, the Egyptian Hall in Piccadilly, underwent a change of function similar to that of the Adelaide Gallery, although it never completely lost its educative purpose. 'Built in 1812', the hall was 'originally intended as a natural history museum' housing the collection of the Liverpool scientist-entrepreneur William Bullock, but 'soon became the most famous exhibition hall in London' where, for example, Napoleon's coach and Gericault's *Raft of the Medusa* were shown,[5] as well as a number of major exhibitions on ancient cultures and displays of live human beings such as 'Laplanders', 'American Indians' and 'Bushmen'.[6] By the time Smith took over the hall for his entertainment, it had thus long been associated with museum displays that pioneered the systematic arrangement of exhibits, as opposed to the older cabinets of curiosities. Such new ground had been broken by the way in which Bullock organised his zoological collection scientifically, becoming 'the first English museum keeper to arrange his specimens in a semblance of what are today called "habitat groups", with careful attention to postures and physical surroundings'.[7] A similar principle of order was followed by diversifying exhibitions according to subject. The Egyptian Hall became famous for showing Napoleana, Egyptian and Mexican art and architecture and, extending the 'zoological' system to ethnic varieties, for displaying live human beings, representatives of pre-civilised humanity, in reconstructions of their 'natural' environments. The highly problematic, racist implications of the latter are weighed up by Altick against the potential improvement which such exhibitions brought to the self-knowledge of city dwellers:

> It is not unlikely that at least some of the more thoughtful Victorians, contemplating the Bushmen and Kaffirs [...], reflected that here [...] they were confronted with possible models of their former selves; or that they murmured with mingled awe and gratitude, "There, but for the grace of the evolutionary process, go we." We cannot know for sure; but to many a

---

5   Fitzsimons (note 3), p. 123; for Géricault's painting see 'Exhibition Catalogue', in *London – World City 1800-1840*, ed. by Celina Fox (New Haven: Yale University Press, 1992), p. 562.
6   See Altick (note 1), pp. 243-50 and 273-87.
7   Ibid., p. 237.

mind and sensibility [...] the experience of gazing on such creatures must have induced thoughts too troubling for easy utterance.[8]

Moves toward a scientific understanding of beings in relation to their environments, reflected by the visual arrangements of museums such as the Egyptian Hall, thus would have helped the spread of evolutionary thinking long before the 'thunderbolt of Darwin's theory' struck.[9] By recreating fractions of a foreign flora, fauna and civilisation in his lecture hall and by setting his own performances in the cognitive context of a natural history museum, Albert Smith clearly made his Continental and Chinese travelogues part of an ethnological enterprise. The main difference between them and the Egyptian Hall's exhibitions was, of course, that Smith's witty performances exposed the audience directly to the self-critical question, 'Who are *we*?' And in this respect the performer had ample experience, namely, as a writer of social 'Physiologies' or 'Natural Histories' during the 1840s.

In the present Chapter, I examine the relationship of sketches to systematic arrangements of knowledge. The natural history museum and zoological garden provide one example of these. In this kind of arrangement, the order is spatial and relates to the century's culture of spectacle. Two collections parodying *Les Français peints par eux-mêmes* are thus entitled *Muséum parisien* and *Scènes de la vie privée et publique des animaux* (Scenes from the private and public lives of animals), the latter being advertised by its frontispiece as *Les Animaux peints par eux-mêmes*.[10] Both collections allude to the Jardin des Plantes and its display of the natural world in its zoo and Muséum d'histoire naturelle. *Muséum parisien* is subtitled *Histoire physiologique, pittoresque, philosophique et grotesque de toutes les bêtes curieuses de Paris et de la Banlieue, pour faire suite à toutes les éditions des œuvres de M. de Buffon* (Physiological, Picturesque, Philosophical and Grotesque History of All the Strange Beasts of Paris and its Suburbs, As a Sequel to All the Editions of

---

8 Altick (note 1), p. 287.
9 Ibid.
10 The parodistic reference of *Scènes de la vie privée et publique des animaux: études de mœurs contemporaines publiées sous la direction de M. P.-J. Stahl* is also to Balzac's *Scènes de la vie privée*, the collection of narratives of *mœurs* (first edition in two volumes: 1830) which forms one of the seedcorns of *La Comédie humaine*. Balzac also contributed five stories to *Scènes de la vie privée et publique des animaux* and collaborated on one written by P.-J. Stahl, pseudonym of the editor Hetzel; see Stéphane Vachon, *Les Travaux et les jours d'Honoré de Balzac. Chronologie de la création balzacienne* (Paris: Presses du CNRS, Presses Universitaires de Vincennes, Les Presses de l'Université de Montréal, 1992), p. 197.

The Encyclopaedic Order: Reviewing the Nation and the Century 255

Monsieur de Buffon's works). The collection lines up its types according to their status in the Vanity Fair of fashionable society, arguing that 'by a truly bizarre quirk, *fashion* has borrowed the main terms of its jargon from the Dictionary of natural history and taken pleasure in choosing the names of quadrupeds which normally inhabit the wildest of deserts'.[11] Thus, the most 'civilised' of human beasts in terms of fashion are classed as the 'lions' of society, male and female, followed by 'la panthère' (the would-be lioness) and 'le tigre' (the coachman in the service of high society). Others include 'le loup-cervier' (the financial lynx stalking the area of La Bourse), 'la mouche' (the fly or police informer), and all kinds of 'rats' (of the ballet, church and wine cellar). Therefore *dictionaries* of natural history, apart from offering society the vocabulary to denote contemporary types, serve as a parodistic reference point for social encyclopaedias in their specific function as media of print.

This medial affinity can also be detected between sketch collections and reviews as well as encyclopaedias in the proper sense. Apart from print, the link here lies in the tradition of 'letters', a genre encompassing scholarly, scientific and literary works alike. In his sketch discussed above, 'The Casino',[12] Albert Smith drily comments that 'poor Science', after eventually being ousted from the Adelaide Gallery, 'declined into the *Gazette*'.[13] The *Literary Gazette* to which, for example, Michael Faraday contributed scientific articles, was 'one of the most influential populd popularisers of artistic, literary and scientific activity around Britain during the first half of the nineteenth century'.[14] This journal is exemplary in the field of review publishing where the epithet 'literary' denotes the sphere of 'letters' in the comprehensive sense.[15] Art, literature and science are strands of an encyclopaedic order of letters,[16] as the

---

11 'Par un caprice vraiment bizarre, la *fashion* a emprunté les principaux termes de son argot au Dictionnaire d'histoire naturelle, et a pris plaisir à choisir les noms des quadrupèdes qui d'ordinaire habitent les plus sauvages déserts.' [Louis Huart], 'Le Tigre', in *Muséum Parisien [...]* (Paris: Beauger, Aubert, 1841), pp. 27-34 (pp. 27-8).
12 See pp. 243-8 of this study.
13 Albert Smith, 'The Casino', in *Gavarni in London*, ed. by A. Smith (London: Bogue, 1849), pp. 13-16 (p. 14).
14 James Hamilton, *Faraday. The Life* (London: Harper Collins, 2002), p. 152.
15 The term 'review' was used in a general sense denoting quarterly, monthly or weekly periodicals with a more or less comprehensive, 'philosophical', that is to say, not directly political content, as opposed to the daily press. See Edward Lytton Bulwer, *England and the English* (Paris: Baudry, 1833), p. 250.
16 Encyclopaedias in the modern understanding, which began to appear in the eighteenth century well before Diderot's and D'Alembert's *Encyclopédie*, referred to the circle of knowledge united in them as one of the sciences and the arts, often pre-

subtitle of *Muséum parisien* also suggests, referring as it does to the picturesque and grotesque as well as the philosophical and physiological history of Parisian types. It has been argued that the French understanding of literature in this universal way informs the educated 'interdisciplinary' discourse of Diderot's and D'Alembert's *Encyclopédie*.[17] The same could be said of the German *Konversationslexikon*, the innovative type of encyclopaedia created by the publisher Brockhaus in response to a need for wide-ranging, nonspecialist knowledge to support the art of conversation in the early nineteenth-century salon.[18] Periodicals of the type of the *Literary Gazette* must therefore be seen as living encyclopaedias, reviewing contemporary knowledge before it turns into various alphabetically sorted encyclopaedia entries. Due to the principle of serial publication, the differences between periodicals, sketch collections and encyclopaedic reference works (which often came out in inexpensive monthly instalments),[19] were not that marked anyway. The sketch industry, of which Smith's Egyptian Hall performances were a continuation, formed an essential part of the century's living encyclopaedia. It fully participated in popularising knowledge by working as an entertaining as well as instructive medium alongside the reviews and the (increasingly) illustrated encyclopaedic publications.[20]

---

sented by a society of gentlemen of letters. See 'Dictionary', in *The Penny Cyclopædia of the Society for the Diffusion of Useful Knowledge*, 27 vols (London: Knight, 1833-43), VIII (1837), pp. 481-4 (p. 484).

17 See Peter M. Schon, 'Naturwissenschaft und "Les Physiologies" im 19. Jahrhundert in Frankreich. Ein Beitrag zur Geschichte der Beziehungen zwischen Naturwissenschaft und Literatur', *Alma Mater Aquiensis*, 6 (1968), 70-6 (pp. 71-2).

18 See Ulrike Spree, *Das Streben nach Wissen. Eine vergleichende Gattungsgeschichte der populären Enzyklopädie in Deutschland und Großbritannien im 19. Jahrhundert* (Tübingen: Niemeyer, 2000), pp. 272-83.

19 See ibid., p. 231. Subscribers to periodicals would occasionally receive free numbers of a new encyclopaedic work as an incentive.

20 As already indicated in Chapter 1, Charles Knight's illustrated *Penny Magazine*, itself a hybrid between periodical and encyclopaedia (published weekly from March 1832), had its equivalents in France and Germany in *Le Magasin Pittoresque* and *Das Pfennig-Magazin für Verbreitung gemeinnütziger Kenntnisse*, both appearing from 1833. The *Penny Cyclopædia* which appeared in monthly numbers from 1832 until 1843 was echoed, not in volume but in popularising intention, by the *Pfennig-Encyclopädie oder neues elegantes Conversations-Lexikon für Gebildete aus allen Ständen* (4 volumes, Leipzig: Kollmann, 1834-7; supplement 1839-41). Brockhaus's illustrated *Bilder-Conversationslexikon* (4 volumes, 1837-41) appealed both to national and to democratic sentiment in adding *für das deutsche Volk* to its title and presenting itself as a 'manual' offering useful instruction

The Encyclopaedic Order: Reviewing the Nation and the Century 257

Smith's own *Natural History of the Flirt* literally illustrates this parallel by juxtaposing, on two facing pages, the vignette of a type encountered in a physiological sketch, and the sort of zoological illustration found in the *Penny Cyclopædia of the Society for the Diffusion of Useful Knowledge*:

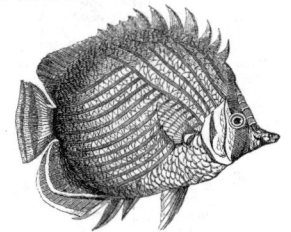

Illustration 41a
Gavarni (left) and Gilbert and/or Henning (right), vignettes in Albert Smith, *The Natural History of the Flirt* (London: Bogue, 1848), pp. 16-17. Wood engravings.

The illustration of the strikingly beautiful fish has been copied – reduced in size and necessarily in the form of a mirror image – from the article on the 'Chætodon (Linnæus)' contained in the seventh volume of the *Penny Cyclopædia*:

---

and entertainment at the same time: *Ein Handbuch zur Verbreitung gemeinnütziger Kenntisse und zur Unterhaltung.*

CHÆ 459 CHÆ

Its abbey, founded by St. Columbanus in the beginning of the sixth century, as well as another abbey of Bernardines at St. Jean d'Aulps, in a neighbouring valley, are now suppressed. On the coast of the lake towards the borders of Valais, was a town called Tauretunum, which was destroyed by the fall of a mountain, A.D. 563. The rocks of Meillerie, celebrated by Rousseau, are in this neighbourhood. The highest summits in the Chablais are, the Dent d'Oche, on the borders of the Valais, 7000 feet above the sea; the Col de Jouxplane, a corruption of Jovis planities, or the plain of Jupiter, which rises between the Chablais and Faucigny above the valley of the Giffre, and is about 100 feet higher than the Dent d'Oche; and the Roc d'Enfer, which rises above the valley of the Dranse, near the centre of the province, and is about the same height as the latter. (Keller's *Map of Switzerland*.)

CHABLIS. [YONNE, DEPARTMENT OF.]

CHA'BRIAS, a distinguished Athenian general, who, in B.C. 388, sailed to Cyprus to assist Evagoras in the reduction of the island (Xen. *Hell.* iv., 8. 24), of which his father had been deprived by the Persians. In B.C. 376 he gained the sea-battle at Naxos. (Demosth. *Aristocrat.*, p. 686; Clinton, *Fast. Hell.*) In 373 he and Callistratus acted as colleagues of Iphicrates at Coragra. (Xen. *Hell.* vi., 2. 39.) He was despatched to settle the affairs of Thrace in 360. (Demosth. *Aristocrat.*, p. 677.) In 357 Chabrias and Chares were sent from Athens with an army to besiege Chios, which, with Rhodes, Cos, and Byzantium, had revolted. (Diodor. Sic. xvi., 7.) Chares led the land forces and attacked the walls from shore. Chabrias no sooner approached the harbour than he engaged in a desperate sea-fight; his ship was shattered by the enemy; most of his men escaped, but the general himself preferring, as Diodorus says, a glorious death to a disgraceful surrender, fell fighting. (Diod. Sic. xvi., 7; Corn. Nep., c. 4.)

CHÆRONE'A, an old city of Bœotia, on the borders of Phocis, near the pass which led to Delphi by Panopeus and Parnassus (Thucyd. iv. 72); it was twenty stadia from

several subgenera; those to which the name *Chætodon* is now restricted have the body more or less elliptical, the rays of the dorsal fin forming a tolerably uniform curve, the snout more or less produced, and the pre-operculum sometimes furnished with a small tooth.

In some of this section, one or more of the soft rays of the dorsal fin are much produced and form a long filament; and others are distinguished by their having very few spines to the same fin.

Chætodon vagabundus, a species which inhabits the coasts

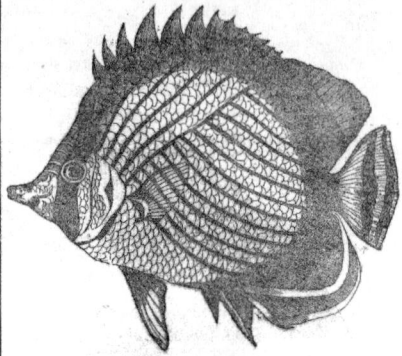

[Chætodon vagabundus.]

of Ceylon, has the body of a pale yellow colour, with numerous oblique brownish-purple lines; the dorsal fin is blackish, and has thirteen spinous rays; the caudal fin, or tail, is yellow

Illustration 41b
'Chætodon vagabundus', in *The Penny Cyclopædia of the Society for the Diffusion of Useful Knowledge*, 27 vols (London: Knight, 1833-43), VII (1836), 459.
Wood engraving.

These illustrations make clear the affinity and difference between the media in which they appear. The *Penny Cyclopædia* and the genre of 'natural history' sketches are both popular, working with cheap, 'useful' wood-engraved illustrations; both are committed to zoology as a lead science, and both define and describe their subjects within an encyclopaedic order. The difference between them which Smith's sketch wittily points out is the absence of a sociological dimension from the *Cyclopædia*. While the term 'Flirt' is glossed unsatisfactorily in Johnson's Dictionary as 'a pert young hussey' and likewise in Maunder's *Treasury of Knowledge* (1830), though without the 'young', Charles Knight's epoch-making popular reference work does not include it at all. Being wised up about the 'Flirt' is obviously not considered part of the 'useful knowledge' to be diffused among less well-off readers. Smith addresses this flaw by satirically presenting his own 'natural history' of a type as the kind of article one would like to see in the *Penny Cyclopædia* instead of yet another boring zoological entry.[21] But the satire indicates that the opposite is true. Showing itself once more as a meta-medium, the sketch absorbs the visual-cognitive ensemble of a contemporary print medium into a parodistic form which allows associative and critical freedom. 'The Flirt' would die the death if confined to the columns of a general encyclopaedia. It is precisely as living beings that women habitually behaving in a flirtatious manner have their place in society, and only the ephemeral sketch, as an entry for an encyclopaedia of contemporary mores, will do justice to the phenomenon. By virtue of its status as a meta-medium, such a moral 'encyclopaedia' makes it necessary to imagine its denomination between inverted commas. Series and collections of 'encyclopaedic' sketches, including the *Physiologies*, are *not* intended to offer 'useful knowledge', and therefore means of control, as Richard Sieburth suggests. 'Armed with the appropriate *physiologie*', he argues, 'the Parisian could from now on be reassured' in the sense that, for example, 'the anonymous *passante* perceived in the crowd' could be ruled out to belong to this class or that, but most probably to another, for example, 'the species known by the name of *La Lorette*'.[22] This argument misses the fundamental point that the 'alterity' thus defined and made 'legible' includes to a large extent the viewer's own social self. The woman is precisely not a species and genus of fish catalogued in an encyclopaedia, but a type whose categorisation has much to do with the eye of the beholder and the unstable relationship between viewing and knowing, as well as with the review of existing knowledge and its forms of organisation.

Sketches organised according to an encyclopaedic principle differ from those following a panoramic order in terms of subject matter. Rather than the metropolis, they are concerned with wider themes such as the national body politic or the times and their mores. This is also methodologically relevant. They do not present kaleidoscopic variety synthesised in a totalising view, but address orders of knowledge and systems of classification, in other words, divisions and subdivisions, and this is why they are able to parody not only other media of classification, but each other. The industrial reproduction of types by sketches, as well as their breaking-down of a grand theme into ever smaller special units, has been criticised as a reflection of the petit-bourgeois

---

21 See Albert Smith, *The Natural History of the Flirt* (London: Bogue, 1848), pp. 14-17.
22 'Armé de la *physiologie* appropriée, le Parisien pouvait désormais être rassuré: la passante anonyme aperçue dans la foule n'était pas [...] un spécimen de *La Femme Honnête* [...] ou *La Grisette* ou *Le Bas-bleu*, mais plutôt un élément représentatif de l'espèce connue sous le nom de *La Lorette*.' Richard Sieburth, 'Une idéologie du lisible: le phénomène des physiologies', *Romantisme*, 47 (1985:1), 39-60 (p. 48).

limitations of the *Physiologies*, for example, by Sieburth who follows Benjamin in this respect as in others.[23] This criticism can only be maintained if one denies sketches their capacity to respond cognitively to a given reality of reproduction and specialisation. Neither Benjamin nor Sieburth take account of the 'panoramic' and the 'encyclopaedic' mode as two distinct forms in which specialisation and multiplication are faced as realities and appropriated as an epistemological and creative principle. As can be gleaned from Janin's 'Introduction' to *Les Français peints par eux-mêmes*, the collaboration of many is necessary because the great subject, the depiction of contemporary mores, breaks down into an infinite number of subordinate and sub-subordinate portraits, each requiring its own expert.[24] The synthesis of such a multitude of specialisms takes different forms. While the emphasis of the panoramic *Livre des Cent-et-un* was on 'multiplicity', *Les Français* places it on 'classification', and the 'beau désordre' of the panoramic *Diable à Paris*, published a few years later, is again created in declared opposition to the structured method of *Les Français* and the *Physiologies* of 1840-42. Since these individually published little books constitute a kind of encyclopaedic order of their own, they will also be discussed in this Chapter, although the main focus will again be on collections. I will, however, first draw attention to two single-authored works that were not even compilations of previously published sketches, but were each conceived as a whole. In Bulwer's *England and the English* (1833) and Gutzkow's *Die Zeitgenossen* (1837), specialisation and classification constitute the methodological principles of sociological enquiry. Both works can be seen as early examples in the field of sociology of knowledge, and significantly, as encyclopaedic forms of publication, they hover between review publishing and sketch production.

Edward Lytton Bulwer, *England and the English*, and Karl Gutzkow, *Die Zeitgenossen*

It could be said that Bulwer and Gutzkow, both extremely erudite men of letters, personified the *orbis* of knowledge assembled in periodicals of the 'literary review' type. They were, of course, also active as review editors. Under Bulwer's editorship the *New Monthly Magazine*, hitherto a rather 'nondescript'

---

23 See Sieburth (note 22), pp. 49-50.
24 'Il est donc nécessaire que cette longue tâche de l'étude des mœurs se divise et se subdivise à l'infini [...].' Jules Janin, 'Introduction', in *Les Français peints par eux-mêmes*, 8 vols (Paris: Curmer, 1840-2), I (1840), iii-xvi (p. ix).

journal, became a politically 'determinate' review of contemporary letters.[25] The experience was essential for the creation of *England and the English*. For Gutzkow, editing a review of Western European format was an almost life-long project, beginning in 1835 with the *Deutsche Revue*, which censorship nipped in the bud, and ending in 1862 with the last number of *Unterhaltungen am häuslichen Herd* (Conversations at the Hearth of the Home; comparable in some ways, and contemporaneous with Dickens's *Household Words*).[26] The suppression of the *Deutsche Revue* and its immediate successor, *Deutsche Blätter*, meant that a single-authored review-type outlet, the bi-monthly serial *Die Zeitgenossen*, was Gutzkow's next-best option. This serial was allegedly written by the celebrated author of *England and the English* and presented as a German translation 'aus dem Englischen des E.L. Bulwer'.[27]

Bulwer's portrait of the nation in *England and the English* and Gutzkow's of the nineteenth century in *Die Zeitgenossen* are encyclopaedic in that both arrange their components according to various fields of knowledge – physiognomy or characterology, education, mores and morality, theology, politics, the arts, sciences and letters being the most prominent ones. Bulwer emphasises the

---

25 See Michael Sadleir, *Bulwer and his Wife. A Panorama 1803-1836* (London: Constable, new edn 1933), p. 288.
26 On the inter-discursivity of the *Deutsche Revue* see Wulf Wülfing, 'Stil und Zensur. Zur jungdeutschen Rhetorik als einem Versuch von Diskursintegration', in *Das Junge Deutschland. Kolloquium zum 150. Jahrestag des Verbots vom 10. Dezember 1835. Düsseldorf 17.-19. 2. 1986*, ed. by Joseph A. Kruse and Bernd Kortländer (Hamburg: Hoffmann & Campe, 1987), pp. 193-217, and idem, '"Das europäische Panorama" findet nicht statt. Bemerkungen zu einem diskursiven Streit um Öffentlichkeit im Vormärz', in *Vormärzliteratur in europäischer Perspektive I: Öffentlichkeit und nationale Identität*, ed. by Helmut Koopmann and M. Lauster (Bielefeld: Aisthesis, 1996), pp. 41-53.
27 As an author affected by the decree of the Federal Diet (Bundestag) in Frankfurt of 10 December 1835, banning the writings of the oppositional 'Young Germans' (*Jungdeutsche*), Gutzkow was forced to publish anonymously or under a false name. Bulwer's roaring success in Germany, where three publishers brought out his collected works in translation simultaneously, was one of the reasons why Gutzkow, struggling to make a living as a journalist and banned author, plumped for the Englishman as a mystification. Moreover, their genuine affinity as social observers and sketchers in the tradition of La Bruyère must also have been a strongly motivating factor in this particular choice of mask. See M. Lauster, 'Bulwer, Edward Lytton', in the 'lexicon' part of *Gutzkows Werke und Briefe. Kommentierte Digitale Gesamtausgabe*: <http://www.gutzkow.de>, Digitale Gesamtausgabe, Lexikon (English translation of article by R.J. Kavanagh; see particularly its section 'The importance of Bulwer for Gutzkow').

knowledge-led structure of his work particularly by dedicating individual parts to prominent men of letters, men of the world or scholars. The knowledge unfolded in both works is that of the universally educated gentleman who 'reviews' the state of the national or European polity. Since it deals with the contemporary body politic, Gutzkow entitles his work *Die Zeitgenossen* – 'Our Contemporaries', rather than *Die Zeit*, 'Our Time'. In other words, review knowledge is turned into comprehensive sociology, and this is also why *England and the English* and *Die Zeitgenossen* are eminent examples of physiological sketch-writing. The discursive texts are laced with sketches, although Gutzkow does not reveal this in his contents table. Bulwer does provide special sections entitled 'illustrations of character', for example, the one at the end of the first book which illustrates the contemporary national physiognomy, including satirical portraits of 'William Muscle, of the Old School of Radical', 'Samuel Square, a Pseudo-philosopher of the New', 'My Lord Mute, the Dandy Harmless', 'Sir Paul Snarl, the Dandy Venomous', 'Mr. Warm, the respectable Man' and 'Mr. Cavendish Fitzroy, a corollary from the theorem of Mr. Warm'.[28] Bulwer also indicates, in the detailed breakdown of each chapter in the table of contents, where the reader can expect 'dialogues', 'portraits' and 'characters' as illustrations of the argument (see the example on p. 266).

I begin my discussion of the structures of the two works with a synopsis of Gutzkow's serial, which provides an impression of encyclopaedic range centering on the discussion of mores:

Die Zeitgenossen

Vol. 1 (parts 1-6 of the serial)

    An Sir Ralph **** (einen berühmten Staatsmann)
    (To Sir Ralph **** [a famous statesman])
    Der Mensch des neunzehnten Jahrhunderts (Nineteenth-century man)
    Das Jahrhundert (The century)
    Die neue Welt (The New World)
    Das Moderne (What is modern)
    Die Existenz (Material existence)
    Der Stein der Weisen (The philosophers' stone)
    Das Leben im Staate (Life in the *civitas*)
    Die Erziehung (Education)
    Sitte und Sitten (Morality and mores)

---

[28] Bulwer, *England and the English* (note 15), p. viii.

Vol. 2 (parts 7-12 of the serial)

Sitte und Sitten (Morality and mores)
Religion und Christenthum (Religion and Christianity)
Kunst und Literatur (Art and literature)
Wissenschaft. Literatur (Science. Letters)
Anhang (Appendix)

This arrangement closes with a discussion of the arts, sciences and letters in the two concluding chapters, having started with depiction of social type(s) in the first. Within each chapter itself, however, the reader finds satirical character portraits which 'make visible' the social dimension of the critique. For example, in 'Die Existenz' it is argued that, while body, soul and intellect have rarely been found in perfect balance through the ages, nowadays there is such a bad imbalance between them, favouring the body at the cost of the soul and of the intellect, that the three seem to be completely separated from each other. This is illustrated by three different types, – the contemporary 'Master Caliban', son of a wealthy brewer, 'a mass of flesh which has accidentally congealed into human shape';[29] 'Sir Ariel' who does not seem to have a body at all but is all sentimental soul and the idol of women; and 'Lord Abstrakt', cold, absent-minded and uncommunicative, the greatest mathematician since Newton.[30] The capitalist middle class has made possible a purely physical existence in material abundance, while the metaphysical and intellectual human faculties are rendered marginal, disembodied and anti-social, even if their social prestige is still high.

According to Gutzkow himself, he was not only attempting, in *Die Zeitgenossen*, to paint 'Charaktertypen' in the style of the first collaborative panorama of Paris, the *Livre des Cent-et-un*, but, significantly in our context, 'to combine' them, 'with the intention of arranging the characteristics and tendencies of our century in certain groups'.[31] The two halves of the work, corresponding to one volume each, have distinct cognitive functions, the first dealing with the century's social world, the second with its moral and intel-

---

29 '[E]ine zufällig zum Menschenbilde zusammengeronnene Fleischmasse'. [Karl Gutzkow], *Die Zeitgenossen. Ihre Schicksale, ihre Tendenzen, ihre großen Charaktere. Aus dem Englischen des E.L. Bulwer*, 2 vols (Stuttgart: Verlag der Classiker, 1837), I, 174.
30 See ibid., pp. 174-6.
31 'Eine Verbindung solcher Charaktertypen mit dem Vorsatz, die Eigenthümlichkeiten und Richtungen des Jahrhunderts in bestimmten Gruppen zu bringen [...].' Karl Gutzkow, *Rückblicke auf mein Leben* (Berlin: Hofmann, 1875), p. 158. See Bibliography for internet edition.

lectual superstructure. The depiction of nineteenth-century society in the first six serial parts breaks down into types, ways of life, perceptions of the accelerating and shrinking world, fashions, 'the social question', technology, inventions and institutions. It is, significantly, the chapter on morality and mores that divides the first from the second half. This chapter is the longest and comes itself in two parts; the first, concluding volume 1, being a satirical genre painting of mores (Sitten) in the form of a fragmentary novel. Its second part, opening volume 2, presents a non-fictional analysis of the century's moral direction (Sitte). From there the investigation moves to the role of established religion and finally to the century's moral, creative and cognitive resources: arts, sciences and letters. The depiction of the empirical social world and that of the realm of ideas are, crucially, linked by the hinge of mores (as part of the social world) and morality (as part of the realm of ideas). This critical review of the century culminates in a critique of 'letters', in other words, of the knowledge amassed in the journals as the most significant media, and in a general view of European politics at the close of 1837 in the appendix.[32] One could describe *Die Zeitgenossen* as a meta-review, and it makes perfect sense for the contemporary critic Albert Heinrich Oppermann to remark that 'a latter-day German quarterly would find enough material' in this work 'to keep itself going for ten years'.[33]

The structure of *England and the English*, Gutzkow's model for *Die Zeitgenossen*, is rather more complex:

England and the English

Book the First. View of the English Character. Inscribed to His Excellency the Prince Talleyrand.

Chapter I. Chapter II. Chapter III. Chapter IV. Chapter V: Supplementary Illustrations of Character.

Book the Second. Society and Manners. Inscribed to ——, Esq.

Chapter I: Society and Manners. Chapter II: Conversation and Literary Men. Chapter III. Chapter IV. Chapter V: The Social Habits of the Population.

---

32 This appendix thus corresponds to Bulwer's appendices providing a critical survey of British popular education and the writings of James Mill and Jeremy Bentham. See p. 105 of this study.

33 [Heinrich] A[lbert] Oppermann, 'Ueber die sogenannten Bulwer'schen Zeitgenossen', in *Jahrbuch der Literatur. Erster Jahrgang. 1839* (Hamburg: Hoffmann & Campe, 1839), pp. 257-310 (p. 262): 'Das Buch ist so gedankenreich, daß eine neuere deutsche Vierteljahrsschrift auf 10 Jahre an dem Stoff genug hätte, der hier aufgespeichert liegt.'

Book the Third. Survey of the State of Education, Aristocratic and Popular, and of the General Influences of Morality and Religion in England. Inscribed to Thomas Chalmers, D.D.[34]
>Chapter I: The Education of the Higher Classes. Chapter II: State of Education among the Middling Classes. Chapter III: Popular Education. Chapter IV: View of the State of Religion. Chapter V: The Sabbath. Chapter VI: State of Morality. Chapter VII: What ought to be the Aim of English Moralists in this Age.

Book the Fourth. View of the Intellectual Spirit of the Time. Inscribed to I. D'Israeli, Esq.[35]
>Chapter I. Chapter II: Literature. Chapter III. Chapter IV: Style. Chapter V: The Drama. Chapter VI: Moral Philosophy. Chapter VII: Patronage. Chapter VIII: The State of Science. Chapter IX: The State of the Arts. Chapter X: Supplementary Characters.

Book the Fifth. A View of our Political State. Inscribed to the English People.
>Chapter I. Chapter II. Chapter III. Chapter IV. Chapter V. Chapter VI: The State of the Parties. Chapter VII. Chapter VIII. Chapter the Last.

Appendix. (A): Popular Education. (B): Remarks on Bentham's Philosophy. (C): Mr. Mill, his Mind and Writings.

England and the English was not published as a serial work. Its architecture of five books, each subdivided into five to ten chapters, shows that it was planned as a scholarly publication in book form. Its appearance (at least in the Parisian edition published by Baudry) as an octavo volume also underlines this, a format conceivably remote from the cheap, pocket-size German Bulwer editions which Gutzkow imitated in *Die Zeitgenossen*, his spoof 'translation from the English of E.L. Bulwer'. In *England and the English*, Bulwer turns into politically serious scholarship the analytical dandyism of his early

---

34 Thomas Chalmers (1780-1847) was Professor of Moral Philosophy at St Andrews, then of Theology at Edinburgh and a champion of popular education – a subject close to Bulwer's heart; see section (A) in the appendix of *England and the English*. He also contributed a volume to the *Bridgewater Treatises*: *On the Power, Wisdom, and Goodness of God as Manifested in the Adaptation of External Nature to the Moral and Intellectual Constitution of Man*, 2 vols (London: William Pickering, 1833).

35 Isaac Disraeli (1766-1848), father of Benjamin Disraeli, epitomises the man of letters. He was the author of the well-known, entertainingly written *Curiosities of Literature* (six volumes, published between 1791 and 1834), of *The Literary Character* (1795) and *Amenities of Literature* (1840), to mention only a few.

novels and of 'Asmodeus at Large'. The destructive anatomising gaze which, in that series, characterised 'Satiety', is converted into a constructive anatomy of society. The figurehead is now not a dandified devil, but a politician of the old school, Talleyrand (then French ambassador in London), to whom the first book is dedicated.[36] This dedication, and the frequent viewing of England from the French diplomat's perspective in Book one, put into practice the epitaph by Lady Mary Montagu which Bulwer chose for his book, proposing that the 'lynx eyes' of the traveller should be applied to conditions at home.[37]

Yet the result is not a panorama of England, however strongly this may be suggested by the viewing of the country through foreign eyes and by three of the 'books' being styled as 'views' and one as a 'survey'. 'View' here clearly means a discerning consideration, required by abstract subjects such as 'the Intellectual Spirit of the Time'. From a judging and inspecting, stock-taking perspective, the individual chapters are thus lined up and 'pass in review' before the reader. The detailed breakdown of three chapters from Book two, 'Society and Manners', for example, reads as follows in the table of contents:

> Chapter II. Conversation and Literary Men.
>
> *Inelegance of Conversation – With us the Court does not cultivate the Graces of Language – Samples of Dialogue – Literary Men; their want of a fixed Position with us – They do not mix enough in Society to refine its Tone – Effect of Night Sittings in Parliament in diminishing the intellectual Attractions of Society – Men of Letters fall into three Classes – Characters of Nettleton, Nokes, and Lofty*
>
> Chapter III.
>
> *The feeling of Melancholy and Weariness; how engendered – We grow out of it with Age – The Philosophy of Idleness, its Sadness – A Reason why we are a Religious People*
>
> Chapter IV.
>
> *Portrait of M– –, an Exclusive Reformed – Causes of his Amelioration – Fashion has received a Shock – Opinions travel upward, Manners downward – View of Society in a Manufacturing Town – The Manufacturers and the Operatives – Cause in Customs for a Movement in Politics – Political Unions injurious to the Popular Cause*

---

36 Gutzkow's dedication of the first chapter of *Die Zeitgenossen* to 'Sir Ralph**** (a famous statesman)' echoes this, and a critical view of Germany through the eyes of an English man of the world and man of letters is likewise implied.

37 See p. 215 of this study.

Sketched-out lines of investigation provide the reader with an overview of each chapter, as was common in nineteenth-century publishing (for example, each instalment of 'Asmodeus at Large' in the *New Monthly* was also provided with an initial synopsis of this kind). In an encyclopaedic work such as *English and the English*, I would argue, this type of contents breakdown has a particular function. Strung together by hyphens, the descriptions, analyses of causes, judgements, classifications and illustrative sketches constitute the snippets of observation from which Bulwer's sociological edifice is constructed, and the whole process is a linear one. The smallest units of observation are aligned to form chapters, the chapters to form books, and the books to form the publication. In an analogy with review publishing, the individual snippets can be compared to the kind of aphoristic contributions often used to fill up a periodical (and some of them, of course, to the sketches and cartoons of a satirical journal). The chapters, on the other hand, are comparable to self-contained critical essays. Each of the five books, then, represents a collection of criticism in a certain branch of knowledge (for example, education, moral philosophy or politics), and is comparable to a section, or to an established strand of critical interest, in a review. The ordering principle of a review is to arrange 'views', criticisms, evaluations and appreciations of a wide range of materials in such a way that an overview of contemporary knowledge is gained by the (regular) reader. This ordering principle is applied in *England and the English* by combining the 'books' which offer informed 'views' into a complete critical 'review' of English society.

The study of mores and morality is as central to Bulwer as it is to Gutzkow. The first two books, 'View of the English Character' and 'Society and Manners', are devoted to the subject of mores, whereas the third book considers 'Morality and Religion' together with 'Education'. Bulwer's review, however, does not culminate in a critique of letters. True, the press, journalism and publishing are dealt with extensively in the monumental fourth book, 'View of the Intellectual Spirit of the Time', and there can be absolutely no doubt that the author sees publishing and the widening dissemination of knowledge as the engine of democratic progress. However, he ties his discussion of the ideal superstructure, 'the Intellectual Spirit', firmly into an *orbis* of knowledge that begins and ends with practical politics. The first book, 'View of the English Character', already shows its political orientation in the dedication to Talleyrand, and the concluding one, besides being dedicated to the 'English People', focuses explicitly on 'the Political State'. Practical politics, however, needs the support of a new branch of knowledge which *England and the English* already represents without having a name for it – sociology. The critique of Bentham in the appendix, arguing that, for all its practicality and effectiveness, his philosophy is lacking the foundations on which social science could be built, is significant.

'Passing in review' before the reader is an image which Janin uses, very appropriately, with reference to the way in which sketches present themselves in *Les Français peints par eux-mêmes*.[38] Uniformly, as head-to-toe portraits, they will pass through the magic lantern one after the other. This standardisation of 'entries' can be seen as analogous to that of a certain type of encyclopaedia,[39] the genre under which *Les Français* is explicitly subsumed by its subtitle from vol. 4 (1841) onwards: *Encyclopédie morale du XIXe siècle*. An encyclopaedic order is, of course, also observed by its model, *Heads of the People*. It is a masterpiece of regularity.

The national review directed by London journalism and its European impact: *Heads of the People, Deutschland und die Deutschen, Wien und die Wiener* and *Les Français peints par eux-mêmes*

Heads of the People presents a national physiognomy in the form of 'English faces, and records of English character', as Douglas Jerrold puts it in his 'Preface'.[40] Kenny Meadows's drawings consistently show half-figures, not complete bodies. Throughout the collection, then, 'the people' are depicted as 'heads', and the title *Heads of the People* refers not only to the paradigm of social physiognomy, but also to the standard format of the work's graphic sketches. Uniformity also extends to the titles of sketches (by definite article and profession or type, for example 'The Housekeeper', 'The Teetotaller', 'The Factory Child') and to the way pictures and texts are laid out. A full-page graphic sketch is placed on an even-numbered, 'lefthand' page opposite the 'right-hand', odd-numbered first page of a written sketch. The text will be precisely eight pages in length, corresponding to an

---

38 '[...] nous nous passons en revue les uns et les autres'. Janin, 'Introduction' (note 24), p. xvi.
39 Pierer's *Enzyklopädisches Wörterbuch der Wissenschaften, Künste und Gewerbe* (26 vols, 1822-36, second edition: *Universal-Lexikon der Gegenwart und Vergangenheit oder neuestes encyklopädisches Wörterbuch der Wissenschaften, Künste und Gewerbe*, 34 vols, 1840-6) is a good example of a standardised encyclopaedia. Its uniform presentation of articles in paragraphs and sub-paragraphs encourages a classifying approach to the subjects. See Spree (note 18), p. 225.
40 [Douglas Jerrold], 'Preface', in *Heads of the People, or: Portraits of the English*, 2 vols (London: Tyas, 1840-1), I (1840), iii-vi (p. iii).

individual number of the serial, without any free space at the end.[41] White expanses of paper are therefore found solely in the margins and on the verso of the engravings, which means that the 'heads' clearly stand out as the raison d'être of the collection. As wood engravings, they are provided with conspicuous inscriptions in type (not the faint, decorative cursive writing found in steel or copper plates; see, for example, illustrations 18, p. 126, and 37, p. 235). These clearly spell out what is depicted, for example, 'The Conductor'. The reader's education in 'letters' being taken for granted, a brief literary quotation pertaining to the type follows, in this case, a cockneyfied travesty of Dante ('By me they goes it now into the city'). The headline of the text on the opposite page repeats 'The Conductor', but instead of the literary reference we read the name of the author, [Thornton] Leigh Hunt, whose text supplies the full contemporary explanation of 'The Conductor' to which the Dante reference acts as a humorous spark. The following illustration shows the first-page layout pattern in three successive sketches of *Heads of the People*, starting with 'The Conductor':

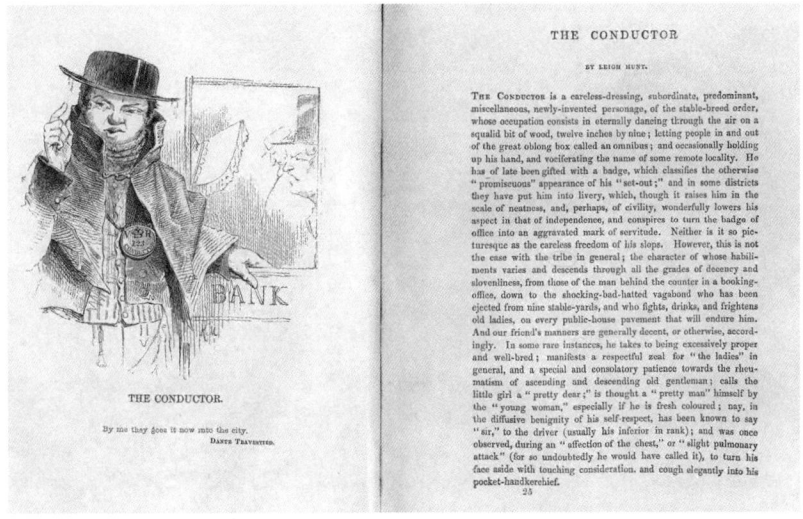

Illustration 42
Kenny Meadows, illustrations in Leigh Hunt, 'The Conductor'; Douglas Jerrold, 'The Common Informer'; Miss Winter, 'The Family Governess', in *Heads of the People, or: Portraits of the English*, 2 vols (London: Tyas, 1840-1), I (1840), 193, 201, 209.
Wood engravings by Orrin Smith.

---

41 A lesser degree of uniformity is found in volume 2, although the graphic sketches there are also always presented opposite the first page of the written sketch.

270 *Sketches of the Nineteenth Century*

THE COMMON INFORMER.

— I confess, it is my nature's plague
To spy into abuses; and oft, my jealousy
Shapes faults that are not.

OTHELLO.

THE COMMON INFORMER.

BY DOUGLAS JERROLD.

"My opinion is,"——
—(And here we solicit of the reader his most respectful attention to the opinion of Viscount Melbourne, Prime Minister, as expressed in the House of Lords, in the second year of the reign of the virgin Victoria.)

"My opinion is, let a man's understanding be as bright as it may; let a man's genius be what it may; that profession (*i. e.*, the profession *of the law*) does little else but cramp the understanding, and fetter the mental faculties; and that almost universally." To this, the chronicler of the speech adds, "great laughter."*

If we believe in Lord Melbourne, we must be visited with throes of pity for all lords-chief-justices past and to come; all judges, sergeants, barristers;—we must, through our tears, behold them dwarfed, distorted, manacled. The shining, constant lights of the courts, are no other than jack-o'-lanterns; the upright pillars of the law are pillars lamentably twisted!

When we shall henceforth read the names of victims called to the bar, we shall look upon the sufferers as doomed men; individuals sentenced to an inevitable decrease of understanding; to a daily discipline that crooks their finest wits; to an atmosphere that dims and tarnishes the brightest capabilities. They have, however, this consolatory reflection, that, with all these manifest disadvantages, they are the chosen and appointed best advisers of their fellows; that though their understanding be "cramped," it is the distorted Mentor to the minds of others; that though their mental faculties be in gyves, they are, for that reason, the surest steps to the fettered capacities of their fellow subjects.

Now, if this be the inevitable condition of men disposed to study the transcendant beauties of the law, what must be the hapless state of the wretched individual self-doomed to ponder on its deformities?

* See Lord Melbourne's Speech on the "Canada Government Act Declaratory Bill," August 10, 1838.

THE FAMILY GOVERNESS.

She only said, "My life is dreary."

TENNYSON.

THE FAMILY GOVERNESS.

BY MISS WINTER.

"It is most vexatious—most distressing!" ejaculated Mr. Burleigh, of Effinghame, as he paced up and down his breakfast-room, awaiting the appearance of his lady. "I cannot think of it with toleration!" he continued, as he stopped before the window, commanding a view of his own spacious park, and of the distant Frith of Forth, with its rocks and islands. Nothing in the view, however, seemed to give ease to his troubled spirit; for, flinging himself into an arm-chair, at one end of the table, which was loaded with the multifarious luxuries of a Scotch breakfast, he resigned himself to gloomy despondency. At length the door opened, and Lady Harriet Burleigh entered.

"I *do* trust, Lady Harriet," he immediately cried, "I do *trust* you now see the necessity of parting with the cook! The dinner yesterday was execrably bad."

"You have only to make up your mind to give the requisite salary," replied the lady, with fashionable indifference.

"I *have* made up my mind, Lady Harriet, provided I can obtain a complete history of the man's training. I will know where he began life; under whom he studied; and every family in which he has since lived," said Mr. Burleigh, solemnly.

"Well, here is the document furnished by Chouffleur, Lord Dytchland's late cook," replied Lady Harriet; "I told you, a week ago, I had received it."

"Highly satisfactory, indeed," said Mr. Burleigh, reading, as he sipped his coffee with additional relish. "Salary, three hundred a-year; three under-cooks, a separate table, and the exclusive use of a gig. Well, well, I agree to this; I will write and conclude the negociation to-day. I must also see about another gardener: our fruit is very imperfect. I shall insist on knowing every particular of *his* life, from his apprenticeship upwards. No ignorant bungler shall pretend any longer to be the cultivator of my grapes and pines."

A silence which ensued was broken by the loud lamentations of two childish voices, proceeding from the terrace outside, with a

27

Heads of the People offers a dictionary of types which readers can use either 'systematically' by consulting the table of contents, or as browsers, leafing through the volumes and fixing their eyes on the regularly recurrent 'heads'. This method comes close to the viewing of images in a magic lantern show with witty accompanying sketches, in other words, the kind of educative entertainment Albert Smith provided in the Egyptian Hall. Multi-media 'lectures' of this kind, and, by analogy, illustrated encyclopaedic sketch publications such as *Heads of the People*, occupy a place somewhere between the popular music-hall revue and the serious learned review.[42]

What is being reviewed in *Heads of the People* is the social and moral state of the nation. The reader is to recognise the 'family-likeness'[43] between the one hundred-or-so members of the 'numerous family' of 'John Bull' as the collection portrays them.[44] A bull's head over a pewter tankard, engraved with an ornate 'E' for 'English', is shown at the beginning of the Preface, and at its end the same beast is depicted as the pot-bellied sitter of a painting (illustration 43, pp. 272-3). The satire on the English beef-and-ale character indicates who is to be understood as the nation. It is the popular majority, 'the people', whose 'heads' can be studied, more often than not, in the ale-house. Therefore it is not surprising that volume one should include a mini-encyclopaedia entitled 'Tavern Heads', subdivided into 'The Landlady', 'The Barmaid', 'The Introducer', 'The Parlour Orator', 'The Man of Many Goes', 'The Sentimental Singer', 'The President' and 'The Last Go'. Focusing the nation around the tavern or (John) Bull's Head, this collection attempts to forge an image not just of an England, but of a Britain of the people. More than half a decade after the Reform Bill and a decade after Catholic

---

42 The genre of the theatrical revue, 'pièce comique qui passe en revue l'actualité', originated in the 1830s. See 'Revue', in *Genres mineurs. Texte zur Theorie und Geschichte nichtkanonischer Literatur (vom 16. Jahrhundert bis zur Gegenwart)*, ed. by Fritz Nies (Munich: Fink, 1978), pp. 95-8. On the proximity between Vaudeville theatre and physiological sketches see Hans-Rüdiger van Biesbrock, *Die literarische Mode der Physiologien in Frankreich (1840-1842)* (Frankfurt a. M.: Lang, 1978), p. 61. Jonathan Crary also points to the affinity between instruction and spectacle in his comments on hypnosis: 'Frequently [hypnosis] would be the centerpiece of the quasi-scientific lecture or demonstration, a specifically nineteenth-century form of didactic entertainment. Just as often, however, the performance of a "magnétiseur" was itself a form of spectacle within a milieu of magic shows, of music hall and proto-vaudeville acts. In fact, many of the important researchers associated with hypnosis in the nineteenth century, including Braid, Charcot, Freud, and the American psychologist G. Stanley Hall, were first exposed to hypnotic practices through such "theatrical" displays and, notably, were convinced by them that there was something important and authentic to study further.' J. Crary, *Suspensions of Perception. Attention, Spectacle and Modern Culture* (Cambridge, MA: MIT Press, 2000), pp. 232-5.
43 [Douglas Jerrold], 'Preface', in *Heads of the People* (note 40), II (1841), iii-iv (p. iv).
44 [Douglas Jerrold], 'Preface', in *Heads of the People*, I (note 40), p. vi.

Illustration 43 Kenny Meadows, vignettes for [Douglas Jerrold], 'Preface', in *Heads of the People*, I (1840), iii and vi. Wood engravings by Orrin Smith.

emancipation, the nation does not (yet) include amongst its political body, for example, types such as 'The Irish Peasant'. Yet he is depicted here with much verve by the Irish writer Samuel Lover, as is his English equivalent, portrayed by William Howitt. True, Howitt's text criticises Meadows's blinkered London perspective on this rural type.[45] Yet these citizens at least have a place in the national encyclopaedia of types, where their 'heads' are represented like everybody else's. This method of national self-inspection was a recipe for international success.

---

45 Samuel Lover, 'The Irish Peasant' and William Howitt, 'The English Peasant', in *Heads of the People*, I (note 40), pp. 298-304 and 257-64. Howitt's critical comments on the 'London prints' of the English peasant, including Meadows's own portrait, are found on p. 257.

A (probably) pirated German translation of *Heads of the People* under the title *England und die Engländer in Bildern aus dem Volke* (England and the English in Popular Pictures)[46] gave rise to *Wien und die Wiener, in Bildern aus dem Leben*, discussed in my Chapter on panoramic collections. Apart from its title being closely modelled on the German translation, the Austrian collection betrays its indebtedness to *Heads of the People* by the very first sketch following Stifter's overview. It deals with the assistant in a draper's shop and shows almost verbatim the same title, 'Der Ladendiener des Modehändlers', as the German translation in *England und die Engländer* of Douglas Jerrold's 'The Draper's Assistant', the twelfth sketch of *Heads of the People*. It seems that Daniel Reibersdorffer, the author of this anonymously published portrait of the 'Ladendiener' and also the original editor of *Wien und die Wiener*, was planning a more or less straight copy of *Heads of the People*, with typological graphic portraits and accompanying written sketches. His text on the draper's assistant actually lifts parts of Jerrold's, most conspicuously its beginning where the assistant's skill in persuading an indecisive female customer is described. Significantly Böhm, the illustrator of *Wien und die Wiener*, produced his drawings before the texts (as did Meadows), and like those of his English model, they are entirely typological. The sketches dealing with Vienna's geographical or topological aspects are not illustrated. It therefore seems safe to assume that the collection had been planned as an encyclopaedia of Viennese types and changed its character to a city panorama after Stifter felt that starting straight away with a sketch of a type and following it with others of the same kind would look too much like a 'soulless' catalogue.[47] Portraits of different kinds, particularly of crowd scenes, were then also included, and, most important of all, the initial overview.

A German collection attempting a review of national conditions or, to quote Jerrold's description of *Heads of the People*, an 'index of the national mind',[48] is *Deutsche Pandora. Gedenkbuch zeitgenössischer Zustände und Schriftsteller* (The German Pandora. Keepsake of Contemporary Conditions and Writers). Except for Karl Buchner's study of the German lawyer ('Der deutsche Advokat'), it contains no typological sketches but concentrates instead on regional portraits. It is remarkable as a major collective work in four

---

46 This translation (see Bibliography) was very probably based on the serial instalments of *Heads of the People* which appeared from November 1838. Many of the contributors are listed under their *noms de plume* (e.g. Henry Brownrigg for Douglas Jerrold) which were dropped in the table of contents of the book edition.
47 See Kai Kauffmann, *"Es ist nur ein Wien!" Stadtbeschreibungen von Wien 1700 bis 1873* (Vienna, Cologne, Weimar: Böhlau, 1994), p. 389.
48 [Jerrold], 'Preface', in *Heads of the People*, I (note 40), p. iii.

volumes (1840-41) with an emphasis on contemporary society and letters. However, it seems an altogether unadventurous, almanac-type publication (not issued as a serial) without an editor or a clear concept. Almost needless to say, it consists of texts only. Some illustrations were, however, included, at least in the form of copper-plate frontispieces, in Eduard Beurmann's *Deutschland und die Deutschen* (Germany and the Germans, four volumes, 1838-40). The work appeared with the same publisher, Hammerich in Altona, who was responsible for Carl von Rotteck's and Theodor Welcker's famous *Staats-Lexikon oder Encyclopädie der Staatswissenschaften* (Civic Dictionary or Encyclopaedia of Political Sciences; 15 volumes, 1834-43). Despite its dry title, this was a politically subversive reference work, edited by two radical professors from Baden and enlightening the virtual German citizen about all aspects of the *civitas* that Germany was not (yet). Beurmann's single-authored work is comparable to this political *orbis doctrinae*. However, his focus is on the actual state of the polity with regard to concepts of modern citizenship, not on these concepts as such. Beurmann's endeavour to produce a socio-political geography of the nation from the critical perspective of the citizen, the *homo politicus*, can perhaps be gleaned from an outline of the contents tables. Volume 1, for example, presents ten chapters dealing with (1) Germany's geographical, cultural and political position between the East and West, North and South of Europe; (2) German rivers, coastlines and merchant cities and their economic, cultural and political significance; (3) the political state of Germany since the Reformation; (4) the German national character; its virtues and its faults; (5, 6) the social fabric of Germany in relation to the various histories and types of the aristocracy; (7, 8) the role of the universities; the isolation of study from public life; (9) school education and the problematic prestige of learning; (10) the state of the German theatre. The following three volumes subject to a similar systematic review individual regions and urban centres mainly in North Germany, from Mecklenburg, Pomerania and Holstein to the Prussian parts of Saxony, Thuringia and Frankfurt am Main. Chapter by chapter the line of investigation is sketched out in the contents tables, as it was in the author's model, Bulwer's *England and the English*.

Unlike Bulwer, however, who was able to review the state of the nation in two densely structured volumes, Beurmann takes four volumes to cover about a third of the nation. The structure of his work reflects the socio-political diversity of a decentralised national body, a diversity to which no single author alone can do justice. A project such as Beurmann's cries out for a looser, panoramic representation by a multitude of contributors supplying political portraits of their own regions (much as *Deutsche Pandora* then did, but with a lack of impetus and direction). Beurmann feels the dilemma himself and gives expression to it in his introduction. As a single author he is embarking on a national survey which must be panoramic because of the great variety of the subject, and he refers to it explicitly as a 'Panorama'. Furthermore, there is the difficulty of not having a 'centre' ('Mittelpunkt'), no national capital or platform from which to co-ordinate the parts of the whole. This is why *England and the English*, written from the secure stance of a metropolitan man of letters, cannot entirely serve as a model for a German writer, even if its critical scrutiny and self-knowledge ('Prüfung', 'Selbsterkenntniß') are exemplary.[49] What Beurmann does produce is not a panorama, but a review of parts of the body politic, and in this respect he follows Bulwer's system of order precisely. However, it is a review that cannot, due to the lack of centralisation in the civic *orbis* it examines, arrange its subject according to branches of knowledge and in the form of subordinated chapters. Instead, it has to be additive and potentially infinite like a serialised collective work. Beurmann's magnum opus breaks off after chapter 60.

The super-encyclopaedia modelled on *Heads of the People* was, of course, *Les Français peints par eux-mêmes*. As in the case of *Wien und die Wiener*, a translation of the running numbers of the English serial (as *Les Anglais peints par eux-mêmes*) acted as the transmission belt. The translation had just become a Parisian success and was in full swing when the first number of *Les Français* appeared in May 1839.[50] The model, *Heads of the People*, had then only been running for six months. The sketch industry was thus producing more or less simultaneously an English 'master' work, a French and a German translation of it, a French and an Austrian 'assimilation', and an English translation of the French 'assimilation'.[51] There were other assimilations in

---

49 See Eduard Beurmann, 'Einleitung', in *Deutschland und die Deutschen*, 4 vols (Altona: Hammerich, 1838-40), I (1838), 1-35 (pp. 18-19 and p. 26).
50 To complicate things slightly, it has to be pointed out that the first instalments of *Les Français* appeared under the title *Les Français, mœurs contemporaines*. It was not until the first volume had been completed at the end of 1839 (dated 1840) that the definitive title *Les Français peints par eux-mêmes* was adopted. The translation of *Heads of the People* as *Les Anglais peints par eux-mêmes* from late 1838 or early 1839 must have been inspired by a Belgian sketch collection, *Les Belges peints par eux-mêmes*, which appeared from September 1838. See Pierre Bouttier, 'Postface', in *Les Français peints par eux-mêmes. Encyclopédie morale du XIXe siècle, éditée par Léon Curmer* ([Paris (?)]: Omnibus, 2003–), I (2003), 1051-1104 (pp. 1071-2).
51 The instalments making up vol. 1 of *Les Français peints par eux-mêmes* (or rather *Les Français, mœurs contemporaines* as it was then still called), and a small number of those from the first volume of the 'Province' series were translated into English as *Pictures of the French: A Series of Literary and Graphic Delineations of French Character* and appeared in book form in 1840 and 1841.

progress or to follow very soon, not of *Heads*, but of the more conspicuous *Les Français*, including *Nashi, spisannye s naturi russkimi* (Our Own People, Painted from Nature by the Russians), 1841-42,[52] and *Los Españoles pintados por sí mismos* (The Spanish Painted by Themselves), 1843-44.[53] What *Les Français* adopted from *Heads of the People* was the graphic representation of the wood-engraved type on a full page outside the text ('horstexte'). The same image-text relationship applies to *Wien und die Wiener*, although it used steel-engraved plates. Wood engravings, the very purpose of which was to be inserted into the text as vignettes or useful illustrations, now appeared on separate pages like traditional plates, a development which testified to the growing significance of this technique of reproduction. Isolated from surrounding text and positioned opposite the first page of the written sketches devoted to them, the wood-engraved types can be seen as an innovation showing the achievements of the medium in developing a 'typology' in its own right, and, at the same time, as a continuation of the 'City Cries' tradition. This traditional genre, which consisted solely of printed image and caption, was in turn modernised by the wood-engraved 'type' in its partnership with a full textual sketch. As in *Heads of the People*, the written sketches of *Les Français* numbered – at least initially – eight pages, the length of an individual 'livraison'.[54] While types of this collection are depicted, as in the English model, against a white background, they are represented as fulllength figurines, not as 'heads'. Janin makes a point of this in his introduction.[55] The emphasis in *Les Français* is therefore not so much on social physiognomy, but on physiology, on the function of the whole professional

---

52 This illustrated collection, edited by A.P. Bashutskii, contained contributions by about half a dozen writers, various draughtsmen and engravers and appeared in St Petersburg as a serial in octavo format; see below, pp. 303-4.
53 Including contributions by the most distinguished writers as well as now obscure journalists, this illustrated collection first appeared in weekly numbers (with the Madrid publisher Boix) and then in two volumes. See J.F. Montesinos, *Costumbrismo y novela. Ensayo sobre el redescubrimiento de la realidad española* (Berkeley & Los Angeles: University of California Press, 1960), pp. 106-7, and H.U. Gumbrecht and J.-J. Sánchez, 'Der Misanthrop, die Tänzerin und der Ohrensessel. Über die Gattung "Costumbrismo" und die Beziehungen zwischen Gesellschaft, Wissen und Diskurs in Spanien von 1805 bis 1851', in *Bewegung und Stillstand in Metaphern und Mythen. Fallstudien zum Verhältnis von elementarem Wissen und Literatur im 19. Jahrhundert*, ed. by Jürgen Link and Wulf Wülfing (Stuttgart: Klett-Cotta, 1984), pp. 15-62 (pp. 30-1).
54 See Bouttier (note 50), p. 1075.
55 '[...] nous nous montrerons [...] non pas seulement peints en buste, mais des pieds à la tête'. Janin (note 24), p. xvi. See also pp. 168-9 of this study.

body in society. In contrast to *Heads of the People*, the written sketches show a vignette of the type's *environment* at the head of the first page ('tête de page') and, in many cases, another one at the end, a tailpiece ('cul de lampe') depicting a scene in the life of the type. This illustrated presentation of the text itself is emphasised by the ornate first letter ('lettre') which shows an often emblematic still life or a significant letter such as 'D' for the grocer's 'delta'. Gavarni's grocer, facing the first page of Balzac's 'L'Épicier', thus appears in the following set-up:

Illustration 44
Gavarni, 'Type, 'Tête de page' and 'Lettre' in [Honoré] de Balzac, 'L'Épicier', in *Les Français peints par eux-mêmes*, 8 vols (Paris: Curmer, 1840-2), I (1840), opposite p. 1 and p. 1. Wood engravings by Lavieille.

Ségolène Le Men sees the regularity with which these clearly defined elements of illustration are employed as a characteristic of the 'ordered' or 'organised' type of sketch collection ('livre ordonné') as distinct from the 'mixed' or 'jumbled' one ('livre-macédoine'), pointing to *Les Français* and

Le Diable à Paris as prime examples of each genre.[56] These two categories correspond to the encyclopaedic and the panoramic order. While the panoramic order of *Le Diable* is composed of a great variety of textual and visual media (scenes, dialogues, essays, narrative, statistics, surveys, topographical and typological sketches, free-standing graphic series such as Gavarni's 'Gens de Paris', and integrated illustrations), the encyclopaedic system of *Les Français* provides for a uniform text type in relation to a predictable range of images, the most important of which being the 'type'. While 'tête de page', 'cul de lampe' and 'lettre' count among the age-old embellishments of print, this 'type', the full-page image presented opposite its accompanying text, is unprecedented.[57]

The term 'type' is consistently used in the table of contents of *Les Français* with reference to these figurines, and thereby a new technical term is introduced into the vocabulary of printing. *Les Français* thus conceptualises the innovation of *Heads of the People* by giving a name to the new kind of typological illustration alongside which the written sketch appears as a kind of encyclopaedia article. This conceptual step forward also clearly manifests itself in a self-consciously encyclopaedic arrangement of the table of contents. While *Heads of the People* lists Meadows's illustrations separately from the written sketches, *Les Français* integrates illustrations and texts in the same contents table, which becomes an illustrated dictionary in its own right (illustration 45, p. 280).

The reader finds the table of contents always set out in this way. Bold letters indicate the name of the type, in other words, the title of the respective sketch, followed by the author's name. The illustrations are then listed as 'Type', 'Tête de page', 'Lettre' and, if applicable, 'Cul-de-lampe', and for each, not only the name of the draughtsman ('dessinateur') is listed, but also that of the engraver ('graveur'). For example, Orrin Smith, the engraver of *Heads of the People*, can be discovered amongst the illustrators of 'Le Bourreau' ('The Executioner'). This order is completed or rather dominated by a tiny replica of the 'type' in both its senses, the social type and his/her graphic representation outside the text. Horizontally, the user's eye is guided from the visual type to the type's denomination, much in the way of a picture lexicon,

---

56 See Ségolène Le Men, 'La Vignette et la lettre', in *Histoire de l'édition française*, ed. by Henri-Jean Martin and Roger Chartier, 4 vols ([Paris]: Promodis, 1983-7), III (1985): *Le Temps des éditeurs. Du Romantisme à la Belle Époque*, 312-27 (pp. 326-7).
57 See Ségolène Le Men, 'Peints par eux-mêmes...', in *Les Français peints par eux-mêmes. Panorama du XIXe siècle* (Paris: Éditions de la Réunion des musées nationaux, 1993), pp. 4-46 (p. 6).

	Dessinateurs. MM.	Graveurs. MM.	Pag.
LE BOURREAU, par M. Félix PYAT.			113
Type.	Pauquet.	Orrin Smith.	ib.
Tête de page.	H. Monnier.	Guillaumot.	ib.
Lettre.	Pauquet.	id.	ib.
Cul-de-lampe.	id.	Orrin Smith.	120

LE SÉMINARISTE, par M. J.-J. PRÉVOST.			121
Type.	Pauquet.	Guillaumot.	ib
Tête de page.	id.	Laisné.	ib.
Lettre.	id.	Caqué.	ib.

LA BOUQUETIÈRE, par madame Mélanie WALDOR.			129
Type.	Gavarni.	Gérard.	ib.
Tête de page.	Pauquet.	Loiseau j.	ib.
Lettre.	id.	Bréval.	ib.

LES AGENTS D'AFFAIRES, par M. Gaetan DELMAS.			137
Type.	Gavarni.	Lavieille.	ib.
Tête de page.	id.	Pervillé.	ib.
Lettre.	Pauquet.	Fontaine.	ib.

LA MAITRESSE DE MAISON, par M. le comte Albert de CIRCOURT.			145
Type.	Eug. Lami.	Lavieille.	ib.
Tête de page.	id.	id.	ib.
Lettre.	Pauquet.	Deghouy.	ib.

LE FIGURANT, par M. Étienne ARAGO.			155
Type.	Gavarni.	Pibaraud.	ib.
Tête de page.	Émy.	Guilbaut.	ib.
Lettre.	id.	Perville.	ib.

Illustration 45
Page from table of contents, in *Les Français peints par eux-mêmes*, III (1841), [356].

while having an array of about a dozen such entries in view on the two facing pages, all ordered in the same way. Read vertically, the tables make a row of figurines file past, one after the other as in the laterna magica show to which Jules Janin compares *Les Français* in his introduction. The types literally pass 'in review' as the contents tables are placed at the end of each volume (if the bookbinder has got it right), thus acting as re- rather than pre-viewing devices. In this way the structuring principle of the collection is made explicit, significantly not by means of discursive text, but through a classifying table combining words and images.

The meticulous listing of 'dessinateurs' and 'graveurs' against the different types of illustration and alongside the names of authors also makes these tables a lexicon of contemporary French writing and graphic art – a dictionary, in other words, of sketchers in words and images. It is easy to see that the model of *Heads of the People*, which also produced a national encyclopaedia through the concerted efforts of one draughtsman, one engraver and a number of 'distinguished writers', is emulated and surpassed through the sheer scale of the enterprise which the publisher Léon Curmer had embarked upon. 137 authors and 44 draughtsmen[58] (not counting the engravers) collaborated on what was to become a monumental eight-volume work in grand-octavo format and 422 instalments,[59] five volumes devoted to Paris and three to the Provinces. Comparable to a major encyclopaedic publication such as Charles Knight's *Penny Cyclopædia*, which appeared in monthly parts over eleven years, such an effort could only be sustained on the basis of a great number of subscribers. 21,000 had initially, according to Pierre Bouttier, put their confidence and money behind *Les Français*.[60] Yet their willingness waned when it became clear that this *Encyclopédie morale du dix-neuvième siècle* was going to exceed its originally envisaged scope considerably,[61] whereupon the publisher issued a free volume with every subscription, *Le Prisme*, which counts as volume nine. The patience of subscribers was, however, tried in other ways too. In addition to the issues of *Le Prisme* starting with the serial's ninety-fifth instalment, Curmer delivered, from number 120 onwards, not only one, but two weekly 'livraisons' – one for the running series on Paris, and one for

---

58 See Bouttier (note 50), p. 1063, note 3.
59 Or 423, as number 26 has a '26 bis'; see ibid., p. 1073.
60 See ibid., p. 1067.
61 The *Penny Cyclopædia*, too, in the end exceeded its proposed limits 'by about one-fourth', as the note to subscribers in the concluding volume, no. 27, dated 20 December, 1843, makes clear. This 'excessive' 25% corresponds exactly to the unforeseen two extra volumes of Curmer's *Encyclopédie morale du XIXe siècle*, bringing the promised maximum of six up to eight. See ibid., p. 1072.

the new series on the Provinces. A subscriber would thus have had to contend with three numbers per week for three different volumes. The serial form of publication of this highly structured work caused chaos. As Bouttier remarks, 'the tables became indispensable'.[62] Not only were individual volumes provided with the enormously detailed tables of contents, but Curmer produced no less than six different tables, forty pages in all, as an ordering device for the entire collection, including *Le Prisme*:

1) a table of contents for the nine volumes,
2) a name index of authors, with their contributions,
3) a subject index based on titles of contributions,
4) a subject index based on categories,
5) a name index of draughtsmen,
6) a synopsis of the 422 'livraisons' and their place within each volume.[63]

Table number four combines the ordering principle of a review (in other words, the subsuming of articles under categories of knowledge) with the alphabetical order of an encyclopaedia. The categories include, for example, 'Armée', 'Beaux-Arts. Peinture. – Musique. – Danse', 'Commerce. Banque. – Bourse', 'Clergé. Mœurs religieuses', 'Éducation. Mœurs universitaires', 'Médecine. – Hôpitaux', and 'Paupérisme. Prisons. – Bagnes'. Since *Les Français peints par eux-mêmes* is intended as a moral encyclopaedia of the nineteenth century, it is worth listing the sub-categories of 'Mœurs' under which sketches are arranged in table four:

Mœurs administratives.
Mœurs coloniales.
Mœurs littéraires.
Mœurs parisiennes.
Mœurs politiques.
Mœurs populaires.
Mœurs sociales.

The device linking the vast numbers of typological sketches is the understanding of the nation as an ensemble of mores. What *Heads of the People* attempted under the sign of John Bull, that is to say, a comprehensive representation of the nation as a popular body, *Les Français peints par eux-*

---

62 'Et les tables s'imposèrent.' Bouttier (note 50), p. 1077.
63 These tables were supposed to be bound at the end of vol. 5; the copy held by the British Library, however, has them at the end of vol. 8.

mêmes attempts through a clear structural division; five volumes for the 'mœurs' of Paris, three for those of the Provinces. These three volumes devoted to the population outside the capital, although started as an afterthought, developed into a sociological project of almost the same weight as the traditional concern with Paris. The *Province* series even includes inhabitants of colonial territories (see above, 'Mœurs coloniales'), and the frontispiece of the volume in which they are represented emphasises the equality of all French people before the law. Such a politically systematic way of depicting French society would, even without the inclusion of overseas citizens, still be an astonishing effort. The sphere of 'mœurs' not only constitutes a link between the enormously different parts of the nation (metropolitan, provincial and colonial) and the categories in which they are classified (administrative, literary, political etc.), but also between the depiction of actual forms of living and the speculation about the general moral direction of the age. The *Encyclopédie morale* of the nineteenth century arises, as in the case of *Die Zeitgenossen*, from a review of existing mores. While in Gutzkow's single-authored serial the systematic arrangement according to social and intellectual categories is made in advance, the monumental collective portrait of the century through typological sketches in *Les Français* is ordered retrospectively by a combination of tables with different functions.

The pivotal role of mores in reviewing the nation lends support not only to politically progressive concepts of citizenship. A Spanish genre defined by the study of mores ('costumbres') and therefore known as *costumbrismo* has a different emphasis, generally critical of the century's tendency to wipe out customs and traditions. Interestingly and significantly, however, *costumbrismo* is closely linked to journalism and would in fact, as Gumbrecht and Sánchez have stressed, be unthinkable without periodical publishing as the engine that mediates knowledge about the times.[64] Despite its appearance in weekly numbers and its text-image correlation, *Los Españoles pintados por sí mismos* is therefore not to be understood as a simple copy of *Les Français peints par eux-mêmes*, but as a 'costumbrist' adaptation responding to the quotidian knowledge and expectations cultivated among a Spanish readership over decades. This adaptation must have been facilitated by the fact that even the French model was by no means free from conservationist views of national or regional identity which were perceived to be threatened by industrialisation. Luce Abélès has drawn attention to a prospectus of the *Province* series of *Les Français* which declares this part of the collection to be essentially backward-looking. 'Before it is too late', Abélès comments, the

---

64 See Gumbrecht and Sánchez (note 53), pp. 22-33.

Province contributors intend to capture the 'particular characteristics of each province – mores, customs, dialects, songs, dances and costumes –' which, according to the prospectus itself, 'give the inhabitants of certain parts of France that veneer *of strangeness* which civilisation is rubbing away day by day'.[65] For the purpose of capturing rural France, the regional portraits follow the old provincial divisions predating the French Revolution. The distinctive 'strangeness' of some provincial citizens would, it seems, not be appreciated if the country were studied in its modern departmental divisions. In other words, it is the pre-modern countryside, not the 'capital of modern civilisation' with its international habits and types, where the body politic is thought to be rooted (an anti-modern emphasis found similarly in *Los Españoles*[66] and, of course, in *Wien und die Wiener* with its focus on popular types and its avoidance of international high[er] society).[67] Abélès detects even in some of the portraits of provincial industrial labourers in *Les Français* a preference for a state of production which is already archaic, and for types that are about to become extinct.[68] Far from furnishing an encyclopaedia of nineteenth-century values, the provinces offer a reservoir of traditional morality. For Édouard Ourliac who contributed the introduction to volume two of the *Province* series, rural France is therefore the home of the true French citizen who has not lost a moral sense.[69] It must, however, be noted that the 'serious' representation of provincial types in *Les Français*, differing quite markedly from the witty depiction of Parisians, is generally free from sentimentality. Paris, after all, takes up five of eight volumes, and the awareness of change pervades the portraiture even of provincial life, literally from start to finish. The table of

---

65 '[...] *Les Français* se donnent pour tâche de fixer, avant qu'il ne soit trop tard, les traits particuliers propres à chaque province – mœurs, coutumes, patois, chants, danses, costumes – "qui donnent aux habitants de certaines parties de la France ce vernis *d'étrangeté* que la civilisation vient effacer chaque jour"'. Luce Abélès, 'La province vue par *Les Français*', in *Les Français peints par eux-mêmes. Panorama du XIXe siècle* (Paris: Éditions de la Réunion des musées nationaux, 1993), pp. 47-61 (pp. 53-5).

66 See Montesinos (note 53), pp. 107-9; on the anti-modern sentiment inherent in the *costumbrismo* genre see also Gumbrecht and Sánchez (note 53), pp. 15-17.

67 On the interest of the *Lebensbild* genre in the 'common people' of the suburbs, perceived as nationally distinctive compared to the educated classes of the inner city, see Kauffmann (note 47), pp. 360-3.

68 See Kauffmann (note 47), p. 53.

69 See Édouard Ourliac, 'Introduction', in *Les Français peints par eux-mêmes. Encyclopédie morale du dix-neuvième siècle. Province*, 3 vols (Paris: Curmer, 1841-2), II (1841), i-viii (pp. iv-v).

contents in the second *Province* volume, for example, is framed by a head vignette representing an arrival at Rouen St Ome by mailcoach, and a tailpiece depicting a departure by train (illustration 46, pp. 286-7). The expansion and acceleration of transport is already bringing the capital and the provinces much closer together, and the provincial 'veneer of strangeness', existing solely in the eye of the metropolitan beholder, may soon have worn off. What makes social encyclopaedias such as *England and the English*, *Heads of the People* and *Les Français* and, in a more limited way, *Deutschland und die Deutschen*, interesting up to the present day is their systematic scrutiny of the national body from the point of view of modernisation, or at least in view of it, whether it is welcomed or not.

Les Français peints par eux-mêmes was not the only French publication reviewing society in series devoted to the capital and to the provinces. Balzac's *Scènes de la vie de province* (1833, 1837) and *Scènes de la vie parisienne* (1834-35), published as parts of a work entitled *Études de mœurs au XIXe siècle* which was to become the *Comédie humaine*, observe the same ordering principle, although the constituent parts are, of course, not sketches but works of fiction. In a less systematic way, this order was also followed by the *Physiologies*, a very important class within the group of encyclopaedic sketch publications. Their peak had been passed by early 1842, up to which time they had focused on Parisian society, although some authors also considered the provinces, for example Balzac and Arnould Frémy in their *Physiologie du rentier de Paris et de province* or Louis Couailhac in his *Physiologie du théâtre, à Paris et en province*. From 1842 provincial *Physiologies*, written by non-Parisian authors and published outside the capital, began to appear more frequently and continued well after the fashion had ebbed.[70]

The encyclopaedic coverage of *Les Français* was thus imitated by a genre that otherwise does not seem to have much in common with Curmer's meticulously organised moral encyclopaedia – the *Physiologies*.[71]

---

70 See Andrée Lhéritier, 'Les Physiologies. Introduction', *Etudes de Presse*, 9:17 (1957), 1-11 (p. 9).

71 The parallel between the *Physiologies* and *Les Français* with regard to Parisian and provincial portraits has been pointed out by Nathalie Preiss-Basset, 'Les physiologies, un miroir en miettes', in *Les Français peints par eux-mêmes. Panorama du XIXe siècle* (Paris: Éditions de la Réunion des musées nationaux, 1993), pp. 62-7 (pp. 62-3).

286 Sketches of the Nineteenth Century

	Dessinateurs MM.	Graveurs. MM.	Pag.
FRONTISPICE.	Delacroix et Pauquet.	Thiébault et Guillaumot.	
INTRODUCTION, par M. Ourliac.			

L'HABITANT DE VERSAILLES,
 par M. Arnould Frémy.   1

Type.	Gavarni.	Birouste.	ib.
Tête de page. Vue du palais et des jardins de Versailles, prise de la cour d'honneur à vol d'oiseau.	Émy.	Orrin Smith.	ib.
Lettre. Bosquet de Trianon.	id.	id.	ib.
Cul-de-lampe. Vue du palais de Versailles, prise de la terrasse à vol d'oiseau.	id.	id.	8

LE PAYSAN DES ENVIRONS DE PARIS, par M. L. Couailhac.   9

Type.	Charlet.	Bara.	ib.
Tête de page.	id.	Guilbaut.	ib.
Lettre.	id.	id.	ib.

Illustration 46
[Hippolyte] Pauquet, 'Arrivée' (engraver: Gusman) ...

The Encyclopaedic Order: Reviewing the Nation and the Century 287

	Dessinateurs. MM.	Graveurs. MM.	Pag.
LE BOURGUIGNON, par M. A. FERTIAULT.			348
Type. COIFFURES BOURGUIGNONNES.	PAUQUET.	GUILLAUMOT.	ib.
Tête de page. Paysage.	JACQUE.	HARRISON.	ib.
Lettre. Armes de la Bourgogne.	DELACROIX.	THIÉBAULT.	ib.
Type. MACONNAISE.	PAUQUET.	BARA.	352
Type. BOURGUIGNON.	JACQUE.	VERDEIL.	360
LE POITEVIN, par M. ED. OURLIAC.			369
Type. POITEVIN.	PAUQUET.	GUILBAUT.	ib.
Tête de page.	GELLÉE.	TAMISIER.	ib.
Lettre.	id.	GUILBAUT.	ib.
TABLE DES MATIÈRES.			
Tête de page. Arrivée.	PAUQUET.	GUSMAND	
Cul-de-lampe. Départ par le chemin de fer.	id.	VERDEIL.	

... and 'Départ par le chemin de fer' (engraver: Verdeil).

Vignettes in the table of contents of *Les Français peints par eux-mêmes. Encyclopédie morale du dix-neuvième siècle. Province*, 3 vols (Paris: Curmer, 1841-2), II (1841), [397, 404]. Wood engravings.

The *Physiologies*: a meta-order of encyclopaedism

At first glance, the little books selling as *Physiologies* which inundated the Parisian book trade in 1840-42 seem indeed little more than a wild commercial offshoot of *Les Français peints par eux-mêmes*. A considerable number (around thirty) of writers and graphic artists who were involved in their production were also contributing to Curmer's serial which had been running since May 1839. It was not, however, the publisher of *Les Français* who profited from the physiological vogue which began to culminate in spring 1841. Curmer only brought out one single *Physiologie* in November 1841 (of the *Jardin des Plantes*, by Pierre Bernard and Louis Couailhac, illustrated by Henry Émy). Other publishers had been jumping on the bandwagon, churning out illustrated monographs on metropolitan types by the dozen. The overlaps between *Les Français* and the *Physiologies* are indeed considerable,[72] including some direct spin-offs. For example, Balzac and Frémy produced their co-authored *Physiologie du rentier* (Physiology of the Man of Independent Means) by combining sketches previously published in *Les Français*, in other words, Balzac's 'Monographie du Rentier' and Frémy's 'L'Habitant de Versailles'.[73] For his *Physiologie* of the metropolitan and provincial theatre, Couailhac, on the other hand, not only drew on his contributions to *Les Français* published in 1839 and 1841 ('La Mère d'actrice', 'Le Sociétaire de la Comédie française' and 'Le Comédien de province'), but simply recycled his Parisian *Physiologie du théâtre* which had appeared in 1841, added a chapter on the provincial stage and then placed the whole thing with a different publisher in 1842.[74]

---

[72] Bouttier (note 50), pp. 1051-9, has drawn attention to the thematic parallels between *Les Français peints par eux-mêmes* and the *Physiologies*. Oddly, however, he seems to suggest that the *Physiologies* predate or set a pattern for Curmer's collection. When the first *Physiologies* started to appear in 1840, well over one hundred typological portraits of *Les Français* had been published and two volumes completed.

[73] See Stéphane Vachon, *Les Travaux et les jours d'Honoré de Balzac. Chronologie de la création balzacienne* (Paris: Presses du CNRS, Presses Universitaires de Vincennes, Les Presses de l'Université de Montréal, 1992), p. 203.

[74] See van Biesbrock (note 42), pp. 106, 162-3; Andrée Lhéritier, 'Répertoire des Physiologies', *Etudes de Presse*, 9:17 (1957), 13-58 (numbers 27 and 28, p. 17). *Physiologie du théâtre, à Paris et en province*, although announced by the *Bibliographie de la France* on the same day as the *Physiologie du théâtre* (15 May 1841), does not seem to have appeared until 1842, the year printed in the publication.

The ferocious commercialism of the *Physiologies*, shared by publishers, authors and illustrators alike, is also evident from the number of titles that appeared in Paris alone (about 120 in 1841-42), the average print run per title (3,500; a high figure as book editions would not normally exceed 2,000 copies), the ratio between the total number of copies sold (about half a million) and the population of Paris (under a million), the relatively cheap price per copy (1 franc; on average, books cost 3 fr. 50), and the aggressive marketing strategies of competing or collaborating publishers.[75] These statistics, testifying to a frenzied, well and truly industrial production of physiological sketches over a span of two years, leave out of account the more or less simultaneous serial appearance of *Les Anglais* and *Les Français peints par eux-mêmes* (Curmer, 1839-42), of *Muséum parisien* (Beauger and Aubert, 1840-41), *Scènes de la vie privée et publique des animaux* (Hetzel, 1840-41) or *Le Musée pour rire*, one hundred lithographs by Daumier, Gavarni, Grandville, Bouchot and Traviès with accompanying texts by Alhoy, Huart and Philipon (Aubert, 1838-39). This phenomenal productivity of sketchers in words and images and their publishers, which becomes even more stupendous when one thinks of its European dimensions around 1840, finds its epitome in the vogue of *Physiologies*. These publications have to be seen (and were clearly seen by their producers) as the culmination point of the ephemeral in the sphere of letters, a development which had started with the eighteenth- and early nineteenth-century *tableaux* and received an unparalleled impetus after the July Revolution. It is the high degree of self-awareness and self-irony, the parodistic trait and the sheer virtuosity of interplay between text and image that makes the *Physiologies* a moral encyclopaedia in their own right.

Following Andrée Lhéritier's pioneering bibliographical work, Hans-Rüdiger van Biesbrock has thoroughly defined the 'genuine' *Physiologie* as opposed to publications of around 1840 merely using this generic title. The characteristics of the genre are, primarily and significantly, found in its uniform presentation.[76] The title *Physiologie de ...* is followed by a noun with definite article, as can be seen, for example, in the typological *Physiologie du garde national*, *Physiologie de l'étudiant* or *Physiologie du flâneur*. There are also topographical, sociological and cultural-semiological variants such as *Physiologie du Jardin des Plantes*, ~ *des bals de Paris*, ~ *du théâtre*, ~ *du vin de Champagne*, ~ *de l'omnibus*, ~ *du calembourg* (of the pun) and even ~ *du parapluie* (of the umbrella) or ~ *du gant* (of the glove). Authors are often

---

75 See Lhéritier, 'Les Physiologies' (note 70), pp. 7-9; van Biesbrock (note 42), pp. 106-12.
76 See Lhéritier, 'Les Physiologies' (note 70), p. 9, and van Biesbrock (note 42), pp. 84-112.

anonymous and may be wittily referred to as types in the title. Thus, for example, the *Physiologie du parapluie* is by *deux cochers de fiacre* (two cabmen), that of the pun, the *calembourg*, by *un nain connu* (which is itself a pun on 'un inconnu'), while *deux buveurs d'eau* (two water-drinkers) take responsibility for the *Physiologie du vin de Champagne*. The vast majority of these books appear in the pocket-size format of 'in-32', that is to say, 16° (approximately 9 x 14 cm or 3 ½ x 5 ½ in.), a quarter of the size of an octavo page, and their number of pages is around 120, typically 128, which corresponds to four folio sheets @ 32 pages. Any unfilled pages at the end are used for publishers' adverts. Normally, a *Physiologie* is illustrated by about 40 wood-engraved vignettes, including 'lettres', 'têtes de page' and 'culs de lampe', and the buff or pale blue paper cover is also illustrated or ornamented (illustration 47).

The well-known publishers of graphic art, Aubert, in partnership with Lavigne, were by far the most active producers of *Physiologies*, but their dominance does not explain the stylistic convergence between these publications. A synoptic table compiled by van Biesbrock proves that the majority of *Physiologies* which deviate from the presentation criteria described above show only minor variations from the norm.[77] This astonishing degree of uniformity achieved between about ten different Parisian publishing houses or consortia suggests that, albeit as competitors, they were collaborating on an undeclared project – 'Les Physiologies' – which emulated and parodied Curmer's monumental national review in *Les Français peints par eux-mêmes*. The *Physiologies* appear like parts of a serial, like standardised contributions to an encyclopaedia of types and mores. The subjects they cover are more wide-ranging than the purely typological ones of *Les Français* and seem to be carefully chosen so that no subject is 'physiologisé' more than once. On the other hand, the fact that the *Physiologies* remain individual publications, in other words, that they are not formally parts of a serial collection, is also important. One could see them as an informal encyclopaedic project that is deliberately left fragmentary. *Physiologies* eschew an aspiration to totality, to universal knowledge, by focusing on one phenomenon only, and (if one views them all together as a corpus of publications) by presenting society in bits and pieces. Nathalie Preiss-Basset has aptly referred to them as a 'mirror in smithereens' ('un miroir en miettes').[78] She has also pointed to the anti-systematic character of some *Physiologies* which deal with fashion, and has drawn attention to a certain anarchic tendency which is achieved by punning

---

77 See van Biesbrock (note 42), pp. 91-7.
78 See Preiss-Basset, 'Les physiologies, un miroir en miettes' (note 71).

The Encyclopaedic Order: Reviewing the Nation and the Century 291

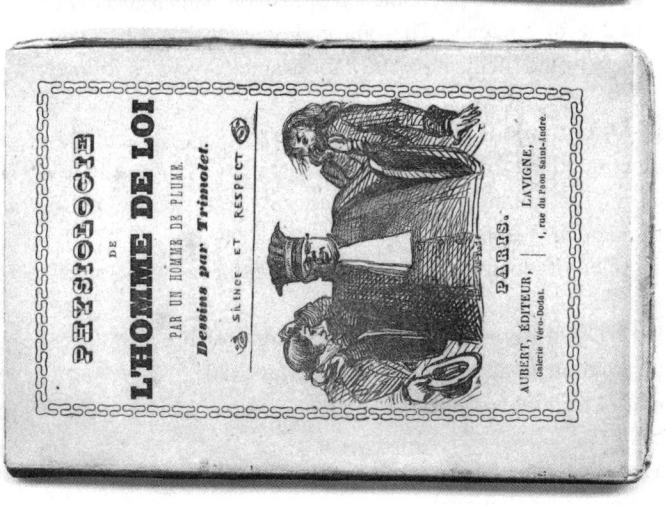

Illustration 47 Covers of:
[Anon.], *Physiologie de l'homme de loi par un homme de plume. Vignettes de MM. Trimolet et Maurisset* (Paris: Aubert, Lavigne, [1841]).
E. Bourget, *Physiologie du gamin de Paris, galopin industriel. Illustrations de Mar[c]kl* (Paris: Laisné; Aubert, Lavigne, 1842).

and other forms of word-play.⁷⁹ The concern of *Physiologies* with fashionable ephemera and their focus on language goes hand in hand with a study of surfaces. In this light they emerge as forerunners of present-day theories of signifiers, an aspect I will develop in my last Chapter. What is of interest in the present context is the suggestion of a fragmentary encyclopaedia.

By the generic title *Physiologie de ...* these sketches indicate the sociological angle from which their subjects are studied. The application of medical and zoological paradigms to the study of society was, by 1840, becoming commonplace. Individual types are thus explicitly portrayed as parts of a social body, an emphasis not found in titles included in *Heads of the People*, *Wien und die Wiener* or *Les Français* where types are simply listed as 'The ...', 'Der ... / Die...' or 'Le .. / La ...' respectively. While the serial collections suggest the physiological or topological interconnections between their parts by systems of order, the individually published *Physiologies* suggest the links between their isolated objects of study by their title. The physiological model thus advertised, they engage in classification. 128 pages as opposed to eight per type in *Heads* or *Les Français* offer ample space, despite the minute format, for subdivisions. A *Physiologie* therefore constitutes a monograph in the original sense, a treatise on a single subject of natural history, for example, a species, or in this case, on a profession, place, institution or a phenomenon of fashion. This is usually clearly indicated in the table of contents. The one in Louis Huart's *Physiologie du médecin* (Physiology of the Medical Doctor), for example, reads as follows:

> CHAPITRE I. – Avant-propos philosophico-médical.
> (Philosophico-medical foreword)
> CHAPITRE II. – Du nombre des médecins qui exercent, ou plutôt qui n'exercent guère en France.
> (Of the number of doctors who practise, or rather do *not* practise in France)
> CHAPITRE III. – Des différents moyens de se rendre célèbre.
> (Of the different methods of making oneself famous)
> CHAPITRE IV. – Les homœopathes.
> (Homeopaths)
> CHAPITRE V. – L'agrément des consultations.
> (The pleasure of consultations)

---

79 See Nathalie Basset, 'Les Physiologies au XIXe siècle et la mode. De la poésie comique à la critique', *Année balzacienne*, 1984, 157-72, and the relevant section in her book: N. Preiss, *Les Physiologies en France au XIXe siècle. Étude historique, littéraire et stylistique* (Mont-de-Marsan: Éditions InterUniversitaires, 1999), pp. 68-87.

CHAPITRE VI. – Les hydropathes.
(Hydropaths)
CHAPITRE VII. – Du magnétisme, du somnambulisme et du jobardinisme.
(Of magnetism, somnambulism and gullibility)
CHAPITRE VIII. – De la médecine et de la philanthropie.
(Of medicine and philanthropy)
CHAPITRE IX. – Deuxième classe de médecins philanthropes. Les docteurs en jupon.
(The second class of philanthropical physicians. Doctors in skirts)
CHAPITRE X. – Le médecin des eaux.
(The doctor of waters)
CHAPITRE XI. – Le médecin des dames.
(The ladies' doctor)
CHAPITRE XII. – Du chirurgien militaire et du médecin de campagne.
(Of the military surgeon and the country doctor)
CHAPITRE XIII. – Les empiriques voyageurs.
(Itinerant empirics)
CHAPITRE XIV. – Prodiges de la chirurgie.
(Wonders of surgery)
CHAPITRE XV. – Quelques mots sur les pharmaciens.
(A few words on pharmacists)
CHAPITRE XVI. – Epilogue et morale.[80]
(Epilogue and moral)

This structure shows a sequence of sixteen more or less independent sketches (their number may vary, but the table shown here is representative). The chapters do not represent a synthetic order as, for example, those of *England and the English* or *Die Zeitgenossen* which construct society or the century from various strands of knowledge, which are in turn synthesised from the study of types and phenomena. A *Physiologie* presents the opposite, that is to say, an analytical order, dividing a single social subject into many parts. A key profession is here split up into its classes, including fashionable types such as the homeopath; the doctor prescribing water as a panacea, either normal drinking water (the hydropath) or special spa water (the doctor of waters); the neo-Mesmerite believing in magnetism; or the ladies' doctor who specialises in the caprices of the bored, spoilt middle-class woman, has achieved the same function that was once her confessor's, and what is more,

---

80 Louis Huart, *Physiologie du médecin. Vignettes de Trimolet* (Paris: Aubert, Lavigne, [1841]), p. 123.

is 'in supreme control of his patient's body and soul'.[81] Analysing the medical profession in this way is almost tantamount to writing a sociology of the century's lead science, or of the medical paradigm that has replaced religion. However, the numerous specialisations of the profession are shown to be anything but beneficial to medicine or to society. They are indicative of the fact that this science has not only ousted religious belief, but that it has also clearly begun to play the role of a new faith. Therefore it has become an eldorado for charlatans, speculators and careerists. What is typical of a *Physiologie* is the unremitting satire in depicting differentiation, specialisation and fragmentation and its materialist aspects, without, however, moralising about a lost unity or a functional totality to be achieved.[82] Thus, in *Physiologie du médecin*, no notion of a unifying function of the medical profession is developed. The 'Epilogue et morale', the shortest chapter in the book, states that there is no moral to be drawn from the study of doctors since the subject is utterly devoid of morality:

> Following our laudable habit we did not wish to take leave of our readers without making them painstakingly aware and appreciative of the moral of the work they have just read.
> However, all our greatest efforts have been in vain; we have been unable to arrive at any result but the following; – which is to say that the conduct of all the medical charlatans of our age lacks even the slightest moral standards.[83]

If all the varieties of doctors are immoral, not even sharing a basic professional ethos, they cannot be synthesised into a moral type. 'The' physician of the nineteenth century therefore does not exist. Readers are to evolve for themselves, from the immoral *mœurs* depicted, what the *Physiologie* refuses to posit, which is a notion of medical practice as it should be, according to the needs of the individual organism and the social body as a whole. A *Physiolo-*

---

81 '[...] le souverain directeur de l'âme et du corps de sa cliente'. Huart (note 80), p. 78.
82 On specialisation as a prominent subject of *Physiologies* see van Biesbrock (note 42), p. 235, and Sieburth (note 22), pp. 49-50.
83 'Suivant notre louable habitude nous n'avons pas voulu prendre congé de notre lecteur sans lui faire soigneusement remarquer et apprécier toute la morale de l'ouvrage qu'il vient de lire. / Mais c'est en vain que nous avons fait les efforts les plus grands, nous n'avons pas pu arriver à un autre résultat que celui-ci: – C'est que dans la conduite de tous les charlatans médicaux de l'époque il n'y a pas la moindre morale!' Huart (note 80), p. 122.

gie is thus often a 'pathologie', confining itself to the satirical depiction of social ills and follies. The sensitive link between the analysis of existing mores and the synthesis of a moral totality is not made by these monographs. In this respect they differ from earlier *Physiologies*, for example, from Balzac's 'L'Épicier', where a totality of social interaction and moral dispositions is clearly suggested within the analysis. It is not by chance that this sketch opens, in a revised form, the encyclopaedic project of *Les Français*. In the *Physiologies* of 1840-42 the social, moral and cognitive whole of which their subjects form part usually remains a suggestion made by the title, *Physiologie de* ... , and by the 'serial' presentation. Whether or not they formed a deliberate parodistic opposition to the grandiose synthetic project of *Les Français peints par eux-mêmes* and its claim to be a moral encyclopaedia of the century may never be established, but the evidence strongly suggests that this was the case.

The self-conscious ephemerality of the *Physiologies* is another aspect which allows us to see them, somewhat paradoxically, as a kind of encyclopaedic project. Their cheapness and pocket format predestined them to be read and thrown away. As 'run-of-the-mill products of the street' not designed to end up in luxuriously bound coffee-table and library volumes such as the tomes of *Les Français*,[84] they focus on every *dernier cri* and, of course, on their own intimate connection to journalism.[85] The journalist's and the caricaturist's combined eye, touch, wit and commercial nous, applied in a highly self-reflective manner, provides a stylistic and discursive link between all those specialised monographs, a degree of 'inter-discursiveness' which an encyclopaedia would not achieve even under the strictest conventions. This is indicated by the fact that anonymous *Physiologies* repeatedly state their authors' occupations as professional writers. A title such as *Physiologie de l'homme de loi, par un homme de plume* is a good example. The specialism of the man of law is transcended by the discourse of (the man of) letters, which ties the legal system into a meta-order. It also accords perfectly with the self-reflective logic of journalistic writing if the anonymous *Physiologie des Physiologies* launches a fulminant attack

---

84 See Bouttier (note 50), pp. 1057-8. He also remarks on the 'perishable' nature of the *Physiologies*, the cheap products of their day, in relation to their extreme rarity and value today (p. 1056, note 2).

85 It was probably Charles Philipon, former editor of *La Caricature* and in charge of its successor, *Le Charivari* (both published by his brother-in-law, Aubert), who played a leading part in launching the *Physiologies*. Practically the complete 'équipe' of *Le Charivari*, including the draughtsmen Daumier, Gavarni and Grandville and the writers Couailhac, Huart, Delord and Cler, produced *Physiologies* for Aubert which were duly advertised in *Le Charivari*. See Lhéritier, 'Les Physiologies' (note 70), pp. 6-7.

on the vacuousness of the genre. It does so, of course, by applying all the witty ruses of a *Physiologie* within the standard 126 pages (leaving some of them almost blank as an illustration of the subject), and by re-using illustrations already published in other *Physiologies* (as was common practice) by one of the busiest producers of vignettes, Henry Émy.[86] The publisher, Desloges, was the second most productive churner-out of *Physiologies* after the Aubert / Lavigne consortium. This text should therefore not be read simply as a satirically distanced comment on the industry, as seems to have become habitual with those writing about *Physiologies*,[87] but very much as a self-reflective part of it. The criticism made in *Physiologie des Physiologies* of the present-day 'homme de lettres' as being on a par with the 'épicier' (both equally driven by mercantile interest, they serve each other as content and form),[88] thus fully applies to the physiology of the *Physiologies* itself. And when this text criticises the catch-word *Physiologie* for being a mere title and nothing else,[89] it formulates both a critique of the genre's commercialism and a shrewd self-analysis. *Physiologies* of 1840-42 indeed do not generally spell out physiological interconnections – their restriction to the particular is their hallmark, and the suggested 'whole' is nothing but an allusive title. Sieburth sees the *Physiologie des Physiologies* as a more or less parodistic farcical treatment of the whole genre ('farce plus ou moins parodique du genre tout entier'), but fails to acknowledge the fundamentally parodistic, self-reflective trait of this 'whole genre' as a journalistic medium. The point is not that the genre provided easy distraction, making sure that its humour never overstepped the limits of perfect harmlessness ('que l'humour n'outrepassait jamais les bornes de la parfaite inocuité'),[90] but that it offered critical keys to the phenomenon of journalism, the century's engine for constituting, diffusing and recycling 'type'.

As one of many examples of this self-analytical spirit, the beginning of the *Physiologie du théâtre. Par un journaliste* may be cited. The author Couailhac

---

86 See Lhéritier, 'Répertoire des Physiologies' (note 74), p. 22.
87 See, for example, Lhéritier, 'Répertoire' (note 74), p. 1; van Biesbrock (note 42), pp. 103-4, pp. 200-01; Preiss-Basset, 'Les physiologies, un miroir en miettes' (note 71), p. 62; Bouttier (note 50), p. 1055-6.
88 'La variété de l'épicier et celle de l'homme de lettres. Ces deux classes de l'humanité si utiles l'une à l'autre, la première pour le contenu, et la seconde pour le contenant.' ('The variety of the grocer and that of the man of letters. These two classes of humanity so useful to one another, one for the content, the other for the containing.') [Anon.], *Physiologie des Physiologies* (Paris: Desloges, 1841), p. 18.
89 'Une Physiologie est un titre. [...] Le volume entier est sur la première page.' ('A Physiologie is a title. [...] The entire volume is on the first page.') Ibid., pp. 96-7.
90 Sieburth (note 22), p. 43 and p. 45.

chose to remain an anonymous man of the press, in order to lend credibility, as he himself purports, to his depiction of the backstage world. To gain access to this 'sanctuary, you need to be one of the priests in charge of the cult, a comedian, an author' or – now comes the typically ironic self-reference – or 'at the very least a journalist'.[91] Couailhac was already active as an author of vaudevilles (and would be on a regular basis in the 1850s, like his English counterpart Albert Smith who wrote stage extravaganzas in the 40s), but introducing himself as a penny-a-liner was obviously much more appropriate to the medium of the cheap physiological sketch. Journalism is the essential make-up of the *Physiologie du théâtre*. This is the real reason why the author introduces himself as a humble writer of play reviews whose life depends on his good standing with the theatre world. A portrait of this type is found in *Physiologie de la presse*, and with explicit reference to our author:

L. Couailhac, dealer in economic articles who produces everything, sells everything, and writes everywhere; one of the supporting pillars of all the publications paid at two *sous* per line [...].[92]

The self-introduction of the anonymous hack in *Physiologie du théâtre* contains his own portrait 'after nature'. Even if he does not wish to disclose his name so as not to jeopardise his free access to the stages of Paris, he wants to be recognised by the reader should they ever meet; for, he argues (alluding to the reader's daily encounter with journalism), one always likes running into an old companion. After 'Here I am' ('Me voici'), the reader finds the picture of a grumpy, pedantic-looking eighteenth-century fellow in breeches and buckled shoes, in other words, the very opposite of the fashionable 'homme de plume' who trades in all sorts of writing for the day. The design of the figure is equally coarse, in the style of eighteenth-century caricature. This image could be a humorous travesty of the man in a top hat who has entered the back-stage space, facing the viewer, in Émy's frontispiece of this *Physiologie*. The two illustrations are separated by only three pages:

---

91 'Pour pénétrer dans le sanctuaire, il faut être l'un des desservants du culte, comédien, auteur ou tout au moins journaliste.' [Louis Couailhac], *Physiologie du théâtre. Par un journaliste. Vignettes par MM. H. Émy et Birouste* (Paris: Laisné; Aubert, Lavigne, 1841), pp. 5-6.

92 '[...] marchand d'articles économiques, qui fait de tout, qui vend de tout, qui écrit partout; l'un des soutiens obligés de toutes les publications à deux sous la ligne [...].' [Anon.], *Physiologie de la presse. Biographie des journalistes et des journaux de Paris et de la province* (Paris: Laisné; Aubert, Lavigne, 1841), p. 64.

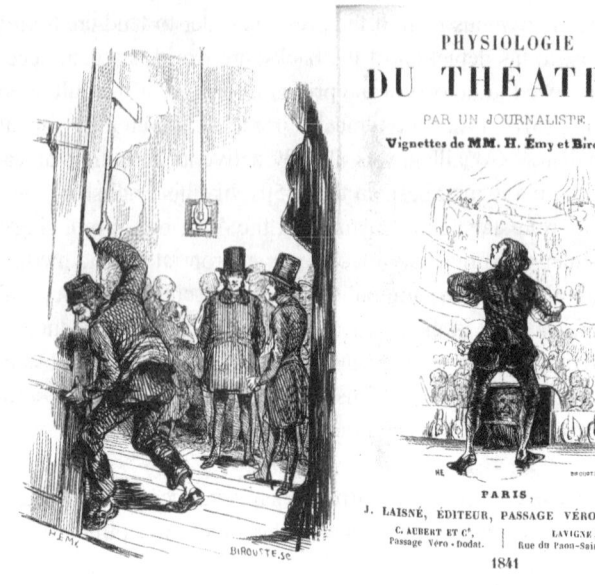

Illustration 48   Henry Émy, frontispiece, title illustration and vignette (p. 7) in [Louis Couailhac], *Physiologie du théâtre. Par un journaliste* (Paris: Laisné; Aubert, Lavigne, 1841). Wood engravings by Birouste.

The Encyclopaedic Order: Reviewing the Nation and the Century   299

The reader, well familiar with the physiognomy of modern journalism anyway, knows that the pen-and-pencil self-portrait of the journalist is a comic distortion and that the true face of the profession is to be found within the pages of the *Physiologie* itself, in the wit and allusiveness of its style. The journalist himself will remain un-portrayed; his personal identity is immaterial.

Self-referentiality also characterises, as can be expected, the anonymous *Physiologie de la presse*. Its frontispiece shows a journalist who also remains unidentifiable, literally faceless as his drooping head disappears behind the top hat he is about to put on:

Imprimerie de Ve Dondey-Dupré, rue St-Louis, 46, au Marais.

Illustration 49 [Anon.], frontispiece in [Anon.], *Physiologie de la presse. Biographie des journalistes et des journaux de Paris et de la province* (Paris: Laisné; Aubert, Lavigne, 1841).

Ironically, the *Physiologie de la presse* then offers individualised portraits in the form of a 'biographical' lexicon of present-day journalists and journals. The links between the *Physiologies* and journalism are thus made very obvious, as Nathalie Preiss has remarked in pointing out the prominence this genre gives to current affairs and actual personalities (thus continuing the business of political caricature under the guise of social portraits):

> [...] if the *Physiologistes* inscribe themselves into the tradition of the seventeenth-century moralists, they also know how to innovate by taking a deliberate interest in the most topical news. This is exemplified by the *Physiologie de la presse* which, instead of presenting general types, takes the form of a Biography of journalists and of a 'Biography in action', since even minor fluctuations in the direction of a journal are registered. [...] And this link that unites *Physiologies* with current events seems fundamental in that it distinguishes these works [...] from the series *Les Français peints par eux-mêmes* (to which they come close [...] in several respects).[93]

Yet, however closely the topicality of their references may link the *Physiologies* to journalism, they often expose it as an immoral or at least questionable business, as is illustrated by the comments on Louis Couailhac quoted above. The *Physiologie de la presse* is designed to make the reader think about journalism as 'the fourth power' which has nearly eclipsed the traditional three, in other words, executive, legislature and judiciary.[94] It lists journals by their method of publication (dailies, weeklies, reviews etc.) and provides brief

---

93 '[...] si les *Physiologistes* s'inscrivent dans la tradition des moralistes du XVIIe siècle, ils savent aussi innover et s'intéresser délibérément à l'actualité la plus proche, témoin la *Physiologie de la Presse* qui, au lieu de présenter des types généraux, prend la forme d'une Biographie des journalistes et d'une "Biographie en action" puisque les moindres fluctuations dans la direction ou la rédaction d'un journal sont enregistrées. [...] Et ce lien qui unit les *Physiologies* et l'actualité apparaît fondamental, dès lors qu'il distingue ces ouvrages [...] de la série *Les Français peints par eux-mêmes* (dont ils se rapprochent [...] par plusieurs aspects) [...].' Preiss, *Les Physiologies en France au XIXe siècle* (note 79), pp. 67-8.

94 '[...] le journalisme [...] n'est pas seulement un quatrième pouvoir dans l'état, il est le plus puissant et le plus influent de tous les pouvoirs, et il menace d'absorber les trois autres, déjà passablement amoindris.' ('[..] journalism is not only the fourth power within the state, it is the most powerful and most influential of all the powers and is threatening to absorb the three others which are already fairly weakened.') *Physiologie de la presse* (note 92), pp. i-ii.

sketches of their stance in the political spectrum of the July Monarchy, complete with the latest information on their chief staff and collaborators. The fact that, of all the publications of the vogue, the *Physiologie de la presse* appears as a simple reference work, provides a clue with regard to the encyclopaedic character of the *Physiologies*. Their *orbis* of social knowledge, it has been argued, is fragmented as far as their subjects are concerned (Lorettes, bourgeois, umbrellas, omnibuses etc.). With regard to the *way in which* they treat their objects, however, the *Physiologies* represent an unbroken mirror, a full self-critical review and complete dictionary of professional journalism, the 'fourth power' which is the engine of social knowledge and public opinion. Each *Physiologie* is in fact an indirect self-portrait of journalism through the object that is 'physiologised', so that together they constitute an encyclopaedia in the figurative sense, a witty universe of the century's sociophysiological medium and of the 'métalangage' which points the reader to the journalistic features of the genre.[95] Günter Oesterle's comments on the *feuilleton* apply in every sense equally to the genre of the *Physiologie* and may serve to illuminate my argument that this genre constitutes an encyclopaedia of itself as a medium:

> The feuilleton thrives on self-criticism, on the awareness of its own inevitable *piquanterie* and going-in for effects, inextricably linked as they are to a quest for daguerreotypical precision, for the crucial point in the description of new modes of behaviour that are appearing. [...] The *feuilleton* is a self-reflective genre particularly in the sense that it knows about the peculiarity of its own medium, the difference between book and journal, and that it seeks to respond to this difference by a language that is self-critical.[96]

---

95 See Basset, 'Les Physiologies au XIXe siècle et la mode' (note 79), p. 162, and Preiss, *Les Physiologies en France au XIXe siècle* (note 79), p. 76.
96 'Das Feuilleton lebt von der Selbstkritik, vom Bewußtsein der notwendigen Pikanterie und Effektproduktion und der gleichzeitigen Suche nach der daguerreotypischen Genauigkeit, nach dem *punctum saliens* in der Beschreibung neu aufkommender Verhaltensweisen. [...] Das Feuilleton ist eine selbstreflexive Gattung gerade auch in dem Sinne, daß es um die Eigenart seines Mediums, um die Differenz von Buch und Journal weiß und darauf sprachkritisch zu reagieren versucht.' Günter Oesterle, '"Unter dem Strich". Skizze einer Kulturpoetik des Feuilletons im neunzehnten Jahrhundert', in *Das schwierige neunzehnte Jahrhundert*, ed. by Jürgen Barkhoff, Gilbert Carr and Roger Paulin (Tübingen: Niemeyer, 2000), pp. 229-50 (p. 235).

The connections between *Physiologies* via self-referentiality also work at a cross-cultural level. Albert Smith's *Natural Histories*, produced to exactly the same formula as their Parisian models and sold at one shilling each,[97] would have fully participated in the vogue if they had appeared about six years earlier. In Smith's description of the English 'Ballet Girl' as the nearest approximation to a Parisian Grisette, we find a tiny vignette of a bard singing the praise of the type:

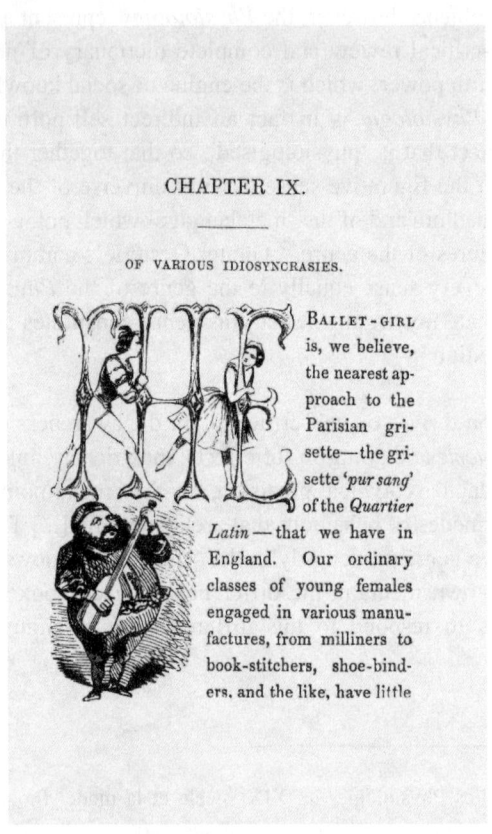

Illustration 50   Archibald S. Henning, vignette in Albert Smith, *The Natural History of the Ballet Girl* (London: Bogue, 1847), p. 93. Wood engraving.

---

97 Apparently all 2,000 copies of his *Natural History of the Gent*, the first of his '*Physiologies*', sold out in a day. The work was an early 'best-seller'; see 'Smith, Albert Richard', in *Oxford Dictionary of National Biography*, ed. by H.C.G. Matthew and Brian Harrison, 60 vols (Oxford: Oxford University Press, 2004), LI, 29-30 (p. 29).

An 'invocation' often introduces a *Physiologie* (see *Physiologie de la Lorette* discussed in Chapter 3),[98] and this is what the image of the singer in Smith's *Natural History of the Ballet Girl* alludes to. Moreover, the rotund minstrel bears the features of Jules Janin, who had written the sketch on the Grisette in the first volume of *Les Français peints par eux-mêmes*. Thus, the comparison between Ballet Girl and Grisette is mediated by an implicit comparison between the sketchers. Whether Smith and Henning refer to the icons of French journalism, Janin and Gavarni (the illustrator of Janin's 'La Grisette') to heighten the physiological portrait of the English dancer, or whether they imply their own journalistic kinship with them seems relatively unimportant; what matters in our context is the self-referentiality of the medium. In the same *Natural History* we find a modification of Émy's frontispiece for Couailhac's *Physiologie du théâtre* (illustration 51, p. 304). The re-use of wood engravings already published was common in *Physiologies*, as indicated above. By adapting the Parisian sketch of the scene-shifter, the London illustrator Henning alludes to this practice. He has changed the theatre staff behind the scenes to include ballet dancers, but gives similar prominence to the male intruder with a top hat who is not part of the theatre world – in other words, to the class including the journalist who has free access to this sphere and who 'physiologises' the ballet girl.

Like the model of *Les Français peints par eux-mêmes* itself, its reflection in the vogue of *Physiologies* became an international phenomenon. I have, however, drawn the line at checking cross-national connections between Spanish, Russian and French physiological sketches. Suffice it to say that the genre of the *Fisiología* or *Fisiologiya* respectively was very successful in Spain and in Russia, where the 'lion' of critics, Vissarion Belinskii, acted as its 'great promoter'.[99] He also wrote an important laudatory review of *Nashi, spisannye s naturi russkimi*, the Russian equivalent of *Les Français*, which stresses the fact that this *'de luxe'* edition, particularly the refinement of its wood-engraved sketches, mark Russia's catching-up with Western European publishing.[100]

---

98 See pp. 112-13.
99 See Montesinos (note 53), pp. 102-06; Joachim T. Baer, 'The "Physiological Sketch" in Russian Literature', in *Mnemozina. Studia litteraria russica in honorem Vsevolod Setchkarev*, ed. by J.T. Baer and Norman W. Ingham (Munich: Fink, 1974), pp. 1-12 (p. 3).
100 'Not for nothing does the cover of *Nashi* read: "the first Russian *édition de luxe*". Indeed, until now hardly anyone would even have dreamt of such as publication in Russia. The enterprising A.P. Bashutskii (to whom the original idea for *Nashi*

Illustrations 51a and b

Archibald S. Henning, vignette in Albert Smith, *The Natural History of the Ballet Girl* (London: Bogue, 1847), p. 45. Wood engraving.

Henry Émy, frontispiece in [Louis Couailhac], *Physiologie du théâtre. Par un journaliste* (Paris: Laisné; Aubert, Lavigne, 1841). Wood engraving by Birouste.

---

belongs, and under whose editorship the publication now proceeds) has shown that as far as elegant *éditions de luxe* are concerned, we do not in fact lag behind Europe itself. In actual fact *Nashi* is as refined a publication as it is sumptuous. The drawings of Messrs. Timm, Shchedrovskii, and Shevchenko are remarkable for their characteristic originality and faithfulness to reality; woodcuts of these have been produced by Baron Klodt, Deriker, and Baron Nettel'gorst. This alone is already sufficient evidence of the publication's *refinement*.' Untitled review by Belinskii in *Otechestvennye zapiski* (Notes on the Fatherland), 2 (1842), pp. 45-6. Translated by Carol Adlam, in *Russian Visual Arts: Art Criticism in Context, 1814-1909*, ed. by C. Adlam, R. Russell and A. Makhrov (Sheffield: HRI Online, 2005). <http://hri.shef.ac.uk/rva/texts/belinskii/belin02/belin02.html>, accessed 09/06. I am grateful to Carol Adlam, Exeter, for supplying this reference.

Perhaps one could venture the following hypotheses. In their own national as well as in the international context, the 1840s *Physiologies* (or *Natural Histories*) constitute an encyclopaedic meta-system, partly by parodying collective sketch publications which follow an encyclopaedic order, partly by constructing a network of self-references which focus on the industrial scale of sketch production, its ephemerality, its commercialism, its connections to journalism, and, above all, the function of journalism as a medium which popularises the cognitive paradigm of physiology. *Physiologies* form an order of journalistic self-knowledge. On the other hand, the genre's encyclopaedic character is not confined to the level of discourse and presentation. Its systematic analysis of types and phenomena one by one constitutes an *orbis* of social knowledge, however disjointed, which is of great value even (and perhaps especially) for today's research into the nineteenth century.

***

Sketch collections observing an encyclopaedic order attempt to synthesise a contemporary portrait of the nation or of the century on the basis of classifying, systematising, grouping and cataloguing types and manners. This ordering system relies to a considerable extent on sketches that are already pre-structured so that they fit into the encyclopaedic frame in terms of subject matter, style and presentation. Typological sketches informed by the paradigms of physiognomy and physiology therefore prevail, often produced to a standard layout or to a format involving several presentation criteria. Single-authored works that can be called 'encyclopaedic' show the centrality of moral observation very clearly. From it derives all the knowledge about the nation and the century. The language of letters, which forms the bond between the specialised articles in an encyclopaedia, is equally at home in publications by men of letters who are active as review editors, journalists and sketch-writers. The witty, self-referential journalistic discourse of the *hommes de plume* writing *Physiologies* is in fact a major feature linking these fragmented analytical sketches together to an encyclopaedic project *malgré soi*.

As in panoramic sketch productions, the reader is faced with an enormous volume of detailed, and also fragmented, individual observations and is invited to make general sense of them. This seems to be an easier task in encyclopaedic publications because of their structured presentation, the uniformity and comparability of 'entries' and, if applicable, the appeal to a national self-image. On the other hand, the guiding perspective of the visitor from outside which conditions the reading of panoramic collections is not normally found in encyclopaedic ones (with the exception of *England and the English* and *Die Zeitgenossen* where the dedication to a foreign statesman has a similar effect). More importantly, however, encyclopaedic arrangements lack framing devices such as overviewing or lead-in *tableaux* which provide an imaginative grip on the diverse portraits. Encyclopaedic sketch publications are introduced by discursive essays which, as in the case of *Die Zeitgenossen*, may take the form of a dedication to an imaginary kindred spirit, but are usually addressed to the reader and contain reflections on the moral state of the nation and the ways in which the publication proposes to capture it (see Jerrold's prefaces to the two volumes of *Heads of the People*, Janin's to *Les Français peints par eux-mêmes*, and Beurmann's to *Deutschland und die Deutschen*). The reasoning mode of the introduction seems more appropriate for orders guided by, and designed to popularise, knowledge about the social body and the century. In encyclopaedic arrangements, the reader is therefore not as imaginatively guided as in the less structured panoramic collections. The task of piecing together the city requires a visual, associative effort supported by (critical self-)knowledge of the middle class. The panorama is synthesised from a painterly point of view (Gavarni's in *Gavarni in London*, that of the ensemble of comedy viewers/sketchers in *Le Diable à Paris* or of the kaleidoscope in *Wien und die Wiener* which 'paints itself together' in the reader's guided imagination). In contrast, the task of reviewing the mores of the nation or of the century requires a cerebral, critical effort supported by images. Illustrations in encyclopaedic publications are therefore more systematically text-related (or the texts are illustrated to a more predictable scheme) than in panoramic ones. The middle-class readership of these moral encyclopaedias is thus empowered to examine the body politic passing in review from the viewpoint of the educated non-specialist. Inasmuch as 'letters' is an encyclopaedic concept, this view is by definition an inclusive one. Anticipating the aesthetic tenets of Realism, the nation's or century's review must therefore include the most undistinguished, 'un-literary' types such as the uncommunicative old Dutch couple who spend their days looking at the tulips in their immaculate little garden, reading the paper, sipping port, smoking cigars and playing cards, and then go to bed, mute and stiff, at eight o'clock: 'Is not this, too, a scene of our century?' asks Gutzkow, their portraitist in *Die Zeitgenossen*. 'Is it permissible for a reformer to overlook it?'[101] This question is one that middle-class readers were bound to ask themselves when confronted, by their moral encyclopaedias, with the lot of many a lower-class type and with morals that would have been considered beyond the pale. The 'gravity' of 'tone' and the 'moral seriousness' of a work such as *Heads of the People* was thought to have taken those by surprise who had expected no more than humorous distraction from a work of sketches: 'Many took up the first portion

---

101 'Ist dieß nicht auch eine Scene des Jahrhunderts? Darf sie der Reformator übersehen?' Gutzkow (note 29), I, xviii.

only to laugh', according to Douglas Jerrold; 'and, we are proud to say, read on to think.'[102] The combination of amusement and instruction, so typical of nineteenth-century forms of entertainment, extends to the moral encyclopaedias which, as has been suggested, have their equivalent in magic lantern shows and revues or vaudevilles. As a performative genre and as a metamedium of the century's intructively entertaining media, sketches present knowledge ultimately as self-knowledge, that of actor-spectators in a fully commodified theatre of action.

---

102 [Jerrold], 'Preface', in *Heads of the People*, I (note 40), p. iv.

Conclusion
Sketches as a Grammar of Modernity

Sketches of the 1830s and 40s depict the moral state of society on the verge of fully industrialised social relationships. Their cognitive systems are, however, one step ahead of the actual social development. Anticipating the commodification and reification of all aspects of life, they equip the nineteenth-century citizen for a modernity which is, in many ways, yet to develop in material terms.

A good example are sketches by Georg Weerth, one of the sharpest observers of industrial poverty in England's North and author of *Skizzen aus dem sozialen und politischen Leben der Briten* (Sketches from the Social and Political Life of the British, written 1843-48). Applying his socio-physiognomic skills to his home environment in *Humoristische Skizzen aus dem deutschen Handelsleben* (Humorous Sketches from German Commercial Life, 1847-48), he describes the broker ('Makler') of the north and west German trading centres as the epitome of a social physiognomist. Behind the most civil appearances of others, this dyed-in-the-wool materialist is able, at one glance, to detect their basic self-interest, while himself behaving with utmost courtesy. He reads his customers' physiques and actions in much the same way as the analytical sketch reads *him*, in other words, as expressions of an economic system that has replaced social and moral values by exchange value and characters, as Marx explains in the 'Exchange' chapter of *Capital's* first volume (1867), by 'character masks' ('Charaktermasken'). These 'appear on the economic stage' as mere 'personifications of the economic relations that exist between them'.[1] Coupling buyer and seller with the routine of a matchmaker,[2] Weerth's 'Mr Busy' ('Herr Emsig') both understands and signifies the undermining of commercial, social and sex-

---

1 Karl Marx, *Capital [...]*. Translated by Samuel Moore and Edward Aveling [...] (London: Lawrence & Wishart; Moscow: Progress Publishers, 1974), p. 89. The term 'Charaktermasken' is rendered simply as 'characters' in the first English translation of 1887 used here.
2 See Georg Weerth, 'Humoristische Skizzen aus dem deutschen Handelsleben', VII: 'Der Makler', in *Sämtliche Werke*, 5 vols. ed. by Bruno Kaiser (Berlin: Aufbau-Verlag, 1956-7), II (1956), 349-485 (pp. 410-20, esp. 411-12).

ual morality by high capitalism. Yet Germany in the 1840s was only just beginning to show the effects of industrialisation in its economically most advanced areas. Weerth's writing thus exemplifies the epistemologically avant-gardist achievements of sketches.

The industrial proletariat in general features only marginally in the written and graphic sketches discussed in this study, partly because they focus on metropolitan environments which were not necessarily centres of big industry. Capital cities in the 1830s and 40s, while confronting observers with pauperism, did not provide obvious scenarios for the study of regimented, exploited, demoralised and dehumanised industrial existences. For his harrowing portrait of the 'Factory Child' in *Heads of the People*, for example, Jerrold presents a Manchester scene.[3] Nevertheless, the entire epistemological system of sketches is 'industrial' in that it accommodates types, reproducibility, specialisation and 'demoralisation', the latter to be understood in terms of a radical relativity of values or even the absence of any binding moral codes.

The moral implications of specialisation are acutely understood by the sketch-writer and novelist Karl Gutzkow in the 1830s, an understanding which Ute Promies interprets as distinctly modern: 'For Gutzkow, social fragmentation shows itself, amongst other things, in the absence of a superior moral system that could be binding for all members of society'. And she connects this pertinently to acting and role-play as forms of social communication: The 'fragmentary education' of Gutzkow's middle-class types means that they have to resort to the 'role of actor', which changes 'according to supply and demand', so that 'the trickery of bourgeois play-acting becomes the hallmark of modern society, as well as the precondition for surviving in it'.[4] Promies's expression, 'trickery of bourgeois play-acting', formulates, in a nutshell, the complex expe-

---

3   See Douglas Jerrold, 'The Factory Child', in *Heads of the People*, 2 vols (London: Tyas, 1840-1), I, 185-92. The illustrated reports on the conditions of the working class which emerged in the 1840s were the domain of investigative journalism, not of sketch-writing, although (as Jerrold's example shows) there were overlaps. See Celina Fox, 'The Development of Social Reportage in English Periodical Illustration during the 1840s and Early 1850s', *Past & Present*, 74:1 (1977), 90-111.
4   'Die gesellschaftliche Zersplitterung zeigt sich für Gutzkow unter anderem im Fehlen einer übergeordneten Moral, die bindend für alle Mitglieder der Gesellschaft sein könnte.' His characters 'ergreifen [...] von vornherein den Beruf des Schauspielers nicht aufgrund eines höheren Ideals, sondern aufgrund ihrer fragmentarischen Bildung. [...] [Sie] wechseln [...] ihre Rollen je nach Angebot und Nachfrage [...] Fazit: die trickreiche bürgerliche Schauspielerei wird zum Kennzeichen wie auch zum Überlebensgarant in der modernen Gesellschaft.' Ute Promies, *Karl Gutzkow – Romanautor und kritischer Pädagoge* (Bielefeld: Aisthesis, 2003), pp. 103 and 105.

rience of dishonesty, inauthenticity, freedom and virtuosity involved in having to play one's role on a social stage where traditional hierarchies and ties are about to vanish. Nathalie Preiss has examined the extensive lexical field of 'deception' ('tromperie') dominating the social portraiture of the *Physiologies*.[5] Watching themselves play parts for which the script is only written as the performance is going on (and in this way linking the physiological study of the living social body with self-scrutiny, self-portraiture and self-enactment), the middle classes are at once actors, dramatists and spectators in a dynamic social scenario.

French sketches of the 1830s and 40s have forerunners in the humorous 'Codes' of the Restoration in which Balzac was also involved, instructing readers, for example, how to guard themselves against being duped.[6] Not surprisingly, the newly-created popular characters of 1830s social caricature are often mask-bearers, and without exception 'players' in the emphatic sense. Examples are Daumier's and Philipon's money-grabbing con-artist Robert Macaire, able to play in any guise provided by bourgeois society,[7] and Henri Monnier's pre-

---

5 See 'Tableau I. Champ lexical de la tromperie dans les Physiologies', in Natalie Preiss, *Les Physiologies en France au XIXe siècle: étude historique, littéraire et stylistique* (Mont-de-Marsan: Éditions InterUniversitaires, 1999), pp. 85-7.
6 See 'Code des Gens honnêtes ou l'art de ne pas être dupe des fripons', 'Code de la toilette' and 'Code conjugal' in Honoré de Balzac, *Œuvres diverses*, ed. by Pierre-Georges Castex (Paris: Gallimard, 1990–), II (1996), ed. by Roland Chollet and René Guise, 147-294. A bibliography of 'Arts – Codes – Guides – Hygiènes – Manuels' is found in Preiss, *Physiologies* (note 5), pp. 298-9. Douglas Jerrold's *Handbook of Swindling* (1839) and the satirical 'manual' by Augustus and Henry Mayhew, *Whom To Marry and How To Get Married* (1847-48), as well as *Anleitung zur Kunstkennerschaft oder Kunst, in drei Stunden ein Kenner zu werden* (Instructions on Appreciating Art, or The Art of Becoming a Connoisseur in Three Hours; 1834) by the lawyer Johann Hermann Detmold, belong to the same category. They all expose the mastery of codes and jargons as the key to success in bourgeois society.
7 The banning in 1835 of the successful stage play *Robert Macaire, ce cynique scapin du crime*, in which the actor Lemaître satirised the July Monarchy in the figure of the con-man Macaire, motivated Philipon and Daumier to continue the satire in graphic-verbal form. Between 1836 and 1838, one hundred and one *Macaire* lithographs appeared in the 'Caricaturana' section of *Le Charivari*, with captions provided by Philipon: see Raymond Escholier, *Daumier. Peintre et Lithographe* (Paris: Floury, 1923), p. 88, and Judith Wechsler, *A Human Comedy. Physiognomy and Caricature in Nineteenth-Century Paris* (London: Thames & Hudson, 1982), pp. 85-91. Aubert then reissued the series under the title *Les Cent et un Robert-Macaire* with complete verbal sketches complementing the pictures and captions. They were written by Maurice Alhoy and Louis Huart, well-known as authors of *Physiologies*.

tentious petit bourgeois Monsieur Prudhomme, doubling up as stage character and graphic type like Macaire.[8] There are also the numerous down-and-outs who, having 'nothing to lose',[9] represent the jester's penetrating insight. These include Glaßbrenner's and Hosemann's talkative load-carrier, hanger-around at corner pubs and alcoholic good-for-nothing, 'Eckensteher Nante', another hybrid between stage and print; the onlooking sweeps, coalheavers and dustmen in early Victorian graphic satire,[10] and Gavarni's slightly later creation, Thomas Vireloque, the misanthropic rag-picker or *chiffonnier*.[11] By imagining an outcast's perspective, sketches stage the review of contemporary mores as a modern picaresque narrative. But even the outcast may be presented as a swindler, or rather, as one who has completely understood the importance of role-play as a vehicle for survival in modern society.

Hence the prominence of false beggars in London sketches, such as Angus B. Reach's 'Street Beggar', captured by Gavarni (illustration 52). 'Idlers may gather around him', we read in the sketch, 'pitying or gibing words may fall upon his ear, but he gives no token that he has heard them. Either hunger has benumbed and frozen up his faculties and sensations, or he is acting a part, and acting it very well.' Asking which of these alternatives may apply, the writer answers: 'in nineteen cases out of twenty, the latter'.[12] It seems that this lack of sympathy with mendicants results not so much from middle-class complacency, but from the realisation that studied appearances have begun to obscure real deprivation which is being inflicted and endured unseen. The theatrical beggar announces his 'starving' condition in fluent letters written on the pavement, as well as through his body language and rags. By his mute presence and his own handwritten 'caption', a self-advertisement contrasting ironically with the 'Stick No Bills' poster on the wall behind him, this figure holds up a mirror of inauthenticity to a world in which all sorts of visual signifiers, not least written and printed, have replaced the signified. Surfaces no longer 'reveal' anything, but are in themselves as significant as acting masks.

The provenance of this critique of appearances from the moralist tradition has been discussed in my study, and it can be observed here once more. Fake gentlefolk and false mendicants of London's underworld had been portrayed

---

8 On this character, see Wechsler (note 7), pp. 112-29.
9 Ibid., p. 109.
10 On the latter see Brian Maidment, *Dusty Bob. A Cultural History of Dustmen 1790-1870* (Manchester: Manchester University Press, 2007).
11 On this character, see Wechsler (note 7), pp. 109-11.
12 Angus B. Reach, 'The Street Beggar', in *Gavarni in London*, ed. by Albert Smith (London: Bogue, 1849), pp. 7-12 (p. 7).

Illustration 52 Gavarni, 'The Street Beggar', in *Gavarni in London*, ed. by Albert Smith (London: Bogue, 1849), opposite p. 7. Tinted wood engraving by Henry Vizetelly.

since Marcellus Laroon's 'Cries';[13] Gavarni's and Reach's sketch harks back to this tradition while moving it forward into the industrial age. The appearance of the type cast as 'The Street Beggar', this late descendant of the 'Cries' genre, is not simply false. His falseness is 'right' in the sense that it points to role-play, to people acting as 'character masks' in bourgeois society on the one hand, and to the invisibility of authentic suffering which this society produces on the other hand. What the physiognomy of the beggar does not disclose is the 'systematic' starvation of all those plunged into poverty by the process of industrialisation. Yet the written sketch is able to point out precisely the absence of the industrial poor from London's street begging, and to indicate (and morally to stipulate) that 'honest poverty' will rarely resort to

---

13 See Sean Shesgreen, *Images of the Outcast. The Urban Poor in the Cries of London* (New Brunswick: Rutgers University Press; Manchester: Manchester University Press, 2002), pp. 64-76.

'parad[ing] its woes in the crowded street' and to 'pocketing alms'.[14] Whether role-playing is disapproved of or not, the emphasis of the sketch is on acting and performance, aspects so intricately connected to its own generic qualities. It also posits an unbridgeable gulf between the visible world of unprecedented material progress (literate beggars who can make a living from 'starving') and the invisible human cost of such progress (industrial impoverishment); a gulf which is addressed by ever more complex arrangements of sketches into panoramic or encyclopaedic bodies of knowledge.

By translating scientific paradigms into modes of observation, and by observing the social body in action, sketches construct a moral grammar of modernity. It has been shown, however, that their epistemology empowers readers/spectators not simply to control a potentially threatening urban space, the lower classes, and women, but, first and foremost, to look at themselves whilst acting within a shifting universe of signifiers. The code book or *Encyclopédie morale* that sketches provide for the citizen of the nineteenth century is therefore one of critical and humorous self-observation in the role of character mask. The self under scrutiny is the middle-class educated male, provider of society's legal, scientific and moral codes since the Enlightenment. It is significant that one of the early social *Physiologies*, which appeared in 1833, should allude to the (male) society of 'gens de lettres', which figures as an ensemble of authors in the title of Diderot's and D'Alembert's *Encyclopédie*,[15] by calling itself *Physiologie du ridicule, ou Suite d'observations, par une société de gens ridicules* (Physiology of the Ridiculous, or Series of Observations by a Society of Ridiculous People). This parody exposes encyclopaedic discourse as a laughable but necessary mask and could be seen to have a gendered slant since it is authored – albeit anonymously – by a female writer, Sophie Gay. She declares 'the ridiculous' to be the most solid social bond,[16] thereby poking fun at the notion of 'letters' uniting male educated society. Moreover, she hints at the fundamental importance of acting one's part in post-1830 society and launches the business of satirical self-observation which culminates in the spectacle of types passing in review, 'in as ridiculous a fashion' as possible,

---

14 Reach, 'The Street Beggar' (note 12), p. 11.
15 *Encyclopédie, ou Dictionnaire raisonné des sciences, des arts et des métiers, par une société des gens de lettres.*
16 'Vu des hauteurs de la philosophie, le ridicule est le lien le plus solide de tous ceux qui unissent les hommes [...].' [Anon.], *Physiologie du ridicule, ou Suite d'observations, par une société des gens ridicules*, 2 vols (Paris: Vimont, 1833), I, 7.

announced by Janin in his introduction to *Les Français peints par eux-mêmes*.[17] The fact that the 'man of letters' and thus the logocentric order is at the heart of this review becomes more than clear from Balzac's 'Monographie de la presse parisienne' (1843). Here the author, true to form, outdoes the *Physiologies* in subjecting the entire publishing sector and its political power to an 80-page physiological analysis in densely printed octavo, focusing on the human genus of 'gendelettre'. The 'Journalist-cum-Statesman', in his sub-variety of 'Man of Politics', embodies the questionable authority of the logos most strikingly. Acting as political figurehead for a journal (which in turn amplifies the ideas he stands for), this man is revered by the nation who will praise *his* civil courage when he loses his wife rather than mourning *her*, and he is celebrated as an eminent French 'homme politique' – a fusion of letters and politics – in any country honoured by his visit. 'When he sees the Rhine, it's the Rhine that sees him' (illustration 53, p. 316).[18] Yet he is, more often than not, a myth in the true sense, for 'he does not exist'. This paragon of intellectual culture 'has not even two ideas in his head. Make him second in command, and he won't be able to manage the street-cleaning service'.[19] The mythical modern male self is viewed, in the vignette, by an antique river god who wears a lens – a witty visual comment on the present-day Narcissus receiving his reflection not by looking at the mirroring water surface, but by being looked at as a sensational phenomenon from the point of view of the mirror/viewer. Thus sketches, as Sieburth argues with reference to the *Physiologies*, do engage in a narcissistic spectacle revolving around seeing oneself,[20] but the point is that this viewing involves a process of *re*viewing. My study has highlighted the central importance of 'passing in review' as a concept which the intermedial genre of the sketch thrives on. And reviewing amounts to a critique of the act of viewing, in other words, of the admiring gaze which creates Narcissus's mythical status in the first place.

---

17 See pp. 168-9 of this study.
18 'S'il voit le Rhin, c'est le Rhin qui le voit.' Honoré de Balzac, 'Monographie de la Presse parisienne. (Extrait de l'Histoire naturelle du Bimane en société.)', in *La Grande Ville. Nouveau Tableau de Paris comique, critique et philosophique*, 2 vols, 2nd edn (Paris: Maresq, 1844), II, 129-208 (p. 152).
19 'Cet homme est quelquefois un mythe; il n'existe pas, il n'a pas deux idées: vous en feriez un sous-chef, il serait incapable d'administrer le balayage public.' Ibid., p. 150.
20 See Richard Sieburth, 'Une idéologie du lisible: le phénomène des physiologies', *Romantisme*, 47 (1985:1), 39-60 (pp. 57-8).

316 *Sketches of the Nineteenth Century*

Illustration 53   [Anon.], illustration in Honoré de Balzac, 'Monographie de la presse parisienne', in *La Grande Ville. Nouveau Tableau de Paris comique, critique et philosophique*, 2 vols, 2nd edn (Paris: Maresq, 1844), II, 152. Wood engraving.

One sketcher who has been under-represented in my study is W.M. Thackeray. His *Punch* series 'The Snobs of England, by One of Themselves' (28 February 1846 – 27 February 1847; collected in *The Book of Snobs*, 1848) offers a perfect example of sketches reviewing middle-class civilisation 'narcissistically', so to speak, with the male observer basically viewing himself. One of Thackeray's sketches that exemplifies this critique most impressively is, however, an individual one, first published in *Punch* in 1850 and included in *Sketches and Travels in London* (1856). 'Waiting at the Station' questions male middle-class educated selfhood by confronting the observing ego – including the narrator and reader as a directly addressed 'you' – with the sight of lower-class women awaiting their departure from Fenchurch Street Station in London under the 'Female Emigration Scheme'. In Australia, where women are in short supply, they hope to find a materially more secure future as wives of settlers. The thoughts crowding the observer's mind make him feel distinctly uneasy within his own skin. He puts himself in the position of the women, wondering what they must feel at this particular moment. He also adopts the stance of the man choosing a wife amongst them and decides (for reasons of personal taste and social etiquette, as he shamefacedly admits) that he would rather stay a bachelor. Finally he pictures the typical situation of the educated gentleman addressing the simple girl:

> If you go up and speak to one of these women, as you do (and very good-naturedly, and you can't help that confounded condescension), she curtsies and holds down her head meekly, and replies with modesty, as becomes her station, to your honour with the clean shirt and the well-made coat. And so she should; what hundreds of thousands of us rich and poor say still. Both believe this to be bounden duty; and that a poor person should naturally bob her head to a rich one physically and morally.[21]

The woman will, so the observer muses, have performed one of her last curtsies to her posh interlocutor. The new-world society she will soon settle into knows no 'Gothic' hierarchies. What is expressed in this way is a 'physical and moral' self-critique of the dominating old-world class, gendered as male, in opposition to the female-gendered lower (implicitly up-and-coming) class. The critique centres on the depiction of codes which have become second nature in the civilised world, such as gestures, attitudes, speech and dress.

Moral codes of any age or time can be seen as a 'grammar' that contemporaries need to master in order to interact. What turns Thackeray's critique, when read as an example of the moral review provided by the sketch industry as a whole, into a 'grammar of modernity' is

a) the sense that the age-old sign-system by which rich and poor, men and women, educated and uneducated people 'naturally' communicate forms but an arbitrary layer of manners, bound to be swept away by the dynamism of the times,

b) the awareness that social relationships are, to a large extent, of a semiotic kind, in other words, that signs, however transient, are invested with real social power (the lower-class woman curtsying before a 'clean shirt' and 'well-made coat'), and

c) the consciousness of the moment, that shortest unit of lived time, in which a mundane experience such as 'waiting at the station' before the train sets off condenses past, present and future into reflections on modes and manners.

---

21 William Makepeace Thackeray, 'Waiting at the Station', in *Miscellanies*, 8 vols (Leipzig: Tauchnitz, 1849-57), V (1856), 1-232 (p. 178).

This grammar of modernity represents an early form of cultural semiology, which is not to say that the critique of mores found in sketches is without its limitations. For example, Thackeray dubs the presumably more humane morality of the new world that of a 'manly brotherhood',[22] perhaps to imply degeneracy and a lack of Christian values in the old. But 'manly' observation is precisely what is at stake in the sketch. The observer is himself subject to the dynamics of what is seen.

I would argue that the fluctuating position of the observer, the hallmark of 1830s' and 40s' sketches, centres on theatrical paradigms with which post-1850s metropolitan sketches have little in common. Their preoccupation with the conditions of the urban underclass, heralded by James Grant's *Sketches in London* (1838) and particularly by Henry Mayhew's *London Labour and the London Poor* (first book edition 1851-52), marks a specialisation of sketch-writing which is incompatible with the comprehensive reflections of strolling spectators. It means that the situation of labourers and those inhabiting the underworld of cities becomes the sole object of investigation and that the middle-class observer has to develop a set of navigation tools apt to support him as a 'social explorer'. Arguably, this role reestablishes some of the power strategies that had been subjected to critical review in the 1830s and 40s.

We can infer this from Thackeray's own sketch, 'Waiting at the Station', where he refers to Mayhew's first, daring reports on metropolitan poverty in the 'Labour and the Poor' series of the *Morning Chronicle*:[23] 'A picture of human life so wonderful, so awful, so piteous and pathetic, so exciting and terrible, that readers of romances own they never read anything like to it [...].'[24] According to E.P. Thompson, Mayhew's 'revelations about prostitution among the needlewomen were perhaps the most sensational moment of the series',[25] prompting the intervention of high-ranking individuals to launch the Emigration Scheme for an estimated 500,000 surplus working-class females in England and Wales. While Thackeray obviously admires the 'kind people whose bounty and benevolence organized' the Scheme, referring to the women as their '*protégées*' and to their departure as an act of

---

22 Thackeray, 'Waiting at the Station' (note 21), p. 178.
23 The 82 letters Mayhew wrote for this series were partly incorporated into *London Labour and the London Poor*. For a synopsis, see *The Unknown Mayhew. Selections from the Morning Chronicle 1849-50*, ed. by E.P. Thompson and Eileen Yeo (Harmondsworth: Penguin, 1973), pp. 581-3.
24 Thackeray, 'Waiting at the Station' (note 21), p. 179.
25 E.P. Thompson, 'Mayhew and the "Morning Chronicle"', in *The Unknown Mayhew* (note 23), pp. 9-55 (p. 25).

rescue,[26] he remains true to his role of observer empathising with the women and reflecting on his own position rather than politicising about the wider context. Significantly, he sees investigating the conditions of the underclass as a special vocation of someone like Mayhew who 'travels into the poor man's country for us, and comes back with his tale of terror and wonder'.[27] A division of labour is thus indicated between the observer, such as Thackeray himself, who writes sketches of everyday life, and the explorer whose mission it is to produce 'for us' narratives of an incredibly horrible, yet real world on the metropolitan doorstep. The sketch-writer's moral sensibility is obviously strongly affected by the explorer's 'tales':

> [...] the griefs, struggles, strange adventures here depicted, exceed anything that any of us could imagine. Yes; and these wonders and terrors have been lying by your door and mine ever since we had a door of our own. We had but to go a hundred yards off and see for ourselves, but we never did.[28]

The inquisitive traveller's eyes that sketch-writers apply to home environments have not focused, as Thackeray seems to indicate, on the poor man's land within the metropolis. Yet 'seeing for ourselves' what remains concealed to the middle-class observer would require a deliberate effort and break the convention of casual, speculative viewing. What is more, the autopsy of lower-class living conditions turns Mayhew's depiction, willy-nilly, into something little short of a sensational account. Thackeray's repeated recourse to the vocabulary of 'romance' is telling. As Shesgreen remarks, *London Labour and the London Poor*, with its emphasis on 'those outcast shunned even by other outcasts', became an ethnographic enterprise 'infused with the notion that, lacking conventional evidence and historical testimony, earlier phases of civilization could be understood by observing people still languishing in primal stages of development'.[29] The popularity of Mayhew's investigations (after his 'revelations' had lost their shocking effect), and the number of sketch publications of the second half of the nineteenth century and first part of the twentieth which are devoted to the London underworld,[30] could be explained in terms of an anthropological interest that no longer questions the view of the observer. Mayhew's collection, having grown to

---

26 Thackeray, 'Waiting at the Station' (note 21), p. 180.
27 Ibid.
28 Ibid., p. 179.
29 Shesgreen, *Images of the Outcast* (note 13), pp. 168-9.
30 See ibid., p. 169.

four volumes by 1862, not only focuses decidedly on street existences, which made up only 'one-fortieth of the city's working population',[31] thereby continuing to depict labourers in the mould of 'Cries', but some of the wood-engraved illustrations could be seen almost as falsifications of the real picture: 'They are based on daguerreotypes by James Beard [...] who drove around London in a cab picking up vendors and posing them in the alien surroundings of a photography studio for thirty-second sittings.' These images, 'accessories after the fact',[32] are more like 'scientific' illustrations, conceivably far removed from the graphic sketches engaged in dialogue with the text, and from the epistemology of viewing and reproduction which is one of the chief characteristics of sketches published in the 1830s and 40s.

The implied or explicit text-image relationship of these sketches has a lot to do with the consciousness of the moment, the archetypal modern experience. Like the expression 'visual imagination', the term 'grammar of modernity' under which I have subsumed this Conclusion seems slightly pleonastic. Grammars by definition offer shortcuts through languages, reducing the bewildering variety of forms to a set of patterns. Modernity as an epoch of acceleration, abbreviation and reduction makes visible patterns of life that were concealed before and enables contemporaries to develop semiotic keys to an understanding of culture and society. In this respect, modernity seems by definition 'grammatical', fostering any intellectual developments that move towards abstraction. Yet the expression 'grammar of modernity' with regard to what sketches offer seems appropriate in that the modern tools of cognition are so emphatically turned upon the living body of society and on its smallest unit, the self of the observer. In their attachment to the here-and-now, sketches fulfill a 'canonical' definition of the modern as 'this transitory, fugitive element' which any work must capture in order to outlast its time.[33] This definition, Baudelaire's, is significantly formulated in his discussion of the work of the draughtsman Constantin Guys, in the chapter 'La Modernité' of 'Le Peintre de la vie moderne'. Unlike his interpreter Walter Benjamin, Baudelaire fully appreciated the journalistic sketches of manners ('croquis de mœurs')[34] which succeeded the political caricature of the early July Monarchy. It is true that Baudelaire's hyperbolic description of self-loss in the

---

31 Shesgreen (note 13), p. 168.
32 Ibid., p. 167.
33 'Cet élément transitoire, fugitif, dont les métamorphoses sont si fréquentes, vous n'avez pas le droit de le mépriser [...].' Charles Baudelaire, 'Le Peintre de la vie moderne', in Œuvres complètes, ed. by Claude Pichois, 2 vols (Paris: Gallimard, 1975-6), II (1976), 683-724 (p. 695).
34 See Baudelaire's chapter thus entitled; ibid., pp. 686-7.

crowd as a precondition for the modern sketcher's creativity has a distinctly aestheticist agenda, and that his princely dandy-*flâneur* who sees while remaining unseen is equally incompatible with the concerns of the speculative stroller of 1830-50. Nevertheless, the understanding of the fluctuating moment as the nucleus of visual-cognitive experience in the modern age, which is also at the heart of the 'physiological' concept of writing and reading, makes Baudelaire's comments relevant in our context:

> For the perfect *flâneur*, for the passionate observer, it is an immense joy to establish his home amongst the crowd, in the midst of fluctuation, movement, fugitiveness and infinity. [...] It is an *ego* insatiably attracted by the *non-ego* that, at any given moment, expresses its object in images more lively than life itself, always unstable and fugitive.[35]

One such moment is expressed in Paul de Kock's / Honoré Daumier's sketch 'Les Champs-Elysées': The *promeneur* has here mingled with the crowd weaving its way through the athletic leisure activities of Parisians, and has to dodge rackets, balls, clenched fists and bodies ever so often lest he or she gets knocked over. This risky physical experience is described by the text as a sequence of seconds:

> Look out, you imprudent strollers who do not spot that big ball of white leather flying through the air with the speed of a bomb; the player who can see the chance to make a splendid shot is running up to you, covered in sweat..... make way... there's still time.... You haven't made way... So much the worse for you, as the young man in shirtsleeves has hurled himself at you and roughly knocked you aside so as to catch and punch back the ball which was coming straight at your head; as you were not prepared for this violent clash, you have lost your balance and are now rolling on the lawn... Everyone laughs at your fall, and I advise you to do likewise, for the player was perfectly entitled to do as he did, and your complaints will be ill-received.[36]

---

35 'Pour le parfait flâneur, pour l'observateur passionné, c'est une immense jouissance que d'élire domicile dans le nombre, dans l'ondoyant, dans le mouvement, dans le fugitif et l'infini. [...] C'est un *moi* insatiable du *non-moi*, qui, à chaque instant, le rend et l'exprime en images plus vivantes que la vie elle-même, toujours instable et fugitive.' Baudelaire, 'Le Peintre de la vie moderne' (note 33), pp. 691-2.

36 'Prenez garde à vous, promeneurs imprudents qui ne remarquez pas ce gros ballon en peau blanche qui traverse les airs avec la rapidité d'une bombe; le joueur qui voit un beau coup à faire accourt tout en sueur de votre côté..... rangez-vous... il en est

The image then captures the energy of the player as he reaches back a long way to punch the ball within the next fraction of a moment, while his partner is already anticipating the return shot:

Illustration 54   Honoré Daumier, illustration in Paul de Kock, 'Les Champs-Elysées', in *La Grande Ville*, 2 vols, 2nd edn (Paris: Maresq, 1844), I, 294. Wood engraving by Verdeil.

The low angle from which the sketch is made suggests a dodging movement on the part of the viewer, while emphasising the statuesque, yet dynamic figure of the player. This picture clearly foreshadows the achievements of photography, yet we have before us an artistically conceived sketch of the

> temps.... Vous ne vous êtes pas rangé... Tant pis pour vous, le jeune homme en manche de chemise s'est jeté contre vous, et vous a rudement repoussé de côté, afin de recevoir et de renvoyer le ballon qui venait droit sur votre tête; comme vous ne vous attendiez pas à ce choc violent, vous avez perdu l'équilibre, et vous roulez sur le gazon... Tout le monde rit de votre chute, et je vous conseille d'en faire autant, car le joueur était dans son droit, et vos plaintes seraient mal reçues.' Paul de Kock, 'Les Champs-Elysées', in *La Grande Ville* (note 18), I, 289-96 (p. 293).

moment uniting what is typically modern (in Baudelaire's terms, the fleeting and the fugitive) with the time-resistant, 'classical' body language of the athlete. The imprint of modernity, literally and figuratively, can be seen in the engraver's name and the heap of clothes in the foreground. Fashion and print are essential ephemera of nineteenth-century civilisation. The arrangement dominated by the top hat exemplifies the art of semiotic abbreviation providing a grammar of modernity.

Like all modern language grammars, this grammar is crucially mediated through print. Contemporary mores 'passing in review' can be compressed into tiny printed figures, as was discussed with regard to the tables in *Les Français peints par eux-mêmes*. The diminutive presentation of figures may also serve to emphasise the historical relativity or 'ridiculousness' of manners, as in Bertall's vignettes (illustration 55, p. 324) for P. Pascal's sketch 'Comment on se salue à Paris' (How People Greet Each Other in Paris). The written sketch analyses the 'nuances' in various forms of greeting which seem indicative of social differences, if only for the moment in which people physically acknowledge one another:

> Before the two greeters have regained their position on both legs, you can judge, from a distance, what separates them; once they are back on their feet and the ballet has finished, their uniformly black habit effaces any inequality.[37]

The sketch tellingly ends in a vignette by Bertall of a top hat, reducing both the uniformity of the male citizen and his ostentatious 'difference' (when lifting the hat in greeting) to a printed cipher.

---

[37] 'Avant que les deux salutateurs se soient raffermis sur leurs jambes, vos jugez de la distance qui les sépare; et une fois raffermis sur leurs pieds et le ballet terminé, le niveau de l'habit noir efface l'inégalité.' P. Pascal, 'Comment on se salue à Paris', in *Le Diable à Paris*, 2 vols (Paris: Hetzel, 1845-6), I, 82-4 (p. 84).

324 *Sketches of the Nineteenth Century*

Illustration 55
Bertall, vignettes in P. Pascal, 'Comment on se salue à Paris', in *Le Diable à Paris*, 2 vols (Paris: Hetzel, 1845-6), I (1845), 83. Wood engravings by 'B-Gs'.

The fact that the nineteenth-century citizen should feel compelled to show 'difference' in this way when there really is none between men all wearing black civil uniform makes the sketch-writer express his resignation. Yet he also hopes that, should future generations (who will mock the manners of the past) read this sketch, they will at least become aware that contemporaries themselves already had an acute sense of their own ridiculousness. Thus, their *croquis de mœurs* in which graphic gestures constitute a 'ballet' of mores and the text supplies the codes, offer a moral grammar. Its prime purpose is not to be followed, but to be studied so that people will understand the conceitedness behind 'difference', or only fine gradations of it, being acted out in contemporary society. As everything modern, the action – a brief lifting of the hat, a glance, perhaps a shake of hands – and its decoding by the observer are a matter of moments. The physiological mode of observation, including the writer/viewer/reader in mundane depictions 'more lively than life itself', to use Baudelaire's words, once more allows for a dynamic form of cognition.

My study has put much emphasis on the cross-cultural dimensions of sketch production in the 1830s and 40s. I ought to end this Conclusion by considering 'abbreviation' as a transnational phenomenon. Writing as 'E.L. Bulwer' and in an alleged translation from the English, Karl Gutzkow imagines two English gentlemen of good breeding but moderate means in fashionable, that is to say, wordless conversation:

> Now they are silent for a quarter of an hour, during which they communicate solely by facial expressions [...], in short, they look at one another like telegraphs, achieving, by all sorts of pantomimic quirks, a result amounting roughly to a novel and requiring, if it were to be printed, sixteen octavo pages in order to reflect all the witty nuances in which they have related it to one another.[38]

This satirical depiction of 'telegraphic' conversation as an ultra-modern achievement has a political subtext. As the *Penny Cycplopædia* informs us, 'telegraphic communications' were 'as remarkable for their impenetrable se-

---

38 'Jetzt schweigen sie eine Viertelstunde, während welcher sie nur mit ihrem Mienenspiele sich verständlich sind [...], kurz, sie betrachten sich wechselsweise wie Telegraphen und erreichen durch allerhand pantomimische Merkwürdigkeiten ein Resultat, das auf einen ungefähren Roman hinauskömmt, und einen Bogen von 16 Seiten brauchen würde, wenn man ihn mit all' den witzigen Nüancen wieder geben wollte, mit welchen sie sich ihn erzählt haben.' [Karl Gutzkow], *Die Zeitgenossen. Ihre Schicksale, ihre Tendenzen, ihre großen Charaktere. Aus dem Englischen des E.L. Bulwer*, 2 vols (Stuttgart: Verlag der Classiker, 1837), I, xiv-xv.

crecy as for their rapidity'[39] because they worked with coded signals. Gutzkow alludes to the semaphore, common before the introduction of the electric telegraph, with its adjustable arms fixed to poles. The intelligence travelling from pole to pole was often of a military, political or financial kind and not meant for public consumption. The first telegraph line in Prussia opened in 1832, being extended westwards to the Rhineland in 1833, but making no difference, of course, to the stifling of public discourse in Prussia. Gutzkow hints, however, at another form of telegraphy that has begun to undermine the regime of censorship, in other words, the imaginary and imaginative communication of German journal writers with Western Europe from where they adopt the codes of modernity, down to the latest developments in sign-reading and sketch-writing. No system of censorship will be able to suppress this rapid process of subversive modernisation.

There is now, Gutzkow alias Bulwer observes, a special jargon in every branch of knowledge and walk of life, which makes communication amongst the initiated brief and comfortable.[40] Sketches, as has been shown, engage in this process of specialisation on a grand scale by their divisions and subdivisions, following the paradigm of zoological classification. But the meta-language they develop, the self-reflection of journalistic print media, offers a critique of specialisation, as I have discussed in my section on the *Physiologies*. This meta-language, which could also be called one of the *feuilleton*, has to be seen as the lasting heritage of the European sketch industry of the 1830s and 40s, a language always able to reflect its own abbreviations, its own 'grammar of modernity', up to the point where punning brevity puts an end to itself, as in the following illustration:

A GRAMMARIAN DECLINING TO BE

Illustration 56 'A Grammarian Declining To Be'. Vignette in *Punch*, 1 (July-December 1841), 275. Wood engraving.

---

39 'Telegraph', in *The Penny Cyclopædia of the Society for the Diffusion of Useful Knowledge*, 27 vols (London: Knight, 1833-43), XXIV (1842), 145-55 (p. 145).

40 'Die Religion hat ihren Jargon, die Moral, die Politik, die Industrie, die Liebe. Man kann sich mit Redensarten weit kürzer und bequemer ausdrücken, als wenn man vernünftig spricht. [...] Denn Jeder, der eingeweiht ist, versteht diese Abkürzungen [...].' [Gutzkow], *Die Zeitgenossen* (note 38), p. xiii.

The contribution of physiological sketches to the genesis and understanding of modernity is that of a popular print medium reflecting its own status. This medium helps us to revise a one-sided concept of modernity, Benjamin's which follows Baudelaire's aesthetics of self-loss in the fugitive, unstable, momentary experience of the city, in terms of a dynamically growing public sphere and in terms of expanding cultural and social self-knowledge. In recognising the social relativity of norms, values and even of science, the new religion of the century, physiological sketches certainly break the ground for the fictional realms of Realism. Yet they also anticipate twentieth-century sociological and semiological thought by a long way in the acuteness of their cultural semiotics developed in the analysis of contemporary mores. Their awareness that there is a close connection between 'modes' and 'modernity' is at the heart of the matter. During two decades framed by revolutionary upheavals, and at a time of 'visible transition', European society reconfigured its moral systems in accordance with the 'March of Intellect' and the significance of the ephemeral. The sketch industry acted as the chief engine of this process at the level of quotidian knowledge. After 1848-49 this cognitive re-orientation feeds into various channels, such as the 'exploration' of poverty. Its European, cross-cultural dimensions are largely superseded by national competition (for example, between hosts of Great Exhibitions). This can be seen as a retrograde step compared to the openness of an intercultural process that found its epitome in the transfer of printed 'types'.

Bibliography

1 Primary texts

1.1 Sketches[1]

1.1.1 Sketches by single authors, published individually, serially and/or in book form

Alhoy, Maurice, *Physiologie de la Lorette. Vignettes de Gavarny [sic]* (Paris: Aubert, Lavigne, [1841]).
[Anon.], *Physiologie du calembourg, par un nain connu. Dessins de Henry Émy* (Paris: Raymond-Bocquet, 1841).
[Anon.], *Physiologie de l'homme de loi, par un homme de plume. Vignettes de MM. Trimolet et Maurisset* (Paris: Aubert, Lavigne, [1841]).
[Anon.], *Physiologie des Physiologies* (Paris: Desloges, 1841).
[Anon.], *Physiologie de la presse. Biographie des journalistes et des journaux de Paris et de la province* (Paris: Jules Laisné; Aubert, Lavigne, 1841).
Balzac, Honoré de, 'Complaintes satiriques sur les mœurs du temps présent. Exorde', in *Œuvres diverses*, ed. by Pierre-Georges Castex (Paris: Gallimard, 1990–), II (1996), ed. by Roland Chollet and René Guise, in collaboration with Christiane Guise, pp. 739-48.
—— 'L'Épicier' (1830), *Œuvres diverses*, II (1996), 723-7.
—— 'L'Épicier' (1839), in *Les Français peints par eux-mêmes*, 8 vols (Paris: Curmer, 1840-2), I (1840), 1-8.
—— 'L'Épicier' (1839), in *Les Français peints par eux-mêmes. Encyclopédie morale du dix-neuvième siècle publiée par Léon Curmer*, ed. by Pierre Bouttier ([Paris (?)]: Omnibus, 2003–), I (2003), 23-33.
—— 'L'Épicier' (1839), in *Œuvres complètes illustrées*, 26 vols, ed. by Jean A. Ducourneau (Paris: Les Bibliophiles de l'originale, 1965-76), XXVI (1976), 130-9.
—— 'Monographie de la presse parisienne. (Extrait de l'Histoire naturelle du Bimane en société)', in *La Grande Ville. Nouveau tableau de Paris, comique, critique et philosophique, par MM. Paul de Kock, Balzac, Dumas, Soulié, Gozlan, Briffault, Ourliac, E. Guinot, H. Monnier, etc. Illustrations de Gavarni, Victor Adam, Daumier,*

---

1 This section lists sketches referred to in this book only and is by no means comprehensive.

D'Aubigny, H. Emy, Traviès, Boulanger, Henri Monnier et Thenot, 2 vols, second edn (Paris: Marescq, 1844), II, 129-208.

— 'Monographie de la presse parisienne. (Extrait de l'Histoire naturelle du Bimane en société)', in Œuvres complètes illustrées, XXVI (1976), 234-94.

— 'Nouvelle théorie du déjeuner', in Œuvres diverses, II (1996), 762-8.

— Physiologie du mariage ou Méditations de philosophie éclectique sur le bonheur et le malheur conjugal, publiées par un jeune célibataire, in La Comédie humaine, ed. by Pierre-Georges Castex, 12 vols (Paris: Gallimard, 1976-81), XI (1980), 865-1205.

— 'Théorie de la démarche', in La Comédie humaine, XII (1981), 259-302.

— and Arnould Frémy, Physiologie du rentier de Paris et de province (Paris: Martinon, 1841).

Beurmann, Eduard, Frankfurter Bilder (Mainz: Kupferberg, 1835).

— Skizzen aus den Hanse-Städten (Hanau: König, 1836).

— Deutschland und die Deutschen, 4 vols (Altona: Hammerich, 1838-40).

[Blessington, Marguerite, countess of], The Magic Lantern; or, Sketches of Scenes in the Metropolis (London: Longman, Hurst, Rees, Orme & Brown, 1822).

Bourget, Émile, Physiologie du gamin de Paris, galopin industriel. Illustrations de Mar[c]kl (Paris: Laisné; Aubert, Lavigne, 1842).

Bulwer, Edward Lytton [Anon.], 'Asmodeus at Large', New Monthly Magazine, 34 (January-June 1832), 38-48; 112- 20; 312-20; 423-32; 35 (July-December 1832), 24-32; 104-14; 409-17; 494-504; 36 (January-June 1833), 61-8; 155-68.

Book edn: Philadelphia: Carey, 1833. Preceded by anon. Engl. edn of the same year.

— England and the English (Paris: Baudry, 1833). First edn: 2 vols (London: Bentley, 1833).

— England and the English, ed. by Standish Meacham (Chicago: University of Chicago Press, 1970).

[Couailhac, Louis], Physiologie du théâtre. Par un journaliste. Vignettes par MM. H. Émy et Birouste (Paris: Laisné; Aubert, Lavigne, 1841).

Dickens, Charles, Sketches by Boz. Illustrative of Every-Day Life and Every-Day People. With Forty Illustrations by George Cruikshank (London: Chapman & Hall, 1839).

— Sketches by Boz, ed. by Dennis Walder (London: Penguin, 1995).

— Sketches of Young Gentlemen. Dedicated to the Young Ladies. With Six Illustrations by "Phiz" (London: Chapman & Hall, 1838).

— Sketches of Young Couples; with an Urgent Remonstrance to the Gentlemen of England (Being Bachelors or Widowers), on the Present Alarming Crisis. With Six Illustrations by "Phiz" (London: Chapman & Hall, 1840).

— Pictures from Italy. The Vignette Illustrations on Wood, by Samuel Palmer (London: Bradbury & Evans, 1846).

Dronke, Ernst, Berlin, 2 vols (Frankfurt a. M.: Literarische Anstalt [J. Rütten], 1846).

— Berlin, ed. by Rainer Nitsche (Darmstadt, Neuwied: Luchterhand, 1987); abridged.

Bibliography 331

Egan, Pierce, *Life in London; or, The Day and Night Scenes of Jerry Hawthorn, Esq. and his Elegant Friend Corinthian Tom, Accompanied by Bob Logic, the Oxonian, in their Rambles and Sprees through the Metropolis. Embellished with Thirty-Six Scenes from Real Life, Designed and Etched by I.R. & G. Cruikshank; and Enriched Also with Numerous Designs on Wood, by the Same Artists* (London: Sherwood, Neely and Jones, 1821).

Eichler, Ludwig, *Berlin und die Berliner. Neue Folge. Schilderungen*, parts 1-5, with frontispieces by Theodor Hosemann (Berlin: Klemann, 1841-2). Continuation of: Ludwig Lenz, *Berlin und die Berliner. Genrebilder und Skizzen*, parts 1-3, with frontispieces by Theodor Hosemann (Berlin: Klemann, 1840-1).

[Gay, Sophie], *Physiologie du ridicule, ou Suite d'observations, par une société de gens ridicules*, 2 vols (Paris: Vimont, 1833).

Glaßbrenner [pseud. Brennglas], Adolf, *Berlin wie es ist und – trinkt*, parts 1-32, 1832-50. (Parts 1-4: Berlin: Bechthold & Hartje. Part 5: Berlin: Curths. Parts 6-10: Leipzig: Vetter & Rostosky. Parts 11-12: Leipzig: K.A. Rostosky / Rostosky & Jackowitz. Parts 13-50: Leipzig: Ignaz Jackowitz).
Reprint: *Berlin wie es ist und – trinkt. Vollständiger Nachdruck der Ausgaben 1835-1850*, ed. by Paul Thiel, 2 vols (Leipzig: Zentralantiquariat der Deutschen Demokratischen Republik, 1987).

Gutzkow, Karl, 'Naturgeschichte der deutschen Kameele', *Phönix. Frühlings-Zeitung für Deutschland*, 49 (26 February 1835), 193-5.

— 'Naturgeschichte der deutschen Kameele', ed. by Martina Lauster, in *Gutzkows Werke und Briefe*, ed. by Editionsprojekt Karl Gutzkow (Exeter, Berlin: www.gutzkow.de, 2003). <http://www.gutzkow.de>, Digitale Gesamtausgabe, Schriften zur Politik und Gesellschaft.

— 'Papilloten', *Berliner Don Quixote*, 146 (19 September 1833), [1-2].

— *Die Zeitgenossen. Ihre Schicksale, ihre Tendenzen, ihre großen Charaktere. Aus dem Englischen des E.L. Bulwer*, 2 vols (Stuttgart: Verlag der Classiker, 1837).

— *Die Zeitgenossen*, ed. by Martina Lauster, in *Gutzkows Werke und Briefe*, ed. by Editionsprojekt Karl Gutzkow (Exeter, Berlin: www.gutzkow.de, 2001). <http://www.gutzkow.de>, Digitale Gesamtausgabe, Schriften zur Politik und Gesellschaft.

Grant, James, *Sketches in London. With Twenty-Four Humourous Illustrations by "Phiz", and Others* (London: Orr, 1838).

Huart, Louis, *Physiologie du médecin. Vignettes de Trimolet* (Paris: Aubert, Lavigne, [1841]).

Jouy, Etienne, *L'Hermite de la Guiane, ou Obervations sur les mœeurs et les usages français au commencement du XIXe siècle*, 3 vols (Paris: Pillet, 1816-17).

— *L'Hermite en Italie, ou Observations sur les mœurs et usages des Italiens au commencement du XIXe siècle*, 4 vols (Paris: Pillet ainé, 1824-5).

Lenz, Ludwig, *Berlin und die Berliner. Genrebilder und Skizzen*, parts 1-3, with frontispieces by Theodor Hosemann (Berlin: Klemann, 1840-1). Continued by Ludwig Eichler as *Berlin und die Berliner. Neue Folge. Schilderungen*, parts 1-5, with frontispieces by Theodor Hosemann (Berlin: Klemann, 1841-2).

Lewald, August, *Panorama von München*, 2 vols (Stuttgart: Hallberger, 1835).

Mayhew, Henry, *London Labour and the London Poor; a Cyclopædia of the Condition and Earnings of Those that **Will** Work, Those that **Cannot** Work and Those that **Will Not** Work [...]*. [Vols 1-3:] *The London Street-Folk; Comprising, Street Sellers. Street Buyers. Street Finders. Street Performers. Street Artizans. Street Labourers. With Numerous Illustrations from Photographs* [Vol. 4:] *Comprising, Prostitutes. Thieves. Swindlers. Beggars. By Several Contributors. With Introductory Essay on the Agencies at Present in Operation in the Metropolis for the Suppression of Vice and Crime. By the Rev. William Tuckniss, B.A., Chaplain to the Society for the Rescue of Young Women and Children. With Illustrations.* 4 vols (London: Griffin, Bohn, 1861-2; repr. London: Cass, 1967).

— *The Unknown Mayhew*, ed. by E.P. Thompson and Eileen Yeo (Harmondsworth: Penguin, 1973; first edn London: Merlin Press, 1971). A selection from the eighty-two letters Mayhew published for the 'Labour and the Poor' series of *The Morning Chronicle*, 19 October 1849 – 12 December 1850.

Mercier, Louis Sébastien, *Tableau de Paris. Nouvelle édition. Corrigée & augmentée.* 12 vols (Amsterdam, 1782-8; repr. Genève: Slatkine, 1979).

"Quiz" [Edward Caswall], *Sketches of Young Ladies: In Which These Interesting Members of the Animal Kingdom are Classified According to their Several Instincts, Habits, and General Characteristics. With Six Illustrations by "Phiz"* [Hablot Knight Browne] (London: Chapman & Hall, 1837).

[Seymour, Robert], *Seymour's Sketches, Illustrated in Prose and Verse by Alfred Crowquill* [Alfred H. Forrester], 2 vols (London: Wallis, [1838]).

Smith, Albert, [Anon.], 'Physiology of the London Medical Student', *Punch*, 1 (July-December 1841), 142, 154, 165, 177, 185, 201, 213, 225, 229, 244, 253, 265.

— *The Natural History of the Ballet Girl. Illustrated by A. Henning* (London: Bogue, 1847).

— *The Natural History of the Flirt. Illustrated by Gavarni, Gilbert, and Henning* (London: Bogue, 1848).

Thackeray, William Makepeace, *The Book of Snobs* (New York: Appleton, 1852; first edn 1848). Serial in *Punch*: 'The Snobs of England, by One of Themselves', 28 February 1846 – 27 February 1847.

— 'Sketches and Travels in London', in *Miscellanies*, 8 vols (Leipzig: Tauchnitz, 1849-57), V (1856), 1-232.

— *Vanity Fair*, 2 vols, in *The Works of William Makepeace Thackeray. With Biographical Introductions by his Daughter Lady Ritchie*, 26 vols (London: Smith, Elder, 1910-11), I-II (1910). First book edn 1848; 20 monthly parts (*Vanity Fair. Pen and Pencil Sketches of English Society*) January 1847 – July 1848.

— 'Waiting at the Station', *Punch*, 18 (9 March) 1850, 92-3. Incorporated into 'Sketches and Travels in London'.

Weerth, Georg, 'Humoristische Skizzen aus dem deutschen Handelsleben', in *Sämtliche Werke*, ed. by Bruno Kaiser, 5 vols (Berlin: Aufbau-Verlag, 1956-7), II (1956), 349-485.

— 'Skizzen aus dem sozialen und politischen Leben der Briten', in *Sämtliche Werke*, III (1957), 11-475.

1.1.2 Collective works in serial parts and/or in book form[2]

Les Cent et un Robert-Macaire, composés et dessinés par M. H. Daumier, sur les idées et les légendes de M. Ch. Pilipon, réduits et lithographiés par MM.*** ; texte par MM. Maurice Alhoy et Louis Huart, 2 vols (Paris: Aubert, 1839-40). Text-image parts. The plates are reduced and reversed copies of Daumier's lithographs, with captions by Philipon, originally published, without the texts by Alhoy and Huart, in the 'Caricaturana' section of *Le Charivari*, 1836-8.

Deutsche Pandora. Gedenkbuch zeitgenössischer Zustände und Schriftsteller, 4 vols (Stuttgart: Literatur-Comptoir, 1840-1).

Le Diable à Paris. Paris et les Parisiens. Mœurs et coutumes, caractères et portraits des habitants de Paris, tableau complet de leur vie privée, publique, politique, artistique, littéraire, industrielle, etc., etc., 2 vols (Paris: Hetzel, 1845-6; repr. [only vol. 1?] Paris: Collection Capitale, 1992). 106 text-image parts, April 1844 – December 1845.

Los Españoles pintados por sí mismos, 2 vols (Madrid: Boix, 1843-4). Weekly text-image parts.

Les Français peints par eux-mêmes. [From vol. 4:] *Encyclopédie morale du dix-neuvième siècle*, 8 vols (Paris: Curmer, 1840-2). Vols 1-5 covering Paris, vols 6-8 the provinces. Vol. 9: *Le Prisme. Encyclopédie morale du dix-neuvième siècle* (Paris: Curmer, 1841). 422 text-image parts altogether, April 1839 – August 1842.

— *Les Français peints par eux-mêmes. Encyclopédie morale du dix-neuvième siècle éditée par Léon Curmer*, ed. by Pierre Bouttier ([Paris (?)]: Omnibus, 2003–). New edition in progress, presenting two volumes in one, including the illustrations.

Gavarni in London: Sketches of Life and Character, with Illustrative Essays by Popular Writers, ed. by Albert Smith (London: Bogue, 1849). Monthly parts, each containing three plates.

La Grande Ville. Nouveau Tableau de Paris, comique, critique et philosophique, par MM. Paul de Kock, Balzac, Dumas, Soulié, Gozlan, Briffault, Ourliac, E. Guinot, H. Monnier, etc. Illustrations de Gavarni, Victor Adam, Daumier, D'Aubigny, H. Emy, Traviès, Boulanger, Henri Monnier et Thenot, 2 vols (Paris: Marescq, 1843). Serial parts appeared from May 1842. The second edition of 1844 adds 11 wood-engraved plates to vol. 1.

Heads of the People: or, Portraits of the English. Drawn by Kenny Meadows. With Original Essays by Distinguished Writers, [ed. by Douglas Jerrold], 2 vols (London: Tyas, 1840-1). According to the *Cambridge Bibliography of English Literature*, IV: *1800-1900*, 3rd edn, ed. by Joanne Shattock (Cambridge: Cambridge University Press, 1999), col. 2004, the serial appeared as *Heads of the People Taken off by Quizzfizz* in 1838 (first series) and 1839 (second series), each series in 13 parts (as 12); then as a composite series in 20 parts (1839-40).

— *Les Anglais peints par eux-mêmes. Dessins de Kenny Meadows, traduction d'Émile de La Bédollière*, 2 vols (Paris: Curmer, 1840-1).

---

2 Where known to me, I indicate the appearance of serial parts preceding a book publication. Translations are listed if referred to in my study.

334 Bibliography

— *England und die Engländer in Bildern aus dem Volke mit Zeichnungen nach Kenny Meadows* (Pforzheim: Dennig, Finck, 1840). Corresponds to vol. 1.

— *England und die Engländer in Bildern aus dem Volke. Mit Zeichnungen von Kenny Meadows. Mit Original-Aufsätzen ausgezeichneter Schriftsteller. Zweiter Band. Aus dem Englischen übertragen von Dr Künzel, Mitglied der Londoner Camden Society etc.* (Pforzheim: Dennig, Finck, 1843). Corresponds to vol. 2.

Le Livre des Cent-et-un: see *Paris, ou Le Livre des Cent-et-un*

Le Musée pour rire. Dessins par tous les caricaturistes de Paris; texte par MM. Maurice Alhoy, Louis Huart et Ch. Philipon, 2 vols (Paris: Aubert, 1839). Text-image parts.

Muséum parisien. Histoire physiologique, pittoresque, philosophique et grotesque de toutes les bêtes curieuses de Paris et de la Banlieue, pour faire suite à toutes les éditions des œuvres de M. de Buffon. Texte par M. Louis Huart. 350 vignettes par MM. Grandville, Gavarni, Daumier, Traviès, Lécurieur et Henri Monnier (Paris: Beauger, Aubert, 1841).

Nashi, spisannye s naturi russkimi, [ed. by A.P. Bashutskii], 14 vols (St Petersburg: Isakov, 1841-2; repr. Moskva: Kniga, 1986).

Nouveau Tableau de Paris au XIXe siècle, 7 vols (Paris: Madame Charles-Béchet, 1834-5).

Paris, ou Le Livre des Cent-et-un, 15 vols (Paris: Ladvocat, 1831-4). Of the numerous reprints abroad, the one appearing in Brussels deserves special mention as it was published, with the permission of Ladvocat, more or less simultaneously with the Paris edition (Bruxelles: Meline, [from vol. 3:] Bruxelles: Peeters; Leipzig: Allgemeine Niederländische Buchhandlung, 1831-4). Other reprints of the French original appeared in Frankfurt (Schmerber) and Berlin (Schlesinger, up to vol. 10).

Scènes de la vie privée et publique des animaux: études de mœurs contemporaines publiées sous la direction de M. P.-J. Stahl, 2 vols (Paris: Hetzel & Paulin, 1842). Serial parts appeared from the beginning of 1841.

Wien und die Wiener, in Bildern aus dem Leben [ed. by Adalbert Stifter, Franz Stelzhamer and Carl Edmund Langer] (Pesth: Heckenast, 1844). Serial parts appeared from 1841.

— *Wien und die Wiener, in Bildern aus dem Leben*, in Adalbert Stifter, *Werke und Briefe. Historisch-kritische Gesamtausgabe*, ed. by Alfred Doppler (Stuttgart: Kohlhammer, 1978–), IX,1 (2005): reprint of texts and illustrations; IX,2 (2007): critical commentary, ed. by Johann Lachinger.

1.2 Other texts / materials

[Anon.], 'A Defence of Plagiarism', *New Monthly Magazine*, 34 (January-June 1832), 301-2.

[Anon.], 'The State of the Poor in a Manufacturing Town', *New Monthly Magazine*, 35 (July-December 1832), 53-7.

Balzac, Honoré de, 'Gavarni', in *Œuvres diverses*, ed. by Pierre-Georges Castex (Paris: Gallimard, 1990–), II (1996), ed. by Roland Chollet and René Guise, in collaboration with Christiane Guise, pp. 777-82.

— [Anon.], 'Physiologie du mariage, ou méditations de philosophie éclectique sur le bonheur et le malheur conjugal; publiées par un jeune célibataire. Deux vol. in-8°. Paris, Levavasseur et Urbain Canel. 14 F. 14 F net.', in *Œuvres diverses*, II (1996), 673-5.

— 'Prospectus' [for *La Caricature*], in *Œuvres diverses*, II (1996), 795-8.

Baudelaire, Charles, 'Le Peintre de la vie moderne', in *Œuvres complètes*, ed. by Claude Pichois, 2 vols (Paris: Gallimard, 1975-6), II (1976), 683-724.

— 'Quelques caricaturistes français', in *Œuvres complètes*, II (1976), 544-63.

Berliner Don Quixote. Adolf Glaßbrenner [Pseud. Brennglas], reprint edn in 2 vols (Hildesheim: Olms, 2001), I: *1. Jgg. Nr. 1-55*; II: *2. Jgg., 1833, Nr. 1-204. Mit einem Nachwort von Hugh Powell*.

Börne, Ludwig, *Briefe aus Paris*, in *Sämtliche Schriften*, ed. by Inge and Peter Rippmann, 5 vols (Düsseldorf [from vol. 4 Darmstadt]: Melzer, 1964-8), III (1964), 3-867.

— 'Monographie der deutschen Postschnecke', in *Sämtliche Schriften*, I (1964), 639-67.

Boulevards de Paris [foldout panorama] (Paris: L'Illustration, 1846).

Brentano, Clemens, 'Der Philister vor, in und nach der Geschichte', in *Werke*, 4 vols, ed. by Wolfgang Frühwald, Bernhard Gajek and Friedhelm Kemp, 2nd edn (Munich: Hanser, 1973-8), II (1973), 959-1016.

Büchner, Georg, 'Mémoire sur le système nerveux du barbeau (Cyprinus Barbus L.)', in *Sämtliche Werke, Briefe und Dokumente*, ed. by Henri Poschmann in collaboration with Rosemarie Poschmann, 2 vols (Frankfurt a. M.: Insel, 2002), II, 69-156.

Buckland, William, *Geology and Mineralogy Considered with Reference to Natural Theology*, 2 vols, The Bridgewater Treatises on the Power of Wisdom and Goodness of God as Manifested in the Creation, 6 (London: William Pickering, 1836).

Charivari. Redigirt von Eduard Maria Oettinger (Leipzig: Reclam), vol. 4, numbers 118-168 (January-December 1845).

Damen Conversations Lexikon. Herausgegeben im Verein mit Gelehrten und Schriftstellerinnen von Carl Herloßsohn, 10 vols (Leipzig: Volckmar [from vol. 3: Adorf], 1834-8). *Neusatz und Faksimile der 10-bändigen Ausgabe Leipzig 1834 bis 1838*, Digitale Bibliothek, 118 (Berlin: Directmedia, 2005).

Detmold, Johann Hermann, *Anleitung zur Kunstkennerschaft oder Kunst, in drei Stunden ein Kunstkenner zu werden: ein Versuch, bei Gelegenheit der zweiten Kunstausstellung* (Hannover: Hahn, 1834).

—*Die Kunst, in drei Stunden ein Kunstkenner zu werden. Mit Bildern von Daumier und Adolf Schrödter*, ed. by Bruno Kaiser (Berlin: Rütten & Loening, 1954).

Düsseldorfer Monathefte. Erster und zweiter Jahrgang (1847-1849). Repr. in one vol. (Düsseldorf: Schwann, 1979).

Goethe, Johann Wolfgang von, '*Principes de philosophie zoologique. Discuté en Mars 1830 au sein de l'académie royale des sciences par Mr. Geoffroy de Saint-Hilaire. Paris 1830'*, in *Goethes Werke*, ed. by Erich Trunz, 14 vols (Munich: Beck; Hamburg: Wegner, 1973-6), XIII (1975), ed. by Dorothea Kuhn and Rike Wankmüller, pp. 219-50.

Gutzkow, Karl, *Briefe eines Narren an eine Närrin*, ed. by R.J. Kavanagh, in *Gutzkows Werke und Briefe*, ed. by Editionsprojekt Karl Gutzkow, *Erzählerische Werke*, 1 (Münster: Oktober Verlag; Exeter, Berlin: www.gutzkow.de, 2003). <http:www.gutzkow.de>, Digitale Gesamtausgabe, Erzählerische Werke.
— [Anon.], 'Frankfurter Bilder. Von Ed. Beurmann. Mainz, Kupferberg. 1835', *Phönix. Frühlings-Zeitung für Deutschland*, 108. Literatur-Blatt, 18 (7 May, 1835), 431-2.
— *Rückblicke auf mein Leben*, ed. by Peter Hasubek, in *Gutzkows Werke und Briefe*, ed. by Editionsprojekt Karl Gutzkow, *Autobiographische Schriften*, 2 (Münster: Oktober Verlag; Exeter, Berlin: www.gutzkow.de, 2006). <http://www.gutzkow.de>, Digitale Gesamtausgabe, Autobiographische Schriften.
— [Anon.], 'Vater Goriot, Familiengemälde aus der höheren Pariser Welt. Nach dem Französischen des Balzac. Zwei Bände. Stuttgart, Hallberger. 1835', *Phönix. Frühlings-Zeitung für Deutschland*, 156 (4 July 1835), 623-4.
— 'Vorrede', in *Novellen*, ed. by Gert Vonhoff, in *Gutzkows Werke und Briefe*, ed. by Editionsprojekt Karl Gutzkow (Exeter, Berlin: www.gutzkow.de, 2000). <http://www.gutzkow.de>, Digitale Gesamtausgabe, Erzählerische Werke.
— *Wally, die Zweiflerin. Roman*, ed. by Günter Heintz (Stuttgart: Reclam, 1979).
— [Anon.], 'Werke der Industrie', *Phönix. Frühlings-Zeitung für Deutschland*, 138. Literatur-Blatt, 23 (23 June 1835), 549-51.
— 'Zur Philosophie der Geschichte', in *Schriften*, ed. by Adrian Hummel, 2 vols plus one vol. of materials (Frankfurt a. M.: Zweitausendeins, 1998), I, 553-728.
Heine, Heinrich, 'Préface' [30 May 1855] of 'Lutèce. Lettres sur la vie politique, artistique et sociale de la France', in *Historisch-kritische Gesamtausgabe der Werke*, ed. by Manfred Windfuhr, 16 vols (Hamburg: Hoffmann und Campe, 1973-97), XIII,1 (1988), 163-9.
[Jerrold, Douglas], *The Hand-Book of Swindling by Captain Barabbas Whitefeather. Edited by John Jackdaw; with Illustrations by 'Phiz'* (London: Chapman & Hall, 1839).
La Bruyère, Jean de, *Les Caractères de Théophraste traduits du grec avec Les Caractères ou les Mœurs de ce siècle*, ed. by R. Garapon (Paris: Garnier, 1990).
Le Sage, Alain René, *Asmodeus; or, The Devil on Two Sticks. [...] With a Biographical Notice of the Author, by Jules Janin. Translated by Joseph Thomas; and Illustrated by Tony Johannot* (London: Thomas, 1841).
[Mayhew, Henry and Augustus], *Whom to Marry, and How to Get Married! or, The Adventures of a Lady in Search of a Good Husband. Edited by the Brothers Mayhew. Illustrated by George Cruikshank* (London: Bogue, [1848]). Six monthly numbers, November 1847 – April 1848.
The New Monthly Magazine and Literary Journal (London: Bentley), 34 (January-June 1832), 35 (July-December 1832), 36 (January-June 1833).
Oken, Lorenz, *Allgemeine Naturgeschichte für alle Stände*, 7 vols (Stuttgart: Hoffmann, 1833-41). First issued in 90 parts.

Oppermann, [Heinrich] A[lbert], 'Ueber die sogenannten Bulwerschen Zeitgenossen', in *Jahrbuch der Literatur. Erster Jahrgang. 1839* (Hamburg: Hoffmann & Campe, 1839; repr. Frankfurt a. M.: Athenäum, 1971), pp. 257-310.

Panorama der Straße Unter den Linden vom Jahre 1820 (Berlin: Nicolai, 1991). Foldout reprint of the original scroll panorama.

The Penny Cyclopædia of the Society for the Diffusion of Useful Knowledge, 27 vols (London: Knight, 1833-43).

Phönix. Frühlings-Zeitung für Deutschland. Herausgegeben von Eduard Duller. Mit einem Literaturblatt. Redaktion Karl Gutzkow (1835), Athenäum Reprints. Die Zeitschriften des Jungen Deutschland, ed. by Alfred Estermann, 2 vols (Frankfurt a. M.: Athenäum, 1971), I: January-June 1835, II: July-December 1835.

Punch, or The London Charivari (London: Bryant), 1 (July-December 1841).

Saphir, Moritz Gottlieb, 'Papillotten', in *Gesammelte Schriften*, 4 vols (Stuttgart: Hallberger, 1832), IV, 195-248.

The Spectator; with a Biographical and Critical Preface, and Explanatory Notes, 4 vols (London, New York: Routledge, Warne and Routledge, 1860).

The Tatler: By Isaac Bickerstaff, Esq., vols. 1-271 (1709-10), republished as: *The Lucubrations of Isaac Bickerstaff, Esq. Revised and Corrected by the Author*, 4 vols (London: Nutt, Knapton, Sprint et al., 1733).

Walker, Alexander, *Physiognomy Founded on Physiology, and Applied to Various Countries, Professions, and Individuals: With an Appendix on the Bones at Hythe – the Sculls of the Ancient Inhabitants of Britain and its Invaders. Illustrated by Engravings* (London: Smith, Elder, 1834).

2 Secondary literature

Abélès, Luce, 'La province vue par *Les Français*', in *Les Français peints par eux-mêmes. Panorama du XIXe siècle*, Les Dossiers du Musée d'Orsay, 50 (Paris: Éditions de la Réunion des musées nationaux, 1993), pp. 47-61.

Abraham, J.H., *The Origins and Growth of Sociology* (Harmondsworth: Penguin, 1973).

Ackroyd, Peter, *London. The Biography* (London: Chatto & Windus, 2000).

Adburgham, Alison, *A Punch History of Manners and Modes: 1841-1940* (London: Hutchinson, 1961).

— *Silver Fork Society. Fashionable Life and Literature from 1814 to 1840* (London: Constable, 1983).

Adhémar, Jean and Jean-Pierre Seguin, *Le Livre romantique* (Paris: Le Chêne, 1968).

Altick, Richard, *The English Common Reader: A Social History of the Mass Reading Public*, 1800-1900 (Columbus: Ohio University Press, 1998; first edn 1957).

— *Punch: The Lively Youth of a British Institution 1841-1851* (Columbus: Ohio University Press, 1997).

— *The Shows of London* (Cambridge, MA: The Belknap Press of Harvard University Press, 1978).

338 Bibliography

Amossy, Ruth, *Les Idées reçues. Sémiologie du stéréotype* (Paris: Nathan, 1991).
Anderson, Patricia, *The Printed Image and the Transformation of Popular Culture 1790-1860* (Oxford: Oxford University Press, 1991).
Ansart, Pierre, *Saint-Simon* (Paris: Presses Universitaires de France, 1969).
Arac, Jonathan, *Commissioned Spirits. The Shaping of Social Motion in Dickens, Melville and Hawthorne* (New Brunswick: Rutgers University Press, 1979).
Art social und art industriel. Funktion der Kunst im Zeitalter des Industrialismus, ed. by Helmut Pfeiffer, Hans Robert Jauß and Françoise Gaillard; Theorie und Geschichte der Literatur und der schönen Künste, 77 / Ästhetik, Kunst und Literatur in der Geschichte der Neuzeit, 3 (Munich: Fink, 1987).
Baer, Joachim T., 'The "Physiological Sketch" in Russian Literature, in *Mnemozina. Studia litteraria russica in honorem Vsevolod Setchkarev*, ed. by Joachim T. Baer and Norman W. Ingham, Centrifuga. Russian Reprintings and Printings, 15 (Munich: Fink, 1974), pp. 1-12.
Barbéris, Pierre, *Balzac et le mal du siècle. Contribution à une physiologie du monde moderne*, 2 vols (Paris: Gallimard, 1970), I: 1799-1829; II: 1830-1833.
Barnes, John, *Precursors of the Cinema. Shadowgraphy, Panoramas, Dioramas and Peepshows Considered in their Relation to the History of the Cinema*, Catalogue of the Collection 1 (St. Ives: Barnes Museum of Cinematography, 1967).
Basset, Nathalie, 'Les Physiologies au XIXe siècle et la mode. De la poésie comique à la critique', *Année balzacienne*, nouv. sér., 5 (1984), 157-72. [See also Preiss, Nathalie]
Benjamin, Walter, *Charles Baudelaire. A Lyric Poet in the Era of High Capitalism. Translated from the German by Harry Zohn* (London: Verso, 1983).
— *The Arcades Project. Translated by Howard Eiland and Kevin McLaughlin* (Cambridge, MA: The Belknap Press of Harvard University Press, 1999).
—, *Gesammelte Schriften*, ed. by Rolf Tiedemann and Hermann Schweppenhäuser, 7 vols (Frankfurt a. M.: Suhrkamp, 1991).
Bernstein, Carol, 'Nineteenth-Century Urban Sketches: Thresholds of Fiction', *Prose Studies*, 3:3 (1980), 217-40.
Biesbrock, Hans-Rüdiger van, *Die literarische Mode der Physiologien in Frankreich (1840-1842)* (Frankfurt a. M., Berne, Las Vegas: Lang, 1978).
Blachon, Remi, *La Gravure sur bois au XIXe siècle* (Paris: Les Éditions de l'amateur, 2001).
Bosch-Abele, Susanne, *La Caricature (1830-1835): Katalog und Kommentar*, 2 vols (Weimar: Verlag und Datenbank für Geisteswissenschaften, 1997).
Bouttier, Pierre, 'Préface' and 'Postface', in *Les Français peints par eux-mêmes. Encyclopédie morale du XIXe siècle, éditée par Léon Curmer*, ed. by Pierre Bouttier ([Paris (?)]: Omnibus, 2003–), I (2003), i-vii and 1051-1104; II (2004), i-xx and 1037-1053.
Brake, Laurel, 'Writing, Cultural Production, and the Periodical Press in the Nineteenth Century', in *Writing and Victorianism*, ed. by J.B. Bullen (London, New York: Longman, 1997), pp. 54-72.
— *Print in Transition, 1850-1910: Studies in Media and Book History* (Basingstoke: Palgrave, 2001).

Brantlinger, Patrick, *The Spirit of Reform: British Literature and Politics, 1832-1867* (Cambridge, MA: Harvard University Press, 1977).

Buck-Morss, Susan, *The Dialectics of Seeing: Walter Benjamin and the Arcades Project* (Cambridge, MA: MIT Press, 1990).

Buddemeier, Heinz, *Panorama, Diorama, Photographie: Entstehung und Wirkung neuer Medien im 19. Jahrhundert*, Theorie und Geschichte der Literatur und der schönen Künste, 7 (Munich: Fink, 1970).

Burton, Richard D.E., *The Flâneur and his City. Patterns of Daily Life in Paris 1815-1851* (Durham: University of Durham, 1994).

Butler, E.M., *The Saint-Simonian Religion in Germany* (Cambridge: Cambridge University Press, 1926).

Byerly, Alison, 'Effortless Art: The Sketch in Nineteenth-Century Painting and Literature', *Criticism*, 41:3 (Summer 1999), 349-64.

The Cambridge Bibliography of English Literature, IV: *1800-1900*, 3rd edn, ed. by Joanne Shattock (Cambridge: Cambridge University Press, 1999).

Chambers, Helen, 'Theodor Fontane, Albert Smith und Gordon Cumming', in *Theodor Fontane im literarischen Leben seiner Zeit: Beiträge zur Fontane-Konferenz vom 17. bis 20. Juni 1986 in Potsdam*, Beiträge aus der Deutschen Staatsbibliothek, 6 (Berlin: Deutsche Staatsbibliothek, 1987), pp. 286-302.

Chittick, Kathryn, *Dickens and the 1830s* (Cambridge: Cambridge University Press, 1990).

Chollet, Roland, *Balzac journaliste. Le tournant de 1830* (Paris: Klincksieck, 1983).

Collet, Collet Dobson, *History of the Taxes on Knowledge. Their Origin and Repeal*, 2 vols (London: Fisher Unwin, 1899).

Comment, Bernard, *The Panorama* (London: Reaktion Books, 1999). Revised and expanded version of *Le XIXe siècle des panoramas*, 1993.

Crary, Jonathan, *Suspensions of Perception. Attention, Spectacle and Modern Culture* (Cambridge, MA: MIT Press, 2000).

— , *Techniques of the Observer. On Vision and Modernity in the Nineteenth Century* (Cambridge, MA: MIT Press, 1990).

Curtis, Gerard, 'Dickens in the Visual Market', in *Literature in the Marketplace. Nineteenth-Century British Publishing and Reading Practices*, ed. by John O. Jordan and Robert L. Patten (Cambridge: Cambridge University Press, 1998), pp. 213-49.

— 'Shared Lines. Pen and Pencil as Trace', in *Victorian Literature and the Victorian Visual Imagination*, ed. by Carol T. Christ and John O. Jordan (Berkeley: University of California Press, 1995), pp. 27-59.

De Kuyper, Eric, and Emile Poppe, 'Voir et regarder', *Communications*, 34 (1981), 85-96.

De Toro, Alfonso, 'Formen des *Sehens* im französischen Kultursystem unter besonderer Berücksichtigung von Roman und Lyrik', in *Rhetorische Seh-Reisen. Fallstudien zu Wahrnehmungsformen in Literatur, Kunst und Kultur*, ed. by Alfonso de Toro and Stefan Welz (Frankfurt a. M.: Vervuert, 1999), pp. 41-86.

Easson, Angus, 'Who Is Boz? Dickens and his Sketches', *Dickensian*, 81:1 (1985), 13-22.

Eisermann, Gottfried, 'Balzac als Soziologe', *Französisch heute*, 19:2 (1988), 99-119.

— 'Zur Rezeption von Balzacs "Soziologie"', *Französisch heute*, 21:1 (1990), 1-20.

Escholier, Raymond, *Daumier. Peintre et lithographe* (Paris: Floury, 1923).

Everitt, Graham, *English Caricaturists and Graphic Humourists of the Nineteenth Century. How They Illustrated and Interpreted their Times. A Contribution to the History of Caricature from the Time of the First Napoleon Down to the Death of John Leech, in 1864* (2nd edn, London: Swan Sonnenschein, 1893).

Farrant, Tim, *Balzac's Shorter Fictions. Genesis and Genre* (Oxford: Oxford University Press, 2002).

Feltes, Norman N., 'The Moment of *Pickwick*, or the Production of a Commodity Text', *Literature and History*, 10:2 (Autumn 1984), 203-17.

Fitzsimons, Raymond, *The Baron of Piccadilly. The Travels and Entertainments of Albert Smith (1816-1860)* (London: Bles, 1967).

Flint, Kate, *The Victorians and the Visual Imagination* (Cambridge: Cambridge University Press), 2002.

Forster, John, *The Life of Charles Dickens* (London: Chapman and Hall, 1893).

Fox, Celina, *Graphic Journalism in England during the 1830s and 1840s*, Outstanding Theses in the Fine Arts from British Universities (New York: Garland, 1988).

— 'The Development of Social Reportage in English Periodical Illustration during the 1840s and Early 1850s', *Past & Present*, 74:1 (1977), 90-111.

Genres mineurs. Texte zur Theorie und Geschichte nichtkanonischer Literatur (vom 16. Jahrhundert bis zur Gegenwart), ed. by Fritz Nies, in collaboration with Jürgen Rehbein; Kritische Information, 78 (Munich: Fink, 1978).

Goncourt, Edmond and Jules, *Gavarni. L'Homme et l'œuvre* (Paris: Fasquelle, 1925; 1st edn 1870).

J. J. Grandville. Karikatur und Zeichnung. Ein Visionär der französischen Romantik (Ostfildern-Ruit: Hatje Cantz, 2000). Exhibition catalogue of the Staatliche Kunsthalle Karlsruhe and the Wilhelm-Busch-Museum Hannover – Deutsches Museum für Karikatur und kritische Grafik.

Guerche, Raymond, 'La Réalisation ambitieuse d'un éditeur romantique: *Français peints par eux-mêmes*', *Bulletin de la librairie ancienne et moderne*, 145 (1972), 84-95.

Guichardet, Jeannine, *Balzac 'archéologue' de Paris* (Paris: Sedes, 1986).

Gumbrecht, Hans-Ulrich and Juan-José Sánchez, 'Der Misanthrop, die Tänzerin und der Ohrensessel. Über die Gattung 'Costumbrismo' und die Beziehungen zwischen Gesellschaft, Wissen und Diskurs in Spanien von 1805 bis 1851', in *Bewegung und Stillstand in Metaphern und Mythen. Fallstudien zum Verhältnis von elementarem Wissen und Literatur im 19. Jahrhundert*, ed. by Jürgen Link and Wulf Wülfing; Sprache und Geschichte, 9 (Stuttgart: Klett-Cotta, 1984), pp. 15-62.

Hamilton, James, *Faraday. The Life* (London: Harper Collins, 2002).

Hanebutt-Benz, Eva-Maria, *Studien zum deutschen Holzstich im 19. Jahrhundert. Sonderdruck aus dem 'Archiv für Geschichte des Buchwesens'. Bd. XXIV, Lieferung 3-6. Frankfurt a. M. 1983* (Frankfurt a. M: Buchhändler-Vereinigung, 1984).

Harden, Edgar F., *A Checklist of Contributions by William Makepeace Thackeray to Periodicals, Books and Serial Part Issues, 1828-1864* (Victoria, B.C.: English Literary Studies, University of Victoria, 1996).

Hess, Günter, 'Panorama und Denkmal. Erinnerung als Denkform zwischen Vormärz und Gründerzeit', in *Literatur in der sozialen Bewegung. Aufsätze und Forschungsberichte zum 19. Jahrhundert*, ed. by Alberto Martino (Tübingen: Niemeyer, 1977), pp. 130-206.

Hick, Ulrike, *Geschichte der optischen Medien* (Munich: Fink, 1999).

Histoire générale de la presse française, ed by Claude Bellanger and others, 5 vols (Paris: Presses Universitaires de France, 1969-76), II (1969): *De 1815 à 1871*.

Hollington, Michael, 'Adorno, Benjamin and *The Old Curiosity Shop*', *Dickens Quarterly*, 6:3 (1989), 87-95.

— 'Dickens and Cruikshank as Physiognomers in *Oliver Twist*', *Dickens Quarterly*, 7:2 (1990), 243-54.

— 'The Live Hieroglyphic: *Physiologie* and Physiognomy in *Martin Chuzzlewit*, *Dickens Quarterly*, 10:1 (1993), 57-68.

— 'Monstrous Faces: Physiognomy in *Barnaby Rudge*', *Dickens Quarterly*, 8:1 (1991), 6-15.

— 'Physiognomy in *Hard Times*, *Dickens Quarterly*, 9:2 (1992), 58-66.

Hughes, Linda K. and Michael Lund, 'Textual/Sexual Pleasure and Serial Publication', in *Literature in the Marketplace. Nineteenth-Century British Publishing and Reading Practices*, ed. by John O. Jordan and Robert L. Patten (Cambridge: Cambridge University Press, 1998), pp. 143-64.

Jervis, Simon, 'Rudolph Ackermann', in *London – World City 1800-1840*, ed. by Celina Fox (New Haven: Yale University Press, 1992), pp. 97-110.

Kainen, Jakob, 'Why Bewick Succeeded: A Note in the History of Wood Engravings', *United States National Museum Bulletin*, 218, Paper 11 (1959).

Kauffmann, Kai, *'Es ist nur ein Wien!' Stadtbeschreibungen von Wien 1700 bis 1873. Geschichte eines literarischen Genres der Wiener Publizistik*, Literatur in der Geschichte – Geschichte in der Literatur, 29 (Vienna, Cologne, Weimar: Böhlau, 1994).

Koch, Ursula E., '*Le Charivari* (Paris), *Punch* (London) und *Kladderadatsch* (Berlin). Drei Satire-Journale zwischen Kunst und Journalismus', in *Forum Vormärz Forschung Jahrbuch*, 11 (Bielefeld: Aisthesis, 2006), 17-61.

— *Der Teufel in Berlin. Von der Märzrevolution bis zu Bismarcks Entlassung. Illustrierte politische Witzblätter einer Metropole 1848-1890* (Cologne: Informationspresse – Leske, 1991).

— and Pierre-Paul Sagave, *Le Charivari. Die Geschichte einer Pariser Tageszeitung im Kampf um die Republik (1832-1882)* (Cologne: Informationspresse – Leske, 1984).

Lauster, Martina, 'Anatomie und Enzyklopädie als Muster literarischer Verfahrensweisen im Werk Karl Gutzkows', in *Zeitdiskurse. Reflexionen zum 19. und 20. Jahrhundert*, ed. by Roland Berbig, M. Lauster and Rolf Parr (Heidelberg: Synchron, 2004), pp. 43-54.

— 'Englische "Anatomie" gegen deutsche "Konstruktion" der Geschichte: Gutzkows Versuch, den Sonderweg zu korrigieren', *Chroniques allemandes*, 7 (Grenoble: Université Stendhal-Grenoble III, 1999), 57-68.

— 'Physiognomy, Zoology and Physiology as Paradigms in Sociological Sketches of the 1830s and 40s', in *Physiognomy in Profile: Lavater's Impact on European Culture*, ed. by Melissa Percival and Graeme Tytler (Newark: University of Delaware Press, 2005), pp. 161-79.

— 'The Quest for the German Citizen. Physiognomies of 'Bürgerlichkeit' in Sketches of the Vormärz', in *Politics in Literature. Studies on a Germanic Preoccupation from Kleist to Améry*, ed. by Rüdiger Görner; London German Studies, 9 (Munich: iudicium, 2004), pp. 52-82.

— 'Walter Benjamin's Myth of the "Flâneur"', *Modern Language Review*, 102:1 (January 2007), 92-109.

Le Men, Ségolène, 'Peints par eux-mêmes ...', in *Les Français peints par eux-mêmes. Panorama du XIXe siècle*, Les Dossiers du Musée d'Orsay, 50 (Paris: Éditions de la Réunion des musées nationaux, 1993), pp. 4-46.

— 'La Vignette et la lettre', in *Histoire de l'édition française*, ed. by Henri-Jean Martin and Roger Chartier, 4 vols ([Paris]: Promodis, 1983-7), III (1985): *Le Temps des éditeurs. Du Romantisme à la Belle Époque*, pp. 312-27.

Lengauer, Hubert, *Ästhetik und liberale Opposition. Zur Rollenproblematik des Schriftstellers in der österreichischen Literatur um 1848*, Literatur in der Geschichte – Geschichte in der Literatur 17 (Vienna, Cologne: Böhlau, 1989).

Lhéritier, Andrée, 'Les Physiologies. Introduction', *Etudes de presse*, 9:17 (1957), 1-11.

— 'Répertoire des Physiologies', *Etudes de presse*, 9:17 (1957), 13-58.

Lindenstruth, Gerhard, *Edward Bulwer Lytton. Eine Bibliographie der Veröffentlichungen im deutschen Sprachraum* (Giessen: Lindenstruth, 1994, repr. 2001).

Literature in the Marketplace. Nineteenth-Century British Publishing and Reading Practices, ed. by John O. Jordan and Robert L. Patten (Cambridge: Cambridge University Press, 1995).

Lloyd Jones, I.D., 'Charles Fourier: the Faithful Pupil of the Enlightenment', in *Philosophers of the Enlightenment*, ed. by Peter Gilmour (Edinburgh: Edinburgh University Press, 1989), pp. 151-79.

London – World City. 1800-1840, ed. by Celina Fox (New Haven: Yale University Press, 1992). [Catalogue of an exhibition in the Villa Hügel, Essen, 6 June – 8 November, 1992].

Macleod, Roy, *The 'Creed of Science' in Victorian England* (Aldershot: Ashgate, 1984).

Maidment, Brian, *Into the 1830's. Some Origins of Victorian Illustrated Journalism. Cheap Octavo Magazines of the 1820s and their Influence* (Manchester: Polytechnic Library, 1992).

— *Reading Popular Prints 1780-1870* (Manchester: Manchester University Press, 1996).

— *Dusty Bob. A Cultural History of Dustmen 1790-1870* (Manchester: Manchester University Press, 2007).

Manevy, Raymond, *La Presse française de Renaudot à Rochefort* (Paris: Foret, 1958).

Mansel, Philip, *Paris between Empires 1814-1852. Monarchy and Revolution* (London: Phoenix, 2003).

Martin, Henri-Jean and Odile Martin, 'Le monde des éditeurs', in *Histoire de l'édition française*, ed. by Henri-Jean Martin and Roger Chartier, 4 vols ([Paris]: Promodis, 1983-7), III (1985): *Le Temps des éditeurs. Du Romantisme à la Belle Époque*, pp. 158-216.

Marx, Karl, *Capital. A Critical Analysis of Capitalist Production. Translated from the Third German Edition by Samuel Moore and Edward Aveling and Edited by Frederick Engels. Volume 1* (London: Lawrence & Wishart; Moscow: Progress Publishers, 1974).

Meacham, Standish, 'Editor's Introduction', in Edward Lytton Bulwer, *England and the English* (Chicago: University of Chicago Press, 1970), pp. ix-xxv.

Melot, Michel, 'Le texte et l'image, in *Histoire de l'édition française*, ed. by Henri-Jean Martin and Roger Chartier, 4 vols ([Paris]: Promodis, 1983-7), III (1985): *Le Temps des éditeurs. Du Romantisme à la Belle Époque*, pp. 286-312.

Moers, Ellen, *The Dandy. Brummell to Beerbohm* (New York: Viking Press, 1960; repr. Lincoln: University of Nebraska Press, 1978).

Montesinos, José F., *Costumbrismo y novela. Ensayo sobre el redescubrimiento de la realidad española* (Berkeley: University of California Press, 1960).

Morus, Iwan, Simon Schaffer and Jim Secord, 'Scientific London', in *London – World City. 1800-1840*, ed. by Celina Fox (New Haven: Yale University Press, 1992), pp. 129-42.

Neuburg, Victor, 'Introduction', in *Henry Mayhew, London Labour and the London Poor*, ed. by Victor Neuburg (Harmondsworth: Penguin, 1985), pp. xii-xxiii.

Oesterle, Günter, 'Das Komischwerden der Philosophie in der Poesie. Literatur-, philosophie- und gesellschaftsgeschichtliche Konsequenzen der "voie physiologique" in Georg Büchners *Woyzeck*', *Georg Büchner Jahrbuch*, 3 (1983), 200-39.

— '"Unter dem Strich". Skizze einer Kulturpoetik des Feuilletons im neunzehnten Jahrhundert', in *Das schwierige neunzehnte Jahrhundert. Germanistische Tagung zum 65. Geburtstag von Eda Sagarra im August 1998*, ed. by Jürgen Barkhoff, Gilbert Carr and Roger Paulin (Tübingen: Niemeyer, 2000), pp. 229-50.

Oesterle, Ingrid, 'Bewegung und Metropole: Ludwig Börne, "der gegenwärtigste aller Menschen, die sich je in den Straßen von Paris herumgetrieben haben"?', in *Vormärzliteratur in europäischer Perspektive II: Politische Revolution – Industrielle Revolution – Ästhetische Revolution*, ed. by Martina Lauster and Günter Oesterle (Bielefeld: Aisthesis, 1998), pp. 179-206.

— 'Metropole und Landschaft, verzeitlichte Geschichte und geowissenschaftlicher Raum. Das Pariser Reisetagebuch von Carl Gustav Carus', in *Vormärzliteratur in europäischer Perspektive III: Zwischen Daguerreotyp und Idee*, ed. by Martina Lauster (Bielefeld: Aisthesis, 2000), pp. 65-99.

— 'Paris, die Mode und das Moderne', in *Nachmärz. Der Ursprung der ästhetischen Moderne in einer nachrevolutionären Situation*, ed. by Thomas Koebner and Sigrid Weigel (Opladen: Westdeutscher Verlag, 1996), pp. 156-74.

— 'Peripherie und Zentrum – Kunst und Publizistik – Wahrnehmungsgrenzfall "große Stadt". Die Aufzeichnungen Friedrich Hebbels in Paris', in *Das schwierige neunzehnte Jahrhundert. Germanistische Tagung zum 65. Geburtstag von Eda Sagarra im August 1998*, ed. by Jürgen Barkhoff, Gilbert Carr and Roger Paulin (Tübingen: Niemeyer, 2000), pp. 187-206.

Oettermann, Stephan, *Das Panorama. Die Geschichte eines Massenmediums* (Frankfurt a. M.: Syndikat, 1980). English translation: *The Panorama. History of a Mass Medium* (New York: Zone Books, 1997).

Parejo Vadillo, Ana, *Women Poets and Urban Aestheticism. Passengers of Modernity* (Basingstoke: Palgrave Macmillan, 2005).

Park, Roy, '*Ut Pictura Poesis*: The Nineteenth Century Aftermath', *Journal of Aesthetics and Art Criticism*, 28 (1969), 155-64.

Patten, Robert L., *George Cruikshank's Life, Times, and Art*, 2 vols (New Brunswick: Rutgers University Press, 1992).

— 'Serialized Retrospection in *The Pickwick Papers*', in *Literature in the Marketplace. Nineteenth-Century British Publishing and Reading Practices*, ed. by John O. Jordan and Robert L. Patten (Cambridge: Cambridge University Press, 1998), pp. 123-42.

Pennell, Elizabeth Robins, 'The Modern Comic Newspaper: the Evolution of a Popular Type', *Contemporary Review*, 50 (October 1886), 509-52.

Pelzer, John and Linda, 'Coffee Houses in Augustan London', *History Today*, 32 (October 1982), 40-7.

Physiognomy in Profile. Lavater's Impact on European Culture, ed. by Melissa Perceval and Graeme Tytler (Newark: University of Delaware Press, 2005).

De la Poire au parapluie. Physiologies politiques, ed. by Nathalie Preiss (Paris: Champion, 1999).

Popular Print Media 1820-1910, ed. by Andrew King and John Plunkett, 3 vols (London: Routledge, 2004).

Powell, Hugh, 'Nachwort', in *Berliner Don Quixote. Adolf Glaßbrenner [Pseud. Brennglas]*, 2 vols (Hildesheim: Olms, 2001), II, 1-18.

Pratt, Mary Louise, *Imperial Eyes. Travel Writing and Transculturation* (London: Routledge, 1993).

Preiss, Nathalie, *Les Physiologies en France au XIXe siècle: étude historique, littéraire et stylistique* (Mont-de-Marsan: Éditions InterUniversitaires, 1999).

— *Pour de rire! La Blague au XIXe siècle ou la représentation en question* (Paris: Presses Universitaires de France, 2002).

——Basset, 'Les Physiologies, un miroir en miettes', in *Les Français peints par eux-mêmes. Panorama du XIXe siècle*, Les Dossiers du Musée d'Orsay, 50 (Paris: Éditions de la Réunion des musées nationaux, 1993), pp. 62-7. [See also Basset, Nathalie].

Promies, Ute, *Karl Gutzkow – Romanautor und kritischer Pädagoge* (Bielefeld: Aisthesis, 2003).

Rasch, Wolfgang, *Bibliographie Karl Gutzkow*, 2 vols (Bielefeld: Aisthesis, 1998).

—— 'Zur Geschichte des *Telegraph für Deutschland*', *Forum Vormärz Forschung Jahrbuch*, 1 (Bielefeld: Aisthesis, 1996), 131-60.

Rebel, Ernst, *Druckgrafik. Geschichte. Fachbegriffe. Mit 55 Abbildungen und Risszeichnungen* (Stuttgart: Reclam, 2003).

Reid, John Cowie, *Bucks and Bruisers: Pierce Egan and Regency England* (London: Routledge & Kegan Paul, 1971).

Rignall, John, *Realist Fiction and the Strolling Spectator* (London: Routledge, 1992).

Riha, Karl and Gerhard Rudolph, 'Nachwort', in *Düsseldorfer Monathefte. Erster und zweiter Jahrgang (1847-1849). Unveränderter Nachdruck in einem Band*, ed. by Karl Riha and Gerhard Rudolph (Düsseldorf: Schwann, 1979), pp. 471-82.

Ritzer, Monika, 'Die Tatsachen der Wahrnehmung. Zur Relation von Naturwissenschaft und Literatur im Realismus am Beispiel von Hermann Helmholtz und Conrad Ferdinand Meyer', in *Rhetorische Seh-Reisen. Fallstudien zu Wahrnehmungsformen in Literatur, Kunst und Kultur*, ed. by Alfonso de Toro and Stefan Welz (Frankfurt a. M.: Vervuert, 1999), pp. 203-25.

Robinson, David, *The Lantern Image. Iconography of the Magic Lantern 1420-1880* (London, Nutley: The Magic Lantern Society, 1993).

Sadleir, Michael, *Bulwer and his Wife. A Panorama 1803-1836* (London: Constable, new edn 1933).

Schlicke, Paul, *Dickens and Popular Entertainment* (London: Unwin Hyman, 1988).

Schmid Noerr, Heidegert, 'Die illustrierte Presse', in *Kunst der bürgerlichen Revolution*, ed. by Volkmar Braunbehrens and others, 2nd edn (Berlin: Neue Gesellschaft für Bildende Kunst, 1973), pp. 151-6.

Schon, Peter M., 'Naturwissenschaft und "Les Physiologies" im 19. Jahrhundert in Frankreich. Ein Beitrag zur Geschichte der Beziehungen zwischen Naturwissenschaft und Literatur', *Alma Mater Aquiensis*, 6 (1968), 70-6.

Science in the Nineteenth-Century Periodical: Reading the Magazine of Nature, ed. by Geoffrey Cantor and others (Cambridge: Cambridge University Press, 2004).

Sha, Richard C., *The Visual and Verbal Sketch in British Romanticism* (Philadelphia: University of Philadelphia Press, 1998).

—— 'The Power of the Nineteenth-Century English Visual and Verbal Sketch: Appropriation, Discipline, Mastery', *Nineteenth-Century Contexts*, 24:1 (2002), 73-100.

Shesgreen, Sean, *Images of the Outcast. The Urban Poor in the Cries of London* (New Brunswick: Rutgers University Press; Manchester: Manchester University Press, 2002).

Shorter, Clement, 'Illustrated Journalism; its Past and its Future', *Contemporary Review*, 75 (April 1899), 481-94.

Sieburth, Richard, 'Une idéologie du lisible: le phénomène des "Physiologies"', *Romantisme*, 47 (1985:1), 39-60.

Slater, Michael, *Douglas Jerrold. 1803-1857* (London: Duckworth, 2002).

Spielmann, M.H., *The History of 'Punch'. With Numerous Illustrations* (London, Paris, Melbourne: Cassell, 1895).

Spree, Ulrike, *Das Streben nach Wissen. Eine vergleichende Gattungsgeschichte der populären Enzyklopädie in Deutschland und Großbritannien im 19. Jahrhundert* (Tübingen: Niemeyer, 2000).

Stein, Richard L., 'Street Figures: Victorian Urban Iconography', in *Victorian Literature and the Victorian Visual Imagination*, ed. by Carol T. Christ and John O. Jordan (Berkeley: University of California Press, 1995), pp. 233-63.

Stierle, Karlheinz, 'Aura, Spur und Benjamins Vergegenwärtigung des 19. Jahrhunderts', in *Art social und art industriel. Funktionen der Kunst im Zeitalter des Industrialismus*, ed. by Helmut Pfeiffer, Hans Robert Jauß and Françoise Gaillard (Munich: Fink, 1987), pp. 39-47.

— 'Baudelaires *Tableaux Parisiens* und die Tradition des "tableau de Paris"', *Poetica*, 6 (1974), 285-322. English translation: 'Baudelaire and the Tradition of the *Tableaux de Paris*', *New Literary History*, 11 (1979-80), 345-61.

— *Der Mythos von Paris. Zeichen und Bewußtsein der Stadt* (Munich, Vienna: Hanser, 1993).

Strosetzki, Christoph, *Balzacs Rhetorik und die Literatur der Physiologien*, Akademie der Wissenschaften und der Literatur. Abhandlungen der geistes- und sozialwissenschaftlichen Klasse, 1985:6 (Mainz: Akademie der Wissenschaften und der Literatur; Stuttgart: Steiner, 1985).

Uglow, Jenny, *Hogarth. A Life and a World* (London: Faber & Faber, 1998).

Unknown London: Early Modernist Visions of the Metropolis, ed. by John Marriott; consulting editors Masaie Matsumara and Judith Walkowitz, 6 vols (London: Pickering & Chatto, 2000).

The Unknown Mayhew. Selections from the 'Morning Chronicle' 1849-50, ed. by E.P. Thompson and Eileen Yeo (Harmondsworth: Penguin, 1973).

Vachon, Stéphane, *Les Travaux et les jours d'Honoré de Balzac. Chronologie de la création balzacienne* (Paris: Presses du CNRS, Presses Universitaires de Vincennes, Les Presses de l'Université de Montréal, 1992).

Victorian Literature and the Victorian Visual Imagination, ed. by Carol T. Christ and John O. Jordan (Berkeley: University of California Press, 1995).

Victorian Print Media, ed. by Andrew King and John Plunkett (Oxford: Oxford University Press, 2005).

Vonhoff, Gert, '"Eine frische Literatur". Georg Weerths *Skizzen aus dem sozialen und politischen Leben der Briten*', in *Mutual Exchanges. Sheffield-Münster Colloquium I*, ed. by R.J. Kavanagh (Frankfurt a. M.: Lang, 1998), pp. 80-95.

Walder, Dennis, 'Introduction', in *Charles Dickens, Sketches by Boz*, ed. by Dennis Walder (London: Penguin, 1995), pp. ix-xxxiv.

Warman, Caroline, 'What's behind a Face? Lavater and the Anatomists', in *Physiognomy in Profile*, ed. by Melissa Percival and Graeme Tytler (Newark: University of Delaware Press, 2005), pp. 94-108.

Weber, Wolfgang, *Johann Jakob Weber. Der Begründer der illustrierten Presse in Deutschland* (Leipzig: Lehmstedt, 2003).

Wechsler, Judith, *A Human Comedy. Physiognomy and Caricature in Nineteenth-Century Paris* (London: Thames & Hudson, 1982).

Wilkinson, Ian, *Narrative Strategies in Charles Dickens's 'Sketches by Boz'* (PhD thesis, Keele University, 2002).

Winston, Brian, *Media, Technology and Society. A History: From the Telegraph to the Internet* (London: Routledge, 1998).

Wissen in Literatur im 19. Jahrhundert, ed. by Lutz Dannenberg and Friedrich Vollhardt (Tübingen: Niemeyer, 2002).

Wittmann, Reinhard, *Ein Verlag und seine Geschichte. Dreihundert Jahre J.B. Metzler Stuttgart* (Stuttgart: Metzler, 1982).

The Wonders of Light and Shadow. Published under the Direction of the Committee of General Literature and Education, Appointed by the Society for the Promotion of Christian Knowledge (London: The Society for the Promotion of Christian Knowledge, 1851).

Wülfing, Wulf, '"Das europäische Panorama" findet nicht statt. Bemerkungen zu einem diskursiven Streit um Öffentlichkeit im Vormärz', in *Vormärzliteratur in europäischer Perspektive I: Öffentlichkeit und nationale Identität*, ed. by Helmut Koopmann and Martina Lauster (Bielefeld: Aisthesis, 1996), pp. 41-53.

— 'Stil und Zensur. Zur jungdeutschen Rhetorik als einem Versuch von Diskursintegration', in *Das Junge Deutschland. Kolloquium zum 150. Jahrestag des Verbots vom 10. Dezember 1835. Düsseldorf 17.-19. 2. 1986*, ed. by Joseph A. Kruse and Bernd Kortländer (Hamburg: Hoffmann & Campe, 1987), pp. 193-217.

— 'Die telegraphischen Depeschen als "Chronik des Jahrhunderts". Karl Gutzkows "Ahnungen" von einem Medium der Moderne', in *Karl Gutzkow. Liberalismus – Europäertum – Modernität*, ed. by Roger Jones and Martina Lauster (Bielefeld: Aisthesis, 2000), pp. 85-106.

Zahn, Eva, 'Geschichte der Fliegenden Blätter', in *Facsimile Querschnitt durch die Fliegenden Blätter* , ed. by Eva Zahn (Munich, Berne, Vienna: Scherz, 1966), pp. 8-18.

Zeldin, Theodore, *France 1848-1945*, 2 vols (Oxford: Clarendon Press, 1973-7).

Index

Page numbers in **bold** indicate illustrations.

À Beckett, Gilbert Abbott (1811-56) 32, **38**, 47
Abélès, Luce 283-4
Acceleration / abbreviation: see Modernity; Transport
Ackermann, Rudolph (1764-1834) 131
Ackroyd, Peter 152, 154-5
Addison, Joseph (1672-1719) 134, 148 and note 48, 149-52 and note 55
Alhoy, Maurice (1802-56) 48, 52-**53**, **56**-7, 111-14 (**112**), 289, 303, 311 note 7
Alibert, Jean-Louis-Marc (1766-1827) 91 note 15
Allgemeine Naturgeschichte für alle Stände (Oken) 116, 117-18, 122
Altick, Richard 64 note 14; 82 note 45; 245, 251, 253-4
Amossy, Ruth 88-9, 111-13
Anatomy (see also Observation; Physiology) 114-15, 173-5, 178-9, 180, 181
Les Anglais peints par eux-mêmes 54, 110, 168 note 93; 276 and note 50 ; 289
Les Animaux peints par eux-mêmes 254
Arago, Etienne (1802-92) 48
Arcades Project (Benjamin) 11, 15, 16, 67 note 22
Aristocracy: see Class
The Ascent of Mont Blanc (Mr Albert Smith's) 251-4 (**252**)
'Asmodée' (Janin) 132-3, 140, 162
'Asmodeus at Large' (Bulwer) 134, 151, 178, 179-85, 187, 193, 265-6
Asmodeus, or the Devil in London 134
Asmodeus, or The Devil on Two Sticks (Le Sage) 129-36, **172**

Aubert, Gabriel (print dealer and publisher) 43, 289, 290, 295 note 85; 296, 311 note 7
Auger, Hippolyte (1797-1881) 162 note 85
Azaïs, Hyacinthe (1766-1845) 91

Balzac, Honoré de (1799-1850) 17, 19, 32, 39 note 30; 48, 89, 92-103, 132 note 6; 163, 175
'Avant-propos' of *La Comédie humaine* 110-11, 115
'Codes' 311 and note 6
'Les Comédies qu'on peut voir gratis à Paris' 221
'Complaintes satiriques sur les mœurs du temps présent' 92-3, 102 note 42; 181 note 28; 182
'L'Épicier' 94-103 (**95**), 108, 128, **278**, 295
'Gavarni' 110
'Histoire et physiologies des Boulevards de Paris' 65-75 (**68**, **72**, **74**); 77, 83-4, 88, 136, 155, 217
'Monographie de la presse parisienne' 97 note 29; 315-**16**
'Nouvelle théorie du déjeuner' 99 and note 35
Physiologie du mariage 92, 93-4
Physiologie du rentier 285, 288
'Prospectus' for *La Caricature* 28, 40-1, 110
Scènes de la vie parisienne 285
Scènes de la vie privée 254 note 10
Scènes de la vie de province 285
'Théorie de la démarche' 174, 212, 246

Barker, Robert (1739-1806) 213 note 4
Bashutskii, Aleksandr Pavlovich (1801-76) 277 note 52
Baudelaire, Charles (1821-67) 6, 8, 10 and note 19; 14 and note 32; 16, 145, 175-6, 186, 320-1, 323, 325, 327
Baudry (publisher of English books in Paris) 265
Beard, James (photographer) 320
Beauger (publisher) 289
Beaumarchais, Pierre-Augustin Caron de (1732-99) 164 note 89
Les Belges peints par eux-mêmes 276 note 50
Belinskii, Vissarion (1811-49) 303 and note 100
Benjamin, Walter (1892-1940) 3-4, 6-17, 22, 41-2; 53, 67 note 22; 175-6, 213, 260, 320-1, 327
translation into English 11-12
Bentham, Jeremy (1748-1832) 27, 104-5, 175, 179, 265, 267-8
Berlin (Dronke) 17, 177, 194-201 and note 71; 237
Berlin und die Berliner (Lenz / Eichler) 46
Berlin wie es ist und – trinkt (Glaßbrenner) 46, 158-**59**, 169, 195-**96**
Berliner Charivari 137 (see also *Satan. Berliner Charivari* and *Der Teufel in Berlin*)
Berliner Don Quixote 48-52 (**50**)
Berliner Figaro 47 and note 53
Bernard, Pierre (*Physiologie du Jardin des Plantes*) 288
Bernstein, Carol 3-4
Bertall, Charles Albert [Charles Albert, vicomte d'Arnoux] (1820-83) **72**, **74**, 201-02, **203**, **224**, 323-5 (**323-4**)
Bertrand (draughtsman, collaborator on *Le Diable à Paris*) **68**, **72**
Beurmann, Eduard (1804-83) 75-79, 81, 117, 119, 237, 275-6, 306

Bewick, Thomas (1753-1828) 33, 42, 110
Bichat, Xavier (1771-1802) 91, 93
Bickerstaff, Isaac [Richard Steele] 152
Biedenfeld, Ferdinand von (1788-1862) 131
Biesbrock, Hans-Rüdiger van 289-90
Bilder-Conversationslexikon 256 note 20
Birouste, Jean (1813-after 1840) **298**, **305**
Blessington, Marguerite, countess of (1789-1849) 83
Blumenbach, Johann Friedrich (1752-1840) 118
Bogue, David (1807-56) 239
Böhm, Wilhelm (draughtsman) 166, **167**, 226, **235**, 274
Le Bon Sens 160, 161
Börne, Ludwig (1786-1837) 18, 118-19
Bossange, Martin (1766-1865) 35
Bouchot (lithographer, collaborator on *Le Musée pour rire*) 289
Boulevards de Paris (foldout panorama) 69-71 (**70**)
Bourget, E. (*Physiologie du gamin de Paris*) 291
Bouton, Charles-Marie (1781-1853) 62
Bouttier, Pierre 281-2, 288 note 72
Braid, James (1795-1860) 271 note 42
Braun, Kaspar (1807-77) 45
Brecht, Bertolt (1898-1956) 22
Brentano, Clemens (1778-1842) 122 and note 95
Brevière, Louis Henri (1797-1869) **172**
The Bridgewater Treatises 124, 265 note 34
Brillat-Savarin, Jean Anthelme (1755-1826) 92 and note 16
Brockhaus, Friedrich Arnold (1772-1823) 256 and note 20
Browne, Hablot Knight [pseud. 'Phiz'] (1815-82) 124, 125, **126**
Brugnot, Louis (1814-45) 7, **68**, **72**, 217, **219**

Buchez, Philippe Joseph Benjamin (1796-1866) 92 and note 17; 115, 162 note 85
Büchner, Georg (1813-37) 116, 175 note 10
Buchner, Karl (1800-72) 274
Buckland, William (1784-1856) 124-5
Buffon, George-Louis Leclerc, comte de (1707-88) 121, 254-5
Bullock, William (early 1780s – after 1843) 253
Bulwer, Edward Lytton [later Bulwer Lytton] (1803-73) 19, 325-6
  'Asmodeus at Large' 134, 151, 178, 179-85, 186, 187, 265-6, 267
  The Coming Race 184
  Devereux 151 note 55
  England and the English 5, 18, 23, 24-8, 43, 79, 80, 104-5, 151 and note 55; 174, 178, 215, 255 note 15; 260-8 and note 27; 275, 293, 306
  New Monthly Magazine (editorship) 260-1
  Pelham or the Adventures of a Gentleman 174, 178
Bunyan, John (1628-88) 163
Burton, Richard 9-10, 193-4 and note 67; 201
Byerly, Alison 3

Cabanis, Georges (1757-1808) 91 and note 15; 93
Cabet, Etienne (1788-1856) 160
The Cabinet Cyclopædia (Lardner) 124
Camera obscura: see Media of visual entertainment
Caqué, Joseph Hippolyte Jules (1814-85) **74**
Les Caractères (La Bruyère) 140, 141-3 and note 26; 152
Caricature (see also Censorship) 32, 37, 39-40, 42, 89, 110-14, 125-**26**, 153, 158, 238, 297-**98**, 300, 311-12, 320

La Caricature 28, 32, 39-41 and notes 28, 29; 42, 110 and note 65; 295 note 85
Carlyle, Thomas (1795-1881) 180
Carus, Carl Gustav (1789-1869) 232-3
'The Casino' (Albert Smith) 151, 243-9 **(244, 245)**
Caswall, Edward [pseud. 'Quiz'] (1814-78) 123-8 **(126)**
Censorship (direct and indirect) 14, 26 and note 6; 39 note 29; 41-2, 45, 46, 48, **50**-2, 237, 261 and note 27; 311 note 7; 326
Les Cent et un Robert Macaire (Daumier / Alhoy, Huart) 311 note 7
Cervantes Saavedra, Miguel de (1547-1616) 164 note 89
Chalmers, Thomas (1780-1847) 265 and note 34
Champin, Jean-Jacques (1796-1860) **217**-18, **219**
Chapman & Hall (publishers) 124
Charakteres (Theophrastus) 140
Charcot, Jean-Martin (1825-93) 271 note 42
Le Charivari (Paris) 39, 41-3 and note 44; 164, 295 note 85; 311 note 7
Charivari (Leipzig) 43, 47 note 53; **137**
Charles II, king of England, Scotland and Ireland (1630-85) 156-7
Charles V, king of France (1338-80) 65
Charton, Édouard (1807-90) 35
Chaussard, Publicola [Pierre Jean Baptiste Chaussard] (1766-1823) 131
Chittick, Kathryn 187, 192 and note 62
Cholera 134, 178-9, 180
Chollet, Roland 39-40
Cities (see also Rural populations)
  Berlin 16, 17, 46-7, 69 and note 25; 131, 135, 136-7, 158-9, 194-201, 237
  Frankfurt 75-9, 81, 82, 237, 275
    Bundestag 261 note 27

Judengasse 77-8
Museum(sgesellschaft) 117, 119, 123
Leipzig 35, 43, 45 note 47; 47 and note 53; 137
London 16, 17, 37-9, 55, 83, 115-16, 131, 134, 149-53, 154-5, 156-8, 174, 178, 180, 187-92, 198, 238-49, 266, 273, 302-3, 313, 316-20
    Adelaide Gallery / The Casino 83, 151, 243-9 (**244**), 253, 255
    British Museum 158, 243
    Egyptian Hall 251-4 (**252**), 256, 271
    Houses of Parliament 181
    Regents Park Colosseum 214
    Stanley's Rooms 83
    Willis's Rooms 251
Madrid 129-30, 277 note 53
Manchester 178, 310
Munich 46, 79-82, 237
Paris 15-16, 17, 37-9, 43, 47, 55, 65-75, 115-16, 119, 131-2, 133-4, 143, 144-8, 153, 159-61, 180, 181-3, 193-4, 195, 202-9, 216-25 (**217, 219, 222**), 239-40, 246, 263, 265, 276, 282-3, 284-5, 289, 297, 302-3, 323-**24**
    Champs-Elysées 321-3 (**322**)
    Jardin des Plantes 73, 115, 218-20 (**219**), 254
    Muséum d'histoire naturelle 218-20, 254
    Place de la Concorde 218
St Petersburg 67-9, 277 note 52
Vienna 15, 21-2, 46, 131, 132-3, 145, 156, 225-37, 247, 274
    Counter-image to Western metropolis 229, 231, 236-7
City Cries
    street vendors 71-**72**, 152-3
    print genre 153-61, 237, 313, 320
Class (see also Types)
    aristocracy 25-7, 83, 182-3, 234

middle class / bourgeoisie (see also Observation: middle-class) 13, 21, 25, 27, 63, 161, 179, 187, 193-4, 195, 198, 202, 209, 240-1, 248, 259-60, 263, 293, 306-7, 310-20
working class / industrial class / mechanics / proletariat (see also Poverty) 13, 17, 24-7, 65-6, 71-3 (**72**), 97, 160-1, 178, 197-201, 202, 220, 310, 317
Classification: see Physiology; Sketches: specialisation
Cler, Albert (1804-?) 295 note 85
Codes 311 and note 6
Columbus, Christopher (1451-1506) 89
Combe, William (1742-1823) 82, 131 and note 3
La Comédie humaine (Balzac) 152, 163, 254 note 10; 285
'Les Comédies qu'on peut voir gratis à Paris' (Balzac) 221
The Comic Almanack 37-**38**
Comment, Bernard 11-12
Communist Manifesto 201 note 87
'Complaintes satiriques sur les mœurs du temps présent' (Balzac) 92-3, 102 note 42; 181 note 28; 182
Comte, Auguste (1798-1857) 92, 103
The Condition of the Working Class in England (Engels) 17
Condorcet, Marie Jean Antoine Nicolas Caritat, marquis de (1743-94) 91
Costumbrismo 283-4
Cotta, Georg von (1796-1863) 135
Couailhac, Louis (1810-85) 285, 288 and note 74; 295 note 85; 296-7, **298**, 300, 303, **305**
'The Country Schoolmaster' (Howitt / Meadows) 106-10 (**107**)
'Coup d'œil général sur Paris' (Sand / Français) 148, 204-8 (**204-5**), 216, 220, 223

Cousin, Victor (1792-1867) 93, 98-9, 103
Coyne, Joseph Stirling (1803-68) 240-1
Crary, Jonathan 59, 194 note 67; 271 note 42
Cries: see *City Cries / Cryes*
Cries of London: Exhibiting Several of the Itinerant Traders of Antient and Modern Times (John T. Smith) 158
'Les Cris de Paris' (Joseph Mainzer) 155, 156
'Les Cris de Paris' (Henry Martin) 159-61
Cromwell, Oliver (1599-1658) 153
Cruikshank, George (1792-1878) 3, 37, 39 and note 30; 41, 42, 113, 135
Comic Almanack 37-**38**
Life in London 37, 39, 82-3
Sketches by Boz 5, 30-1, 45 note 47
Cruikshank, Isaac Robert (1789-1856) 32, 37, 39, 42, 82-3, 134
The Cryes of the City of London (Laroon) 155
Curmer, Léon (1801-70) 110, 281-2 and note 61; 285, 288-9 and note 72; 290
Curtis, Gerard 52, 186 note 44
Cuvier, Georges de (1769-1832) 115, 116, 124, 219

Daguerre, Louis-Jacques Mandé (1787-1851) 60, 62, 232
Daguerreotype: see Graphic/reprographic art
The Daily News 60
D'Alembert, Jean le Rond (1717-82) 255 note 16; 256, 314
Damen Conversations Lexikon 125 note 98
Dancing 226, 243-**44**, 246-8, **302**-3
Dante Alighieri (1265-1321) 269
Darwin, Charles (1809-82) 114-15, 254
Daumier, Honoré (1808-79) 32, 41, 43, 289, 295 note 85; 311, 321-**22**, 323
Delord, Taxile (1815-77) 295 note 85
Deriker, G.V. (? - 1847) 304 note 100

Desenne, Alexandre (illustrator of Jouy) 33 note 22
Desloges, Louis-Camille-Auguste (late C18-c.1870) 296
Destutt de Tracy, Antoine-Louis-Claude, comte (1754-1836) 91 note 15
Detmold, Johann Hermann (1807-56) 311 note 6
Deutsche Pandora 274-5
Deutsche Revue 116, 261 and note 26
Deutschland und die Deutschen (Beurmann) 79, 275-6, 285, 306
Devil (of observation) / Satan (see also Religion; Sketches: Moralist heritage) 7, 101, 128, 129-40 (**136**, **137**), 160-1, 167, 170, 175, 177, 186-7, 200-1, 202-3, 205-9, 216, 220, 223-**24**, 266
The Devil upon Crutches in England 131
The Devil upon Two Sticks (Foote) 131, 152
The Devil upon Two Sticks in England (Combe) 131
Le Diable à Paris 13, 19, 65-75 (**68, 72, 74**), 135-6, 148, 201-2, **203**, 204-10, 213, 216-25 (**217, 219, 222, 224**), 224 note 27, 225 note 29; 238, 239, 323-5 (**323-4**)
Gavarni's frontispiece 6-**7**, 21, 128, 136-7, 170, 212-13, 216-**17**, 223, 229-30, 232
Prologue 216, 220-1, 260
Conclusion 223-**24**
panoramic paradigm; 'un beau désordre' 220-1, 225, 260, 278-9, 306
Le Diable boiteux (Le Sage; see also Asmodée / Asmodeus) 21, 129-36, 145-6, 170, **172**, 179, 184
English translation 135
Le Diable boiteux (early department store) 132
Le Diable boiteux. Feuilleton littéraire 132
El Diablo cojuelo (Vélez de Guevara) 130

Dickens, Charles [Boz] (1812-70)   17, 19, 21, 105, 124, 181
   'The First of May'   198, 200
   Household Words   261
   Nicholas Nickleby   31 note 18; 43 and note 43
   'Our Next-Door Neighbour'   188
   Pickwick Papers   28, 29-31, 124
   Pictures from Italy   60-4, 193
   'A Rapid Diorama'   60-4
   'Shops and their Tenants'   187, 188-93, 206, 209
   Sketches by Boz   3, 4-5, 15, 30, 31 and note 18; 33, 45 note 47;   187, 188-93, 198, 200, 206
      German translation   45 note 47
   Sketches of Young Couples   124
   Sketches of Young Gentlemen   124
   'Street Sketches'   187
   'Travelling Sketches Written on the Road'   60-4
Diderot, Denis (1713-84)   161, 255 note 16; 256, 314
Diogenes of Sinope (?-323 B.C.)   134
Diorama: see Media of visual entertainment
Diorama anglais, ou Promenades pittoresques à Londres   62
D'Israeli, Isaac (1766-1848)   265 and note 35
Dronke, Ernst (1822-91)   17, 177, 194-201 and note 71; 208, 209, 237
Düsseldorfer Monatshefte   43-5 (**44**)

Egan, Pierce (1772-1849)   37, 39, 62, 82-3, 132, 174, 176
Eichler, Ludwig (1815-70)   46
Émy, Henry (productive betw. 1840 and 1852)   140, 288, 296, **298**, 303, **305**
Encyclopaedism   150, 256, 314-15
   (man of) letters   150-1, 180, 183, 255-6, 260-8 and notes 35, 36;   276, 295-6, 305-6, 314-15

Encyclopédie, ou Dictionnaire raisonné des sciences, des arts et métiers   173, 183, 255 note 16;   256, 314
Encyclopédie méthodique   173-4
Engels, Friedrich (1820-95)   16-17 and note 41;   195 note 71;   201 note 87
England and the English (Bulwer)   5, 18, 23, 24-8, 30, 43, 105-5, 151 and note 55;   178, 215, 255 note 15;   260-8 and note 27;   285, 293, 306
   Influence in Germany   79, 80, 261 and note 27;   275-6, 325
England und die Engländer in Bildern aus dem Volke   274
Enzyklopädisches Wörterbuch der Wissenschaften, Künste und Gewerbe (Pierer's)   268 note 39
'L'Épicier' (Balzac)   94-103 (**95**), 108, 128, **278**, 295
Los Españoles pintados por sí mismos   277 and note 53;   283-4
St Étienne du Mont (Daguerre's diorama)   60
Étrennes mignonnes   146 and note 41
Europa (journal ed. by Lewald)   79
Everitt, Graham   113
Evolution (see also Zoology)   114-15, 253-4
The Examiner   104 note 46

Faraday, Michael (1791-1867)   255
Fashion (see also Modernity: abbreviation; Semiology)   25-6, 46, 65-6, 87, 132, 143, 174, 180, 183, 188-9, 197, 236, 243, 255, 290, 292-3, 317, 323-5 (**324**)
   cigar   55, 182, 191-2 and note 62;   240-1, 306
   dandyism   6, **7**, 83, 128, 183-7, 192, 216
   monocle   **7**, 136, 212, **222**-3
   top hat   52-**53**, 55, 243-**44**, **299**, 303-4, **322**-3, **323**-4
Faust (Goethe)   185
Faust legend   140, 184

Le Feuilleton des journaux politiques 92, 93 note 22
Le Feuilleton littéraire 132 note 6
Fielding, Henry (1707-54) 148 note 48
Le Figaro 39, 47-8
Figaro in London 32, 37, 39, 47, 134
Figaro (Berlin / Leipzig): see *Berliner Figaro*
Fisiología (Spanish genre) 303
Fisiologiya (Russian genre) 303
Flâneur 3, 6-11, 14-17, 150, 175-7, 193-4, 214, 321
Flint, Kate 1 and note 1; 59-60, 60-1, 184
Foote, Samuel (1721-77) 131, 152
Forster, John (1812-76) 31 note 18
Fourier, Charles (1772-1837) 62 and note 22; 89 and note 8
Fox, Celina 32, 37 note 25; 48
Français, Louis (1814-97) **204-5**
Les Français peints par eux-mêmes 5, 13, 14, 16, 19, 33, 42, 45, 54, 94-**95**, 103, 105, 110, 134, 135, 138-40 (**138-39**), 140, **141**, 154, 155, 156, 210, 220, 222, 223, 226, 285 note 71; 289, 292, 300, 303, 323
   encyclopaedic paradigm 276-87 (**278, 280, 286-7**), 295
   Heads of the People as a model 276-81 and note 50
   Janin's Introduction 85, 140-4, 152, 161-2, 168-9 and note 93; 260, 268, 277, 281, 306, 314-15
   overlap with *Physiologies* 288 and note 72
   parodies 254-5, 290, 295
   Le Prisme 281-2
   Province volumes 283-7 (**286-7**)
   tables 282-3
   translation into English 276 note 51
Frankfurter Bilder (Beurmann) 75-9, 237
Frémy, Arnould (1809-?) 285, 288
Freud, Sigmund (1856-1939) 271 note 42

Gall, Franz Joseph (1758-1828) 13
Garrick, David (1717-79) 152
Gavarni [Sulpice Hippolyte Guillaume Chevalier] (1804-66) 43, 154 note 65; 239 notes 68, 69; 289, 295 note 85; 312
Cris de Paris 154
Le Diable à Paris 221-**22**, 223, 239, 279
   Frontispiece 6-**7**, 21, 128, 136-7, 170, 212-13, 216-**17**, 223, 229-30, 232
Les Français peints par eux-mêmes 94-**95**, 101-2, **278**, 303
   Frontispiece in vol. 2 140-**41**
Gavarni in London 5, 156, **157**, 238-49 (**242, 244, 245**), 305, 312-**13**
'Les Gens de Paris' 221-**22**, 239, 279, 306
The Natural History of the Flirt 257
'Les Parisiens de Paris' 222-3
Physiologie de la Lorette 52-**53**, **56**-7, 111-14 (**112**), 303
Gavarni in London 5, 31, 151, 156, 215, 238-49 (**242, 244, 245**), 306, 312-14 (**313**)
Gay, John (1685-1732) 161
Gay, Sophie (1776-1852) 92 note 16; 314-15
Gender (see also Prostitution) 48-9, 51-2, 52-7, 89, 111-14, 123-8, 143, 156-8, 185-6, 192-3, 195, 204-9, 243-4 (**244**), 247, 259, 303, 314-17 (**316**), 318-19
Geoffroy de Saint-Hilaire, Etienne (1772-1844) 115
Geography / topography 216-20 (**217, 219**), 225, 229-37, 275
Geology 124-5, 233-6
George IV, king of Great Britain (1762-1830) 132
Géricault, Théodore (1791-1824) 253
Gilbert, Sir John (1817-97) **257**

Gillray, James (1757-1815) 113
Glaßbrenner [pseud. Brennglas], Adolf (1810-76) 16, 46, 48-52 (**50**), 118, 158-**59**, 164 note 89; 169, 195-**96**, 198, 201 note 87; 312
Goethe, Johann Wolfgang (1749-1832) 115, 121, 185
Goldsmith, Oliver (1728[?]-94) 109, 148 note 48
Goncourt, Edmond (1822-96) and Jules (1830-70) 113-14, 238-9
Göttsche, Dirk 18 note 43
Grand Dictionnaire Universel du XIXe siècle (Larousse's) 88
La Grande ville 97 note 29; 315-**16**, 321-23 (**322**)
Grandville, J.J. [Jean Ignace Isidore Gérard] (1803-47) 32, 41, 43, 289, 295 note 85
Grant, James (1802-79) 318
Graphic / reprographic art (see also Print media)
 daguerreotype 87, 114, 166-**67**, 232, 301, 320
 lithography 41, 69 note 25; 176, 239
 photogravure 85
 photography 322
 steel/copper plate / etching 37, 46, 226, 269, 275, 277
 woodcut 153, 158
 wood engraving 33-9, 42, 43-6 (**44**), 110, 111, 238-9, 258, 269, 277, 290, 320
Greuze, Jean-Baptiste (1725-1805) 147, 161
Gumbrecht, Hans-Ulrich 283
Gusman, Adolphe (1811-1905) **286**
Gutzkow, Karl (1811-78) 6, 19, 46-7, 79, 174-5 and note 10; 310
 Briefe eines Narren an eine Närrin 6
 Deutsche Revue (editorship) 116, 261
 'Naturgeschichte der deutschen Kameele' 117-23, 128
 'Papilloten' 48-52 (**50**)

Richard Savage 151 note 55
'Die Singekränzchen' 135
Unterhaltungen am häuslichen Herd (editorship) 261
Wally, die Zweiflerin 185-6
Die Zeitgenossen 29-30, 151 and note 55; 174, 260-8 and note 27; 283, 293, 306-7, 325-6
Zur Philosophie der Geschichte 118
Guys, Constantin (1805-92) 8, 321
Gwyn(ne), Nell (1651[?]-87) 156-7
Le Gymnase 162 note 85

Hall, G. Stanley (1844-1924) 271 note 42
Hamlet (Shakespeare) 169 note 97
Hammerich (publisher) 275
Haussmann, Georges-Eugène, Baron (1809-91) 66, 193, 194 note 67
Haydon, Benjamin Robert (1786-1846) 165 note 91
Heads from Nicholas Nickleby (Meadows) 43 and note 43
Heads of the People, or Portraits of the English 16, 19, 31 and note 18; 42-3 and note 42; 46, 85-8 (**86**), 105-6, **107**, 132, 175, 198-**99**, 210, 226, 238, 239, 285, 292, 310
 Jerrold's Prefaces 54, 85, 87, 89, 268, 271, **272-3**, 307
 translation into French 42, 54, 110, 168 note 93; 276 and notes 50, 51; 289
 translation into German 42-3, 274
 European impact 268-74 (**269-70**, **272-3**)
Hegel, G.W.F. (1770-1831) 93, 118 and note 86
Heine, Heinrich (1797-1856) 16-17, 18, 96 note 27
Henning, Archibald S. (1803-64) **165**, **257**, **302**, 303, **305**
Hess, Günter 64

Hetzel, Pierre-Jules [pseud. P.-J. Stahl] 208-9, 216, 220-1, 223-**24**, 254 note 10; 289
Hick, Ulrike 169-70
Hoare, Quintin 11-12
Hoffmann, E.T.A. (1776-1822) 16-17 and notes 38, 42
Hogarth, William (1697-1764) 110, 152, 155, 161, 243
Homer (end of 8th cent. B.C.) 142
Hone, William (1780-1842) 37, 39, 41
Hopf, Albert (Berlin democrat) 137
Hosemann, Theodor (1807-75) 46, 158, **159**, 312
Household Words 261
Howitt, William (1792-1879) 106-10 (**107**), 273
Huart, Louis (1813-65) 289, 292-4, 295 note 85; 311 note 7
Hughes, Linda K. 28-9
Hugo, Victor (1802-85) 96, 116
Hunt, Thornton Leigh (1810-73) 269-70

The Illuminated Magazine 238
The Illustrated London News 45 note 47; 238, 239 and note 69
L'Illustration (Paris) 69-**70**, 239
Illustrirte Zeitung (Leipzig) 45 note 47
Industrialisation 134, 198, 234, 236, 241-2, 248, 283-5, 309-10, 313-14

Janin, Jules (1804-74) 48; 135, 140, 174, 303
'Asmodée' 48, 140, 132-3
Introduction to *Les Français peints par eux-mêmes* 85, 140-4, 152, 161-2, 168-9 and notes 93, 94; 260, 268, 277, 281, 306, 314-15
Jean Paul [Jean Paul Friedrich Richter] (1763-1825) 119
Jerrold, Douglas (1803-57) 42, 43 and note 43; 269, 274, 310, 311 note 6
Prefaces to *Heads of the People* 54, 85, 87, 89, 268, 271-3 (**272-3**), 274, 307, 310

Johannot, Tony (1803-52) 135, 170, **172**
Johnson, Samuel (1709-84) 258
Journal des dames 144 note 33
Journal des sciences morales et politiques 115
Journalism (see also Print media; Types: Journalist)
 early forms of 134, 148-53
 journalistic revolution / print revolution 2, 5-6, 23,-4, 36-7, 42, 52, 57, 134, 175
 creation of new metropolitan maps / sign systems 5-6, **7**, 77-8, 326
 (see also Geography)
 cross-cultural networks 35, 39-40, 42-3, 47-8, 54-7
 feuilleton 2, 5, 8, 20, 48, 102, 140, 301, 326
 illustrated periodicals 32-3, 37-47, 238-9
 Physiologies offering critical key to 296-304, 326
 reviews 211, 255-6 and note 15; 260-8, 271 and note 41
Jouy, Victor Joseph Etienne de (1764-1846) 33-**34** and note 22; 37, 133 and note 13
July Monarchy 9, 10, 14, 39, 138, 163, 22 note 29 ; 301, 320-1
July Revolution: see Revolution

Kafka, Franz (1883-1924) 120
Kaleidoscope: see Media of visual entertainment
Kauffmann, Kai 10 note 18; 145, 225-6, 230-2
Klodt [fon Iurgensburg], Konstantin Karlovich, baron (1807-79) 304 note 100
Knight, Charles (1791-1873) 35, 37 note 25; 256 note 20; 258, 281 and note 61
Kock, Paul de (1794-1871) 97 note 29; 321-2
Konversationslexikon (Brockhaus's) 256 and note 20

La Bruyère, Jean de (1645-96) 129, 140-3 and notes 24, 26; 152, 162 note 83; 261 note 27
Ladvocat, L. (1790-1854) 134
Lamarck, Jean Baptiste de Monet de (1744-1829) 115
Landells, Ebenezer (1808-60) 42
Langer, Carl Edmund (1819-85) 226
Langer, C.F. (contributor to *Wien und die Wiener*) 132-3
Lardner, Dionysius (1793-1859) 124
La Rochefoucauld, François, duc de (1613-80) 129
Laroon (the elder), Marcellus (1648/9-1702) 155, 156, 243, 313
Latouche, Henri de (1785-1851) 48
Lavallée, Théophile (1804-67) 217-20, 225, 230
Lavater, Johann Caspar (1741-1801) 13, 92 note 15; 106, 132-3, 173-4
Le Lavater des tempéramens et des constitutions (Morel de Rubempré) 91-2 note 15
Lavieille, Adrien Jacques Eugène (1818-62) **95**, **141**, **203**, **278**
Lavigne (publisher) 290, 296
Lebensbilder 225-6, 228, 232, 284 note 67
Leblanc, Félix Ferdinand Clément (1822-after 1867) **222**
Leech, John (1817-64) 116
Legoyt, Alfred (1815-69) 224-5
Leigh, Percival [pseud. Paul Prendergast] (1813-89) 116, 174 note 4
Lemaître, Frédérick (1800-76) 311 note 7
Le Men, Ségolène 53-4, 140, 154, 278-9
Lemon, Mark (1809-70) 42
Lenz, Ludwig (1813-96) 46
Le Sage, Alain René (1668-1747) 21, 129-36, 140, 146, 149, 170, 172, 179, 183
Lewald, August (1792-1871) 79-82, 83, 237

Lhéritier, Andrée 289
'Lindenrolle' (scroll panorama of Unter den Linden) 69 note 25
Linné, Carl von (1707-78) 124, 125
The Literary Gazette 255-6
Lithography: see Graphic art
Le Livre des Cent-et-un: see *Paris, ou Le Livre des Cent-et-un*
London: see Cities
Louis Philippe, king of France (1773-1850) 138, 182
Lover, Samuel (1797-1868) 273
Ludwig I, king of Bavaria (1786-1868) 80
Lully, Jean-Baptiste (1633-87) 67
Lund, Michael 28-9

Le Magasin Pittoresque 35, 256 note 20
Magic lantern: see Media of visual entertainment
Mahlknecht, Carl (1810-93) 226, **235**
Maidment, Brian 24 note 4; 166-7 note 92
Mainzer, Joseph (1801-51) 155 and note 69; 156
The Man in the Moon 238
Man of letters: see Encyclopaedism
Manet, Édouard (1832-83) 194 note 67
March of Intellect (see also Journalism; Print media) 4, 24-8, 37, 134, 160, 327
Marckl, Louis (1807-?) **291**
Martin, Henry (contributor to *Nouveau tableau de Paris*) 159-61
Marx, Karl (1818-83) 17 and note 41; 78, 102, 195 note 71; 201 note 87; 309 and note 1
Materialism (see also Money) 97, 99-103, 294, 309-10
Maunder, Samuel (1785-1849) 258
Maurisset, Théodore (first ment. 1834, last ment. 1859) **291**
Mayhew, Augustus (1826-75) **38**, 311 note 6
Mayhew, Henry (1812-87) 32, **38**, 42, 47, 311 note 6

Comic Almanack 38
London Labour and the London Poor 4, 318-20 and note 23
Meacham, Standish 104 notes 44, 46; 105 note 51
Meadows, Kenny (1790-1884) 43 and note 43; 54, 85-8 (**86**), 106-10 (**107**), 134, 135, 165, **166**, 168 note 93; 198-**99**, 268, **269-70**, **272-3**, 273, 274, 279
The Mechanism of the Heavens (Somerville) 124
Media of visual entertainment (see also Science and technology institutions; Sketches: visual paradigms) 23, 59-84
    camera obscura 69 note 25
    diorama 11-12, 59, 60, 62, 80, 232, 251
    kaleidoscope 236
    magic lantern 59, 152, 169-**171**, 221, 246, 248, 270-1, 281, 307
    microscope 83, 245
    moving panorama 62, 67-9 (**70**)
    panorama 11-12, 78, 79-80, 211, 213-15, 251, 275-6
    peepshow 169
    phantasmagoria 59, 170
Medicine (see also Physiology) 292-5
Mercier, Louis Sébastien (1740-1814) 144-8 and note 33; 152, 161, 216
Meteorology 233-4
Metternich, Klemens Prince (1773-1859) 225
The Microcosm of London (Combe / Rowlandson) 82, 131
Microscope: see Media of visual entertainment
Middle class: see Class
Mill, James (1773-1836) 265
Mill, John Stuart (1806-73) 104, note 46; 105
La Mode 99 note 35
Modernity
    abbreviation (see also Telegraph; Transport) 323-6

jargon 255, 326
significance of the moment 317, 320-3
punning / word play 37-**38**, **44**-5, 47, 48, 51, 78 and note 35; 159, 201, note 87; 290-2, **326**
cities as textbooks of 231-2
flâneur as an icon of 6-11, 320-1
and print media 229-30
sketches as a grammar of 22, 309-27
Moers, Ellen 178
Molière [Jean-Baptiste Poquelin] (1622-73) 142-3, 152
Money / currency 150, 175, 231
exchange value 101-2, 309-10
Monnier, Henry (1799-1877) 13, 32, 34, 39-40 and notes 29, 30; 41, 110 and note 65; 311-12
Title vignette for *Paris, ou Le Livre des Cent-et-un* 134, 148 and note 48; 167-**68**, 175
Montagu, Lady Mary Wortley (1689-1762) 215, 266
Montaigne, Michel de (1538-92) 129
The Monthly Magazine 187
Moralische Wochenschriften 156
Moreau de la Sarthe, Jacques Louis François (1771-1826) 105-6, 173-4
Morel de Rubempré, M.J. (medic) 92 note 15
Morgenblatt für gebildete Stände 135
The Morning Chronicle 187, 318 and note 23
Moving panorama: see Media of visual entertainment
Le Musée pour rire 289
Muséum parisien 254-5, 256, 289
Music 125-7 (**126**), 152-3, 155 and note 69; 237, 246, 247, 251, **302-3**
Music hall 251, 271 and note 42; 307

Napoleon I, emperor of France (1769-1821) 253
Nashi, spisannye s naturi russkimi 277 and note 52; 303 and note 100

Natural Histories 1, 104, 115, 124, 239 and note 69; 302, 304
The Natural History of the Ballet Girl (Albert Smith) **302**-3, **305**
The Natural History of the Flirt (Albert Smith) 257-9 (**257-8**)
The Natural History of the Gent (Albert Smith) 302 note 97
'Naturgeschichte der deutschen Kameele' (Gutzkow) 117-23, 128
Nelson, Horatio, Viscount (1758-1805) 169 note 97
Nettel'gorst, Otto Petrovich, baron (mentioned 1842) 304 note 100
Neue Rheinische Zeitung 195 note 71
Newman, John Henry (1801-90) 123
The New Monthly Magazine 134, 151, 178-85, 260-1, 267
Newton, Sir Isaac (1642-1727) 263
Nicholas Nickleby (Dickens) 31 note 18; 43 and note 43
Nouveau Tableau de Paris 159-61, 225 note 29; 238
The Novelist's Library 135

Observation (see also Social Explorers; Travel writing) 46-7, 61-2, 111-13, 128, 134, 136, 150, 318
 basis of empirical science 93, 162, 267
 dandy / swell 21, 132, 178, 183-7, 191-2
 democratisation of 175-7, 193, 214
 flâneur 3, 6-11, 14-17, 150, 175-7, 193-4, 214, 321
 limitations of physiognomic reading 21, 194-210
 middle-class self-observation 12-13, 215-6, 239-49, 276, 310-11, 314
 mobility / fluctuating position of observer 62-4, 65-75, 76-7, 79, 81-4, 318
 observers as actors 162, 166, 307, 311
 paradigm of anatomy / autopsy 13, 15, 130, 132, 173-7, 180-1, 184-7, 190, 200, 201-4 (**203**), 209-10, 266, 319
 paradigm of physiognomy 6, 8, 13-14, 17-18, 21, 66-7, 71-5, 85-8, 132-3, 145-6, 175-7, 188-90, 194-201, 206, 209-10, 268, 277, 309-10, 312
 sketch enacting observation 25-6, 63, 73
 speculative strolling 4, 10, 21, 187, 188-93, 319, 321
Oesterle, Günter 20, 91 note 15; 113, 122, 301
Oesterle, Ingrid 218, 232-3
Oettermann, Stephan 214
Oettinger, Eduard Maria (1808-72) 43, 47 and note 53; **137**-8
Ogden, John (contributor to *Heads of the People*) **199**
Oken, Lorenz [Lorenz Ockenfuß] (1779-1851) 116, 117-8, 122
Oppermann, Heinrich Albert (1812-70) 174-5, 264
Otechestvennye zapiski 304 note 100
Ourliac, Édouard (1812-48) 284

Panorama: see Media of visual entertainment
Panorama der Straße Unter den Linden vom Jahre 1820 69 note 25
Parent-Duchâtelet, Alexandre Jean Baptiste (1790-1836) 112
Paris: see Cities
Paris, ou Le Livre des Cent-et-un 9, 11, 21, 32, 34, 46-7, 48, 132-5, 144, 160-1, 193, 202, 212, 213-14, 221, 225 note 29; 238, 260, 261
 'Au Public' 133-4, 143-4, 148
 German translation 134-5
 title vignette 134, 148 and note 48; 167-**68**
Pascal, P. (contributor to *Le Diable à Paris*) 323-5
Patten, Robert L. 29, 39 note 31; 164
Pauquet, Hippolyte (1797-last ment. c.1869) **138**-9, 154, **286-7**

Peepshow: see Media of visual entertainment
Pelham or the Adventures of a Gentleman (Bulwer) 174, 178
The Penny Cyclopædia 33, 35 and note 23; **36**, 37, 114, 124, 214, **258**, 281 and note 61; 325-6
German equivalent 256 note 20
The Penny Magazine 25, 33, 35, 37 note 25
European equivalents 256 note 20
The People's Journal 108
Périer, Casimir (1777-1832) 183
Pfennig-Encyclopädie 256 note 20
Das Pfennig-Magazin 35, 256 note 20
Phantasmagoria: see Media of visual entertainment
Philipon, Charles (1802-62) 32, 39, 43, 138, 164, 289, 295 note 85; 311
'Phiz': see Browne, Hablôt Knight
Phönix. Frühlings-Zeitung für Deutschland 75, 81, 117, 119-23
Photography: see Graphic/reprographic art
Phrenology: see Physiology
Physiognomy: see Observation; Physiology
Physiology
    connection with anatomy / medicine 91-4 and note 15; 105, 114-16, 118, 173-5, 247-8
    connection with phrenology 85-7 (**86**)
    connection with physiognomy 13, 71-5, 85-8, 105-**07**, 125, 277
    connection with sociology 89-94, 104-5
    connection with zoology 110-28
    epistemological significance in sketch production 73-5, 211, 321, 325
    impact of the 'French school' 91-4, 105, 115-16, 118-19
    key to understanding interaction / unseen connections 10, 88, 90-1, 93-4, 97-8, 104-5, 108, 121-2, 146-7, 161-3, 184, 201, 207, 210, 213, 292-5, 296
    paradigm of life science for sketches 1, 15, 20, 75, 83-4, 114-19, 163, 174-5
Physiologie du bien et du mal, de la vie et de la mort, du passé, du présent, de l'avenir (Azaïs) 91
Physiologie du calembourg 290
Physiologie de l'employé (Balzac / Trimolet) 97 note 29
Physiologie du gamin de Paris **291**
Physiologie du goût (Brillat-Savarin) 92 and note 16
Physiologie de l'homme de loi **291**, 295
Physiologie du Jardin des Plantes 288
Physiologie de la Lorette (Alhoy / Gavarni) 52-**53**, **56**-7, 111-14 (**112**), 303
Physiologie du mariage (Balzac) 92, 93-4
Physiologie du médecin (Huart) 292-5
Physiologie du parapluie 290
Physiologie des passions, ou nouvelle doctrine des sentiments moraux (Alibert) 91 note 15
Physiologie de la presse 297-301 (**299**)
Physiologie des Physiologies 295-6
Physiologie du rentier de Paris et de province (Balzac and Frémy) 285, 288
Physiologie du ridicule (Gay) 92 note 16; 314-15
Physiologie du théâtre (Auger) 162 note 85
Physiologie du théâtre (Couailhac) 288 and note 74; 296-7, **298**, 303, **305**
Physiologie du théâtre, à Paris et en province (Couailhac) 285
Physiologie du vin de Champagne 290
Physiologies (see also *Natural History[ies]*; *Naturgeschichte*; *Fisiología*; *Fisiologiya*) 1, 4, 6, 10-11 and note 18; 14-15, 19, 22, 32-3, 41, 43, 48, 88, 89, 103, 104, 111-14, 124, 148, 195, 220,

222, 259-60, 285 and note 71; 311 and note 7; 314, 315
classification / specialisation 220, 259-60, 292-5, 305
earliest journalistic example 94
encyclopaedic enterprise / meta-encyclopaedia 22, 260, 285, 288-304 and notes 72, 85 (**291, 298, 299, 302**), 305-6
overlap with *Les Français* 288 and note 72
parodistic and self-referential genre 14, 259, 289-90, 295-304, 314, 326
re-use of illustrations 296, 303-**04**
role-play / swindling 310-11 and notes 6, 7
self-portrait of journalism 296-304, 326
uniform presentation 289-92 (**291**), 295
'Physiology of the London Medical Student' (Albert Smith) 55
The Pictorial Times 238, 239
Pinchbeck, Christopher (1709-83) 82 note 45
Plautus, Titus Maccius (before 251-c.184 B.C.) 142
Poe, Edgar Allan (1809-49) 8, 11 note 19; 14 and note 32; 16
Le Populaire 160
Porret, Henri Désiré (1800-?) **138-9**
Poverty / pauperism (see also Class; Types) **44**-5, 134, 147-8, 153, 160-1, 177, 179, 180, 187, 194, 197-201, 206-9, 240-1, 309, 310, 313-14, 318-20, 327
Pratt, Mary Louise 215
Preiss, Nathalie 14, 90, 140 note 24; 162 note 85; 285 note 71; 290-2, 300, 311
Print media (see also Censorship; Graphic / reprographic art; Journalism; March of Intellect; Media of visual entertainment; Sketches) 2, 3, 22, 23, 39-41, 52

cross-national developments 16, 20, 30, 32-48, 54-8, 110, 135-7, 274-9
illustration and reproduction technology 2, 5, 20, 33-58, 110, 136, 153-4, 238-9, 277-81
and modernity 229-30, 323
penny press / media for the working class 24-8, 32-3, 36-7, 42, 134
serials / serialisation 10-11, 19, 21, 28-33, 87-8, 109-10, 117-18, 124, 134, 140, 154, 161-2, 163, 211-15, 216, 223, 226, 232, 256, 261, 262-3, 265, 268-71, 275-6, 277 notes 52, 53; 281-3, 285, 290, 295
vogue of *Physiologies* 288-92 (**291**), 303
vogue of (illustrated) serials 274-7, 289
Le Prisme (supplement to *Les Français*) 281-2
Le Producteur 92 note 17
Promies, Ute 310
Prostitution/'fallen women' (see also Gender) 11 note 20; 57, 112, 192-3, 195-6, 198, 318-19
Provinces: see Rural / provincial populations
Pückler-Muskau, Prince Hermann von (1785-1871) 83, 182-3
Punch, or the London Charivari 32, 37, 39, 42-3, 54-7 (**55**), 104, 116, 132, 134, 137, 164, **165-6**, 174 note 4; 238, 240, 316, **326**
Punning: see Modernity: abbreviation

Quartley, John (active 1835-78) **68**
'Quiz': see Caswall, Edward

Raisson, Horace (1798-1854) 132
Reach, Angus Bethune (1821-56) 312-14 (**313**)
Reform Bill (1832) 6, 134, 178, 180, 181, 271
Régnault (engraver collaborating on *Le Diable à Paris*) **224**

Reibersdorffer, Daniel (contributor to *Wien und die Wiener*) 274
Reid, Thomas (1710-96) 93
Religion (see also Devil) 56-7, 78, 93, 94, 98-100, 112, 115, 119, 121-2, 123, 124-5, 163, 209, 230-1, 245, 263-4, 265 and note 34; 267, 271-3, 294, 327
Rembrandt [Rembrandt Harmensz van Rijn] (1606-69) 152
Revolution (see also Reform Bill)
  July 1830 6, 32, 48, 73, 76, 120, 132-3, 134, 143, 145, 160, 193, 289
  1848 6, 115, 137, 194-5, 209, 239 note 69; 247, 327
Revue des Deux Mondes 155
Rignall, John 8, 14 note 32; 17 note 42
Rivarol, Antoine comte de (1753-1801) 144 note 34
Robert Macaire (play) 311 note 7
Robert Macaire (Daumier's / Philipon's character) 311-12 and note 7
Rothschild family (Frankfurt) 77-8
Rotteck, Carl von (1775-1840) 275
Rowlandson, Thomas (1757-1827) 82, 113, 131
Rural and provincial populations / spectators 108-9, 120-1, 197, 223, 227, 273, 282-7 (**286, 287**)

Sadleir, Michael 131 note 3
Saint-Simon, Claude-Henri, comte de (1760-1825) 89-93, 97-8, 100-3 and note 37; 115, 116, 162 note 85
Saint-Simonianism 97, 99-100 and note 37; 115, 181-2
Sánchez, Juan-José 283
Sand, George [Aurore Dupin, baronne Dudevant] (1804-76) 19, 21, 48, 148, 204-8 (**204-5**), 216, 220, 223
Saphir, Moritz (1795-1858) 47, 48 and note 56; 131
Satan. *Berliner Charivari* **136**-7 (see also *Berliner Charivari* and *Der Teufel in Berlin*)
The Satirist 32

The Saturday Magazine 33, 37 note 25
Scargill, William Pitt (1787-1836) 179
Scènes de la vie privée et publique des animaux 254-5 and note 10; 289
Schelling, Friedrich Wilhelm (1775-1854) 93
Science and technology / cultural institutions
  Adelaide Gallery, London 83, 151, 245-6
  British Museum 158, 243
  Egyptian Hall, London 251-4 (**252**)
  Jardin des Plantes, Paris 73, 115, 218-20 (**219**), 254
  Muséum d'histoire naturelle, Paris 218-**20**, 254
  Museum(sgesellschaft), Frankfurt 117, 119, 123
The Scourge 32
Sedley, Charles (pseud.?) 131 note 3
Semiotics / sign-reading (see also Fashion; Observation: paradigm of physiognomy) 9-10, 22, 36, 48, 52-3, 102, 128, 132-4, 145-6, 163, 168, 170, 175, 176-7, 187, 188-91, 193-5, 201-3, 209-10, 232, 292, 309-10, 312-14, 317-18, 326-7
Serialisation: see Print media
Seymour, Robert (1798-1836) 31, 32, 170-**71**
Sha, Richard 2-3, 4
Shchedrovskii, Ignatii Stepanovich (1815-70) 304 note 100
Shesgreen, Sean 153-4, 155, 319-20
Shevchenko, Taras Grigor'evich (1814-61) 304 note 100
Sieburth, Richard 4, 14, 175-6, 259-60, 296, 315
La Silhouette 39 and note 29; 41, 94, 110 note 65
Simmel, Georg (1858-1918) 10
Sketches
  acting / drama / 'scene' as paradigms 21-5, 61, 71-3 (**72**), 152, 154-6, 158,

162-8, 221-3, 236-7, 248-9, 262, 306-7, 310-14, 318
collaboration 5, 43, 46, 133-4, 143-4, 162, 177, 210, 212-15, 223, 226, 232, 238, 260, 275-6, 281
contents tables **138, 139**, 262-3, 264-5, 266, 279-82 (**280**), 285-7 (**286, 287**), 292-3
cross-cultural processes 3, 54-8, 135, 195, 243-9, 261 note 27; 274-9, 302-3, 325-6
entertainment combined with instruction 5, 12-13, 20, 84, 151, 168-9, 190, 193, 256, 307
exponential growth of production after 1830 132-3, 134, 143, 145, 289
generic characteristics 1-6, 20, 23, 27-8, 31, 36, 48, 52, 94, 113-14, 130, 193, 314
geological orientation 22, 213, 229, 234-7, 249
intermediality 4, 20, 136, 154, **257**-9, 315
meta-medium 4, 20, 23, 28, 64, 83-4, 259, 301, 307
moralist heritage 18, 20-1, 129-72
    Asmodeus 21, 129-40, 164, 167-**68**, 170, **172**, 179-85, 202-3, 208, 214, 216
    City Cries 71, 85, 152-3, 153-61 (**157, 159**), **224**, 237, 277, 312-13, 319
    classification: see below, specialisation
    Commedia dell'arte 163-8
    French moralists 140-8 (**141**), 300
    Tatler / Spectator 129, 149-53
physiological / zoological orientation 1, 13-14, 20, 85-128, 210, 213, 218, 228-9, 234, 249, 292
in relation to clichés / stereotypes 20, 22, 64, 88-9, 96, 102, 110-14, 122, 128, 197

in relation to early sociology 92-102, 211
self-referentiality / self-reflectiveness 3-5, 21-2, 44-5, 49-52, 87, 103, 122-3, 128, 139-40, 169, 183, 216, 232, 289, 295-304, 326
significance of the ephemeral 5, 22, 48-52, 289, 292, 295-304, 327
specialisation / classification 111, 114, 124-5, 143-4, 151, 177, 213, 220, 248, 253-60, 281-3, 292-5, 310-11, 326
text-image relationships 3-5, 20, 23-8, 30-58, 71-5 (**72, 74**), 89, 105, 106-10 (**107**), 128, 145, 210, 232, 268-71, 274, 277, 279, 281, 306, 320
thriving on serialisation 29-32, 134, 145, 177, 212-15
typology 4-5, 9-10, 13, 14, 20-1, 27, 42, 52-7, 85-128, 140, 220, 232, 234, 238, 243, 263-4, 268-73, 274, 277, 279-81 (**280**), 282, 290, 292, 294, 310
visual / cognitive paradigms
    camera obscura 83, 176
    daguerreotype 232, 301
    dictionary 255, 270, 279, 281, 300
    diorama 11-12, 60-4
    encyclopaedia / lexicon 5, 11, 13, 21, 101-2, 131, 134, 151, 211-12, 251-305, 314
    index 274
    kaleidoscope 145, 227-8, 232-3, 236, 247-8, 259, 306
    magic lantern 6-7, 12, 83, 136, 168-71, 212, **224**, 232, 236, 268, 270-1, 281
    microcosm 82 and note 45; 131
    microscope 81-3, 174, 184, 186, 191, 245-6
    mosaic 234-6, 249
    moving panorama 9, 67-71
    museum of natural history 253-6

panorama 11-13, 21, 75-82, 130-1, 185, 211-49, 259-60, 266, 275-6, 279, 305, 314
'peinture multiple' 134, 143, 214, 221, 260
'beau désordre' 220-1, 225, 260
introductory general view / 'coup d'œil général' 145-6, 148, 204-8, 212, 213, 216-**17**, 220, 226, 228-31, 232, 241, 259, 274, 306
peepshow 169
review 3, 12-13, 21, 39, 255-6 and note 15; 260-8, 271 and note 42; 281, 285, 312-20
'passing in review' 168-9, 266, 268, 281, 306, 314-15, 323
tableau 144-8, 160, 161-2, 212-14, 225, 226, 230, 233, 289
telegraph 325-6
Sketches and Travels in London (Thackeray) 316
Sketches by Boz 3, 4-5, 15, 30-1 and note 18; 33, 45 note 47; 165 note 91; 187-93
Sketches by Seymour 170-**71**
Sketches in London (Grant) 318
Sketches of Young Couples (Dickens) 124
Sketches of Young Gentlemen (Dickens) 124
Sketches of Young Ladies ('Quiz' / 'Phiz') 123-8 (**126**)
Sketches or Essays on Various Subjects (Temple) 2
Skizzen aus dem sozialen und politischen Leben der Briten (Weerth) 309
Skizzen aus den Hanse-Städten (Beurmann) 79, 117, 237
Smith, Albert (1816-60) 115-16, 124, 256, 271, 297, 302
'Acrobats' 241-**42**
Ascent of Mont Blanc 251-4 (**252**)
'The Casino' 243-9 (**244**, **245**)
Comic Almanack 38

Gavarni in London 151, 186, 238-49 and note 69 (**242**, **244**, **245**), 255
The Natural History of the Ballet Girl 302-3, **305**
The Natural History of the Flirt 257-9 (**257-8**)
The Natural History of the Gent 302 note 97
'Physiology of the London Medical Student' (*Punch*) 54-5
Smith, John T. (keeper of prints and drawings at the British Museum) 158
Smith, John Orrin (1799-1843) 43, 54, **86**, **107**, 110, **199**, 239, **269-70**, **272-3**, 279-80
Smoking: see Fashion: cigar
Social Explorers 4, 318-20, 327
Socialism / radicalism (see also Saint-Simonianism) 92, 116, 134, 160-1, 180, 182-3, 194-5, 200-1, 204, 209, 220
Society for the Diffusion of Useful Knowledge 124, 257-8
Sociology (see also Sketches in relation to sociology)
connection with life science / physiology / zoology 13, 20, 89-94, 173-5, 257-9 (**257**, **258**), 292
connection with review publishing 261-8
connection with socialism 92
in relation to Bentham's utilitarianism 104-5
of knowledge / science of sciences 19, 91 and note 15; 260-8
of medicine 292-5
sketches as a distinct form of early s. 19, 20-1, 88-9, 103-4, 211, 267-8
Somerville, Mary (1780-1872) 124
The Spectator 149-52 and note 55; 156
Sporting activities 321-3 (**322**)
Staats-Lexikon oder Encyclopädie der Staatswissenschaften 275
Stahl, P.-J.: see Hetzel, Pierre-Jules

Statistics 224-5, 228
Steele, Richard (1672-1729; see also Bickerstaff) 129, 151-3 and note 55; 155
Stelzhamer, Franz (1802-68) 226, 227, 234, 236
Sterne, Laurence (1713-68) 148 note 48
Stierle, Karlheinz 15, 91, 128, 133 note 13; 145, 161, 209
Stifter, Adalbert (1805-68) 19, 226-34, 236-7, 274
Superstition 37, 169-70
Surbled, H., Madame (engraver) **112**

Tableau de Paris (Mercier) 144-8 and note 33; 152, 161, 216
Tableaux parisiens (Baudelaire) 145
Talleyrand, Charles Maurice de, prince of Benevento (1754-1838) 264, 266, 267
Tamisier, Charles Ange François (1813-?) **74**
The Tatler 129, 151 and note 55; 156
Telegraph (see also Transport) 6, 134, 325-6
Telford, Thomas (1757-1834) 245
Terence [Publius Terentius Afer] (c. 195-59 B.C.) 142
Thackeray, William Makepeace (1811-63) 42, 316
 Comic Almanack **38**
 Paris Sketch Book 3
 Sketches and Travels in London 316-20
 'The Snobs of England, by One of Themselves' 316
 Vanity Fair 163
 'Waiting at the Station' 316-19
Theatre 71-3 (**72**), 151, 154-6, 162-7 and note 85; 221, 224, 226, 236-7, 241, 271 and note 42; 288, 296-7, **298**, **302-4**
Theophrastus (372-287 B.C.) 140, 142
Thiers, Adolphe (1797-1877) 48

Thomas, Joseph (publisher and translator) 135, **172**
Thompson, Charles (1789-1843) 33-**34** and note 22; 134, **168**
Thompson, E.P. 318
Thompson, John (1785-1855) 33
Timm, Vasilii Fedorovich (1820-95) 304 note 100
Tocqueville, Charles Alexis Henri Clérel de (1805-59) 104 and note 44
Toddle, Timothy (itinerant showman) 169
Tomlins, F.G. (contributor to *Heads of the People*) 175
Transport (see also Observation: mobility of observer)
 cab 158, 191
 express coach 76-7, 119
 horseback 66
 mail coach 77, 119, 285-**86**
 omnibus 15, 66, 69-**70**, 182, 301
 railway 76, 109, 134, 231, 285, **287**, 316-17
 travel coach 63-4 and note 14
Travel writing 60-4, 81, 83, 211, 238
 colonising gaze 2-3, 215
 inversion of traveller's view in self-inspection 18, 215, 216, 239-48, 266, 319
Traviès, Charles-Joseph (1804-59) 289
Treasury of Knowledge (Maunder's) 258
Trimolet, Joseph Louis (1812-43) **291**
Tyndall, John (1820-93) 184 note 38
Types (see also Sketches: typology)
 acrobats 241-**42**
 ballet girl **302**-3
 beggar 234, 241, 312-14 (**313**)
 broker / 'Makler' 309-10
 capitalist / man of money 143, 175, 234, 263
 chamber maid / 'Stubenmädchen' 156, 237
 common informer **270**
 conductor **269**
 cook / 'Berliner Köchin' 195-7 (**196**)

crossing-sweeper 241
dandy / swell 128, 183-7, 191-2, 216, **222**-3
doctor / medical student 55, 292-5
draper's assistant / 'Ladendiener des Modehändlers' 274
Dutch couple 306-7
'Eckensteher' 158-**59**, 195, 312
family governess **270**
factory child 268, 310
flâneur 3, 6-11, 14-17, 150, 175-7, 193, 194, 214, 321
fool / harlequin / Punch 63, 164-8 (**165, 166, 167, 168**), 200-1, 241, 312
grisette 143, 195, 302-3
grocer / 'épicier' 94-103 (**95**), **278**, 295, 296
journalist 83, 150, 297-301 (**298, 299**), 315-**16**
lawyer / 'deutscher Advokat' / 'homme de loi 274, **291**, 295
Lorette 52-3, **56**-7, 111-13 (**112**), 128, 259, 301, 303
mechanic 24-8
'natural historian young lady' 127
orange-girl 156-8 (**157**), 243
peasant (English and Irish) 273
philistine / 'Kameel' 96, 102, 117, 119-23, 195
potato vendor 239-41
provincial man 197, **222**-3
rag-and-bone collector / 'chiffonnier' / 'Knochensammler' 234-**35**, 312
rose-girl 158-**59**
street urchin / 'gamin' 143, 195, 198
sweep 166-**67**, 198-201 (**199**), 312
valet 24-8
young lady who sings 125-7 (**126**)

Unterhaltungen am häuslichen Herd 261

Vadillo, Ana Perejo 64

Vélez de Guevara, Luis (1579-1644) 130
Verdeil, Pierre (1812-after 1874) **74, 287, 322**
Vernet, Carle (1758-1835) 147
Vernet, Horace (1789-1863) 96
Vicq-d'-Azur, Félix (1748-94) 91, 173
Vizetelly, Henry (1820-94) **157**, 238-9, **242, 244, 313**
Vizetelly & Co., London 239
Le Voleur 94
Voltaire [i.e. François-Marie Arouet] (1694-1778) 96

Die Wage 119
Wagner, Sylvester (contributor to *Wien und die Wiener*) 234-**35**
Walker, Alexander (1779-1852) 105-6, **107**
Warman, Caroline 173-4
Weber, Johann Jakob (1803-80) 35, 45 note 47
Wechsler, Judith 85, 88, 163
Weerth, Georg (1822-56) 309-10
Welcker, Karl Theodor (1790-1869) 275
Wien und die Wiener, in Bildern aus dem Leben 15, 16, 19, 21-2, 31, 42-3, 46, 132-3, 164, 166-**67**, 210, 213, 226-37, 238, 248, 249, 274, 276, 277, 284, 292
Wiener Theaterzeitung 46, 47
Winter, Miss (contributor to *Heads of the People*) 269-70
Wood engraving: see Graphic art
Working class: see Class
Wülfing, Wulf 211

Die Zeitgenossen (Gutzkow) 29-30, 151 and note 55; 174, 260-8 and note 27; 283, 293, 306-7, 325-6
Zohn, Harry 11-12
Zoology 110-28, 114-19, 253-4, 258